THE REBEL GIRL

Yours for the Freedom of the Toilers,
Elizabeth Gurley Flynn.

Elizabeth Gurley Flynn. Duluth, Minnesota 1908

THE REBEL GIRL with Joe Hill's dedication to the author

THE REBEL GIRL

An Autobiography
My First Life (1906-1926)

by Elizabeth Gurley Flynn

INTERNATIONAL PUBLISHERS   New York

Library of Congress Catalog Card Number: 72-94154
ISBN: (cloth) 0-7178-0367-8; (paperback) 0-7178-0368-6
PRINTED IN THE UNITED STATES OF AMERICA

Dedicated

To the ever living memory of my dearly beloved only son, Fred Flynn, who died March 29, 1940, at the age of 29. He was my friend and comrade—loving, encouraging, humorous, active in progressive labor politics—to whom I promised this book would be written, and to whom I consciously dedicated my life's work, before and after his death.

EDITOR'S NOTE

THIS EDITION of the first part of Elizabeth Gurley Flynn's autobiography has been reedited in accordance with her wishes. She had prepared the manuscript during very trying times. Her trial under the Smith Act took place in Foley Square, New York, in 1952. In the years immediately following, she was engaged in the exhausting processes of appeal and defense, not only in her case but on behalf of the many Communist leaders who were victims of that thought-control prosecution. She began serving her sentence at the Federal Women's Reformatory at Alderson, West Virginia in January 1955 and was not released until May 1957. The book first appeared, under the imprint of Masses & Mainstream, in November 1955. While in prison she was not permitted to see the proofs (nor the book when it appeared). She thus had no opportunity to make final corrections before publication.

Fortunately, Miss Flynn left among her papers a marked copy of the book, in which she noted some corrections. These have been included in the present edition. She had also planned to give the book a more thorough critical reading, but did not manage to do so before her death. However, when she asked International Publishers to reissue the book, she urged that it be completely reedited to correct the errors and smooth out the rough spots. This has been done for the present edition.

Evidently, the author before beginning to serve her prison sentence had no time to round out the full period through 1926. Missing, among other things, is her role in the textile strike in Passaic, New Jersey, and the nationwide tour she made as the newly elected chairman of the International Labor Defense on behalf of Sacco and Vanzetti in a desperate effort to save the lives of these martyrs. It was in the course of this trip that she became seriously ill in Portland, Oregon; it took ten years of cure and convalescence before she could return to public life.

The book was first published under the title "I Speak My Own Piece: Autobiography of 'The Rebel Girl'." In a letter to the editor (San Francisco, May 25, 1962) she expressed the desire that in a new edition, the title be changed to "The Rebel Girl" and that Joe Hill's song of that name be printed in the book. Also found among her papers was an early outline for the autobiography, to comprise two volumes, the first to be subtitled "My First Life (1906–1926)" and the other "My Second Life." These wishes have been honored in the present edition.

The editor has taken the liberty to give a better structure to the book, by dividing it into seven parts, more or less as the author described the book in her Preface. An index has been added.

It is characteristic of Elizabeth Gurley Flynn that in her preliminary outline she wrote under "My Second Life" the motto: "If I could live my life over again!" and then added emphatically "— *I did.*"

After her release from the Alderson prison, she was deeply immersed in the many pressing defense campaigns arising from the McCarthy period and its aftermath. Under the circumstances, she thought it more important to write about her recent prison experiences rather than turn to the second part of the autobiography. She finished her prison book in 1962 and it was published the following year under the title, *The Alderson Story: My Life as a Political Prisoner.* On finishing the manuscript she wrote the editor: "Then I propose, now at last I have my hand to writing again, that I go to work on my second volume of autobiography . . . (from 1927 to 1951, approximately)." She did manage to draft a few pages, which were found among her papers, before setting off hopefully to Moscow in 1964 where, in seclusion from the many demands upon her at home, she planned to complete the book. She had hardly begun, when she died on September 4, 1964, at the age of 74.

As Miss Flynn says in the Preface to the present book, her intention in the second volume was to "portray my life as an active Communist from 1937 to the present day. Many have written as ex-Communists. This second book will be the story of an active American Communist and one who is proud of it. No matter what are the consequences, 'I will never move from where I stand!' "

To clear up any possible misunderstanding as to when her life as an "active Communist" began—"My Second Life"—it would be in place to explain an important change made in the Preface as it appeared in the first edition. There the date of her joining the Communist Party was given as 1937. In her copy of the book she wrote "*1927* correct date" and subtracted 1927 from 1962 (the year evidently in which she made this note) to give the result "35 years"—with the obvious implication that she considered herself a Communist for those 35 years.

According to the draft manuscript already referred to, she applied for membership not in 1927 but in the Fall of 1926, on the request of C. E. Ruthenberg, then general secretary of the Communist Party. As she writes in the Preface, she did so after "careful examination and evaluation of 21 years of previous activities, which led me, to my mind logically and irrevocably" to take this action. Unfortunately, due to the complex factional situation in the party after the death of Ruthenberg in the Spring of 1927, her application was not acted upon. Finally, after her recovery and with the sponsorship of her old friends William Z. Foster and Ella "Mother" Bloor, she became a member of the party, this time for good. "Like vaccination it didn't take the first time," she wrote in her notes. She was soon elected a member of the National Committee and in 1961 became the National Chairman of the party. The year of her first application for membership is given as 1926 in the present Preface.

That Elizabeth Gurley Flynn never completed her autobiography is an inestimable loss. She would have written about the climactic events of the later years, in which she was deeply engaged, with the same understanding, sensitivity, wit, and devotion to working people and socialism that mark her story of the earlier years.

At the time the book first appeared in 1955 it received little general attention, despite the fame, or as some would have it, the "notoriety" of the author. In the general atmosphere of red-baiting and repression which prevailed, the book suffered "prior censorship" in circles where normally it would have aroused the deepest interest. Let us hope that in the new version the autobiography of "The Rebel Girl" will command the attention due this outstanding Communist leader who since the turn of the century had devoted herself so completely to the cause of labor and socialism.

—James S. Allen

Contents

Illustrations

THE REBEL GIRL

Preface

Here is the story of my life. This first book deals with my childhood and early youth; my becoming a Socialist at the age of sixteen; my activities as an IWW agitator and strike leader up to 1918; and my subsequent work in defense of civil liberties and labor's rights in World War I and during its aftermath of the Palmer raids. It ends with the period of 1920 to 1927 and my close identification in those seven years with the struggle to free Sacco and Vanzetti. The second book will deal with my period of inactivity, due to illness, and my careful examination and evaluation of my 21 years of previous activities, which led me, to my mind logically and irrevocably, to apply for membership in the Communist Party in 1926. It will portray my life as an active Communist from 1936 to the present day. Many have written as ex-Communists. This second book will be the story of an active American Communist and one who is proud of it. No matter what are the consequences, "I will never move from where I stand!"

I have tried to write this first book from the viewpoint and in the context of my experiences at the time, avoiding superimposing the viewpoint of the writer at the age of 65, which will be fully developed in the second volume. I feel it is important for me to set down here my personal recollections of this earlier part of the century, a period full of heroic struggles on the part of the American working class, especially the foreign born. As the reader will see, the years 1906 to 1926 were full of "force and violence" used by the ruling class in America against the workers, who gave their lives, shed their blood, were beaten, jailed, blacklisted and framed, as they fought for the right to organize, to strike and to picket. Struggles—for a few cents more an hour, for a few minutes less work a day—were long and bitterly fought. Nothing was handed on a silver platter to the American working class by employers. All their hard-won gains came through their own efforts and solidarity.

It was my privilege to be identified with many of these earlier labor struggles and the heroic men and women, particularly of the "Left," who made labor history in those days. They should never be forgotten. I feel I have a responsibility to share my memories of them with younger generations and to make available this record of their noble words and deeds. They were flesh and blood of the American working class. I hope this book will help to encourage and inspire others to follow in their footsteps, not only along the path they made wider, smoother and clearer for us today, but to travel far beyond, toward the horizons they glimpsed—peace on earth, and an America free from poverty, exploitation, greed and injustice—a Socialist America. To this I have happily dedicated my life.

—ELIZABETH GURLEY FLYNN

ONE

Childhood and Early Youth

PADDY THE REBEL

By birth I am a New Englander, though not of Mayflower stock. My ancestors were "immigrants and revolutionists"—from the Emerald Isle. I was born in 1890 in Concord, New Hampshire, at the end of a most tragic century for "that most distressful country," which had suffered under British rule for over 700 years. There had been an uprising in each generation in Ireland, and forefathers of mine were reputed to be in every one of them. The awareness of being Irish came to us as small children, through plaintive song and heroic story. The Irish people fought to wrest their native soil from foreign landlords, to speak their native Gaelic tongue, to worship in the church of their choice, to have their own schools, to be independent and self-governing. As children, we drew in a burning hatred of British rule with our mother's milk. Until my father died, at over eighty, he never said "England" without adding, "God damn her!" Before I was ten I knew of the great heroes—Robert Emmet, Wolfe Tone, Michael Davitt, Parnell, and O'Donovan Rossa, who was chained hand and foot, like a dog, and had to eat from a tin plate on the floor of a British prison.

When the French army landed at Killalla Bay in 1798, on an expedition planned by Wolfe Tone to help free Ireland, all four of my great grandfathers—Gurley, Flynn, Ryan and Conneran—joined the French. They were members of the Society of United Irishmen, dedicated to set up an Irish Republic. Fired with enthusiasm over the French revolution and the success of the American colonies, they were determined to follow their examples. Young Irishmen for miles around dropped their potato digging when they heard "the French are in the

Bay." The French armed the Irish, who had only pikes for weapons, and together they defeated the British garrison at Castlebar. The story is that Paddy Flynn of Mayo County, known far and wide as "Paddy the Rebel," led the French 18 miles around through the mountains to attack the British from the rear. The Irish revolution was finally crushed in a sea of blood by the same General Cornwallis who had surrendered to George Washington at Yorktown.

A reign of horrible terror and reprisal against the Irish followed— floggings, executions, massacres, exile. Paddy Flynn lay in a ditch near his home all night till he heard that a baby was born. Then he was "On the run!"—again with a price on his head, fed and protected by the peasants, like hundreds of his countrymen. Others fled to France, some came to the Americas, still others were shipped to Australlian penal colonies. Irish songs reflect this period—"Who dares to speak of '98?" and "Here's a memory to the friends that are gone, boys— gone!" Paddy slipped around the hills he knew so well. Once he lay in the center of a ripe wheatfield, while the peasants, knowing he was there, slowly cut and reaped all around him, and the British soldiers rode past looking for rebels. Finally he reached the home of his foster brother, who was a landlord, but who had a loyalty to the son of his peasant wet-nurse and with whom he grew up as a lad. So he hid him away safely in the barn.

My bold adventurous great-grandfather-to-be had a gun, a blunder- buss it was called, that "shot a hatful of bullets." He couldn't resist taking aim at the wild geese as they flew over. A "loyal" (pro-British) weaver heard the shot and came after him with a shuttle board, de- manding his surrender. "A fine challenge!" cried Paddy, and shot the king's spokesman. A neighbor digging peat nearby threw down his spade and rushed to town spreading the news: "Paddy Flynn is in the bog shooting yeomen!" All his friends rushed to his aid while the Brit- ish sent out a searching party. But he was over the hills and far away again. After several years ammesty was granted, and he came home to live to a ripe old age. He had two wives and 18 children, who later scattered as immigrants to all continents. When he was dying, his last words were, "I want to see the French land on this coast once more!"

My grandfather, Tom Flynn, was one of the many sons of Paddy the Rebel. He was arrested in Ireland as a boy of 16 when caught fish- ing for salmon on a Sunday morning, at an hour when everybody was expected to be in church. The river was considered the private property of the landlord. Enraged because hungry people could not have the fish for food in a famine year, Tom Flynn threw lime in the water so the fish floated bellies up, dead, to greet the gentry. Then he ran away to America. His widowed mother, with her other children, followed during the 1840s. The widow Conneran, with her large family had come earlier in the '30s. They travelled on small sailing vessels that took three months, carrying their own pots and pans and doing their cooking on board. The ships were crowded and unsanitary. Cholera would break out and some were to be held in quarantine in St. John's, New Brunswick. Tom, who was there to meet his family, hired a row boat and rescued a brother and sister and as many others as he could load in the boat. He laid them in the bottom, covered them over and started away. A guard shouted, "What have ye there?" Tom boldly replied, "Fish, do you want some?" The guard replied, "No just keep away from here!"—which Tom gladly did, with a hearty "Go to Hell!" which was ever on his lips for a British uniform.

Life was hard and primitive for these early Irish immigrants in isolated settlements in the state of Maine. Grandfather Tom Flynn worked in lumber camps, on building railroads, as an expert river man driving logs, and in the granite quarries of Maine and New Hampshire. The climate was more rigorous than their own mild country. The work was harder than agriculture in Ireland. So many died from tuberculosis that it was called "the Irish disease." Undoubtedly "stonecutter's consumption" was what we know today as silicosis.

Grandfather Flynn had an obsession against living in another man's house. He built a new cabin wherever he moved by setting up a keg of whiskey and inviting all hands to help him. He became an American citizen in 1856. He voted for Abraham Lincoln in 1860. He married my grandmother at Machias, Maine, where my father was born in 1859. She was little and pretty and had a violent temper. (That's where we get it, my sister Kathie says.)

Grandfather died of consumption in 1877 at Pennacook, New Hampshire, then Fisherville, where he is buried. He was only 49 years old. He was ever a fighter for freedom, in the spirit of his father. Dissatisfied with the bad living and working conditions, the lack of education for his children, and the prejudice and discrimination against the Irish, he at one time joined with others in an expedition to overthrow the Canadian government and set up a republic there. They captured an armory from the surprised Canadian militia and then got drunk to celebrate. But when they had to return across the border for lack of supplies, their leaders were arrested by the American authorities. Again in 1870 and 1871, my father remembered, similar attempted raids were made on Canada. Gay, fighting old Paddy the Rebel has lived on, even unto the third generation.

THE NAME "GURLEY"

My mother, Annie Gurley, landed in Boston in 1877 at the age of seventeen. She was very beautiful, with blue-black hair, deep blue eyes, a soft white skin and regular features. She had a clear and cameo-like profile. She came from Galway on the west coast of Ireland where it is reported the people have "Spanish blood," flowing from the shipwrecked sailors of the defeated Spanish Armada who settled there in the 16th century. To this is attributed our black hair. The first of the Gurleys, her aunt Bina and later her uncles James and Mike, had come to Concord, New Hampshire before the Civil War in the migration from 1847 to 1861 which took a million men and women away from Irish famine and political persecution. My mother was the oldest girl of 13 children, but she was brought up away from home by her Gurley grandparents and spoke only Gaelic in her childhood. She had a faint trace of it in her speech.

Her childhood in Loughrea was a happy one. The Gurleys in Galway, where they say "God bless us!" were much more prosperous than the Flynns in Mayo, where they say "God help us!" She lived on a farm where there were all sorts of domestic animals. She was taught at home by her uncles because they boycotted the National (British) schools. Her grandmother, kind to all others, would give nothing to a "uniform." She refused food, milk or even water to British soldiers, who had to go seven miles further to town for supplies. When the Irish labor leader, James Larkin, once criticized American women for smoking, my mother said smilingly: "Well, Jim, I used to light my grandmother's pipe with a live coal from the hearth!" When another Irish friend turned up his nose at "the garlic-eating Italians" she told him that her grandmother used to pull up garlic in her garden like radishes and eat it raw. She had a theory that the Irish were "the lost tribes of Israel" and told us how her grandfather killed animals for food in the same manner as the Jewish people; Saturday began the Sabbath and all work closed on his farm. Mama did not deny the

Thomas Flynn, the author's father. Concord, N.H. 1895

Mother, Annie Gurley Flynn. Concord, N.H. 1895

Elizabeth *(lower right)* from a P.S. 9 class picture, 1903, wearing a N.Y. Times medal for a prize essay

A 1906 newsclip of Elizabeth, age 16, speaking at Rutgers Square, New York City

faults or glorify the virtues of the Irish, as our father did. We were amused at this and often said, "Papa is more Irish than Mama and he never saw Ireland!"

The Gurleys were Presbyterian, but not very devout. My mother knew all about fairies and leprechauns and "the little people" who are supposed to inhabit Ireland. She was not brought up religious and did not go to church. When we asked about this, she would put us off whimsically by saying: "After all, the Irish are pagans at heart!"

She had a few pleasant years here with her relatives in Concord, until her father died in Ireland; her mother hastily sold the good land he had owned and cultivated and brought her brood of nine children to America. They were all in their teens. She left seven here and returned to Ireland with the two youngest, whom she placed in an expensive convent school. My mother was forced to become the head of a new household, to support and bring up her brothers and sisters. To do this she worked as a tailoress on men's custom-made coats for 13 years. She did exquisite hand sewing, especially on pockets and buttonholes. She helped all her brothers to learn trades—Jim and Martin became plumbers, John a leather worker, and Mike a metal worker. All were members of the Knights of Labor, then a secret society. Chalked signs on the sidewalks notified them of its meetings. Two of her sisters were dressmakers. Because of these family responsibilities my mother did not marry until she was 30 years old, an "old maid" in those days.

My mother was always interested in public affairs. She early became an advocate of equal rights for women. She heard many lecturers in Concord—Susan B. Anthony, Frances Willard, Frederick Douglass, Dr. Mary Walker, a pioneer medical woman, and Charles Stuart Parnell, the great Irish orator. She shocked her in-laws and neighbors by having women doctors in the 90s, when her four children were born. This was a radical step at that time, not long after Dr. Elizabeth Blackwell had opened up the practice of medicine to women. I was named after our doctor in Concord, Dr. Elizabeth Kent. I remember her when she vaccinated me to go to kindergarten, a handsome woman dressed in a tailored suit, the first I had seen. In Manchester, Mama also had a "foreign doctor," an elderly French-Canadian woman who drove up in her own horse-drawn buggy.

My mother admired women of intelligence who did "worthwhile

things" in the world. She rebelled against the endless monotony of women's household tasks and after her marriage remained at work in the tailoring establishment as long as she could get caretakers for her children. This too was unusual at that time. She was an excellent cook; she liked to bake pies, make preserves, raise plants, but she hated what she called drudgery—washing, ironing, cleaning, dishwashing. She was happiest when she was sewing. She made over her green silk wedding dress into dresses for us to go to school. During her lifetime she made dresses for her three daughters. In 1913 a Paterson newspaper accused me of wearing an expensive imported linen dress to a strikers' meeting. Mama had made it for me at a cost of three dollars. The last beautiful dress she made for me was in 1937 when I spoke at my first Communist meeting at Madison Square Garden. It was of black velvet and she sewed it all by hand because at her advanced age of 77 she could not run the machine.

Mama was no model housekeeper. But she was interesting and different and we loved her dearly. She read widely—newspapers, magazines and books. After we came to New York City in 1900, she went to night school to improve her penmanship and spelling and to hear lectures on Shakespeare. All during our childhood she read aloud to us —from Irish history, poetry, fairy stories. I recall one of her favorite books was on Greek mythology, *Gods and Heroes*. She had a large set of paper-covered volumes called "Classics and the Beautiful." We have a precious collection of books which were always "Mama's Books." They include a five-volume set of Irish literature, volumes of Burns, Moore, Byron, Whittier, Sheridan, Swift, Mrs. Browning, Mrs. Hemans, Meredith, Longfellow, Synge, Yeats, Lady Gregory, Stephens and Shaw.

When she was nearly 80, she read from William Z. Foster: "My father, James Foster, was born in County Carlow, Ireland, of peasant stock. He was a Fenian and an ardent fighter for Irish independence." She commented aloud to us: "My great grandfather, John Gurley, also came from County Carlow; so did George Bernard Shaw's grandfather, James Gurley. They were brothers. Shaw's mother's name was Elizabeth Gurley. The Larkins also came from there!" She went on reading, leaving us quite overwhelmed with this information. Finally I said: "Mama, why didn't you tell us this before?" She calmly replied: "The occasion never arose."

SHANTY AND LACE CURTAIN IRISH

The Irish who came to this country around the middle of the last century were far from happy. They sought but had not found freedom from religious and political persecution, nor a chance to earn a decent livelihood for their families. My father was very bitter about the hard conditions which prevailed here in his youth among the Irish. They were principally employed at manual labor—building railroads, canals, roads, and in mines and quarries. They lived in shanty towns, even in New York City. One such, consisting of 20,000 inhabitants, was located in what is now Central Park. They were excluded from the better residential areas. In my father's youth there were many signs on empty houses and factories seeking help: "No Irish Need Apply." They were ridiculed by the Protestant Yankees for their "Papist" religion, for their large families, their fighting and drinking—called dirty, ignorant, superstitious, lazy, and what not, as each immigrant group in turn has been similarly maligned. Nor were the Irish united. Bloody battles occurred in my father's youth between Catholic Irish and Orangemen, who were Protestant Irish. A narrow canal was pointed out to me in Lowell, Massachusetts, by an old man who said: "That stream was once red with blood after a battle between Orangemen and Catholics."

However, the Irish had one advantage which other immigrants did not share—they did not have to learn to speak English. They more easily became citizens. My father commented bitterly: "They soon become foremen, straw bosses, policemen and politicians, and forget the Irish traditions of struggle for freedom!" While this was true of many, it was an exaggeration. The majority of the Irish Americans remained workers—on the waterfront, in mining, transport, maritime and the building trades, and in other basic industries. They played a heroic part in early American labor history—in the Knights of Labor, the Western Federation of Miners, and the American Federation of Labor. William Sylvis, Peter Maguire, Terence V. Powderly, Kate Mullaney, Leonora O'Reilly, T. B. Barry, John Collins, Martin A. Foran, J. P. McDonald and John Sincey are a few of the Irish names appearing in early labor history. In fact, in the early days of labor organization they defied their church to be union members. Finally, yielding to the inevitable, the Catholic Church gave its blessing to trade unionism in 1891. Terence V. Powderly in his autobiography, *The Path I Trod,* has an interesting chapter, "Ecclesiastic Opposition," in which he tells of his struggles to defend the Knights of Labor, of which he was the head, against the attacks of priests, bishops and archbishops. Cardinal Gibbons, in his recommendation to the Pope not to condemn the Knights of Labor, saw the danger of the church in the growing cleavage between it and the mass of Catholic workers who were joining unions.

My father, who was then a laborer in the quarries, met my mother in the mid '80s. There were tight social lines drawn between the "lace curtain" Irish of my mother's family and the "shanty Irish" of my father's family. The difficulties he had in courting my mother are indicated by the fact that neither Gurleys nor Flynns came to their wedding. My father was determined to leave the quarry. All but one of his male relatives had died as a result of working there. My father carried the mark of the quarry to his grave. When he was a young boy, working in a quarry in Maine carrying tools, the sight of one eye was destroyed by a flying chip of granite. He lived to be over 80 "thanks to Mama," we always said, who encouraged him in his ambition. He had a keen mathematical mind and through self-study and tutoring he passed the entrance examinations at Dartmouth College in Hanover, New Hampshire. He attended the Thayer School of Engineering and made excellent progress. One of his classmates, later a professor at Ann Arbor, Michigan, told me how he remembered Tom Flynn poring over his book in the failing light of evening, finally taking it to the window to catch the last rays of the sun.

He was suspended from college for a short interval because he refused to give the names of those attending a secret meeting of Catholic students who were organizing to protest the denial of their right to attend Catholic services. The New York *World* of that day had an article commending his stand; the student body supported him, and he was reinstated. I thought proudly of this family precedent in December 1952, over 65 years later, when I entered the Women's House of Detention in NewYork City to serve a 30 days' sentence for contempt of court for refusal to "name names." His brother Pat died of consumption shortly before my father was to graduate. Pat was the breadwinner for his mother and three sisters, who demanded that Tom now go to work. His money gave out, trying to divide with them, and he was compelled to leave college. He was sufficiently grounded, however, so that he worked from then on as a civil engineer.

When he married, his family was highly indignant, but Mama re-mained at work, partially solving the economic problem for a few years. My father got work in 1895 in Manchester, New Hampshire, as a civil engineer for the Manchester Street Railroad Company, which was laying a track for a new mode of transportation, since torn up to make way for buses. "Frogs" and switches were his specialty then. This was 18 miles south of Concord, and we moved there. Here he took his first flyer into politics. He ran independently for City Engi-neer. He had joined the Ancient Order of Hibernians (AOH) and marched in the St. Patrick's Day parade. He sported white gloves and a green sash over his shoulder, with golden harps, and green sham-rocks on it. We children were terribly impressed. We organized pa-rades and pranced around in that sash till we wore it out. Undoubted-ly he got the Irish vote but it was not enough to elect him. He was convinced that he lost because he was Irish and looked around for a job outside of New England. He took a poorly paid map-making job in Cleveland, Ohio. It was an uncertain, seasonal type of work. Collect-ing his pay in full depended upon how many orders the canvassers re-ceived for the finished atlases. Sometimes the operating companies failed or were fly-by-night concerns and in the end nothing was forth-coming. Somebody was always "owing Papa money."

Yet he worked hard, tramping around in all kinds of weather with his small hand-drafting board, plotting in with red and blue pencils the streets, houses, etc. He worked at this for years, making maps of Cleveland, Boston, Baltimore, Newark, Trenton, Kentucky, Nova Sco-tia and many other places. At first we moved around as his jobs changed, from Concord to Manchester, to Cleveland, to Adams, Mas-sachusetts, and finally to New York City. Our greatest fear was "Papa losing his job!" We enjoyed our peaceful life with Mama when she gave us all her attention. We knew that there would be no money when he was at home all day, and that he would become increasingly irritable and explosive. We were selfishly happy when Papa got a new job and went off to another town.

WE GO "OUT WEST"

Our trip way "out west," to Cleveland, Ohio, was high adventure for three small New England children. I was then seven years old. It was a wearisome trek in a dirty day coach for my mother with a nursing baby. We landed at an old wooden station down by the lake shore. It was still there the last time I visited Cleveland. Our stay in Cleveland was brief, about eight months, but vivid impressions remained—of the beautiful blue expanse of water, Lake Erie, of the muddy Cuyahoga River, coiled like a brown snake in the heart of the industrial section, of the great ore docks, and of mansions set back from Euclid Avenue, with beautiful wide lawns. My father was a great walker and often took me with him. He pointed out the home of Mark Hanna, "who owned President McKinley." Papa had voted for William Jennings Bryan in 1896.

We lived in a shaky little one-story house on Payne Avenue, named for a pioneer family. It had an outdoor toilet which shocked us very much. It was reported to be the old Payne family homestead and had barred windows in the cellar, which was entered through a trap door in the kitchen floor. We were told the family took refuge there a century ago and shot through the windows at attacking Indians. True or not, it made living there exciting. There were cable cars then in Cleveland and apparently some shift in gears was made at midnight. Anyhow the little frame house shook and rocked at that time every night, and we loved to pretend the Indians had returned or maybe it was the ghosts of the old Payne family. My father worked at home, using the front room for his big drafting boards, pantographs, blue prints, etc. It was our first direct contact with his work and with him, in fact. He earned $25 a week, but bread cost three cents a loaf and steak was ten cents a pound.

What I particularly remember about our sojourn in Cleveland was the Spanish-American War, which broke out in 1898. My father was vocal and vitriolic in his opposition to it. He said the blowing up of the American battleship *Maine* in Havana Harbor was an inside job to cause hostilities and that Hearst had a hand in it. He had only scorn for Admiral Dewey and his dramatic entrance into Manila, and for Teddy Roosevelt and his Rough Riders. "Shot a Cuban in the back!" he said of Teddy. My father joined the Anti-Imperialist League of that day, founded by Senator Hoar of Massachusetts and other prominent people to oppose the United States taking over the Philippines. We were all ears to hear the animated, heated discussions Papa had with other mapmen who came to our house. There was considerable sympathy for Aguinaldo, the leader of the Filipino people, who wanted to be free from Spain and were not willing to become an American colony instead. He had distinguished himself in 1896 in leading a Filipino revolt against Spain and had defeated the Spanish army. He became provisional president of the islands. Later he carried on guerrilla warfare against the Americans when they did not leave as the Filipino people expected they would, after the war ended. He was captured and capitulated by taking an oath of allegiance to the U.S.A. That ended Aguinaldo—as a hero.

My father was greatly wrought up over the cruelties inflicted upon the people of these faraway islands of the Pacific. He compared them to similar brutalities inflicted on the Irish people. I remember our horror at stories of the "water cure." My father used to march up and down the floor after we came to New York City reciting a poem written by the famous Western poet, Joaquin Miller. It was about a General Jacob H. Smith, entitled "That Assassin of Samar." Some words of it were:

> And Europe mocks us in our shame;
> from Maine to far Manila Bay the
> nation bleeds and bows it head!

As a result of widespread indignation this brutal general was finally court-martialed in 1902 for his infamous "Burn and kill!" order against the revolting Aguinaldo forces.

I will remember my father's contemptuous angry word "hypocrite" when President McKinley pompously and piously announced that he had walked the floor of the White House night after night wondering what to do with the Philippines and finally decided: "there was nothing left for us to do but to take them and uplift and Christianize and civilize and educate them, as our fellow-man for whom Christ died." So the Spreckels family sugar interests and the Dollar Line moved in, as Pop said they would, and the Spanish feudal agrarian system continued, under the rule of American big businessmen residing ten thousand miles away.

My father saw the whole picture clearly, way back in 1898. When one understood British imperialism it was an open window to all imperialism. The U.S.A. embarked on the ruinous path of imperialism in the Philippines. As children, we came to hate unjust wars, which took the land and rights away from other peoples.

I Hate Poverty

From Cleveland we moved back to Adams. Indelible impressions were made upon me as a child of working-class life and poverty in the textile towns of Manchester, New Hampshire, and Adams, the greatest distinction of which in our youthful eyes was that it was the birthplace of Susan B. Anthony, the woman's suffrage leader. The change from the pleasant clean little city of Concord, to the drab bleak textile center of Manchester, was sufficient to impress even a five-year-old child. We lived there nearly three years. The gray mills in Manchester stretched like prisons along the banks of the Merrimac River; 50 per cent of the workers were women and they earned one dollar a day. Many lived in the antiquated "corporation boarding houses," relics of the time when the mills were built. Our neighbors, men and women, rushed to the mills before the sun rose on cold winter days and returned after dark. They were poorly dressed and poverty stricken. The women wore no hats, but shawls over their heads. The "mill children" left school early to take dinner pails to their parents. The mothers took time off in the mills to nurse their babies who were cared for by elderly relatives.

The mills would slow down or shut down for no apparent reason. "Bad times," it was called. Then I saw mill children eating bread with lard instead of butter. Many children were without underwear, even in the coldest weather. A young woman mill worker, showing her hand with three fingers gone due to a mill accident, shocked me immeasurably. Safety devices were still unheard of. Once, while we were in school in Adams piercing screams came from the mill across the street. A girl's long hair had been caught in the unguarded machine and she was literally scalped. My first contact with a jail was watching a policeman put a weeping old man, "a tramp" he was called, into a "lock-up" in Adams. He kept assuring us children he had done no wrong, he had no job and no money and no place to sleep. This episode caused me anxiety about all old people. Would it happen to Grandma? Would it happen to all of us when we were old? Yet in Adams the old millowner lived in a great mansion in the center of the town, drove around in a fine carriage with beautiful horses, and was once visited by President McKinley.

We finally arrived in New York City at the turn of the century, in 1900. My mother was tired of moving around and decided here we would stay. Our school terms had been interrupted and what little furniture we possessed was being smashed up in moving around. We came to Aunt Mary, a widow and a tailoress, who lived with her five children in the South Bronx. Soon they found a flat for us nearby. It was on the inside facing an airshaft, gaslit, with cold water. The only heat was the kitchen stove. We three older children cried, we refused to unpack our toys, and were as heartsick for the green hills of New England as any lonely immigrants for their pleasant native lands. We missed the fields, the flowers, the cows, and beautiful Greylock Mountain we had seen from our window. We hated the big crowded dirty city, where now our playgrounds were empty lots with neither grass nor trees. The flats where we lived, at 833 East 133rd St., are still in use for "welfare families," I understand, although for a while they were condemned and boarded up.

We were horrified, too, at the conditions we had never met in our travels elsewhere—the prevalence of pests in the old slum houses, mice, rats, cockroaches and bedbugs. My poor mother carried on a desperate struggle to rid us of these parasites. And then something horrible happened to us in school—pediculosis is the scientific term; "lousy" the children called it. One child can infect a whole classroom, as every teacher knows. Yet often you will hear a smug prosperous person say: "Well, at least the poor can keep clean." I remember my friend, Rose Pastor Stokes, answering a woman who said this: "Did your mother ever look at a nickel in her hand and decide between a loaf of bread and a cake of soap? Well, mine did!" To be clean requires soap, hot water, changes of underwear, stockings and handkerchiefs, enough sheets and pillow cases and heat in the bathroom. We had none of these in periods of stark poverty. Mama washed our underwear at night to be ready for the next morning.

On cold winter days we'd huddle in the kitchen and shut off the rest of the house. We would do our lessons by a kerosene lamp when the gas was shut off for nonpayment. We'd undress in the kitchen, scurry to the cold bedrooms, all the children sleeping in one bed, where we put our coats over us to keep warm. We might as well have lived on an isolated farm in the Dakotas for all the good the benefits of the great city did us then. Bill collectors harassed my gentle mother—the landlord, the gas man, the milk man, the grocer. Once she bought us an encyclopedia on the installment plan. But she couldn't keep up the payments and our hearts were broken when we lost the beautiful books we treasured so highly.

Our front windows of the long tunnel-like apartment faced the smoky roundhouse of the New York, New Haven and Hartford Railroad. The great engines would chug in day and night and blow off steam there. Many railroad workers lived in the area. In particularly bad times they would throw off chunks of coal and then look the other way when local children came to pick up coal around the roundhouse. There were many accidents to railroad workers. Widows lived around us who had lost their husbands on that dangerous road, and their children starved while the road fought sometimes for years against paying damages.

There were many small factories, veritable sweatshops, in the neighborhood, where children went to work as early as the law allowed and even younger. They made paper boxes, pencils, shirts, handkerchiefs (at three dollars a week and bring your own thread). There were larger factories employing adult labor—piano and refrigerator factories, a drug plant, and others. Mothers worked too and many children were left alone. Sometimes babies fell out of windows; one boy was killed when a huge sewer pipe rolled over him; a widow's only son fell from a swaying pole in a backyard, where he was putting up a clothes line, and was killed. Children lost legs on the railroad and under trucks on the streets. The wife of the corner saloonkeeper made huge kettles of soup for free lunch and sent bowls of it around to the poorest families. People helped each other as best they could. Truly, as some philosopher said, "Poverty is like a strange and terrible country. Only those who have been there can really speak of it with knowledge."

An unforgettable tragedy of our childhood was the burning of the excursion boat, the *General Slocum,* in 1904. It had left the Lower East Side loaded with women and children on a Sunday school picnic of the Lutheran Church. When it reached Hellgate, a pot of fat upset and the kitchen took fire. The captain tried to reach a dock at 138th Street. By then the boat was an inferno. A thousand people died as a result of burns or drowning. The local undertakers' establishments were full of bodies. The Alexander Avenue Police Station was a temporary morgue, where grief-stricken fathers and husbands rushed up from the East Side to claim their dead. It was heart-rending to all of us in the neighborhood, like a disaster in a mining town. Investigation showed that the boat was an old firetrap, with inadequate fire-fighting equipment and life preservers. The captain, who did his best, was sent to prison, which cleared the company of responsibility for negligence. It was considered one of the worst marine disasters up to that time. The lives of working-class mothers and children were sacrificed to greed and corruption.

LIFE IN THE SOUTH BRONX

Childhood casts a glow around some events, even in poverty. It was a great day when we moved one block, from 133rd Street to 511 East 134th Street, on the corner of Brook Avenue. We lived there for 27 years and a whole book could be written around "511," our lives there and our famous visitors. It was a sunny corner flat facing south, but gaslit and without hot water for many years. We never had steam heat, though electricity was finally installed. In the last few years, at our own expense, we put a small fireplace in the parlor which helped to heat the house. We also installed a porcelain tub. As the old tin tub was being carried out our very near-sighted landlord stood on the stairway. Thinking it was a coffin he stood respectfully bareheaded as it passed.

Our long residence was a record in a neighborhood where for years families got one month's rent free, paid a few months, stayed on a few more until they were dispossessed, and then moved on, to repeat the same procedure elsewhere. When we moved in there were red carpets on the floor and shiny brass door knobs and mail boxes. But it became more and more dilapidated with the passing years and each new, indifferent landlord.

Our windows looked out over the Harlem River and Manhattan's skyline. We saw the Hellgate Bridge in construction. We liked the friendly noises of the railroad—the whistles at night, the red glow of the engines, the late night milk trains rumbling in, and sometimes the circus cars from Bridgeport. One night in the midst of a political argument, a crony of Pop's looked out the window and said: "My God, Flynn, is that an elephant?" Pop replied: "It must be the beer!" But it really *was* an elephant, out for a stroll from a circus car. We loved to see the fire engines clatter down the hill from Brown Place, the horses' hoofs striking sparks from the cobblestones. Once there was a terrible fire opposite our house, on Brook Avenue. Three tenement houses were burned out late at night in zero weather. Over 20 families rushed out in their night clothes to escape the flames. They lost everything— their poor furniture and meager clothes. Everyone around opened up their stores and houses, took the victims in, fed and clothed them. They made wash boilers of coffee and piles of sandwiches for the firemen, who were there all night. Hoses froze and had to be thawed out.

One pretty girl on our block met a handsome fireman that night as she gave him coffee and they were married later—a romantic finale to that memorable fire in a working-class district.

In New England we had bought wood by the cord and coal by the ton. But here, in the South Bronx, we bought coal in bushel bags and wood in little bundles which were three for five cents at first. This was sold by Joe, the only Italian in the neighborhood. In the summertime he sold ice, and wine all year round, if he trusted you. There was only one Jewish family for many years, that of Mr. Isaacs, who kept a poolroom. My mother insisted we treat him courteously, though others did not. She approved of his place, which she said he ran like a social hall for the boys of the neighborhood, and it kept them out of trouble. She was firm in teaching us respect for other people's nationality, language and religion. Most of our neighbors were German and Irish. The Germans owned the stores. The saloons were owned by the Irish. Italian women, with colored handkerchiefs over their heads, shawls over their shoulders, and great circular earrings, would come up from Harlem to the open fields in the Bronx to pick dandelion greens, which they carried back in great bundles on their heads. In the evenings Italian laborers would walk back over the bridge, on the way home from work. The children threw stones at them and shouted "Dago." As little children in Manchester and Adams we had lived near Poles and French-Canadians, who were called "Polacks" and "Canucks." My mother would tolerate none of this and would say firmly, "How would you like to be called *Micks?*"—as the Irish were for so many years.

In the early days of our life in the South Bronx, at the turn of the century, there were no amusements for children, or for adults either. There were no movies—the nickelodeon started later—no radios, no television, not even the old-fashioned phonograph, which also came later and by now is a museum piece. Reading was our sole indoor pastime, especially in the long winter nights. We walked over the Willis Avenue bridge to the East 125th Street library for books. We read everything we could understand and some we did not, including all the traditional books for young people at that time—Louisa Alcott, *Alice in Wonderland, Robinson Crusoe* and James Fenimore Cooper, Sir Walter Scott, Mark Twain, George Eliot and the New England poets.

My mother was a kind but reserved woman. She did not allow us to go into other people's houses; she frowned on over familiarity and gossip. But she was a good neighbor in time of need. She helped the sick, advised on domestic problems, and when she baked pies and cakes she shared them with the neighborhood children. It was a calamity to the area when she moved away to Brooklyn in the late twenties. My father ran for N. Y. State Assembly in 1918, on the Socialist ticket. He got over 6,000 votes and ran ahead of the Republican. But lots of people said: "Too bad it wasn't Mrs. Flynn that was running. She'd easily get elected! Everybody knows her!"

I attended the grammar school, P.S. No. 9 on 138th Street. It was a decrepit old building then, with toilets in the yard. I do not know what improvements have been made since, if any, but the school is still in use. My teacher in an upper grade was James A. Hamilton who was studying law and later became a New York State official. He fired me with ambition to be a constitutional lawyer and drilled us so thoroughly in the U. S. Constitution and especially the Bill of Rights that I have been defending it ever since. (I have been arrested at least ten times in my lifetime and in every instance the denial of the Bill of Rights has been involved.) I joined a debating society which Mr. Hamilton had organized and took to it like a duck to water. I won a gold metal for proficiency in debating and one in English at graduation in 1904. I also won a silver medal from the *New York Times* in 1903 for "Merit in an Essay on the City's History." I believe that originals of these essays are in the cornerstone of the *New York Times* building, for posterity to unearth. Typical subjects for debate then were: capital punishment; should women get the vote; and government ownership of the trusts. I remember arguing that women should vote—and strongly believing what I advocated.

NOT A CATHOLIC

Once when I was in a Catholic hospital for a few days in Portland, Oregon, a sister asked me: "Are you a Catholic?" When I replied, "No, I'm not," she said, "With that name, I'm surprised. Are you an Orangeman?" I answered quickly, "Good heavens! No!" She laughed and said, "You see—you ought to be a Catholic!" I was baptized in the Catholic Church, as were my two sisters and brother, but we were not taken to church for this ceremony by either of our parents. We were belatedly brought there by aunts. Neither of my parents went to church nor did they send us to church. My mother's grandparents, who brought her up, were not Catholic. My father had been a Catholic in his youth but had a scientific turn of mind and became a skeptic at an early age. However, he was not violently anti-Catholic as many ex-Catholics are inclined to be, and resented prejudiced and unprincipled attacks upon Catholics.

The oft-repeated question, "Why are the Irish more attached to their religion than other Catholics?" received a political answer from him, as follows: In Ireland, Catholicism was closely identified with the national independence struggles of the people. Unlike other Catholic countries, the church in Ireland was not identified with the ruling state and was persecuted by it. Laws were passed at one time under British rule forbidding Catholic schools or places of worship; nor were Catholics allowed to own property or to be elected to office. Priests were forced to say mass secretly out in the hills. No priest was allowed to enter the country. "Adherence to the Catholic Church came to be a point of honor with the common people of Ireland," as T. H. Jackson remarks in his excellent history, *Ireland Her Own*. And as the Irish had defended their religion against the attacks of the British government, so they defended it with equal vigor against bigoted attacks here, especially prevalent in New England, such as were made by the APA (American Protective Association).

My sister Kathie and I had one brief experience in Cleveland with a Catholic school and church when our parents decided to send us to a day convent around the corner from where we lived. The public school was far away, across two car tracks. Kathie was five and I was seven. The academy was run by German sisters, strict disciplinarians, and we did not like them. On the occasion of the Bishop's visit, Kathie declined to make a proper bow, much to my embarrassment! We took a silver dollar each to school every month for tuition. We were relieved to return to a New England public school with neither prayers nor hymn books.

We did not resume going to church in Adams and nothing was said about it. The reason again was a political one, as we later learned, related to a struggle in the late 1880s and early 90s, which affected not only my parents but many practicing Catholics of their generation. It caused a large number to leave the church. This struggle developed around a progressive pro-labor priest in New York City, Dr. Edward McGlynn, called in Gaelic the "Soggarth Aroon," the good priest.

Father McGlynn first evoked the ire of the hierarchy by championing the public school system and opposing the establishment of parochial schools, contending that the church should confine itself to religious teaching only. He championed Irish freedom and espoused the Single Tax theories of Henry George, whose United Labor Party candidacy for Mayor in 1886 he endorsed. He was ordered to cease these political activities and was suspended when he refused. He was finally removed from his parish in 1877 and excommunicated, because he refused to go to Boston. He insisted that the Pope had no jurisdiction over his political rights. He fought valiantly as an American citizen for the right of the Catholic clergy and laity to espouse any political views or party they saw fit. A storm broke of unexpected proportions, involving both Catholics and Protestants who supported Father Mc-Glynn around the country. He organized the Anti-Poverty League to express his social views.

After five years of militant struggle in which the Catholic Church lost tremendously, not only in terms of Peter's Pence but in prestige, Father McGlynn was declared free of censure by a Papal Legate and restored to his priestly post. He served in Newburgh, New York, for many years. However, large numbers of Catholics, like my father, did not return to the fold. So it was partly on account of what happened to Father McGlynn that we were not brought up Catholic. Father Mc-Glynn remained active in public affairs until his death in 1900. At one time, citizens of Newburgh petitioned him to run for Mayor. He is buried in Calvary Cemetery in Brooklyn, "consecrated ground," and there is a statue to him in non-sectarian Woodlawn Cemetery in the Bronx, where LaGuardia and Marcantonio are buried. The principle he fought for is so important that the famous struggle of Father Mc-Glynn for civil and political rights free from ecclesiastical domination is part of American history and should not be forgotten.

This question, "Why are you not Catholic?" comes up at regular intervals, undoubtedly because of my Irish name. Of course not all Irish are Catholic. Charles Stuart Parnell, the great Irish leader, was not. Yet people do not find it easy to understand that one can be simply nonreligious. When my mother was 78 years old she was in the Lebanon Hospital in the Bronx, which is a Jewish hospital. The young woman checking her in asked me: "What is your mother's religion?" When I replied, "She has none," she answered impatiently: "That's impossible—an old lady like that," as if I were libeling my mother. "Why don't you ask her?" I suggested, which she did. She asked, as my mother lay on the examining table: "What's your religion, Mrs.

Flynn?" Mama opened her eyes and smiled. "I haven't any, my dear," she said gently. Later, when her sister insisted she should read some religious material, Mama asked us to bring her a book she had been reading at home, *The Story of Buddha and Buddhism*. She had just finished *The Story of Confucius*.

Sometimes, however, one finds discernment in unexpected places. An Irish woman officer in the Women's House of Detention made this observation to me on the subject of religion: "I guess Socialism has always been your religion." And, in a certain sense, this is true. I found the Socialist movement at a very young and impressionable age. To me it was the creed of the brotherhood of man or "to do on earth as it is in Heaven," and I was an intense believer in socialism during my whole life.

The Spark from Anthracite

We were conditioned in our family to accept socialist thinking long before we came in contact with socialism as an organized movement. My father had voted for Eugene V. Debs as the Socialist Party candidate for President in 1900. We knew our father was opposed to the "two old parties," as he called them over 50 years ago. He talked about the Populist and Greenback parties and boasted how in his youth, in the state of Maine, they had elected a labor Congressman, Tom Murch. The granite workers were employed at that time on government contracts, quarrying out paving slabs and the ugly gray stone blocks which went into all the federal buildings of that day—post offices, courthouses, jails and public offices. Fortunately, many were torn down and replaced under the Public Works Administration of the New Deal days.

The islands off the coast of Maine—Hurricane, Fox and Dix—were rich in granite and were privately owned. The government paid 15 per cent to the owners on all the stone taken out and gave them the right to run the stores on the islands and to collect rents on all the houses. The pay was $2.50 a day for the skilled men and $1 for others. They worked ten hours a day, although an Act of Congress in 1868 had declared an eight-hour day for all laboring men on government contracts. Murch was elected to press the claims of the men for the extra pay due for the two hours.

One of my first subjects in the public school debating society was "Should the Government Own the Coal Mines?" I enthusiastically took the affirmative. This grew out of the 1902 anthracite coal strike in Pennsylvania, led by John Mitchell, when 150,000 miners demanded nine hours instead of ten and recognition of their union—the United Mine Workers of America. The strike, which lasted five months, hit New York hard. A coal shortage forced the curtailment of the "El" services, then run with coal engines. This was serious in those pre-subway days. The strike won general sympathy, especially after the head of the Operators' Association, George F. Baer, made his arrogant remark that "God in His infinite wisdom gave us possession of the coal mines." Ever after he was called "Divine Right" Baer. An Arbitration Commission, appointed by President Theodore Roosevelt, awarded the miners a nine-hour day and a ten per cent increase. They returned to their dangerous jobs, where daily they took their lives in their hands in the dark earth.

This debate was my first approach to the subject of public ownership of natural resources and industries. It appealed to me. I had begun to feel very strongly that in a rich and fertile country like ours there was no excuse for poverty, unemployment, child labor and long strikes. My mother used to recite a poem, by Whittier I believe, which expressed our hatred of poverty. It ran something like this:

When Earth produces free and fair the golden waving corn,
And golden fruits perfume the air and fleecy flocks are shorn,
Yet thousands cry with aching head the never-ending song,
"We starve! We die! Oh give us bread!"
There must be something wrong!

It was this "something wrong" I was bound to search out.

Needless to say, I was a terribly serious child for my years, the oldest of a poor family, sharing the miseries of the parents. When a family suffers poverty, when children hear their mother and even their father weep sometimes from despair over how to feed their children, when all around are other suffering families—children cannot be light-hearted and happy. We saw "some way out" in the struggles of the labor movement and rejoiced in them.

The subject of labor struggles was not new in our household. We had heard in our very early childhood of the so-called Molly Maguires, 17 young Irish-American miners who had been executed in the 1870s in the anthracite area, for trying to organize a union, and of how they were framed up by a Pinkerton detective, James McParlan. An old woman had told us as amazed children in Manchester about how the imprint of a hand on the jail wall, made by one of "those innocent lads, God rest their souls!" could not be erased. I heard this same weird tale many years later from people in Pottsville, Pennsylvania. We had heard of the Haymarket martyrs, hung in Chicago in the 1880s during the eight-hour struggle, and of Debs, imprisoned for violating an injunction in the railroad strike of the 90s, and of the Danbury Hatters' case of 1902, when the union was fined $234,000 under the Sherman Anti-Trust law and the members had to sell their houses to pay it. We hated the rich, the trusts they owned, the violence they caused, the oppression they represented.

In our household the children listened in on everything. We knew Papa had met a Socialist, a draftsman, who worked with him and who ran for alderman on a Socialist ticket in Massachusetts. Pop had written a joking poem about how "We'll get free soup and plenty beer, when Fronck is alderman!" We heard heated debates over many a "growler" of beer (ten cents in those days) on politics, labor, religion and sports. Prize fights were also a daily subject with my cousins and my father—John L. Sullivan, Sharkey, Fitzsimmons, Corbett were favorites. Ideas were our meat and drink, sometimes a substitute for both. It is not strange, therefore, that in such a household our minds were fertile fields for socialism, when the seeds finally came.

The seeds did come in a very simple way. Throwaway cards were distributed from door to door in our neighborhood, announcing a Socialist Sunday night forum, not too far away, at the old Metropolis Theatre building at 142nd Street and Third Avenue. My father and I attended regularly. When he was away my mother and I went. They were arranged by the local Socialists, who were predominantly German, in an effort to attract English-speaking people. They put forth the best American Socialist speakers they could procure. I recall hearing Elsa Barker, a noted poet—who died while I was writing this— Leonard Abbott, Ben Hanford, John Chase, who had been Socialist mayor of Haverhill, Massachusetts, Algernon Lee and others. We brought home the Socialist weekly paper of that day, *The Worker,* and as many pamphlets as we could afford, and read them avidly. We were surprised to learn how many Socialists had been elected to city offices around the country and how strong the movement was internationally. Our horizons broadened, beyond the South Bronx and the struggle for Irish freedom. Socialism was a great discovery—a hope, a purpose, a flame within me, lit first by a spark from anthracite.

BOOKS FEED THE FLAME

When I was just past my 15th birthday, searching for a solution to poverty, my mother suggested I read *Looking Backward* by a Massachusetts journalist, Edward Bellamy. It was about the year 2000 in a socialist America. The author, who is portrayed as a sufferer from insomnia, had taken a sleeping potion in 1887 and had gone to rest in an underground soundproof chamber of his house in Boston. The house was burned down, the one servant had died in the fire and it was assumed the young man had also perished. He lay there in a trance-like sleep for 113 years, to awaken in a new world when his resting place was unearthed by builders. The book portrayed an ideal society, due to the abolition of banks, landlords and capitalists. It was an imaginative description of what a socialist America could be like, with collective ownership of all natural resources and industries and full utilization of machinery, technical knowledge and the capacities of her people. It appealed to me as practical and feasible. It still does in its basic principles—though the year 2000 is now only 46 years away and socialism should be that much nearer at least, in fact "just around the corner."

This book of Bellamy's pictured an American society built on the principle, "From each according to his ability, to each according to his needs." Some of it seemed quite fantastic then, such as pushing buttons in the wall and hearing plays and operas right in the room, but *children* can do it today with TV sets. This socialist romance of the 19th century was read and discussed by millions of people throughout the world. It was translated into German, French, Russian, Italian, Arabic and Bulgarian. Bellamy Clubs were formed around the country. My mother had belonged to one, in Concord, New Hampshire. The book first popularized the idea of socialism in this country. It was a biting criticism of capitalism, which hit home to many Americans and with which they agreed in the days of rising monopolies.

Naturally, it created much debate. One of my anarchist friends labeled it as "too mechanical a world" and tried to counteract it by giving me another Utopian story, *News from Nowhere* by William Morris, a famous English Socialist, artist and poet. It appeared in a newspaper serially; published in 1891 in book form as a reply to Bellamy, it portrayed a different socialist world after 2000, in which cities were decentralized and craftsmanship predominated. The Morris book was a prose poem, beautifully written, but it did not appeal to me. I felt that to return to handicrafts was not progress, and that machinery could be a more helpful servant of mankind when it was used for the benefit of all and not for the profit of a few. Of the two pictures, Bellamy's conforms more to our scientific age. One marvels on rereading it, over 60 years after it was written, how much of what he prophesied has already come to pass in the capitalist as well as the socialist countries of today, where the subjugation of machinery to the will and needs of humanity is more and more the rule.

The great value of Bellamy's book is that it was an early American socialist work. I read it 18 years after it was written. It made a profound impression on me, as it had done on countless others, as a convincing explanation of how peaceful, prosperous and happy America could be under a socialist system of society.

A pamphlet which I read at about the same time was called *Appeal to the Young* by Peter Kropotkin, born a prince but then a Russian anarchist revolutionist. It was written in 1885 when he was in a French prison. He made a trip to the United States in 1901 in support of the Russian revolutionary struggle and addressed large meetings here. There was great interest in his books, *Conquest of Bread, Mutual Aid* and *The Great French Revolution*. He appealed to young doctors, lawyers, teachers, scientists, artists to "employ the entire vigor of their youth, energy, the full force of their intelligence, and their talents to help the people in the vast enterprise they have now undertaken—*Socialism.*" His appeal to the youth of the poor struck home to me personally, as if he were speaking to us there in our shabby poverty-stricken Bronx flat: "Must you drag on the same weary existence as your father and mother for thirty or forty years? Must you toil your life long to procure for others all the pleasures of well-being, of knowledge, of art, and keep for yourself only the eternal anxiety as to whether you can get a bit of bread?"

Another book I recall, which caused an immediate change in my life, was *The Jungle* by Upton Sinclair. After reading it I forthwith became a vegetarian! He wrote this book in 1906 to expose the terrible conditions of the stockyard workers and to advocate socialism as a remedy. But the public seized rather upon the horrible descriptions of filth, diseased cattle, floor sweepings and putrid meat packed in sausages and canned foods. The sale of meat fell catastrophically for the packers and demands for investigations and legal action rent the air. Still fresh in the public mind were the scandals over poisonous canned meat sold to the U.S. Army, which caused many deaths during the Spanish-American War. Ella Reeve Bloor, then a young woman, was sent to Chicago by Sinclair to gather data to reinforce his charges. Later, after the Pure Food, Drug and Inspection Act of 1906 was passed as a direct result of Sinclair's book, she went to work in the plants again to check on whether the law was enforced and found the Beef Trust was ignoring it. This was the first time I heard her name—in 1906.

MY FIRST BOY FRIEND

After graduation from grammar school, our debating society continued outside as the Hamilton Literary Society. We met weekly during 1905 at the home of a Dr. Cantor on East 143rd Street and were supervised by Joseph Weinstein, a college student, later a school teacher. Many newcomers from other schools joined, most of whom were Jewish. This was my first intimate contact with Jewish people, and I liked them very much. I found them idealistic and progressive. Their mental curiosity and intellectual acuteness were stimulating. Our discussions encompassed every possible social problem. I began to realize that the Irish were not the only national group that had suffered persecution because of their religion, language and culture. I was influenced greatly in my thinking at the time by a youth in high school I met at this club. He was Fred Robinson, the son of Dr. William J. Robinson who edited an unorthodox trail blazer on medicine called *The Critic and Guide*. Dr. Robinson was one of several doctors who were pioneer advocates of birth control, long before Mrs. Margaret Sanger became its chief spokesman.

Fred used to walk me home the nine blocks after our meetings. He was my first boy friend, though he never as much as held my hand. He talked about Walt Whitman, Jack London, Emma Goldman, and other people of whom I had never heard. He wrote me letters full of ideas of "social significance," enclosing clippings and poems. Fred was more of an anarchist than a socialist, I believe, though the words were loose-

ly interchanged in those days. Albert Parsons, for instance, the martyred leader of the eight-hour movement in the1880s, had called himself a socialist and an anarchist and had run for office on a union labor
ticket.

Fred Robinson wanted me to see and meet Emma Goldman. She
had been persecuted considerably after the death of President Mc-
Kinley, and was living quietly then as E. G. Smith, running a hair-
dressing establishment. But her reputation was as a fiery agitator, who
had served a sentence on Blackwell's Island, and as the companion of
Alexander Berkman who was still in prison in Pennsylvania for the attempted shooting of Henry Frick during the Homestead strike. What
type of woman I expected to meet would be hard to say—an Amazon,
undoubtedly. I afterward thought of my own surprise on this occasion,
when later people would say on first meeting me: "Oh! We expected a
different sort of woman—large and redheaded!"

Finally Fred brought me to a little, rather stout woman, with mild
blue eyes, lovely blonde hair, dressed very plainly, with a funny little
flat hat and a flower cocked on one side of it. She greeted me kindly
but with the absent-minded manner of a public speaker who meets
countless people. Later I heard her speak at the Harlem Liberal Alliance and was surprised at the force, eloquence and fire that poured
from this mild-mannered, motherly sort of woman. Her views on subjects like birth control, prison reform, marriage and love, and the social significance of modern drama would seem quite mild today. Then
they were considered dangerously radical, her meetings were broken
up and she was arrested in many cities, particularly after the Berkman
arrest in Pittsburgh and again after the assassination of President
McKinley by a Polish anarchist. She spoke of Berkman, soon to be released from prison, and said dramatically: "We will take up his work
right where he left off!" I thought that boded no good for old Frick!
As long as Emma Goldman spoke to poor people in the small halls
with sawdust on the floor there was an agitational vibrance in her
speeches. Later, with an insufferable buffoon, Dr. Ben Reitman, as
her manager, she blossomed into a lecturer, the idol of middle-class
liberals, and the crowds grew. He used to boast of the "number of
cars" outside the hall, when cars were scarce and expensive. But she
lost her dynamic quality as an agitator on these occasions and became
quite prosaic.

I went to a meeting of welcome to Berkman and you can judge

my youthful pleasure that she remembered me and took me by the hand to introduce me to him. Again he was an unexpected type. He, too, was a gentle, courteous man, aged by his long imprisonment, but with a strong mentality and a kind word for a young and unknown seeker in the radical world. Later, at a Moyer-Haywood* protest meeting at Union Square, he invited me to dinner at a famous German restaurant, Luchow's, on 14th Street, to pass the time till I had to go to Cooper Union to speak in the evening. Hippolyte Havel, the anarchist philosopher, came along, slightly tipsy as usual. He insisted on kissing my hand and telling me how beautiful I was, but as I had heard he said this to all women when inebriated I was embarrassed but not impressed. Once he had been arrested for accosting a lady on the street to tell her how beautiful she was. Berkman was aware of my embarrassment and kept kicking him under the table and telling him to behave himself. Hippolyte would shake his wild hair and say: "What the hell's the matter with you, Sasha? I'm not doing anything!" Berkman saw that I had an excellent dinner and then took me safely to my meeting, where the Socialists were up in arms surrounding my mother, warning her not to let me be seen with this dangerous anarchist.

After all, Berkman had just been released from the Western Pennsylvania Penitentiary in 1905, after serving 13 years. During the Homestead steel strike in 1892, outraged by the brutal murder of strikers, he had made an attempt on the life of Henry Frick, manager of the Carnegie Steel Works. Berkman was a youth who had come from Russia only five years before and was under the influence of the Nihilists who believed in assassination of all tyrants, from the tsar down. He tells in his book, *Prison Memoirs of an Anarchist,* how he met a steel striker in the jail who thought Berkman had "some business trouble" with Frick, because he had gained access to him with an employment agency card. On this basis, he was sympathetic with him. But when Berkman eagerly tried to explain that he had committed the act from sympathy with the strikers, that it was an act of protest for them, the worker indignantly rejected the idea and said it would only hurt them. "The steel workers defended their homes and their families against invaders. But they will have nothing to do with anarchists," he said. "It's none of your business, you didn't belong to the Homestead

* See below, "Undesirable Citizens."

men!" This was a bitter pill for the young idealist, ready to lay down his life for "the people" and now facing a life sentence.

My parents did not object to the debating society or to my friendship with Fred Robinson. But they were alarmed at my fraternizing with the anarchists and the number of pamphlets from that source I was reading. They certainly did not approve of the free love theories of Emma Goldman, upon which she gave lectures which drew large audiences of young people. They probably discussed the problem with some Socialists at the meetings we attended. Someone who took a special interest in my questions at the forums suggested that I read the publications of the Charles H. Kerr Company of Chicago and gave me for a starter the *Communist Manifesto.* I had not yet read anything by Marx or Engels. They did not have a wide circulation in English. It was part of a "Standard Socialist Series," which this company started in 1900.

The *Manifesto,* by Karl Marx and Frederick Engels, was written in 1848. I read it first in 1906. It was introduced as "evidence" of a criminal conspiracy against me and my co-defendants at the Foley Square trial in New York under the Smith Act in 1952. I also read in that long ago day, nearly a half century ago, *Socialism—Utopian and Scientific* and the *Origin of the Family, Private Property and the State,* both by Engels, and the pamphlets *Value, Price and Profit* and *Wage-Labor and Capital* by Marx. The Kerr company issued the first volume of *Capital* in 1906, the remaining two volumes in 1909. All of these books and pamphlets are today not only labeled "subversive" but are introduced by stool pigeons in trial after trial as Smith Act evidence, to show that we are "foreign agents" and advocate the violent overthrow of government. In 1906 they were considered part of an education by all progressive-minded Americans, as Wendell Willkie remarked to the U. S. Supreme Court.

When I began to accumulate scientific socialist literature my father seized upon it. He read everything by Marx and Engels he could lay his hands on. His knowledge of mathematics helped him to master them easily. He read them aloud to his family. He talked and argued about them with anyone who would listen—in the saloon, in the park, on the job. Scientific socialism came as a balm to my father's spirit. It exposed the capitalist system in all its ugly naked greed, and its indifference to human welfare. It showed how it enriched the few and impoverished the masses of people. It explained what caused depressions, "bad times," economic crises.

Scientific socialism made clear that it was not a poor man's fault if he is out of work; it's no proof of incompetence, laziness and lack of ability on his part, said Pop, "if some damned capitalist could not make a profit out of buying his labor power!" And you were not a "failure" because you did not climb to riches on the backs of your fellow men. I believe, however, my long-suffering mother often felt that Pop overworked Karl Marx as an alibi for not looking for a job.

FIRST SPEECH, 1906

In 1906 the Bronx Socialist Forum, which our family attended regularly, closed. We shifted our allegiance to the Harlem Socialist Club, at 250 West 125th Street. In good weather, open-air meetings were held on the corners of 7th Avenue and 125th Street—with women speaking for suffrage—and Socialist meetings arranged by this club. In winter the Socialist meetings were held in their headquarters, up two flights of stairs. We used to walk over from the South Bronx—carfares for a whole family were more than we could afford. Events took a sudden turn during my second year in Morris High School. I had lost a few months in school during that winter due to an infected jaw from an abscessed tooth. During that period I had studied two more books, which helped to catapult me into socialist activities. One was the *Vindication of the Rights of Women* by Mary Wollstonecraft; the other was *Women and Socialism* by August Bebel. (Forty-six years later in 1951 this book was listed as a Government's exhibit in Federal Judge Dimock's court in a trial under the Smith Act. It is now out of print, practically a collector's item.)

Someone at the Harlem Socialist Club, hearing of my debating experience and knowing of my reading and intense interest in socialism, asked me to make a speech. My father was not much impressed with the idea. He thought they should have asked *him* to expound Marxism, on which he now considered himself an expert. I'm afraid my father would be labelled a "male-supremacist" these days. Once I stood up at a meeting and asked the speaker a question. He frowned upon such a performance. Couldn't I have asked him to explain on our way home? But my mother encouraged me and I accepted the offer to speak. I tried to select a subject upon which my father would not interfere too much, something he did not consider too important. It was "What Socialism Will Do For Women."

Wednesday, January 31, 1906, is a date engraved on my memory, the occasion of my first public speech. It was a small place, holding not more than 75 people, but like the Mayflower, legends grew around it. That little boat would have rivalled the gigantic Queen Mary if she had carried all the ancestors now claimed as passengers. And my little hall would have been of Carnegie Hall proportions to accommodate all who have told me, "I heard your first speech!" I do recall some of those present, who included Edward F. Cassidy and his wife Alice. He was an official for many years of Typographical Union No. 6 and a Socialist candidate for mayor. There was a fussy old man, E. S. Egerton, who had charge of a Fall River Day Line Pier in the daytime and these lectures at night. There was also a young Chinese Socialist, who later returned to China, and a young Negro Socialist, the first I had met, Frank Crosswaithe. There was a thin elderly man named Frost, who wrote plays about workers' lives, in which we all took part. There was a young trade unionist, Al Abrams, who was in the Central Labor Body of the AFL. A singer with a lovely voice, Mrs. Van Name, gave cultural content to our meetings. Fred Harwood, later well known as a Communist, was there, as was Tom Lewis, who in later years was the first Communist Party district organizer in California. He was a pioneer Socialist soapbox agitator—"educated on the breakers in the coal mines," he said, "but bring on your college professors who want to debate socialism." It was not an empty challenge. He was a devastating opponent, his mind overflowed with facts and fast, homely illustrations. He made his living selling pest exterminators by day and "worked free to exterminate the pest of capitalism by night," he used to say. He was an able and resourceful organizer.

I was a slender serious girl, not yet 16, with my black hair loose to my waist, tied with a ribbon. I wore a long full skirt down to my ankles, as was proper in 1906, a white shirt waist and a red tie. I had labored to write my speech and had stubbornly resisted all attempts of Egerton, my father and others to tell me what to say or to actually write it for me. Good or bad, I felt it had to be my own. I began to quake inwardly at the start, facing an adult audience for the first time. But they were sympathetic and I was soon sailing along serenely. When I concluded, I asked for questions, as I had heard other speakers do. None were forthcoming. The audience apparently sensed that I was nervous. How they laughed when I said resentfully: "Just because I'm young and a girl, is no reason you shouldn't ask me questions!"

My speech was compounded of my limited personal experience,

which I felt very acutely, however, and my rather wide reading. It was in the spirit of the Wollstonecraft book, which advocated the rights of women in 1792—economic, political, educational and social. That was a period of ferment over "the rights of man" in America and Europe. The substance of my speech was based on the more modern book, by Bebel a German Socialist leader who was a member of the Reichstag for 50 years. Bebel was tried in 1872 with Wilhelm Liebknecht, charged with "high treason" by the Bismarck government, and sentenced to two years in the fortress, Hubertusburg. While there, he worked on this, his most famous book.

It was translated into English by Daniel de Leon, editor of the *Daily People,* organ of the Socialist Labor Party, and published in 1904 by Kerr. I was interested to hear from Steve Nelson, on his return from fighting in Spain in the late 1930s, that the first Socialist book he had read was Bebel's *Women and Socialism.* Lenin well described it as "written strongly, aggressively, against bourgeois society." So great is the author's sympathy with woman, his indignation at the indignities and injustices she has endured, and so strong was his faith in her abilities and capacities as a human being, that one could well believe a woman wrote it.

My advent as a speaker caused no comment outside of the weekly Socialist paper, *The Worker,* which said: "In view of her youth, although knowing she was very bright, the comrades were prepared to judge her lecture indulgently; they found that no indulgence was called for, that she had a surprising grasp of the subject and handled it with skill." With this blessing I was launched on my career as a public speaker.

"WOMAN'S PLACE"

The first socialist speech in 1906 dealt with the status of women, who were then considered inferior and treated as such in every walk of life. "Woman's place" was a subject of considerable debate 50 years ago. Women were denied the right to vote and deprived of all legal rights over their children, homes or property. Many schools, leading colleges and professions were practically closed to them. Only a few succeeded in overcoming these barriers and they were denied appointments and advancement in their chosen field. The "career girl" was discouraged. Women in industry were overworked and miserably underpaid in the jobs open to them—and always paid less than men on the same level. They were denied opportunities to enter skilled trades and had little protection from labor organizations.

The unionization of women, even in occupations like the needle trades where they predominated, had scarcely yet begun. Equal opportunities, equal pay, and the right to be organized, were the crying needs of women wage-earners then and unfortunately these demands remain with us today. Many union leaders, like Samuel Gompers, president of the American Federation of Labor, did not consider women workers organizable or dependable. "They only work for pin money!" was the usual complaint. An outside job was considered by the woman worker herself as a temporary necessary evil—a stop-gap between her father's home and her husband's home. Fathers and husbands collected women's wages, sometimes right at the company office. Women did not have a legal right to their own earnings. There was no consideration for the special needs and problems of working mothers, though they were numerous and pressing. Even the clothes of women hampered them—the long skirts that touched the ground, the big unwieldy sleeves, the enormous hats. You were still "a girl" if your skirt was above your shoe tops.

The struggle for the right of women to vote was nationwide and growing. It had started with the first Equal Rights Convention, at Seneca Falls, New York, in 1848, led by Elizabeth Cady Stanton and Susan B. Anthony, which was addressed by Frederick Douglass, the great Negro leader. The suffragists had been ridiculed, assaulted by mobs, refused halls, arrested for attempting to vote, disowned by their families. By 1904, groups of working women, especially Socialist women, were banding together to join in the demand for the vote. Two years later, International Women's Day was born on the East Side of New York, at the initiative of these women demonstrating for suffrage. It spread around the world and is universally celebrated today, while here it is deprecated as "a foreign holiday."

The suffrage movement was growing more militant and figures like Maude Malone appeared. She organized the Harlem Equal Rights League in 1905. She interrupted Theodore Roosevelt at a meeting of 3,000 people to demand where he stood on woman suffrage. She walked up and down Broadway, at the same time we were holding our street meetings there, with signs front and back, like a sandwich man, demanding "Votes for Women," and lost her post as a librarian in consequence. Once she was speaking at 125th Street and a heckler asked: "How would you like to be a man?" She answered: "Not much. How would you?" (Maude Malone died at 78 in 1951. She had been librarian at the *Daily Worker* for four and a half years.)

Suffragist speakers on streetcorners were invariably told: "Go home and wash your dishes," or, regardless of their age: "Who's taking care of your children?" Others said: "Imagine a pregnant woman running for office," or "How could women serve on juries and be locked up with men jurors?" I recall an experience at Guffanti's restaurant over 40 years ago, when I was with Margaret Sanger and a woman doctor friend, who started to smoke cigarettes. We were ordered by the management to desist or leave. The doctor asked a man smoking a big cigar: "Do you object to my smoking?" He replied: "Hell, no, lady, go right ahead." Finally, the manager ordered a screen placed around our table to shut the "hussies" from view.

There was a prevalent concept that "woman's work" was confined to the domestic scene. "Woman's place is in the home," was the cry. Women were constantly accused of taking "men's jobs." I spoke in my first speech of the drudgery and monotony of women's unpaid labor in the millions of American kitchens, of primitive handicraft jobs done by women at home, a hangover from times when the home was the center of hand manufacture. With the advent of power-operated machinery many tasks which traditionally belonged to women had been taken out of the home into mass production industry, such as spinning, weaving, sewing, baking, soap-making, food-preserving, making dairy products. Women were forced to follow their jobs into the outside world, there to be accused of taking away "men's jobs." I stressed the possibility, at least under socialism, of industrializing all the domestic tasks by collective kitchens and dining places, nurseries, laundries, and the like.

I said then and am still convinced that the full opportunity for women to become free and equal citizens with access to all spheres of human endeavor cannot come under capitalism, although many demands have been won by organized struggle. I referred to August Bebel's views of a socialist society, like those of all of us, as speculative and prophetic—"the personal opinion of the author himself," he said. He foresaw the abolition of prostitution and of loveless, arranged marriages, the establishment of economic independence of women and the freedom of mothers from dependence on individual men, the social care of children, the right of every woman to an education, to work and to participate in government; to be a wife, mother, worker and citizen; to enter the arts and sciences and all the professions. I was fired with determination to fight for all this.

TAKING CHILDREN TO MEETINGS

When I was a girl, parents took the children along wherever they went, either to church, to visit or to Socialist meetings. If both parents wanted to go to a meeting, they had to take the children. There were no baby-sitters in those days. That came over 30 years later, with World War II. Working class families could not afford it. In case of an emergency, such as childbirth or death, the older children, a relative or a neighbor took the young ones over. A child might be asked "to mind the baby" in the carriage outdoors or while the mother did an errand. Ten cents could be ample reward for this chore. On many occasions our whole family of six—parents and four children—all went to a Socialist meeting or social gathering.

When the younger children got tired they were put to sleep on benches along the walls. They woke up if tea and cookies were served. Most parents did this in moderation, but my father had a tendency to overdo it. There were many times we children rebelled and my mother had to intervene. He would drag the children to street meetings where they had to stand around for hours. They would rather stay home to do their homework than to sell literature and help with collections. They lost sleep and were overtired the next day. He tried to turn everything into socialist propaganda and there were endless struggles over school compositions. We would go to school early and rewrite what he had dictated to us. It developed a dislike of my father and his methods and also a distaste for meetings, of which we had an overdose. It took years to overcome this. I shared the rebellion against Pop but was old enough to like meetings. Another habit my father had was to read aloud. "Listen to this, Annie," he would say, regardless of what Mama was doing. He interrupted our homework with "This is part of your education, too, and more important than that stuff!" As a result, none of us to this day read aloud or can bear to listen. There are right and wrong ways with children, who have more recognized rights today than we had when we were young.

I have been in many working-class families during my long life of labor agitation and have heard complaints from both generations. I have heard many discussions on how to pass socialist ideas on to the next generation. It has been particularly hard for intelligent foreign-born workers, who speak and read papers and books in their native language, which their children all too soon rejected as "old country stuff." I've had many young people say to me in surprise: "You're an American and you believe that too?" Often the parents were overcritical of all American ways and this deepened the rift. The "melting pot" concept, that to be an American one must shed and forget one's language, traditions and culture and be molded to a common denominator has caused the second generation to be ashamed of their parents' ways and to reject their ideas. Later, after experience and struggle, they are often amazed to realize how right their parents really were, even if they were "foreigners."

In the days of my youth there were no organized youth activities of any sort. Later, a Socialist youth movement developed, with Socialist Sunday schools. Some of these were horribly sectarian, however. My sister Kathie went to one in the Bronx, where they sang:

> My father had a working man,
> My father had a mule.
> To save my life I couldn't tell
> Which was the biggest fool!

The point here was that the workingmen did not vote the Socialist ticket. After I left the debating society in 1906, I was plunged into an adult world, with no contact with boys or girls of my own age level. I needed a social life, youthful advice, criticism and association. As a result I had no real youth.

But with all its shortcomings, I still think the old-fashioned method of "taking children to meetings" has some real advantages, especially if the parents are selective and take them to those special occasions which they will remember all their lives. Many people have said to me: "I first remember a meeting where my parents took me to hear Debs—or Haywood—or Mother Bloor." Or, "You are the first speaker I ever heard—at Lawrence, or Paterson." Children of today will similarly remember in days to come: "I heard Paul Robeson—or Steve Nelson—or Ben Davis—or Eugene Dennis." A big rally where there are many people and great enthusiasm gives a child a sense of belonging, a feeling of identification with others, that "we are many," and that their parents do not have queer ideas and are not alone.

There are some modern concepts among progressive parents of "security" or "protecting children" by shielding them from problems and struggles, as if one can shut off the impact of schools, radio, television, comic books, atom bomb scares and what not. Of course plain workers—miners, steel, auto, needle and textile workers—cannot shield their children from the impact of unemployment, part-time employment, and the like. "I don't want my children to go through what I did!" is a natural feeling, but sometimes it is used as an excuse to divorce children from all progressive ideas and to deprive them of all antidotes to the daily poison poured into them. The "wrap them up in cotton wool" method is one approach "Let them do what they please, don't frustrate them," is another, which is more likely to develop egocentric reactionaries than defenders of peace and democracy. We've got to fight for the minds of our children lest they become warped and distorted, as were many of the German youth. We must not surrender our children's minds to brutality, cruelty and violence or to anti-social ideas.

Our father's methods were not entirely correct but his purpose was clear, not to allow his children to be "educated" against the interests of the working class. Our family came out of our early tribulations all progressive-minded, members of unions, voting Socialists. For all his faults our father was a fighter with strong convictions as to the rights of the people. This at least he bequeathed to his children.

TWO

Socialist and IWW Agitator, 1906-1912

◆◆◆◆◆◆◆◆◆◆◆◆◆◆◆◆◆

I MOUNT THE SOAP BOX AND GET ARRESTED

My advent as a speaker at the Harlem Socialist Club in 1906 brought me invitations to speak elsewhere. There were many progressive forums held at that time in practically every section of the city and in nearby cities. I visited Newark, Philadelphia, Providence and Boston. One such gathering was extremely popular with "radicals" of all descriptions. It was called the "Unity Congregation" and was conducted like a church, with readings, songs, and a main speech or sermon. Hugh O. Pentecost, an ex-minister then a lawyer, conducted this assemblage. (He had lost his pulpit over the Father McGlynn controversy.) It was held at Lyric Hall on 6th Avenue between 41st and 42nd Streets opposite Bryant Park, where the Automat now is. It was a famous old meeting place, originally called Apollo Hall. A life-sized statue of a Greek god adorned a niche in the side wall. It was here, in 1872, that the Equal Rights Convention had nominated Victoria C. Woodhull for President and Frederick Douglass for Vice-President of the United States.

My friend Fred Robinson and I attended this forum and we gave out circulars at the door advertising a series of printed mottoes by Fred's older brother, Victor, who later became a professor. The only one I recall is: "Progress is written in one word—disobedience." Mr. Pentecost spoke every Sunday and did not ordinarily invite others to share his platform. Imagine how highly honored I felt when he asked me to speak there! I chose for my subject "Education," in which I

61

voiced all my criticism of the school system—too much homework, not sufficient manual work, not enough subjects of practical value to students, especially those who could not go to college. This is remembered by many as my "first speech."

In the summer of 1906 I began to speak on the street. I took to it like a duck to water. So many of our street meetings were held at 125th Street and 7th Avenue that an enthusiast tacked a metal marker on one of the trees, "Liberty Tree." Needless to say, there were no amplifiers or loudspeakers in those days. Tom Lewis, pioneer soapboxer, who could be heard for blocks, taught me to speak, especially how to project my voice outdoors. "Breathe deep, use your diaphragm as a bellows; don't talk on your vocal chords or you'll get hoarse in no time. Throw your voice out." His advice was effective.

I often wonder how modern audiences would receive the fervid oratory popular then. Styles of speech have changed with the radio and public speaking systems, which have compelled modulation of the voice, eliminated action, and calmed down the approach. Then we gesticulated, we paced the platform, we appealed to the emotions. We provoked arguments and questions. We spoke loudly, passionately, swiftly. We used invectives and vituperation, we were certainly not "objective" in our attacks on capitalism and all its works. Even when newly-arrived immigrants did not understand our words they shared our spirit. At all our indoor mass meetings there were speakers in many languages—Jewish, Russian, Polish, Italian, German and others. Our foreign-born comrades, like Pedro Estove in Spanish, Arturo Giovannitti in Italian, and Bill Shatoff in Russian, were magnificent orators. They inspired us to more beautiful and moving language in English.

In August 1906, I was arrested with my father and several others for "speaking without a permit" and "blocking traffic" at 38th Street and Broadway, then the heart of the theatrical district. The chairman was a little old man with a derby hat—Michael Cody, who sold the *Weekly People* for years at all Socialist meetings. The auspices of our meeting was the Unity Club, an attempt to unite Socialist Party and Socialist Labor Party speakers on one platform. One of our number had a flair for showmanship and had devised a striking unity banner, topped by a whirling contraption with the flags of all nations, flanked by red flares for illumination. Someone in the audience objected to the flags and insisted that only the American flag should be displayed.

Naturally our colorful caravan, rivaling a circus, caused a sensation, even on Broadway, and the argument increased the crowd to huge proportions. When the police officer ordered us to stop, we refused and the reserves were called. Our arrests followed.

We were released on bail at 2 a.m. and appeared before Magistrate Walsh in Jefferson Market Court the next day. Our trial was something of a disappointment to Pop, who wanted to tell the judge off, but Mr. Pentecost, who appeared as our lawyer, hushed him up. He spoke of my extreme youth to my great embarrassment, although I did feel a little better when he said I was "the coming Socialist woman orator of America."

We were all discharged, with the judge advising me to go back to school that Fall and be a student a while longer before I become a teacher. He said to the prosecutor: "Better some socialism than a suspicion of oppression!" He said I was wasting my time trying to convert "the tenderloin riffraff" and the idle curiosity seekers of Broadway. Seldom is judicial advice of this sort taken, and we returned forthwith to bigger and better meetings, although the working class districts would have been more appropriate for our purposes. The newspapers featured my arrest as "Mere Child Talks Bitterly of Life." The *New York Times* editorialized in a humorous, patronizing style about "the ferocious Socialist haranguer, Miss Flynn, who will graduate at school in two years and whose shoe tops at present show below her skirts, [who] tells us what to think, which is just what she thinks." Pop never forgave Mr. Pentecost. "That damned lawyer wouldn't let me talk!" he'd rave.

Strangely enough, when I returned to Morris High School in the Fall, no comment was made on the arrest. But attending school by day and meetings by night was a heavy toll, not conducive to proper rest or study. I had an excellent scholastic record in grammar school with all A marks, but it had now declined alarmingly. Mr. Denbigh, the principal, tried to convince me that I should concentrate on my studies and give up the outside activities, of which he expressed no criticism. He said if I finished my education I would be better equipped for work in the labor movement a few years later. My mother agreed with Mr. Denbigh. But I was impatient. It did not seem to me that anything I was learning there had relationship to life or would be helpful to me. With the Revolution on my mind I found it difficult to concentrate on Latin or geometry. And I smarted under the "too young" attitude of adults. So within the next few months I left school, an action I deeply regretted in later years.

"I Don't Want to Be an Actress!"

Shortly after my arrest on Broadway and 38th Street a message came to me from David Belasco, the most famous theatrical producer of that day. He wanted to see me and arranged it by sending two tickets for his current success. My mother and I went to a matinee performance of *The Girl of the Golden West,* with Blanche Bates. After the show ended, a young man escorted us upstairs to Mr. Belasco's office, which was dominated by a large oil painting of a beautiful redhaired actress, his most famous star, Mrs. Leslie Carter. Mr. Belasco was a striking looking man, with a halo of bushy white hair. He wore a reversed collar that made him look like a priest. On our introduction he said to me: "You are very young!" which I answered with hurt dignity: "That will be remedied in time!"

He asked with an amused twinkle in his eyes, had I ever thought of being an actress; he was thinking of producing a labor play and I might be good material to appear in it. "Indeed not!" I answered heatedly: "I don't want to be a actress! I want to speak my own words and not say over and over again what somebody else has written. I'm in the labor movement and I speak my own piece!" He chuckled and said maybe I'd change my mind later. We shook hands and parted friends. My mother was quite overwhelmed at such an offer and slightly stunned, I fear, at my summary rejection of it. Later, she encouraged my younger sister Bina's aspirations for the stage. She had a small part in one of Belasco's plays, *Dark Rosaleen.* He inquired about me and said with a laugh: "She's the only girl I've ever met who did not want to be an actress. Is she still speaking her own piece?" He told her he thought I had made a wise decision, that I belonged to the labor movement.

Another famous person, although then unknown and obscure, whom I met as a result of the Broadway arrest was Theodore Dreiser. Managing editor of the *Broadway Magazine,* he was in his thirties, a large, somber, slow-spoken man. He lived not far from us in the South Bronx, in a poor section called Mott Haven, now known as The Concourse, since it had its face lifted. He invited me to dinner at his home. Apparently he was in the midst of a struggle to live and to write. He had not yet written many of the powerful books which later brought him national and worldwide fame. He wrote a piece about me in the September 1906 issue of the magazine, called "An East Side Joan of Arc." It read as follows:

They call her Comrade Elizabeth Flynn, and she is only a girl just turned sixteen, as sweet a sixteen as ever bloomed, with a sensitive, flower-like face. But she is also an ardent Socialist orator, one of the most active workers in the cause in New York City. It was in January last that she made her first appearance on the lecture platform and electrified her audience with her eloquence, her youth and loveliness. Since then she has been in demand as a speaker wherever in the city there has been a Socialist gathering, at Cooper Union or at Carnegie Hall or on the street corners of the East Side.

The girl is a typical Irish beauty, with the blue eyes, filmy black hair and delicate pink complexion of the race from which she is sprung. She is only a pupil in her second year at the Morris High School, but she has the mature mentality, the habit of thought and finished expression of a woman of twenty-five. Some day she means to study law. She has been reared in the shadow of the red flag of the proletariat, and her Socialist tendencies are inherited. Her father has long been a member of the party. The walls of the humble apartment which is their home in the Bronx are covered with pictures of world-famed men and women who have defied the existing order of society, from Marat and Mirabeau to Byron and George Eliot, and from Tom Paine to Maxim Gorky.

Elizabeth Flynn believes many things that sound strangely enough from the lips of a girl, but they are the tenets of the party with which she has allied herself. Among her statements are these:

"The state should provide for the maintenance of every child so that the individual woman shall not be compelled to depend for support on the individual man, while bearing the child."

"The barter and sale that goes on under the name of love is highly obnoxious."

"The one system of economics that gives every human being an equal opportunity is Socialism."

"The wage-earning class the world over are the victims of society."

The caption under the picture was as follows:

MISS ELIZABETH FLYNN

On the East Side among the hosts of those who are restless and eager, they call her "Comrade Elizabeth Flynn." She is only sixteen but an orator and a thinker, and believes in attempting to do something to relieve the condition of the poor. Mentally, she is one of the most remarkable girls that the city has ever seen.

I am very proud to have had a fleeting glimpse of this great American in his youth. Subsequently he fought in many struggles for American democratic rights, up to his death. He joined the Communist Party in 1945.

It is interesting to glance over this magazine of 58 years ago, edited by Dreiser. There is a story about the progress of the construction of the Grand Central Terminal, which was not finished until 1908; we read that the first public trade school for girls was planned by the Board of Education; that Ruth St. Denis made her first appearance as a dancer; and that Anthony Comstock was hauling publishers to court on "obscenity" charges, one of them being charged with publishing Tolstoy's *Kreutzer Sonata*. But no one took Comstock too seriously.

My first step into the trade union world also occurred in the summer of 1908, when I was invited to speak to striking longshoremen in Hoboken, New Jersey, and in Manhattan and Brooklyn. They left the meetings to go out to picket the docks. Ships bound for all parts of the world were tied up. The majority in New Jersey were German. In Brooklyn they were Irish. I recall an interesting experience in connection with the Brooklyn meeting, which was held in the basement auditorium of a Catholic church. The committee in charge took me to the priest's home to meet him. They asked me not to say anything about socialism as "the Father" might not like it.

Later in the hall the priest said he would like to speak to me and we went into an anteroom. He said: "Miss Flynn, I understand you are a Socialist." I was taken aback, but I would not deny my ideas. I said: "Yes, but I'm only going to talk unionism here tonight." Imagine my surprise when he said: "I'm interested in socialism but don't say anything to the men. They might be shocked." He wanted to know how he could get some socialist literature. We talked quite a while. I promised to send him some literature, which I did. We corresponded after that until his death not long after. He had told me he would like to be more active in the cause of working people but he was not well and he supposed he'd have to leave the church. "The trouble is," he said, with a wry smile, "I don't know how to do anything else except drive a wagon!"

The first parade I marched in was in memory of Bloody Sunday in Russia. This massacre occurred on January 22, 1905, at the Winter Palace in St. Petersburg (now Leningrad), when 15,000 peaceful working men and women marched in a procession to petition the tsar for national representation. They were led by a Russian Orthodox priest, Father Gapon; they were dressed in their Sunday best; they carried their sacred icons and had a written petition to present. Soldiers fired volley after volley at them from three sides, killing and wounding over 1500. Their blood dyed the white snow. This massacre was the spark that set fire to the Russian Revolution of 1905.

A great protest parade was organized in New York City. It started at Rutgers Square and wended its way up the East Side, past Tompkins Square, where the blood of American workers was once shed in the 1880s. At Union Square a monster mass meeting was held for many hours with many speakers. Every marcher carried a small red flag and the streets, fire escapes and windows were crowded with sympathetic cheering and weeping people. Many of them had but recently come from the Old World. Their families were there. Its struggles were a vivid part of their lives. The terrible pogrom committed against the Jews in Kishinev in 1903 and a later massacre at Tiraspol had created great anguish and horror on the East Side, especially among relatives and people who had lived in these towns, as well as all others. My heart and mind were deeply stirred by their grief and I hoped with them for the speedy overthrow of the bloody-handed tsar.

THE EAST SIDE AND "THE REVOLUTION"

It was a long but fascinating trip from the South Bronx to the Liberal Arts Club at 106 East Broadway, where I was often invited to speak in 1906–07. It took an hour to Canal Street on the Third Avenue "El" with its lurching cars pulled by chuggy little coal-burning engines, before the days of the deadly third rail. The East Side opened up another world to me, beside which the South Bronx Irish railroad workers and German piano workers drinking their beer in corner saloons seemed sedate and dull. On the East Side crowded meetings abounded, with animated discussion. I met many "Jews without money" of whom Mike Gold wrote later so graphically. The halls were long and narrow, poorly heated and lighted, with sawdust on the floor to protect it for the dancing. Usually there was a canopy for Jewish weddings with faded velvet hangings and dusty flowers. On the walls were charters of "landsmen" clubs and beautiful red banners of Socialist locals and unions, hung carefully under glass, taken out only for special occasions like May Day.

There was dire poverty among these newly arrived immigrants, who lived crowded together in dingy firetrap tenements. They toiled in vile sweatshops for starvation wages while they struggled to bring other members of their family to America. Not speaking the language, they were cheated and overworked. At all meetings there was a constant moving about and a commotion at the back of the hall, people who did not understand English talking together. These forums were a haven for homesick people. They brought music, art and comradeship before there were any settlement houses or union halls. Professor Platon Brounoff, a talented pianist, presided at the East Broadway forum. He was the composer of an opera based on American Indian music. He entertained with original short stories, witty criticisms of American life, such as "Moses Comes to Hester Street" and "Jesus Comes to Ellis Island." Often, half-starved violinists played for us, some of whom later became famous.

Brounoff always paid everybody a little—up to $5, a fabulous amount. He fed the hungry souls of his audience with intellectual and musical manna. He fed his performers later, including the speakers, in dingy little coffee houses where we ate cake and drank tea with lemon out of a glass. Finally, he left the East Side due to his wife's social ambitions, and was swallowed up in the prosperous mediocrity of what was then Jewish lower Harlem, where he taught music. He did not live too long after being uprooted. I saw him one night at a theater. He boomed through the lobby as of old: "Comrade Flynn! How's the revolution?"

"The Revolution" was on everybody's lips in 1906, when I first knew the East Side. It was the bourgeois-democratic revolution of 1905, greeted from afar by Russian emigres and native radicals of all schools of thought, watched with the greatest joy by many who hoped to return to their native land. Bloody Sunday had been followed by a Russia-wide general strike of printers, railroad, postal and other workers, demanding the vote and a real Duma (parliament). We could not know all the developments there but the news of continued pogroms against the Jewish people and ferocious murders of thousands of workers and peasants by the Black Hundreds aroused great indignation here. The murderous repression of the revolution lasted about three years. The prison cell, the hangman's rope, the sword, the knout and every form of reprisal were visited upon the people. Thousands more fled into exile. The second Duma, a temporary sop to the revolution, was dissolved in June 1907. Its members were arrested, tried and sentenced, or driven into exile.

All of these events created great protest not only on the East Side but among American liberals and even in conservative circles, where support was pledged to the Russian people in their struggle to overthrow the tsar's tyrannical government. Catherine Breshovsky, then an old lady, came here in 1905 to raise funds for the revolution. In 1908 she was sent again to Siberia; she was released by the 1917 revolution. Maxim Gorky, the famous Russian writer, also came to the United States in 1906 to raise funds. Unfortunately, his visit was marred by a vulgar, puritanical attack upon him and his wife, a talented actress, because they were not legally married. They were ordered to leave the Brevoort Hotel—of all places!

In March 1907, Congressman Bennett of New York presented a petition signed by a group of distinguished Americans calling upon Congress to protest against "the perverted use of Government function of which the Russian people are the victims." It recited a list of atrocities practiced by the Russian government in its "prolonged warfare against its people," such as exile to polar regions; the slaughter of the wounded or their burial alive with the dead; the firing on hospitals by regular troops; the slashing with swords and bayonets and the trampling by horses' hoofs of women and children; the wholesale rape by officers and soldiers of women and girls in towns supposedly under military protection. Among those who signed this document were Julia Ward Howe, Mark Twain, Bishop Potter, Dr. Lyman Abbot and Jacob Schiff. A Russian Famine Relief Committee was organized with the Bishop as chairman. This Committee included Felix Adler, Nicholas Murray Butler, J. Pierpont Morgan and Oswald G. Villard.

A meeting was held by the Society of Friends of Russian Freedom at Carnegie Hall on March 10, 1907, "to express indignation and encourage the fight for Russian freedom." Alexis Aladin, a member of the first Russian Duma which had been dissolved in 1906, and N. W. Tchaykovsky, called the publicity "Father of the Russian Revolution," spoke at this meeting. Boxes were taken by Mark Train, Professor Seligman, William Jay Schefflin, Alton B. Parker, Robert E. Ely, Charles Sprague Smith and others. Among the speakers were Felix Adler, Dr. Lyman Abbot, Senator Robert La Follette, George Kennan and Dr. Parkhurst. Mr. Aladin was very outspoken in his remarks before the Ethical Culture Society at that time. He said: "We will fight and continue to fight, if necessary, and as long as necessary, not only the troops of the tsar but combined Europe and America, should we be forced to face an autocracy uphe'd and supported by foreign capital." He urged his audiences not to allow "our Government to get any material aid from America."

This was cheered to the rafters by large American audiences. I do not know who these Russians were or their subsequent roles. What I am pointing out here was the widespread American sympathy that poured out in a flood of support for the Russian revolution.

Forty-seven years later, a Government's exhibit against myself and other Communists on trial at Foley Square in New York City was a quote from a young man, Joseph Stalin, issued from Tiflis in the midst of the fighting in 1905, as follows: "What do we need in order to really win? We need three things—first, arms—second, arms—third, arms and more arms!" We had never heard of Stalin in 1905, nor until years later, but I am sure his words would have met with cheers and dollars to buy guns if they had been relayed here.

"Undesirable Citizens"

Our interest and enthusiasm for the Russian revolution was suddenly cut across by the sharpness of the class struggle here in the United States. The same President of the United States, Theodore Roosevelt, who had sent a cablegram of condolence to the tsar upon the political assassination of Grand Duke Sergius, now publicly branded American labor leaders as "undesirable citizens." They were the imprisoned officers of the Western Federation of Miners who were awaiting trial for the murder of Governor Steunenberg of Idaho—William D. Haywood, George Pettibone and Charles Moyer.

This attack aroused a storm of protest. The struggle to free the framed-up three occupied the center of the labor stage and united all labor groups during 1906 and 1907. It was one of the great labor defense cases of our time. They were arrested on February 17, 1906 in Denver, Colorado, and spirited away in the dead of night by armed guards on a special train to the penitentiary in Boise, Idaho. Vincent St. John, one of the top organizers of this union, was already in jail in Idaho. Such a kidnapping over a state line, without legal process, created great anger among workers everywhere. Theodore Roosevelt's statement added fuel to the fires of indignation.

The Western Federation of Miners had fought valiantly for the interests of the metalliferous miners since its birth at Butte, Montana, in 1893. It included copper, lead, gold and silver miners, and engineers and smelter workers in Montana, Idaho, Colorado, Utah, Nevada and Arizona. It had struggled militantly for the right to organize, for safety and decent working conditions, and to enforce the eight-hour laws in Colorado and Utah which the operators ignored. It had carried on a series of hard-fought strikes—in Coeur d'Alene, Idaho; in Leadville, Telluride and Cripple Creek, which was then one of the world's richest gold camps. A thousand federal soldiers were sent there in 1903 under Adjutant-General Sherman Bell, who became infamous for his remark: "To hell with habeas corpus! We'll give them post-mortems!" Thousands of miners were arrested and put into "bull-pens"—the first concentration camps in America. Many were deported; many were killed.

Defense conferences, which were delegate bodies from Socialist and Socialist Labor Party locals, IWW and AFL unions, and workers' fraternal organizations, were set up and met regularly. Mammoth-sized demonstrations and parades were held from coast to coast; 20,000 people were on Boston Common; May Day 1907 on Union Square in New York (at which I was a speaker) there was a great protest meeting. Fifty thousand marched in Chicago. Interest spread throughout the world. When Maxim Gorky came to New York he sent a telegram of greeting, in the name of the Russian workers, to these imprisoned American labor leaders. The Socialist Party of Colorado nominated Haywood for governor while he was in jail. He got 16,000 votes. The *Appeal to Reason,* a grass-roots Socialist paper in Girard, Kansas, published four million copies of its "Kidnapping Edition," and of Eugene V. Debs' famous appeal, "Arouse Ye Slaves!" As a result the paper was branded the "Appeal to Treason" in an editorial in the Idaho *Daily Statesman.* Debs minced no words. He said: "It is a foul plot; a damnable conspiracy; a hellish outrage." He quoted "the slimy sleuth who worked up the case against them," who said: "They will never leave Idaho alive!" To this Debs replied: "Well, by God, if they don't, the governors of Idaho and Colorado and their masters from Wall Street, New York, had better prepare to follow them!"

William D. Haywood was tried first. He was prosecuted by William E. Borah, later U.S. Senator from Idaho and defended by the eloquent labor lawyer, Clarence Darrow. Haywood, born in Utah, a worker since he was 15, was a young and vigorous man, a powerful leader of this fighting Western union. He had lost the sight of one eye in the mines and bore on his body many scars from saber and gunshot wounds, from attacks by soldiers and mine guards. In June 1905 he had been chairman of the founding convention of the IWW (Industrial Workers of the World) in Chicago, which attempted to band together all independent unions into one big industrial union movement. Eugene V. Debs, Mother Jones and Lucy Parsons, widow of the labor leader hung in Chicago in 1887, were also present as delegates. The majority of the delegates were Socialists. In its preamble adopted then, the IWW called upon "all the toilers to come together on the political as well as the industrial field." There was no doubt in the minds of the advanced American worker that Haywood's role in launching this new organization was partially responsible for the frame-up against him a few months later.

The principal witness against Haywood was Harry Orchard, a stool pigeon, a self-confessed "killer of twenty-five." He had been well trained to testify by James McParlan, then head of the Denver Office of the Pinkerton Detective Agency, the same man who had sworn away the lives of 19 coal miners, known as the "Molly Maguires" in the anthracite area of Pennsylvania, 30 years before. Orchard swore that he had killed Steunenberg and then tried to involve the men on trial as the instigators of his deed. His testimony was torn to bits by the defendants and 87 other witnesses, many of whom came to court to volunteer their testimony after he told his story. The verdict was "Not Guilty." Pettibone was later tried and acquitted. He died shortly afterward of tuberculosis. Moyer was released without a trial. Harry Orchard met the well-deserved fate of a stool pigeon. He had confessed to murder in open court. He was sentenced to life imprisonment. I heard years later from an Idaho newspaper man that he was afraid of the miners and preferred to stay in prison in safety. Stool pigeons were not public heroes then. There was a healthy contempt for their Judas-like trade. The son of Governor Steunenberg went before the parole board to protest several moves to release him. (Orchard died in Boise, Idaho, State Penitentiary, on April 13, 1954.)

"Big Bill" Haywood came out of jail a hero—a fitting symbol of the solidarity of labor. He was described by one reporter as "big in body, in brain, and in courage." He made a triumphal tour of the United States and Canada, under the auspices of the Socialist Party and the labor organizations which had defended him. He was an intensely down-to-earth dramatic speaker. I remember hearing him say: "I'm a two-gun man from the West, you know," and while the audience waited breathlessly, he pulled his union card from one pocket and his Socialist card from the other. Later, in 1910, he was elected a delegate from the American Socialist Party to the International Socialist Congress at Copenhagen by a larger vote than any other delegate. This was the Congress that unanimously designated March 8th as International Women's Day. Many years later when they met in the Soviet Union, Lenin reminded Haywood that they had met in Copenhagen, but that he (Lenin) had then used another name for safety.

JAMES CONNOLLY—IRISH SOCIALIST

In 1907, During the campaign to free Moyer, Haywood and Pettibone, I was invited to speak at a meeting, in Newark, New Jersey, arranged by the Socialist Labor Party. There was protest against my acceptance by the New Jersey Socialist Party, which had either not been invited to participate or had refused. I felt I should go anywhere to speak for this purpose. Our rostrum was an old wagon, set up in Washington Park. The horse was inclined to run when there was loud applause, so he was taken out of the wagon shafts. This meeting is an unforgettable event in my life because it was here I first met James Connolly, the Irish Socialist speaker, writer and labor organizer who gave his life for Irish freedom nine years later in the Easter Week Uprising of 1916 in Dublin.

At the time I refer to he worked for the Singer Sewing Machine Company of Elizabeth, New Jersey, and had a hard struggle to support his wife and six small children. He lost his job when he tried to organize a union in the plant. He was short, rather stout, a plain-looking man with a large black moustache, a very high forehead and dark sad eyes, a man who rarely smiled. A scholar and an excellent writer, his speech was marred for American audiences by his thick, North of Ireland accent, with a Scotch burr from his long residence in Glasgow. On the Washington Park occasion someone spilled a bottle of water in his hat, the only one he possessed undoubtedly, and with a wry expression on his face he shook it out and dried it, but made no complaint.

Connolly and I spoke again in 1907 at an Italian Socialist meeting early one Sunday morning. I wondered then why they arranged their meetings at such an odd hour but discovered it was a substitute for church among these rabid anticlericals, and happily did not interfere with their sacred ritual of the big spaghetti and *vino* dinner later on. I asked Connolly: "Who will speak in Italian?" He smiled his rare smile and replied, "We'll see. Someone, surely." After we had both spoken, they took a recess and gave us coffee and cake behind the scenes, a novel but welcome experience fo us. Stale water was the most we got elsewhere! Then we returned to the platform and Connolly arose. He spoke beautifully in Italian to my amazement and the delight of the audience who *"viva'*d" loudly.

Later he moved his family to Elton Avenue in the Bronx and the younger children of our families played together. Once, Patrick Quinlan, a family friend who had left a bookcase with a glass door at Connolly's house, was horrified to find all the books on the floor and the Flynn-Connolly children playing funeral, with one child beautifully laid out in the bookcase. "Who's dead?" Connolly asked. "Quinlan," they replied serenely. Needless to say, the children did not like Quinlan.

Connolly worked for the IWW and had an office at Cooper Square. He was a splendid organizer, as his later work for the Irish Transport Workers, with James Larkin, demonstrated. Although the Socialist Labor Party had invited him here in 1902 on a lecture tour and he was elected a member of their National Executive Committee, there was obvious jealousy displayed against him by their leader, Daniel De Leon, who could brook no opposition. Connolly had been one of the founders in 1896 of the Irish Socialist Republican Party in Dublin and editor of its organ. Connolly's position that the Irish Socialist Party represented a separate nation from Britain was recognized by the International Socialist Congress in 1900, and the Irish delegates were allowed to take their seats as such. When membership in the SLP became impossible for him here, he joined the Socialist Party and toured the country under its auspices. Connolly was the first person I ever heard use the expression, "Workers' Republic"; in fact, he is called by one biographer, "the Irish apostle of the Soviet idea," though none of us ever heard the word in those days. (Only later did I learn that Soviets first arose in the Russian Revolution of 1905.)

He felt keenly that not enough understanding and sympathy was shown by American Socialists for the cause of Ireland's national liberation, that the Irish workers here were too readily abandoned by the

Socialists as "reactionaries" and that there was not sufficient effort made to bring the message of socialism to the Irish-American workers. In 1907 George B. McClellan, Mayor of New York City, made a speech in which he said: "There are Russian Socialists and Jewish Socialists and German Socialists! But, thank God! there are no Irish Socialists!" This was a challenge to Connolly, my father and a host of others with good Irish names, members of both the Socialist parties. They banded together as the Irish Socialist Club, later known as the Irish Socialist Federation. James Connolly was chairman and my sister Katherine was secretary. She was then 15 years old. Connolly was strong for encouraging "the young people."

The Irish Socialist Federation caused great protest among the other existing federations. The others insisted we didn't need a federation because we weren't foreign-speaking. We wanted a banner we could fight under. The Unity Club required us to be too placating, too peaceful. The Federation was born one Sunday afternoon at our house in the Bronx. Connolly, Quinlan, O'Shaughnessy, Cooke, Cody, Daly, Ray, all the Flynns, were there; also our faithful Jewish friend, Sam Stodel, who was sympathetic to our proposal. But we excluded him as we feared ridicule if we included a Jew.

He went into the kitchen and said to my mother: "Have you anything for this bunch to eat?" She confessed she had not, so he went around the corner and bought ham, cheese, corned beef, beer, crackers, etc., to feed the doughty Irish when their session was over. Nourished by Sam, we went forth to battle. The Federation arranged street meetings to show that Mayor McClellan was an ignoramus and a liar, especially in Irish neighborhoods where such meetings had never been held. It had a large green and white banner, announcing who and what it was, with the Gaelic slogan, *Faugh-a-Balach* (Clear the Way) in big letters surrounded by harps and shamrocks. The meetings were stormy but finally accepted at many corners. A German blacksmith comrade built the Federation a sturdy platform that could not easily be upset, with iron detachable legs that could be used as "shillelaghs" in an emergency. These helped to establish order at the meetings, and won a wholesome respect for the Federation.

The Federation issued a statement of its purposes (written by James Connolly): "To assist the revolutionary working class movement in Ireland by a dissemination of its literature; to educate the working class Irish of this country into a knowledge of Socialist principles and to prepare them to cooperate with the workers of all other races, colors, and nationalities in the emancipation of labor." James Connolly wrote one book, *Labour in Irish History,* one play and many pamphlets. His extensive writings were spread out over many years in various workers' papers and magazines.

He published a monthly magazine, *The Harp.* Many poems from his own pen appeared. It was a pathetic sight to see him standing, poorly clad, at the door of Cooper Union or some other East Side hall, selling his little paper. None of the prosperous professional Irish, who shouted their admiration for him after his death, lent him a helping hand at that time. Jim Connolly was anathema to them because he was a "So'—cialist."

He had no false pride and encouraged others to do these Jimmy Higgins tasks by setting an example. At the street meetings he persuaded those who had no experience in speaking to "chair the meeting" as a method of training them. Connolly had a rare skill, born of vast knowledge, in approaching the Irish workers. He spoke the truth sharply and forcefully when necessary, as in the following from *The Harp* of November 1900:

> To the average non-Socialist Irishman the idea of belonging to an international political party is unthinkable, is obnoxious, and he feels that if he did, all the roots of his Irish nature would be dug up. Of course, he generally belongs to a church—the Roman Catholic Church—which is the most international institution in existence. That does not occur to him as atrocious, in fact he is rather proud than otherwise that the Church is spread throughout the entire world, that it overleaps the barriers of civilization, penetrating into the depths of savagedom, and ignores all considerations of race, color or nationality. . . . But although he would lay down his life for a Church which he boasts of as "Catholic" or universal, he turns with a shudder from an economic or political movement which has the same characteristics.

Connolly published *The Harp* here as the official organ of the Irish Socialist Federation, and moved it to Dublin in 1910.

The IWW "Stirreth Up the People"

When William D. Haywood, then secretary of the Western Federation of Miners, opened the first convention of the Industrial Workers of the World in 1905, he said: "This is the Continental Congress of the working class." George Speed, a veteran trade unionist who had helped to build the Seamen's Union of the AFL and who was later an IWW member for many years, described this gathering as "the greatest conglomeration of freaks that ever met in a convention." Both statements had a grain of truth. Its advent was an important event and it blazed a trail, like a great comet across the American labor scene, from 1905 to the early 1920s. It made labor history, and left an indelible impress on the labor movement.

The IWW was a militant, fighting, working class union. The employing class soon recognized this and gave battle from its birth. The IWW identified itself with all the pressing immediate needs of the poorest, the most exploited, the most oppressed workers. It "fanned the flames" of their discontent. It led them in heroic struggles, some of which it organized. Others jumped in to give leadership after the strike had started. The memorable accusation against Jesus, "He stirreth up the people!" fitted the IWW. It set out to organize the unorganized, unskilled foreign-born workers in the mass production industries of the East and the unorganized migratory workers of the West, who were largely American born and employed in maritime, lumber, agriculture, mining and construction work. In the East and South, it reached workers in textile, rubber, coal maritime and lumber and in a variety of smaller industries. In New York City, for instance, there were IWW locals in clothing, textile, shoe, cigar, rattan, piano, brass and hotels. In the West there was a Cowboys' and Broncho Busters' local of the IWW. The entire working class of the fabulous town of Goldfield, Nevada, was organized in 1906 by Vincent St. John into the IWW. The Italian laborers at the U.S. Army's West Point were once organized in the IWW. I recall speaking to them there, about 1911.

I joined in 1906, belonging to Mixed Local No. 179 in New York City, a sort of catch-all local. How I got by the strict qualification that one must be an actual wage worker, I cannot recall. Possibly it was due to my extreme youth and the fact that all the work I did was for the movement, sometimes paid for and often not. A special provision regarding "Women and juniors," passed at the 1906 convention, may be the explanation. My first experience with the IWW was a trip up the Hudson River to Schenectady, New York, by the night boat to Albany that summer to speak at a Moyer-Haywood-Pettibone protest meeting at Brandywine Park. It was a mass gathering. Later that year the IWW had a strike of approximately 3,000 men against the General Electric Company. They did not leave the plant but stayed by their machines and stopped production. This action was the first "sit-down" strike in the East as far as I know. The AFL threatened to take up the charter of any local which joined the IWW in Schenectady in a sympathetic strike. Our strike ended rather quickly.

My first personal strike experience was in Bridgeport, Connecticut in the summer of 1907 with the Tube Mill workers, largely Hungarian. I was much amused to hear an overenthusiastic young may say to Ella Reeve Bloor in 1938, during the big CIO drive: "Mother, we had a strike in Bridgeport—the first one they ever had there!" She replied indignantly: "I led a strike of corset workers there before you were born. How about you, Elizabeth?" When I told him that my first strike there was actually over 30 years before, he was speechless. Here, for the first time, I participated in strike committee meetings, mass picketing and daily meetings in two languages, with sad Hungarian violin music for entertainment. For a short time I stayed in the home of a striker, sleeping with the woman and the baby, while the men slept on the kitchen floor. Later, a strike sympathizer got me a room for myself. The strike meetings were in the vicinity of the mill, where the workers lived. In the evening we went downtown and held street meetings on a main thoroughfare to acquaint the people of the city with the conditions and the demands of the striking workers. We gained considerable support this way, which helped to settle the strike.

The first IWW convention I attended was in Chicago in 1907—I had just passed 17 years, and was still in high school. My family and friends were hesitant about letting me go, but I was determined. Local 179 elected me as its delegate. They had no funds, but sufficient was collected among the members of the Unity Club. I paid $18 fare and sat up all the way in a daycoach. Arriving in Chicago at the Wabash Avenue Station of the Pennsylvania Railroad, I was quite appalled to be all alone, so far from home. I had the address of a friend, Mrs. Josephine Conger Kanako, who had invited me to stay with her while there. She was the editor of a magazine, *The Socialist Woman*. She was a tall, thin, plain-looking woman, whose husband was Japanese, and quite short. They were an incongruous but apparently happy pair. He subsequently returned to Japan and died there of tuberculosis.

I made my way to where she lived and found her a charming woman. But it was way out on the South Side, on Cottage Avenue, and the convention was on North Clark Street at the old Brandt Hall. After a few days I moved to the home of William E. Trautman, who was then Secretary of the IWW.

I loved Chicago and still do. It's a big sprawly town—dirty, dingy, alive, real, no hypocrisy or false frills there; teeming with life much closer to the heart of America than any Eastern city. I was amazed at its lack of civilization. I saw rats run across the wooden streets on Milwaukee Avenue; visited the stockyards—and couldn't stand to see the animals killed. The frightened squeals were dreadful. I remained a vegetarian. It smelled bad, looked bad, and left a bad taste for days afterward. But it was a lasting impression of workers in a great production plant and the job that lay ahead of us, to organize them.

I sat in the top gallery of a theater with other delegates and saw E. H. Southern in *Crime and Punishment*. We visited the White City and some buildings that were still left from the World's Fair—museums, I believe. I had childishly wonderful time being "West," and became quite enamored with "Westerners."

At this convention I was thrilled to meet Mrs. Lucy Parsons, widow of Albert Parsons, who had been executed 20 years before in the yard of the Cook County Jail in the heart of Chicago. While he was hanged she was held a prisoner in the Clark Street Station House, not far from where we were then meeting. I met Oscar Neebe, one of Parson's co-defendants and the imprisoned martyr of the eight-hour day struggle who was pardoned by Governor Altgeld. I remember Mrs. Parsons speaking warmly to the young people, warning us of the seriousness of the struggles ahead that could lead to jail and death before victory was won. For years she traveled from city to city, knocking on the doors of local unions and telling the story of the Chicago trial. Her husband had said: "Clear our names!" and she made this her lifelong mission.

I can recall nothing particularly exciting happening at this IWW convention. It was a great adventure in itself for me to make this trip all alone.

I MEET TOM L. JOHNSON

After the IWW convention of 1907 I returned home to New York, stopping off at several Midwestern cities on the way. I spoke first at Cincinnati. The red houses with blinds, the hills, the German atmosphere, even a canal called the Rhine, fascinated me. I was disappointed, years after, to find the canal gone and a road there instead. There I saw pigs driven through the streets to a slaughterhouse. I particularly recall visiting Cleveland, where I had lived as a child. I stayed with a family who were members of the Socialist Labor Party, under whose auspices my meetings were held there. The first was a noonday rally at the Public Square on one of the stone platforms built for free speech by order of Tom L. Johnson, mayor of Cleveland. He was well known as a reformer, an advocate of municipal ownership, a fighter against monopolies, especially the transit system, and had fought to secure the three-cent fare. He was born poor, started as a newsboy, and finally landed in the streetcar business, where he was a phenomenal success as a capitalist and threatened the "Consolidated," owned by Mark Hanna. He became a rich man. Then somebody gave him Henry George's *Progress and Poverty*. Books and ideas are potent. He sold his business and went into politics to fight the system that had made him rich but, as he now felt, at the expense of thousands who were poor. He fought it well, according to his lights.

While I was speaking that noon in 1907, a pleasant, smiling, round-faced man came across the park, accompanied by several others, and stood quietly on the edge of the crowd, listening to me. When I had concluded he came through the crowd and someone said: "Shake hands with Mayor Johnson, Miss Flynn." I liked him but wasn't sure whether my class-conscious socialist principles would allow me to be friends with him. However, he resolved that quickly enough by saying: "Come on for lunch with us!" And I was lifted right off the platform. Some of my comrades looked very dubious. I feared I was being a traitor to the working class right then and there, but others said: "Sure, go ahead, what's the harm?"

So off I went in a big car to his home on Euclid Avenue. I remember meeting Fred Howe and Mrs. Howe and Peter Witt. I was quite embarrassed though I tried to appear calm, as if being whisked away by mayors was an everyday occurrence to me. He took me for a ride all over the city and told me his plans for its improvement. He was proud of the three-cent fare in vogue there. He was direct and forthright. He told me of his disappointment that his daughter had left the stage to marry some titled foreigner and he hoped she'd quit him for good. The politicians and big interests crushed him later and his heart broke. (Some five years later I saw Peter Witt who was then mayor of Cleveland and he gave me a contribution for the Lawrence strikers* in memory of Tom Johnson!) Marie Jennie Howe and Frederick G. Howe, to whom Johnson introduced me the day of the luncheon, took

---

* See below, "The Lawrence Strike of 1912."

me to hear him speak that evening, and remained my good friends for years. Fred Howe was in charge of Ellis Island in the Wilson administration. His talented wife was a minister and a suffrage leader.

It was quite an experience hearing Tom Johnson speak that night —he was informal, used simple language, argued with the audience. He had a good sense of humor, was always pleasant, yet sharp and quick in retort. He was loved by the people and hated by the rich as "a traitor to his class." He described himself as a convert from plutocracy to democracy, a rarity in all periods.

When I left Cleveland, he gave me a letter of introduction to the mayor of Youngstown, so "you won't have any trouble there." My unusual experience greatly puzzled the local Socialist Labor Party, whose party was "purest of the pure." The young daughters of the house where I stayed were excited and thrilled over it, but the SLP elders were worried as to whether I had compromised them beyond repair by my socializing with a "capitalist mayor." Tom L. Johnson corresponded with me after that. He gave my unemployed father an engineering job that lasted quite a while. He died a few years later. There is a statue of him in the square in Cleveland, near the stone platform where I spoke—a belated tribute to a man who did so much for his city. I always waved a greeting as I passed by in later years.

Roaring Pittsburgh

From Cleveland I went to Warren, Elyria, Akron, Youngstown and Pittsburgh. Youngstown was uneventful. I did not need my letter to the mayor. It's great to be young and to see places like these with the eyes of wonder and enthusiasm. In Elyria I visited a glass factory and saw workers blow electric bulbs on the ends of long glass tubes. In Pittsburgh I lived up on a hill, where we had to go through a tunnel or up an incline railroad to get there. In the daytime we couldn't see the city below for smoke.

I will never forget my first visit to Pittsburgh—the great flaming mills on both sides of the Ohio River, the roar and crash of the blast furnaces, the skies lit up for miles around at night, the smoke, gas-laden air, the grime and soot that penetrated every corner. Industries fascinate me and wherever possible I visited them. This was much easier years ago. I visited the Heinz plant of the 57 varieties in Allegheny City, now the North Side of Pittsburgh. The fingers of the girl packers moved so fast as the jars and cans passed along the belt-line, you could hardly see them. Visitors were treated to a plateful of samples and given a souvenir spoon with a pickle-shaped handle. The horses were well cared for, I noted, in tiled stalls, groomed and well fed. In my speeches, I contrasted this with the hotels workers lived in there.

I also visited the Homestead plant, scene of the grim battle of 15 years before, when 300 armed Pinkerton detectives came up the Allegheny River in boats and fired upon the strikers gathered on the shore. A battle ensued in which six workers were killed. The Pinkertons were taken captive by the strikers and driven out of town. I was allowed to go through the plant, but had to sign a paper first absolving the company of all responsibility for accidents which might happen there. I felt as if I were entering an inferno. It was fascinating—the crashing noises, the unexpected bursts of flame, the heat, the sweating toilers, some stripped to the waist, attending the great furnaces and caldrons. We walked miles, saw all the processes that turned the raw red ore into a finished product. My speeches were improved by all this first-hand information.

I also was taken to visit a coal mine somewhere near Pittsburgh. It was in the side of a mountain, not down a shaft. I heard the cracking of the coal roof, an ominous sound. Water dripped down the sides. This was long before the noisy cutting and loading machines used today. Then the sad-faced mules, who did all the hauling, were stabled down in the depths of the earth. It is a saying that miners are superstitious about women coming into the mines, but I found no resentment, only friendly smiles. The little lamps in their caps lit up the gleaming eyes in the dust-covered faces of the coal diggers. To me they were then, and have remained, the unsung heroes of labor, who daily take their lives into their hands that we may have light, heat and power. They were then, and are now, the source of tremendous profits for absentee mine owners. They live in shacks in remote backwood camps, in lonely hills and hollows, or drab little towns, without adequate hospitals, sanitation, water supply, light, housing, roads, social recreation or educational facilities. Whatever they have gained, and it is little enough, has been by the strength of their union in bitter struggles. No wonder that no American coal miner ever wants his son to follow his footsteps into the dark, dangerous bowels of the earth!

Wherever I traveled in my earlier years I always tried to see the local industrial establishments. Later I become too "notorious" to be allowed inside a plant and the rules became stricter during and after World War I. In my early years, I saw the Ford plant in Detroit, the Dayton, Ohio, cash register factory, a lumber mill in the northwest, a pottery plant in Cincinnati, a copper mine in Butte so deep that the earth was hot, a silver mine in British Columbia, a textile mill in Olneyville, Rhode Island, with all the windows closed on a hot summer day so the fabrics in the looms would not be disturbed by the currents of air. In all such trips I saw, of course, only what the guides were allowed to show visitors. But I also saw what could not be concealed— labor-saving machinery, speedup on belt lines, mass production and the hazards of such work. Workers told me at my meetings of conditions in these plants, of wages and hours, of attempts to organize and employers' efforts to thwart them. I was a listener, anxious to overcome the handicap of youth and inexperience. I soaked up a lot of information on the lives of the workers in all my travels.

When I left Pittsburgh after about two weeks' stay, the local surprised me, giving me two weeks' organization salary—$36. (The IWW paid $18 a week and expenses.) It included a $20-gold piece. But I had not been rated an organizer before and had never drawn so much money at one time. I felt proud and affluent.

Mesabi Range

After reporting to the various IWW locals in New York on the convention and my trip, life became singularly dull. I had tasted of travel and the wanderlust was in my blood. I did not want to return to school. I resented the adult interference with my life by the members of the Unity Club and by my father especially. He had a penchant for personal conflicts, had quarreled with Connolly and others, and expected me to carry all his grudges. In August 1907 I had my 17th birthday. When the comrades assembled, my mother said to my father: "It's ridiculous. There isn't a person under forty!"

That summer I tried my wings again in a visit to Paterson, New Jersey. I stayed there a week or ten days, speaking every night in the large IWW Hall, which was located on one of the main streets of the Silk City. I met many workers during my stay, whom I came to know six years later at the time of our big IWW strike there.

One of the delegates to the recent IWW convention, J. A. Jones of Minnesota, began a correspondence with me, urging me to come on a speaking trip to the Mesabi Range, north of Duluth. I needed little persuasion; I was anxious to go. My parents agreed but quite unwillingly, and I was off again. Jones was the local IWW organizer at this time. He had previously been an organizer for the Western Federation of Miners. I met him in Duluth in December of 1907, and spoke there for the local Socialist and IWW branches. Then we went to the iron-ore country, about 60 miles north of Duluth. It was controlled then, as now, by the U.S. Steel Corporation.

Jones had arranged a series of meetings in the bleak and primitive towns of the 60-mile range—stretching from Hibbing to Biwabik. I spoke in miners' halls and in auditoriums belonging to the local Finnish societies. It was sub-zero weather and the people gathered around the huge potbellied stoves that glowed red hot. A few feet away it was cold. Water froze in the pitcher in the bedroom during the night.

The snow-covered landscape, beautiful with fir and pine trees, was scarred by the great open-pit mines, from which rich red iron ore was scooped with huge steam shovels. The Oliver Iron Mining Company, a subsidiary of U.S. Steel, owned the mining rights to the land under the towns. When they exhausted a pit location they moved the mining operations to another place. In the process, the towns were often shifted to make available the ore below. All structures were therefore of a temporary character, shabby and cheap. However, a few years later the population became weary of living in shacks at the mercy of the company. They elected progressive mayors who were not at the beck and call of the company. They picked permanent sites for the towns, and put a stiff tax on the mining companies. They used it to pave streets, lay sidewalks, build schools and public buildings, install lighting systems and generally turn "locations," as they were called, into model towns. They even had drinking fountains on the streets. In Hibbing, the old Carnegie Library came down in one of the last "moves" and they built a brand new city public library—with no thanks to Carnegie. The "Range" as I knew it in 1907 was like the primitive frontier days in the West. All these changes came later.

The ore was loaded into open ore cars, sent to the Duluth docks and shipped down the Great Lakes, when they were not frozen, to Eastern steel mills in Ohio and Pennsylvania. It was basic industry in the raw, in a rough wild country. I was young, not yet eighteen. I romanticized the life—so different from New York—and the organizer who lived and worked there, under conditions of hardship. I fell in love with him and we were married in January 1908.

A joking remark made by Vincent St. John on my marriage hurt me at the time, but expressed a keen insight. He said: "Elizabeth fell in love with the West and the miners and she married the first one she met." Jack Jones was an ore miner. The glamour of the Western Federation of Miners was around Jack Jones. Compared to my current New York admirer of over 40 years, who was a clerk in a cutlery store, Jones was indeed romantic to me at 17. Jones was in his early thirties, he was youthful and vigorous, of medium height, with a nice friendly smile and deep blue eyes. He was of Scotch-English ancestry and had worked all over the Western country.

Almost immediately after we were married I had to go to Minneapolis and St. Paul to fill some IWW speaking dates, which were of long standing. No sooner had I left than Jack got arrested with two miners, charged with attempting to dynamite a mine captain's residence at Aurora, Minnesota. Lurid publicity appeared even in the New York papers. "Law Breaks in on Honeymoon of Girl Orator" was headlined in the New York *World,* and "Girl Orator Whose Husband of Ten Days is in Jail," was another. The Duluth *News Tribune* carried an Aurora dispatch: "A young woman named Elizabeth Gurley Flynn was recently here and her speech was particularly inflammatory. . . . Some of the ignorant miners took what she said for granted and when it was decided to lay off the night shift and confine the work to the day force, some of the men who lost their positions conceived the idea that Nicholas, the man immediately in charge, was responsible."

But nothing serious came of it. Jack was held for eight days and then released for lack of evidence. At his insistence and because of my family's great alarm, I returned home. Apparently, the romance was a possibility they had not anticipated and the arrest topped it off. I returned to Duluth in the spring, when Jones got a job in that city on a railroad tunnel, and brought my unemployed father out to work as an engineer. But they "agitated" so much on the job that they were both fired. All three of us went to New York, and I can see my mother's pale face as this unemployed army appeared with suitcases full of dirty clothes. It was a hard summer. We were all very poor. The men remained out of work.

My mother resented Jones' presence. She felt he should not have married me, so young a girl, so far away from home, without the knowledge of her parents, although she felt guilty for letting me go alone. She hated poverty and large families and was fearful that my life would become a replica of her own. It was bad enough to have one man around the house out of work, spouting ideas and reading books, while she toiled to keep our small crowded quarters clean and make ends meet—but to have two of them was just too much. It was an unhappy time for all of us.

LIFE IN CHICAGO, 1908-1909

By fall Jones was anxious to pull out of New York City. He felt his chances for employment were better in Chicago. We decided to go to the IWW convention there. I went first to Philadelphia to speak for a week to get enough money to pay my fare to Chicago. He hoboed his way out to Chicago. My mother had made me a red broadcloth cape, which I wore, with a broad-brimmed gray hat, for several winters. It kept me warm and was quite picturesque. Somebody gave me a pair of red silk stockings, but I never wore them. They were considered immodest and indecent, worn only in burlesque shows. No "good woman" wore silk stockings in those days. Black cotton was the conventional hosiery attire.

After the 1908 convention was over, Jack made arrangements with a railroad man, a member of the organization who lived at Blue Island, Illinois, for me to stay at home for a while until Jack got a job. But the man's wife was extremely resentful and treated me like an intruder. That I had books and pamphlets, almost a suitcase full, and read and wrote all the time, did not fit her idea of what a young wife and expectant mother should do. I became so uncomfortable there that I urged Jones to get a room anywhere in Chicago so I could leave. We moved to Oak Street, on the North Side. We had a back room next to the kitchen which was heated by a small gas stove. The landlady was extremely kind and gave us credit on our rent during that hard winter. Jones got a job shoveling coal. Some other IWWs lived in the same house, among them B. H. Williams, later editor of the IWW paper *Solidarity,* and Joe Ettor, then 22 years old, smiling, rosy-cheeked, telling us of his adventures during the San Francisco earthquake when he worked in the kitchen of the St. Frances Hotel, below the street level. They thought the racket was the cook throwing the pots around. Later, he and Jack London sat on a hillside across the Bay and watched the city burn.

Joe Ettor almost always used to wear a black shirt with a red tie and carried a small suitcase full of IWW applications and membership cards, literature and buttons. He was on his way to become the organizer in the anthracite region. I was the only woman in the group and rations were extremely slim. But they managed to provide me with milk and an egg a day on account of my "condition."

Jones was a teetotaler, but St. John and the other "fellow-workers" of the IWW used to take me with them to the North-Side Turner Hall on Clarke Street, where they played chess and checkers. With a five-cent glass of beer they could help themselves to all the free lunch they could eat—frankfurters, sliced ham, potato salad, rye bread and pickles. They would bring me all I could eat, too—at the table, of course, as ladies did not go to the bar in those days. The proprietor, who was also a sympathizer, said he would surely go out of business if he didn't have the IWW to eat up the free lunch.

Jones frequented a nearby library a great deal and became interested in developing a better plan of industrial organization than the 13 hypothetical departments then projected but nonexistent in the IWW. These departments were presented to the public in a wheel-shaped diagram which Samuel Gompers derisively called "Father Haggerty's wheel of fortune." Thomas J. Haggerty was an ex-priest, editor of the *Voice of Labor* of the American Labor Union, and one of the founders of the IWW. Jones drew great diagrams on oilcloth, painted with bright colors. They were spread all over the floor and walls. Spirited arguments ensued on his scheme, which was all on paper, of course, and if adopted would have made little difference. But the other men blamed the smell of paint and turpetine for what happened to me and gave Jones hell.

One morning, after Jack had left for his coal shoveling job, I was gripped with excruciating pains. Finally, I knocked on the folding doors between our room and the front room which was occupied by Ben Williams and another IWW. Ben was an angular New Englander, who had been a school teacher. He immediately surmised that I had labor pains and called the landlady, who got a neighborhood doctor. The baby was born prematurely a few hours later. Jones came home, but the baby boy, whom we had named John Vincent, died in the night. All I remember of this fleeting first child of mine was his big blue eyes—opened wide on a world so soon to be forsaken. We were grief-stricken. If he had lived, it might have drawn Jack and me together. Instead, I sought solace in greater activity.

We were in debt and owed the landlady, the doctor and undertaker.

On New Year's Day, I only had three cents to buy a postcard and stamp to write to my mother. Then my friend Vincent St. John, now in charge of the IWW, took a hand and sent Jones to Cobalt, Ontario, to get a job through the Western Federation of Miners local. It wasn't long before he arranged for me to come to speak there, as well as at another camp still further north, to which we went by stage coach, a trip that took two days. It was an exciting trip, but the National Office of the IWW, or rather the Saint, as we called St. John, cut it short. He sent for me to return to Chicago to make a speaking trip to the Pacific Coast. I accepted with joy. It would be my first cross-country tour.

MOTHER JONES—LABOR AGITATOR

The Greatest woman agitator of our time was Mother Jones. Arrested, deported, held in custody by the militia, hunted and threatened by police and gunmen—she carried on fearlessly for 60 years. I first saw her in the summer of 1908, speaking at a Bronx open-air meeting. She was giving the "city folks" hell. Why weren't we helping the miners of the West? Why weren't we backing up the Mexican people against Diaz? We were "white-livered rabbits who never put our feet on Mother Earth," she said. Her description of the bullpen, where the miners were herded by federal troops during a Western miners' strike, and of the bloodshed and suffering was so vivid that, being slightly dizzy from standing so long, I fainted. She stopped in the middle of a fiery appeal. "Get the poor child some water!" she said, and went on with her speech. I was terribly embarrassed. I was with my husband and James Connolly, who lived nearby. Connolly caught me as I fell and told my husband I should not be there. They walked me home from 148th to 134th Street, a long, silent, somber walk. Neither of them had the carfare to ride. Connolly said to my mother: "Put her to bed and give her a hot drink!" Apparently he realized I was pregnant.

The next winter I saw Mother Jones again in Chicago at a meeting in Hull House of the Rudewitz Committee, to which I was a delegate from Local 85, IWW. I heard her hot angry defiant words against the deportation of a young Jewish worker on the vile pretext of "ritual murder." (Jane Addams and others saved him from certain death by their spirited defense). Mother Jones was dressed in an old-fashioned black silk basque, with lace around her neck, a long full skirt and a little bonnet, trimmed with flowers. She never changed her style of dress throughout her lifetime. She may sound like Whistler's Mother but this old lady was neither calm nor still, breathing fearless agitation wherever she went.

She was born in Cork, Ireland, and came here as a girl. She lost her husband, an iron molder, and her four children in a yellow fever epidemic in Memphis, Tennessee. The union buried them. Alone and desolate, she went to Chicago. She did dressmaking for the rich. While she sewed in the magnificent mansions along the Lake front, she saw poverty and misery in the city. After the Chicago fire she attended meetings of the Knights of Labor in their scorched building. Following the first of May massacre of workers in 1886, outside the McCormick Harvester Works, and the subsequent Haymarket frameup of labor leaders, she became a restless labor pilgrim, going from strike to strike— agitating, organizing and encouraging. She began in West Virginia, going on to the anthracite area, and from then on she was with the coal miners in practically every struggle for the next 20 years, in the East, in Colorado—everywhere.

She was put out of hotels. Families who housed her in company towns were dispossessed. She spoke in open fields when halls were closed. She waded through Kelly Creek, West Virginia, to organize miners on the other side. Tried for violating an injunction, she called the judge a "scab" and proved it to him. She organized "women's armies" to chase scabs—with mops, brooms and dishpans. "God! It's the old mother with her wild women!" the bosses would groan. In Greensburg, Pennsylvania, when a group of women pickets with babies were arrested and sentenced to 30 days, she advised them: "Sing to the babies all night long!" The women sang their way out of jail in a few days to the relief of the sleepless town. She was asked at Congressional hearing: "Where is your home?" and she answered: "Sometimes I'm in Washington, then in Pennsylvania, Arizona, Texas, Alabama, Colorado, Minnesota. My address is like my shoes. It travels with me. I abide where there is a fight against wrong."

In 1903 she led a group of child workers from the textile mills in the Kensington district of Philadelphia, Pennsylvania, to Oyster Bay, Long Island, to confront President Theodore Roosevelt with proof of child labor. In Colorado, after the Ludlow massacre in 1914, she led a protest parade up to the governor's office. In West Virginia, time after time, she led delegations to see various governors and "gave them hell," as she said. One of the last strikes she participated in, when she was nearly 90, was the great steel strike of 1919; she was arrested several times with William Z. Foster. She said of Foster: "Never had a strike been led by a more devoted, able and unselfish man."

When she was a very old lady, she warned the rank and file against leaders who put their own interests ahead of labor. Until her death she stoutly affirmed her one great faith: "The future is in labor's strong, rough hands!" She died in 1930, at the age of 100, in Washington, D. C. at the home of Terence V. Powderly, who had been the Master Workman of the Knights of Labor back in the 1880s. She is buried in Mt. Olive Cemetery, Illinois, surrounded by the graves of miners. In death as in life she is with "her boys."

She inspired me a great deal when I first heard her in New York and Chicago in those early days, though I confess I was afraid of her sharp tongue. But when I reminded her of the meeting in the Bronx and told her I had lost my baby, she was very sympathetic and kind. Her harshness was for bosses, scabs and crooked labor leaders.

"THE SAINT"

I never met a man I admired more than Vincent St. John. He was a fabulous figure who came out of the class struggle of the West; he was only 30 years old in 1907, when he became General Organizer of the IWW. He was an American, born in Kentucky, of Irish and Dutch ancestry. His father before him had been an adventurous character who rode the Wells Fargo pony express, carrying the U.S. mails through the Southwest, and had lost his arm, shooting it out with Indians during a holdup. He is buried somewhere along the Arizona trail. Young Vincent went to work at 18 for the Bisbee Copper Company and became a union member. By the time he was 24, he was president of the Telluride, Colorado, local union of the militant Western Federation of Miners. It was a large silver and gold camp.

A strike was declared there under his leadership, in the Smuggler-Union mine, on May 1, 1901. It was one of the biggest mines and at first the struggle was in the nature of a sit-down strike, the first in the United States. The Governor's Commission, sent there to perhaps investigate, reported that instead of leaving the mine and picketing, as usual in strikes, "everything was quiet in Telluride and the miners were in peaceful possession of the mines." The cause of the strike was the piece-contract system, introduced by the manager, Arthur Collins, under which the miners were charged for board, room, tools, powder, candles, sharpening of drills and what not. They were paid per fathom to break ore, cut it to suitable size and load it into chutes. The result was that the miners' wages were actually pared to a minimum.

Collins organized a Citizens' Alliance of the businessmen, who were egged on by the *Telluride Journal* until a pitched battle ensued in which several people, Collins among them, were killed. St. John, as president of the union, was charged with the murder of Collins. To frame a strike leader, stick him in jail and keep him there for the duration of the strike was a usual tactic. He was defended by Judge Orrin N. Hilton, who was chief counsel for the miners' union. (Hilton was the lawyer who, many years later, defended Joe Hill.) He used to say with a chuckle: "That little fellow, St. John—I was his lawyer in a dozen murder charges that never came to trial!" Among these occasions, one was in Idaho when Moyer, Haywood and Pettibone were on trial in 1907. He was released on bail after the acquittal of Haywood.

He became an executive board member of the Federation, in the earlier days. Wherever there were miners in gold, silver, copper and lead, battling to build their union, he was a legendary figure of courage and resourcefulness. The *Rocky Mountain News* of February 28, 1906, quoted a company detective as saying: "St. John has given the mine owners of Colorado more trouble in the past years than twenty other men up there. If left undisturbed, he would have the entire district organized in another year." He was damned as a dynamiter, a gunman, a dangerous agitator; he entered camps with a price on his head, used his mother's name—Magee—and organized hundreds of men, often single-handed. He was one of the greatest labor organizers this country ever produced.

The chronic bronchial condition from which Saint suffered in his later years and which contributed to his untimely death in 1929, at the age of 53, was the result of a terrible mine disaster at Telluride in one of the tunnels of the Smuggler-Union mine. Burning hay (for the mules), lumber and timber caused a dense smoke to fill the mine. Collins was mainly concerned with removing Winchester rifles and ammunition from a nearby storehouse. Many miners were trapped in the mine. St. John led a rescue party, which had great difficulty because of smoke and gas. They brought out the wounded and 25 bodies of men who had been choked and smothered to death. Three thousand men marched in their funerals and covered the graves with evergreen.

The place which is most identified in labor history with the name of Vincent St. John is Goldfield, Nevada. At the turn of the century it was the biggest, busiest, richest gold camp in the world. Today it is a ghost town. It was the scene of an intense labor struggle, led by Vincent St. John. The Miners Federation was still a part of the IWW in 1906, and the "town workers" were also organized by the Saint in another IWW local. Miners and dishwashers, engineers and stenographers, teamsters and clerks—all were union members. The newsboys were organized and when the Tonapah *Sun* attacked the IWW they refused to sell it. St. John described the efforts to make Goldfield a model union town as follows:

> Under the I.W.W. sway in Goldfield, the minimum wage for all kinds of labor was $4.50 a day and the eight-hour day was universal. No committees were ever sent to any employer. The unions adopted scales and regulated hours. The secretary posted the same on the bulletin board outside the union hall and it was the LAW. The employers were forced to come and see the union committees.

Of course, this could not last very long in an isolated community, controlled by big capitalist interests. The Mine Owners' Association engineered a nasty jurisdictional fight between the American Federation of Labor and the Western Federation of Miners, which brought federal troops to the camp. The fight cost the mine owners over $100,000 and St. John nearly lost his life. He had been tricked into lending his gun and was carrying a smaller one that belonged to his wife. He had trouble in drawing it quickly. A company stool pigeon, Paddy Mullaney, shot him in both hands. Weakened by loss of blood, he was first thrown into jail and then inadequately treated at a company hospital. His friends virtually kidnapped him, rushed him to a Chicago hospital and secured from the governor of Illinois a promise that he would not sign extradition papers. Saint's life was saved, but his right hand was permanently crippled as a result.

He was short and slight in build, though broad-shouldered, quick and graceful in his movements, quiet, self-contained, modest, but his keenness of mind and wit outmatched any opponent. Daniel De Leon called him "the little Napoleon of Western labor" until Saint wiped the floor with him in a debate in 1907 at the IWW convention, when there was a revolt against De Leon's attempt to tie the industrial union movement to the apron strings of the Socialist Labor Party. After that, De Leon called St. John "a Western desperado." Socially, the Saint was very companionable, with a lively sense of humor. He and my father had a tussle in one convention over Pop's "decentralization" position. I brought Saint home a few years later and I said anxiously as we approached the house: "Don't mind if the old man is unfriendly." Saint laughed and said: "Oh no! Don't worry. I'll just tell him I've come to stay a month!" But since Saint had just left prison, Pop forgot all the old scores and treated to beer.

In a real fight, Saint's mild blue eyes became steely and cold. He fought only on principle and then as mercilessly as the enemies of the workers did. His loyalty to the working class was boundless. For eight years, from 1907 to 1915, he struggled with lack of funds and the uneven development of the IWW, whose strength he never exaggerated. His wife, a friendly Western woman, was devoted to him and managed marvelously with very little. Once, I recall, she sent me for a ten-cent pail of beer to go with the boiled dinner. I met Saint on my way and he said, with a twinkle in his eyes: "Well! Well! Joan of Arc rushing the growler!"

Preston-Smith and Conspiracy

One of the by-products of the Goldfield struggle was the Preston and Smith case. Morrie R. Preston and Joseph W. Smith were officers of the Goldfield Miners Union in 1907. On March 10 of that year there was a picket line around the restaurant of John Silva. The place had been declared unfair because the boss had held back one day's pay from a waitress when she quit. Preston had successfully turned away several customers. Silva came rushing out the door in a blind rage, waving an automatic pistol. He ordered Preston: "You go away or I'll kill you!" and raised his gun to fire. Preston drew his gun and fired twice, killing his assailant. Silva had previously exhibited the gun in the restaurant and told several customers he would "get" Preston or Smith if they came to picket.

In a defense pamphlet published after their arrest, it was explained:

In the more settled East, the question sometimes arises as to Preston's right to carry arms. The point being prejudicial, it is well to explain that "packing a gun" is so customary in the West, especially in the mining districts, that nothing is thought of it. On the contrary, a miner from the hills, or a ranger, without his "six-shooter" in plain sight would have excited more curiosity and should not be confused with the Eastern "gangster" practice of "carrying concealed weapons'."

To bear arms is the Constitutional right of every American. The prosecution did call attention to Preston being armed but put no emphasis on the point, for the jury, well acquainted with local conditions, would not have given it any weight. This will be better understood when it is recalled that Goldfield was then a "new strike"—a rough and ready mining camp with the "lid off"—born overnight, and full of "claim jumpers," adventurers, fortune hunters and gamblers, which the boom and the gold fever had attracted like flies from every district in the West. Dance halls, gambling houses and saloons crowded the main street and men carried arms as a characteristic part of their dress. In addition to the warrant of custom, Preston had the urge of a "Special Danger," for he, as business agent of the union, had been threatened on several occasions and self-protection counseled him to prepare against assault.

The dragnet theory of "conspiracy" was resorted to by the state, which charged that at a meeting at the Miners Union Hall, a plot was hatched to kill Nixon, the U.S. Senator, Winfield, a millionaire mine owner and others, including Silva, the owner of a little beanery—an unlikely story. Gunmen and labor-baiters were the so-called witnesses, but since there was no evidence that anything or anybody had even threatened the alleged victims, the case was dropped against the 17 union members on trial. Smith, although proved to have been at home eating supper, a mile from the scene of the trouble, was convicted of "manslaughter," which is defined as "taking a human life in the heat of passion and without malice or deliberation." He was sentenced to ten years in prison. Preston was convicted of murder in the second degree and recommended to the mercy of the court by the jury. He was sentenced to 25 years in the State Penitentiary. He was 25 years old.

The Western Federation of Miners financed their appeals and many subsequent efforts by Judge Hilton to secure their release. In 1911 a parole was finally secured for Smith. By 1914 one of the special hired prosecutors in the case and chief counsel for the prosecution, J. F. Douglas, wrote a letter to the Board of Pardons and Parole at Carson City, Nevada, in which he stated:

Relative to my opinion of the testimony given by Claiborne and Bliss at the trial of M. R. Preston, I have no hesitancy in stating that I became convinced at the time of the trial and from information which came to me subsequently thereto, that both of the above witnesses perjured themselves at that trial. Certainly, enough of their testimony was perjured to create grave doubt as to the truth of any of it.

Finally in April 1914, after seven years in prison, Preston was released on parole. This case helped to establish the parole system in the state of Nevada. In the defense pamphlet which was issued on his behalf, of which I have a copy autographed by Preston, there is a very interesting section on the subject of "conspiracy." Based on the Common Law of England, it is less difficult to secure convictions on the charge of "conspiracy" than on any other charge, and this is why it is generally used as a basis for the prosecution in labor cases. I quote these wise remarks of 40 years ago which are applicable now to Communists and labor, under present legislation:

The Union men must face all the allied forces of States as represented by the State's Attorney, his help and court attaches, if not, indeed, the court itself; money, as represented by hired prosecutors, crooked deputies and purchased liars; and thugdom, as represented by gunmen, strikebreakers, and private detectives. The Union men must contend with malfeasance in office on the part of the prosecutor and his henchmen; malpractice on the part of hired prosecutors, garbled reports in the press, and other tricks on the part of money; and finally, perjury, lies, jury-tampering and a thousand and one other despicable devices on the part of deputies, thugs and detectives.

This is an accurate description not only of what Preston and Smith were confronted with in Goldfield in 1907, but in a host of similar labor and political cases from then to the present day, at Foley Square in New York City. I have witnessed it over and over again and been personally a victim of the conspiracy law more than once.

WESTWARD HO!

It was in a spirit of high adventure that I set out in the summer of 1909 to see my country and to meet its people. I went as far as Puget Sound and up into Canada. I traveled alone and was surrounded by men in the IWW halls, where there were only a few women members. Yet, I never had a disagreeable experience (outside of getting arrested). The IWW used to say: "Gurley is as safe with us as if she was in God's pocket!"

The western country still had traces of the frontier. It was sparsely settled and had a natural wild beauty. All cities did not look alike as they do today, with the same chain stores and hotels, movies and illuminated advertisements, chromium fronts and cars. There were Indians, horses, cowboys, men in big wide hats, wearing lumber jackets and calked boots. Silver dollars and five-dollar gold pieces were in circulation. People were more original. They did not all look alike, talk alike, think alike. From place to place there were different styles of clothing, speech and architecture. I fell in love with my country—its rivers, prairies, forests, mountains, cities and people. No one can take my love of country away from me! I felt then, as I do now, it's a rich, fertile, beautiful land, capable of satisfying all the needs of its people. It could be a paradise on earth if it belonged to the people, not to a small owning class. I expressed all this in my speeches for socialism.

As I left Chicago, where I had lived for nearly a year, I had a sensation of excitement, which I have never lost, no matter how many trips I take over the spacious bosom of my country—whether I go by the far north route through snow and fir trees, or the southern way that takes you to palm and olive trees. Sprawled-out Chicago soon lay behind us, as we went along Lake Michigan to Milwaukee, then to Minneapolis and St. Paul. I saw the Mississippi River. On my earlier trip to the Mesabi Range, I had visited Lake Itasca, the small source of this mighty river, where it is but 12 feet wide and 18 inches deep. In my speeches this became an allegory of human progress. Leaving the Mississippi behind, the next strange sight was "the bad lands" of South Dakota, in the Black Hills—mile on mile of weird shapes, grotesque mounds of clay and sandstone. Then came the grandeur of the snow-capped Rocky Mountains. On the Continental Divide, I made my first stop—Butte, Montana.

My lifetime traveling habits were conditioned in my early youth by my great desire to see all I could of my country. Trains were slow in those days. In spring there were floods. In winter there were snow slides. Sometimes yesterday's overland express pulled in today. But even now I prefer a slow train that makes plenty of stops *en route* so you can get out a few minutes and look around—no mad rushing streamliner with a blur outside the window for me, or fast flying airplane with the earth out of sight, riding on cream-puff clouds. Except to go over oceans, I do not prefer a plane. I love to look out of train windows at night to see the low hanging stars and the Big Dipper, or to glimpse Mt. Hood or Mt. Shasta, or the disappearing ghost of the Great Salt Lake. I like to pull into stations in remote places, where signboards say so many miles from Chicago, so many miles to San Francisco. For short trips, I prefer a bus where one meets the simple good people of our country from whom I learn so much in friendly conversation.

Butte was my main destination. I came as the honored guest speaker to an all-day annual affair of the miners, celebrating the founding of the Western Federation of Miners in 1898. Their Butte local was No. 1. They put me up in "the best hotel in town," where I had a room and parlor, with a balcony overlooking the main street. A famous speculator who fought the Anaconda Company, named Heinz, had once occupied it several years before, and used the balcony to receive the cheers of the populace, which was predominantly Irish. A man named Paddy Flynn was now president of the union. Butte is situated nearly a mile above sea level and should have been a healthy place. Instead it was a blighted city. The mines were in the very heart of the city, which has grown up around them.

A practice then prevailed to burn the sulfur out of the copper in great piles near the mines before it was sent to the smelters. The poisoned fumes pervaded the city and killed all vegetation. Not a blade of grass, a flower, a tree, could be seen in this terrible city. A sprawly, ugly place, with dusty shacks for the miners, it had an ever-expanding cemetery out on the flat lands. The city of the dead, mostly young miners, was almost as large as the living population, even in this very young city. "Human life was the cheapest by-product of this great copper camp," wrote Bill Haywood of his visit there in 1898. After years of civic effort the Anaconda Copper Company was forced to abandon the ore burning at the mines and the ore was shipped to the smelters. People have nursed the foliage so Butte looks more like a human habitation today. But its gutted landscape is permanently scarred and defaced by the ravages of the mines.

Before I left Butte they gave me $100 (a fabulous amount in those days) for Vincent St. John. They wanted him to use it to go to the next convention of the Western Federation of Miners, where they figured there was a chance of getting the Federation back into the IWW. They gave me as a personal memento of the occasion a beautiful gold

On tour through Senator Clark's Original Mine, Butte Montana, June 16, 1909. The author is at the *center* with P. W. Flynn, President of the Butte Miners Union at her *left*.

In 1909 with Big Bill (William D.) Haywood, then head of the I.W.W. and Hubert Harrison, Socialist speaker

The author with her son Fred (nine-months of age). 1911

Minersville, Pa. May 16, 1911. Eugene Debs, *(right rear),* Con Foley and Elizabeth *(front),* Mrs. Foley and the town barber *(rear).*

Portrait of Elizabeth Gurley Flynn by the famous Alfred Steiglitz. 1907

locket with a replica of a miner's sifting pan, with nuggets, pick and shovel around it, reminiscent of the early days when gold mining predominated. It is one of my most precious possessions. Whenever I return to Butte I take it with me and it is always open sesame to the miners' hearts. President Flynn and a committee also escorted me down into a mine. We donned miners' caps and overalls to make the trip. The mine was so deep that the earth was actually hot. They also took me through a smelter, where a friendly worker ran an iron bar an inch or two into the molten copper and then cooled and hardened it, so I had another odd souvenir which served as an ash tray in my home in New York for years afterward.

THE MIGRATORY WORKERS

From Butte I went to Kalispell, Montana, where the IWW was leading a lumber strike. It took about 18 hours to go from Butte over the Continental Divide of the Rockies and around the mountains. It is in the northwest section of the state. I arrived there at about 3 a.m. There was no one to meet me at the station. The whole town was sleeping. But a railroad worker said: "Are you Gurley Flynn? Mrs. Heslewood said to go to the hotel," which he pointed out nearby. There I found a room waiting for me. Fred Heslewood, a giant of a man, had been one of the top organizers of the Western Federation of Miners. He was there in charge of the strike of timber workers. He was greatly embarrassed by the presence of an IWW musical band which had set up camp in town, like gypsies. They had red uniforms and went out on the street corners like the Salvation Army.

Their leader, named Walsh, had previously organized the so-called "Overalls Brigade" to go to the 1908 Chicago Convention. There they had contributed to expelling De Leon and he had dubbed them "The Bummery." Heslewood was able to bring the strike to a successful conclusion and he and his wife went on to Spokane with me. The band traveled around a while longer and then split up. They were workers and preferred the camps to a minstrel's life. That they could descend upon a strike, and the organizer there had no control over them, indicated one of the fatal weaknesses of the IWW. It was "rank-and-file-ism" carried to excess, which I saw in many later strikes.

I remained in Spokane the rest of the summer, speaking three and four times a week in the IWW hall to an ever-changing audience of migratory workers. We had a custom in those days to send a speaker into a district for an indefinite period—until the speaker was worn out or the local audiences got tired. It was a good plan, for both the speaker and for the organization. Instead of being a fly-by-night lecturer, voicing generalities, one was compelled to study and deal with the conditions confronting the workers in that area and the remedies the organization proposed, and to speak about these matters. I came to know the people as they really were, their strengths and weaknesses. The speaker had to speak in a manner to interest people to whom he was not a passing novelty. It was hard on the lazy ones—speech orators—of which we had a few.

I learned a great deal about the lives of the migratory workers. The majority were American-born Eastern youth of adventurist spirit, who had followed Horace Greeley's advice: "Go West, young man and grow up with the country!" Out there they became floaters, without homes or families. The IWW hall was their only social center, where they were able to park their blankets and suitcases, take a shower, or —more important—"boil up" their clothes and blankets in order to delouse themselves. Here they discussed their grievances and exchanged experiences which led to placing some particularly bad lumber camps on a blacklist. Here were lectures, discussions, and even parties.

I recall one Christmas the IWW in Tacoma, Washington, had a beautiful tree dedicated to "Fellow-worker Jesus" with many of his sayings about workers and common people decorating the hall. Ministers came from local churches to see for themselves how the IWW honored the Carpenter of Nazareth and the Fisherman of Galilee. They came to criticize but were impressed with the simplicity and sincerity of the tribute.

The bad conditions in the lumber camps of those days were notorious. The food was poor, the sleeping bunks dirty and crowded, sanitary facilities inadequate. The working hours were long, speedup prevailed, there were many accidents. Life was dreary and monotonous, the lengthy seasons out in the woods were broken only by July 4th and the Christmas holidays. The IWW carried on a crusade against drink. Many of these lonely men came to town with a substantial sum in accumulated wages. Before they bought much needed shoes or clothing, they were "rolled" (robbed) in a saloon or house of prostitution and thrown out in the gutter penniless.

The IWW organizers were volunteers who worked on the jobs for wages. They carried small suitcases with supplies. Thousands of dollars were collected for initiations, dues, literature, subs, etc. The percentage defaulted was amazingly low. If an organizer was fired by the boss, he moved on to another job and somebody came shortly after to take over the first one. The language of the Western IWW was picturesque, earthy and salty. The street meetings often conflicted with the Salvation Army. Peaceable arrangements to follow them were finally made in most places. The IWW developed the use of songs as a medium to hold the crowd and for propaganda purposes. Many of them were written to religious airs, others to popular tunes. Some were written by Joe Hill, with original words and music. They were collected together in various editions of the little *Red Song Book* and sold in millions of copies. They are now part of the folklore of America.

The life of the migratory workers was isolated from that of the stationary workers in the cities. They seldom left the skid row areas of the various cities. They were not welcome "uptown." They traveled by freight cars. Their work was hard and laborious. They were strong and hardy, tanned and weather-beaten by summer suns and winter snows. They regarded the city workers as stay-at-home softies—"scissorbills." They referred to a wife as "the ball and chain." But the free-speech fights and mass strikes helped to break all this down, when support from other workers became a necessity.

Free Speech in Montana

Jack Jones came to organize in Missoula, Montana, in the Fall of 1908, sent there by St. John. I was happy to rejoin him. It was the first and only time we actually lived and worked together for any length of time. My first participation in an IWW free speech fight and my second arrest occurred in this little place, not an industrial town but a gateway to many lumber camps and mining areas. It was surrounded by mountains, the air clear and invigorating. It was a clean and attractive little place, the site of a State University.

We held street meetings on one of the principal corners and drew large crowds, mainly the migratory workers who flocked in and out of town. We had rented as an IWW hall a large roomy space in the basement of the leading theater and were rapidly recruiting members into the organization. The storekeepers objected to our meetings, especially the employment agencies, which we attacked mercilessly. Under their pressure the City Council passed an ordinance making street speaking unlawful. We decided to defy this ordinance as unconstitutional, a violation of the First Amendment guaranteeing freedom of speech. Only five or six of us were in town at that time. One was Frank Little, who was lynched in Butte, Montana, eight years later, during World War I. When we tried to hold meetings, two were arrested the first night and dismissed with a warning not to speak again. Four were arrested the second night, including my husband Jones, Frank Little and a stranger to us, Herman Tucker. He was employed by the U.S. Forestry Department which had an office in a building overlooking the corner. He rushed downstairs when he saw a young logger dragged off the platform for attempting to read the Declaration of Independence. Tucker took it over, jumped on the platform and continued to read until he was arrested. (A few years later this young man, an aviator of World War I, lost his life in San Francisco Bay while distributing "Hands Off Russia" leaflets from the air over the city.) Our Missoula free speechers were sentenced to 15 days in the county jail. Those of us who were left planned the mass tactics which were advocated in free speech fights, of which Missoula was one of the first examples.

We sent out a call to all "foot-loose rebels to come at once—to defend the Bill of Rights." A steady stream of IWW members began to flock in, by freight cars—on top, inside and below. As soon as one speaker was arrested, another took his place. The jail was soon filled and the cell under the firehouse was turned into an additional jail. The excrement from the horses leaked through and made this place so unbearable that the IWW prisoners protested by song and speech, night and day. They were directly across the street from the city's main hotel and the guests complained of the uproar. The court was nearby and its proceedings were disrupted by the noise. People came to listen to the hubbub, until finally all IWWs were taken back to the county jail.

The fire department turned the hose on one of the meetings, but the townspeople protested vigorously against this after several people were hurt. College professors at the university took up the cudgels for free speech, especially when another woman, Mrs. Edith Frenette, and I were arrested. We were treated with kid gloves by the sheriff and his wife, although my husband had been badly beaten up in the jail by this same Sheriff Graham. Senator La Follette spoke at a public forum in the theater over our hall. One of our members gave him a copy of a fighting paper defending our struggle, the *Montana Socialist,* published by a woman, Mrs. Hazlett, in Helena, Montana. He made a favorable comment in his speech. Butte Miners Union No. 1, the biggest local in Montana, passed a strong resolution condemning the local officials for "an un-American and unjust action in preventing men and women from speaking on the streets of Missoula" and commending "our gallant fight for free speech." They sent it to the Missoula papers, stating that my arrest had caused them to investigate the matter and adopt the resolution.

There were some humorous aspects to our efforts. Not all the IWW workers were speakers. Some suffered from stage fright. We gave them copies of the Bill of Rights and the Declaration of Independence. They would read along slowly, with one eye hopefully on the cop, fearful that they would finish before he would arrest them. One man was being escorted to jail, about two blocks away, when a couple of drunks got into a pitched battle. The cop dropped him to arrest them. When they arrived at the jail, the big strapping IWW was tagging along behind. The cop said in surprise: "What are you doing here?" The prisoner retorted: "What do you want me to do—go back there and make another speech?"

Eventually, the townspeople got tired of the unfavorable publicity and excitement. The taxpayers were complaining of the cost to the little city, demanding it be reduced. An amusing tussle then ensued between the IWW and the authorities as to who should feed our army. We held our meeting early so the men would go to jail before supper. The police began to turn them out the next morning before breakfast, forcing us to provide rations for the day. Finally, the men refused to leave the jail although the door was thrown wide open. They had been arrested. They demanded a trial, and individual trials and jury trials at that! At last one man "broke solidarity." He was married and he sneaked out to see his wife. But when he returned the door was locked. He clamored to get in—he did not want the fellow workers to think he was a quitter. The cop said: "You're out. Now stay out!" The townsfolk, gathered around and roared with laughter.

Finally, the authorities gave up. All cases were dropped, and we were allowed to resume our meetings. We returned to our peaceful pursuit of agitating and organizing the IWW. I liked Missoula and hated to leave. The distant purple mountains seemed close at hand. The air was clear and invigorating. Our second IWW hall was a small cabin on the river bank. We used the front room for an office and had a bedroom and kitchen in the back. When Jones went out to the camps, a daughter of one of the college professors stayed with me. I could never hear enough of the life and adventures of the lumberjacks and miners who dropped in regularly. But Spokane called me to their free speech fight. "When loud and clear the call I hear, I must arise and go!" I went in December 1909, although I was again pregnant. I expected Jones would come later.

DEFENDING THE CONSTITUTION IN SPOKANE

Before our battle for free speech had ended successfully in Missoula, the much more famous Spokane free speech fight had already begun, in November 1909. It was a far bigger and tougher battle than Missoula. The IWW, although it considered itself nonpolitical, carried on 26 such political struggles for the rights of free speech and assemblage between 1906 and 1916. Some, like San Diego, were even more bitter and bloody. Spokane is the center of "The Inland Empire" of eastern Washington and western Idaho, a rich mining, lumber and agricultural area. Due to the nature of the work and the climate the workers were largely migratory or "floaters," shipping out from Spokane. Their wages were low, the work was hard, conditions unsanitary, and hours were long. But their most pressing grievance, especially in the depression years of 1907 and 1908, was the way the employment agencies cheated them in the sale of jobs.

The IWW systematically collected evidence of hundreds of cases where workers were either sent to nonexistent jobs or were fired after their first pay, out of which they had to pay a fee for the job. The "shark" was usually in cahoots with the foreman on the job. There was a grim joke among the migratory workers that the employment sharks had discovered perpetual motion—"one man going to a job, one man on the job, and one man leaving the job." The IWW found, too, that this trickery interfered with organizing workers, as there was no permanence in a working crew and the "organizer" on the job could not stay there long enough to be effective.

The IWW hall was situated in the heart of the skid row, surrounded by cheap flop houses and employment agencies. Signs hung outside for "help wanted" in all sorts of jobs. In the spring, summer and fall of 1909, the IWW held street meetings directly in front of these places, exposing their practices and naming time, place, amounts and names of workers who were fleeced. It called for a boycott of these agencies and demanded that the companies should hire through the union hall. Naturally, the "sharks" fought back. They were "respectable" businessmen who paid rent and taxes. They attacked the IWW as hoboes, tramps and "bindle-stiffs" (from the rolls of blankets they carried on their backs).

In December 1908, at the instigation of the employment agencies, a city ordinance was passed forbidding all street meetings in the business section of Spokane. Meetings were permissible in public parks which were situated in residential areas, far from the scene of the struggle. However, the IWW took advantage of this to hold meetings in the parks and bring the issues before the residents of Spokane. It succeeded in mobilizing considerable local support in trade unions and women's clubs. Over 600 members came in response to the call of the IWW from the four corners of the country. When they tried to speak on the streets they were arrested for disorderly conduct, which evaded a test as to the constitutionality of the ordinance. The IWW hall was raided in November and four of its officers—James Wilson, editor of the *Industrial Worker*, James P. Thompson, Spokane organizer, A. E. Cousins, assistant editor, and C. R. Filigno, secretary of the Spokane local—were arrested and charged with "criminal conspiracy," the old dragnet charge used so much in labor struggles.

Spokane was the scene of vicious police brutality throughout this struggle. Police officers kicked, struck and abused the prisoners. A newspaper reporter, Fred Niederhouser, characterized the herding of the men in the city jails as "monstrous." Twenty-eight men were forced into a cell seven-by-eight feet. It took four cops to close the cell door. This was called "the sweat box." The steam was turned on until the men nearly suffocated and were overcome with exhaustion. Then they were placed in ice-cold cells and "third degreed" in this weakened state. When the jail became overcrowded an abandoned unheated schoolhouse, the Franklin School, was used as a jail.

A moving diary kept there by James Stark reads today like something from a later Nazi concentration camp. He describes how the men were covered with blood after their arrest; "teeth kicked out, eyes blackened, and clothes torn." One man had a broken jaw. Food at the school was "one-third of a small baker's loaf twice a day" because the men refused to work on the rockpile. Stark describes how "turkey for

Thanksgiving" was the work of a fellow-worker artist who drew it on the blackboard. He tells how scurvy and intestinal trouble developed, how men were too weak to walk and 16 had to be taken to the hospital. On their release, men had to be carried to the IWW hall. Three deaths occurred after their release. A young man died of diabetes. The day of his funeral, arranged by the IWW, not a policeman was visible on the streets of Spokane.

The heroism of the migratory workers who came from all over the country was remarkable. Men gave their addresses on arrest, as McKees Rocks, Chicago, Milwaukee, Los Angeles, San Francisco, Seattle, Portland, and towns in Montana. There was a Civil War veteran among the free speech prisoners, who said that the conditions in the Franklin School reminded him of Libby and Andersonville prisons. There were two youths of 18 years who were offered a suspended sentence by Judge Mann if they would promise not to speak again and to leave town. Both refused and were sentenced to 30 days in jail and $100 fines, to be worked out on the rock pile. One woman was arrested who had also been with us and arrested in Missoula, Mrs. Edith Frenette, a camp cook. She was struck by a policeman on the way to jail. Another woman, Agnes Thecla Fair, who came from Alaska and had written a volume of poems called *Songs of the Sourdoughs,* went out among the farmers to collect money and food for the Spokane fighters. She met with a generous response. Socialist papers, such as the Oakland *World,* the *International Socialist Review* and others, supported our free speech efforts. The Socialist Party of Washington made an investigation and issued a public report strongly condemning the denial of free speech and police brutality.

MY FIRST CONSPIRACY TRIAL, 1910

When I came to Spokane in December 1909 the all-male committee was somewhat disconcerted to be told that I was pregnant. They decided I was not to speak on the forbidden streets but confine myself to speaking in the IWW hall, to clubs and organizations willing to give us a hearing, and in nearby places to raise defense funds. I made trips to Seattle, British Columbia, Idaho and Montana. A few months later, after five editors of the *Industrial Worker* had been arrested and it was harder for me to travel, I was put in charge of the paper. I felt fine, but my co-workers were disturbed about having me appear in public.

In those days pregnant women usually concealed themselves from public view. "It don't look nice. Besides, Gurley'll have that baby right on the platform if she's not careful!" one fussy old guy protested. One night on my way to the IWW hall. I was arrested, charged with "conspiracy to incite men to violate the law," and lodged in the county jail. I was only in jail one night and was released the next day on bail, put up by a prominent club woman.

There had been such an orgy of police brutality in Spokane that my friends back East were greatly concerned. I struck the Spokane authorities a real blow, however, by describing in the next issue of the *Industrial Worker* my overnight experiences in the county jail. The entire edition of the paper was confiscated and suppressed. But the story went all over the country and hundreds of protests poured in. I took my story to the local Women's Club, and they demanded a matron be placed in the jail.

When I came in there were two prostitutes in the women's quarters. They were kind to me, gave me fruit and a blanket. But during the night a jailer came, opened the door and took one of the women downstairs, ostensibly to see her sweetheart. After a long time she returned. This was repeated several times during the night. She told the other woman the jailer had said they'd "have brought Jack up here only for *her* being here"—indicating me. I said in my article that the performance looked to me as if she were expected to ply her trade inside the jail. In the morning, the chief jailer came with our breakfasts —sour bread and weak coffee. He opened the door, marched right into our quarters where we were in bed and put his hand on my face to wake me up. I was startled and insulted and told him so. I also told the whole world or as much of it as I could reach through the press. It caused a furor in the city of Spokane.

The unspeakable Chief Sullivan (who was shot sitting at his window a few months later after the fight was over, undoubtedly by one of the thousands he had brutally attacked), said he had been in office for 20 years and no woman had ever complained before. Therefore I must be lying. The sheriff said the grand jury had recommended that women matrons be put in the jails but the commissioners had done nothing. One of the police captains evoked a storm of protest from women when he said: "Those women back there don't want a woman to care for them; only hardened or low women are kept in jail." My story helped to focus nation-wide attention on the much more terrible experiences of the male IWW prisoners. Matrons were installed in the county jails for the first time in Spokane history.

A peculiar system of trials prevailed there. I was tried first in a lower court with a jury of six—two retired farmers and four businessmen —one in real estate, one in mining, and another the president of a drygoods company; no worker or woman on the jury, of course. The newspapers said I was considered "one of the most dangerous of the IWWs." I was convicted, sentenced to 90 days and released the same day on bail. The second trial, on appeal, took place before a higher court with a jury of twelve. C. L. Filigno, the secretary, and I were tried together as co-conspirators. The prosecutor said of me: "If she had not formed a dangerous organization, had not sung the Red Flag song, had not called Justice Mann an illiterate old fool, had not preached the gospel of discord and discontent, I would have ignored her."

I was ably defended by Fred Moore, then a young local attorney. Mrs. Stafford, an officer of the Women's Club, testified she had heard me speak and there was nothing wrong with my remarks. The president, Mrs. House, was ready to substantiate this, but was not allowed to testify. During my testimony the judge asked me upon what I based my speeches. I replied: "The Bill of Rights." He said: "But you're not a lawyer. How can you interpret them?" I answered: "They are in plain English, your Honor, anyone can understand them. They were not written for lawyers but for the people!" To my great embarrassment, I was acquitted and Filigno was found guilty. By this time I was obviously pregnant and even the fast-fading Western chivalry undoubtedly came into play.

It was during the Spokane free speech fight that I recall first meeting William Z. Foster. He mentions in his book* having been in Missoula, so I may have met him earlier. He came there as a reporter for a Seattle left-wing Socialist paper, Dr. Titus' *Workingman's Paper,* formerly the *Seattle Socialist.* I only wish I had changed as little in appearance in the last 50 years as has Foster. When I met him in Spokane during the free speech struggle, he was 28 years old. He was tall, slender, blue-eyed and soft spoken, much thinner than he is now—a regular "skinny marink," he described himself. His hair was not quite so thin as it is today. But in spite of serious illness he has not aged as

* *Pages from a Worker's Life,* International Publishers, 1939, New York.

much as most men of his years and anyone who knew him then would easily recognize him today at 74 years of age. He was arrested, served two months, and joined the IWW while in jail. On his release he was placed on the committee in charge of the fight.

The hall had been closed down, the defense office had been moved to Coeur d'Alene, Idaho, in charge of Fred Heslewood. Over 600 men had been arrested. Our forces were seriously depleted, although we were boldly and publicly announcing a spring renewal of the free speech fight. The committee resorted to a tactical move at the suggestion of Foster. They approached the mayor offering to negotiate an end of hostilities. The city was full of floaters and the authorities feared they were all IWWs.

The mayor was tired of the whole business. It was costing the city $1,000 a week. The taxpayers were grumbling. He had previously said that he knew the employment agencies were crooks and claimed he had helped men get thousands of dollars back. He offered to put the ordinance on ice, allow the IWW to open up their hall and hold street meetings unmolested. It was accepted as a practical victory. All prisoners were released and pending cases dropped. So ended this famous struggle.

I Meet Tom Mooney

One of my speaking trips on behalf of the Spokane fight took me into the mining area of Idaho, which included the towns of Wallace, Mullen and Burke. I came with a spoken credential that opened every miner's door and purse: "St. John sent me!" That area had been the scene of violent class struggle just a few years before—and Vincent St. John, under the name of John Magee, had been there to represent the Western Federation of Miners. Saint told me to look up certain people, especially an old lady in Mullen who kept a boarding house. I went to this strange little town in a deep narrow canyon, built along one street with the railroad track in the middle. It was so close to the houses that you could step off the train on to the porches. The little old lady welcomed me warmly and told me hair-raising stories of the Saint and his narrow escapes from spies and company thugs. "Only a few of us knew it was him, St. John, and we never told!" she said proudly. She told me of the bull pen, built to imprison the striking miners and of armed camps of guards, how mines were dynamited and miners killed and it was all blamed on the union. And she told me about that grand man, St. John, whom they arrested for "murder" because he organized the miners. He was her hero—and mine.

In the town of Wallace I spoke from a small carriage called a "buggy" against the backdrop of a sheer wall of mountain as a sounding board. When I told the miners gathered around that I spoke for the IWW now fighting in Spokane and that Vincent St. John told me to be sure to come here, they gave me a royal welcome. I can still see them, the circle of miners and lumberjacks in their high boots and big hats, listening attentively. Bill Haywood, who was on a tour, had been advertised to speak in Wallace, but he became ill and a young Socialist and I filled in for him. His name was Tom Mooney, a rosy-cheeked, black-eyed, laughing young Irishman, who had been on the Red Special with Debs. He was engaged at that time in a subscription contest for the *International Socialist Review*. The prize was a "trip around the world," but later he told me he came in second and went instead to the 1910 International Socialist Congress in Copenhagen, Denmark.

Probably I would not have remembered meeting Tom at that time except that he had an accident while I was there. A ring on his little finger caught on a nail in the bannister of the hotel staircase and tore his finger so badly he had to have it amputated. Oddly, this town and meeting have remained in my memory for years. I met a woman in New York a few years later who told me that she and her husband had listened to me speak that day. He was the local doctor. A few months later he and a number of the men who listened to me that day lost their lives in a desperate battle against forest fires. It was a wild and rugged country where both nature and greed snuffed out human life.

MARRIAGE GOES ON THE ROCKS

By April 1910, I had to make a serious decision. The free speech fight was ended. I could not speak anymore at present. My baby was due in a few weeks. Either I had to return to Jones or know that my marriage had ended. I had lived with the Heslewoods during my stay in Spokane. They were puzzled and critical that Jones had not come to Spokane once during my stay there, even after my arrest or during my two trials. By this time I, too, felt hurt and angry that he had remained in Missoula. I had conscientiously advised him to attend to his work, but it was only an overnight trip and I did not expect he would take me so

literally. Some of the fellow-workers who came through said he resented my friendship with the Heslewoods and was jealous of Fred Moore,
the IWW lawyer. Finally, he came to Spokane to insist that I return to
him.

It is hard to say now, after so many years, why I had so completely
fallen out of love with him. But I knew I had. Whether it was the age
difference or a difference in temperament and approach to my work,
I knew that it had come to an end and I said so. He wanted me to go
with him to Butte, where he would get a job in the mines. He proposed
I should give up speaking and traveling and settle down to live with
him in one place. We had been married two years and three months,
but had lived together very little of that time. His attitude was undoubtedly a normal one, but I would have none of it. I did not want
"to settle down" at nineteen. A domestic life and possibly a large family had no attractions for me. My mother's aversion to both had undoubtedly affected me profoundly. She was strong for her girls "being
somebody" and "having a life of their own." I wanted to speak and
write, to travel, to meet people, to see places, to organize for the
IWW. I saw no reason why I, as a woman, should give up my work for
his. I knew by now I could make more of a contribution to the labor
movement than he could. I would not give up. I have had many heartaches and emotional conflicts along the way but always my determination to stick to my self-appointed task has triumphed. But it wasn't
easy in 1910.

I talked to the Heslewoods first. Fred thought I was a little off my
mental balance, "maybe affected by pregnancy," he said anxiously.
Otherwise why should I want to leave my husband at that time? Myr-
tle Heslewood was all sympathy, but she frightened me by proposing
that she adopt my baby. I decided to go home to my mother. I knew
she would understand and help me solve my problem. I did not want
to give my baby away. So I turned my face homeward. It took five
days by train from Spokane to New York, changing at Chicago. It is a
wonder with the jolting of the train in those days that I did not have
the baby *en route*. But I made it home in safety. I had to stay over a
couple of hours in Chicago. St. John met me at the station. I told him
of my decision, which did not seem to surprise or shock him. After he
took one look at me, his main concern was to get me on a homebound
train as soon as possible. He went to the ticket office to find what was
the first train out.

My mother and sisters and my quiet brother Tom met me with open arms at the station. My mother was happy that I had come home and glad about my decision. She and my sister Kathie helped take care of my child from the day of his birth. My son Fred arrived in a little hospital near Mt. Morris Park, on May 19, 1910. The night before, Halley's Comet flashed across the sky, and the whole family went on the roof to see it, but I could not climb the stairs. The next morning Mama called a nearby livery stable for a "hack" and all I could think of now was leaving a box of strawberries on the window that I wanted for my breakfast. I met Bertha Mailly of the Rand School in the hospital and we became friends.

After I had been home a few months, Jack came to New York to see if I would change my mind. He talked to my father who called me into the living room to discuss it. I was just 20 then, but I was determined in my refusal to live with him. Finally my father, in some embarrassment, said: "But surely you can give the man some reason!" All I could say, and it seemed enough to me, was: "I don't love him any more. Besides, he *bores* me!" It was the cruelty of youth, yet the best I could do to explain. My father tried not to smile but I felt he understood.

Jones was a good man, but erratic. His father had been a drunkard, and Jack was so set against drink that when a dentist in Missoula told me to take some whiskey after a tooth was pulled he was highly indignant. When Fred was a baby and ill, a local doctor prescribed a few drops of whiskey. Jones cried and threatened to put the baby in a Masonic home if it happened again. True, I was high-spirited and headstrong and not ready to attempt to adjust myself to another person. But it was especially difficult with him. His hobby was "system." He nearly drove me crazy in Chicago with his wheels and charts on the IWW and a complicated plan he worked out to revise the calendar. Foster, who was a personal friend of his, told me years later: "I always felt sorry for Jones and blamed you for leaving him until I lived with him myself. Then I understood." I felt better, though I also felt the fault was mine to have agreed to marry so young. My parents felt guilty for allowing me to go on the trip in 1907. But I was now back home again and happy to be there, with my two sisters and brother. We were a close-knit family.

My son, Fred, boasted as he grew up that he had been in jail twice for free speech before he was born—in Missoula and in Spokane.

Then, he said jokingly that in a family with four women he had to fight for it all his life!

CARITAS ISLAND

The summer of 1910 was extremely hot and my friends were concerned about me and my baby after the ordeal of Spokane. Dr. Strunsky had taken care of me during childbirth. His sister was Anna Strunsky Walling, whose husband was reputed to be a "millionaire Socialist." So was J. G. Phelps Stokes, recently married to Rose Pastor, a beautiful and talented working woman from the East Side of New York. There had been much publicity about this romantic marriage of a well-to-do Christian settlement worker and a Jewish cigarmaker, and quite a furor in orthodox Jewish circles. It antedated a similar fuss made by the upstart Irish capitalist, Mackay, when his lovely daughter married the Jewish songwriter, Irving Berlin. Religious mixed marriages are accepted sufficiently today that such bitterness would be hard to understand if it did not still exist in relation to interracial marriages. But that will pass, in time.

The Stokes family lived on an island in Long Island Sound, off Stamford, Connecticut, called Caritas Island. Another family, the writer Miriam Finn and Leroy Scott, lived there too. Mrs. Stokes invited me to spend the summer. I had a large downstairs room and bath all to myself, next to the spacious library. I sat outdoors in the sun reading a great deal with the baby asleep in a basket. Many interesting people came there. I recall Horace Traubel and Shaemus O'Sheel, then a budding young poet. There I first met Ella Reeve Bloor, who was the Socialist Party organizer for Connecticut.

Ella Reeve Bloor was in her forties when I met her in 1910. She was strong and vigorous and moved as if she were flying rather than walking. She had dark hair, done up very simply in a little knot on top of her head, and very bright, snapping black eyes. I remembered she wore a lace collar pinned with a brooch. All here life Ella was a dressy little lady and loved jewelry. She was animated and vivacious. I thought she resembled a busy little brown bird. Her voice was clear and resonant and could be heard in the largest hall or on the noisiest street corner.

She was then the mother of six living children; two more had died in childhood. She was divorced from her first husband, Lucian Ware, who remained her friend and took care of their four children at Arden, Delaware, and sometimes the other two as well. She had the two youngest children of her second marriage, Dick and Carl, with her in Connecticut. She described to me the battle she had with the "conservatives" of the Socialist Party there in 1905, when she was first proposed as organizer. Two Catholic Socialists objected on the ground she was "a divorced woman." Some objected simply because she was a woman. But with the tremendous persistence for which Ella was noted, she moved into the state anyhow and worked unofficially, until she wore down the opposition. They finally decided she was "a good woman" (women were either "good" or "bad" in those days) and in 1908 they elected her their organizer.

She helped support her family by writing for the Waterbury *American* until an article against child labor caused her to lose her job. She told me how Emmeline Pankhurst, the militant British suffragette, had come to Connecticut to speak and had criticized her for lending her energies to "a man's party." Ella retorted she was working hard through that party to help get suffrage in that state, cooperating with Mrs. Hepburn who headed the movement—the mother of Katherine Hepburn, the actress. I liked and admired this spirited and peppery little Socialist agitator, who in later years became one of my dearest friends and closest co-workers, although I had only a short visit with her at that time. It took courage in those days to barnstorm for socialism in front of factories, out among the farmers, in every nook and cranny of a New England state, as she did.

THE GIRLS' STRIKE

While I had been away in the West, several large strike struggles had taken place in the East. One, in 1909, was centered in New York's East Side, involved 20,000 waistmakers and was called "the girls' strike." Sixty per cent in the trade were women and 70 per cent between 16 and 25 years old. They worked 56 hours a week in seasonal work, speeded up in dirty firetraps known as "sweat shops." "Learners" wages were $3 to $6 per week. The highest paid to operators was $18. The strike started in two shops, one the notorious Triangle Shirtwaist Company. A meeting was held at Cooper Union with union officials and prominent sympathizers as speakers, cautiously discussing if a general strike was possible. The overflow filled all the halls in the vicinity. After two hours, a girl striker demanded the floor. She said: "I am tired of listening to speakers. I offer a resolution that a general strike be declared now." Her motion was enthusiastically carried. Her name was Clara Lemlich, and today she is known as an active and progressive worker.

The strike lasted two months. The picket lines were broken up again and again by the police. Over 1,000 strikers were arrested. Twenty-two young girls were sent to Blackwell's Island Workhouse, a horrible, filthy place. The Women's Trade Union League and the suffrage organizations came to the aid of the strikers. Five hundred school teachers, led by Henrietta Rodman, president of The Teachers' Association (there was no union then), met at the New Amsterdam Theatre to pledge aid to the strikers. Mary Dreier, then President of the Women's Trade Union League, was arrested on the picket line. A meeting to protest against police brutality was held at the Hippodrome; Dr. John Howard Melish was chairman. A similar meeting at Carnegie Hall was addressed by Rabbi Stephen Wise.

Young girls told at these meetings of violence and insults by the police and of how the prostitutes in jail jeered at their low wages and told them they could do much better at *their* trade. When the strike started, there were two union shops. When it ended, there were over 300 union shops, with shorter hours and more pay. This heroic struggle of women laid a firm base for the International Ladies Garment Workers Union. In 1910 over 45,000 men and women were out in a general strike. Yet it took years for one woman to be elected to their executive board. It has always been a male-run organization, with the biggest local unions of women in existence.

Another hard-fought IWW strike struggle in the East took place while I was in the West. It started in July 1909, and involved 8,000 workers in the Pressed Steel Car Company plant at McKees Rocks, Pennsylvania. There were 16 nationalities employed mostly as unskilled workers at the customary long hours and low wages. It was hard and dangerous work and there were many accidents. This strike lasted eleven weeks.

Picket lines were brutally charged by the state constabulary known as the Coal and Iron Police, whom the strikers called "Cossacks." When one striker was killed, the strikers drove the constabulary into the plants. Several were killed on both sides in the battle that ensued and 50 were wounded. But the fight-back mood of the strikers brought an end to further violence against them. At the end of the strike all strikebreakers were fired. All employees became members of the IWW.

I do not know the exact economic gains won at that time. But Bill Haywood wrote: "It was the only strike of the lower paid workers that had ever been won against the Steel Trust." Vincent St. John, then secretary-treasurer of the IWW, jubilantly wired all over the country that it was a complete victory. A Spokane paper headlined "INDUSTRIAL WORKERS RULE AT MCKEES ROCKS." It was the first big step toward the IWW spreading eastward. It helped break ground for the great steel strike led by Foster just ten years later, in 1919.

GIANTS OF LABOR—HAYWOOD AND DEBS

That fall James Connolly came to say goodbye to our family. He had been called back to Ireland and was glad to go. He said he was not sorry he had come to America and not sorry to leave. Movements were on foot to organize industrial unions in Ireland. We sat and talked quite a while. The baby was very fretful that day. Connolly, who was well experienced with babies, having had seven, took the baby from me, laid him face down across his knees and patted his back until he burped soundly and then went to sleep. We all felt very sorry to see Connolly go. His family left shortly afterward—the older children not too willingly. This was the last time I saw this good friend.

In the winter of 1910–11, after my baby had been weaned, I began to do occasional speaking again. My father was out of work and we were very hard up. I had refused to take any money from my husband, if I could possibly help it. I became involved in a strike in Brooklyn, and the IWW paid me a part-time wage for that, which helped a great deal. This was an IWW shoeworkers' strike of highly skilled craftsmen, who did custom work on made-to-order shoes for the rich, which sold for as high as $75 a pair. They were dissatisfied with the terms the Boot and Shoe Workers Union of the AFL had made with their employers. Some of them received as little as $10 a week, they were speeded up, and the work was seasonal. Many were Italians. They sent for Joseph J. Ettor, who was fast emerging on the labor scene as an excellent organizer. The strike lasted four months and ended with some concessions by the employers and the AFL union. I spoke at their mass meetings two and three times a week.

One striker, Vincent Buccafori, was sentenced to ten years in prison as a result of defending his life against the murderous attack of a foreman in the Dodd factory. I spoke around the city for his defense, taking his wife and two children to some gatherings. On his behalf I appealed to the May Day Conference at the Labor Temple on East 84th Street on April 7, 1911. I went with his wife to visit him in Sing Sing, which was the first of my many visits to grim prisons where labor and political prisoners were incarcerated. He was released a few years later. The Buccafori case was my first direct experience in labor defense work, which later became my specialty.

In the midst of this shoeworkers' strike, Haywood returned from his European trip. He had not spoken under IWW auspices anywhere since his release from jail. But the Socialist Party official leadership was becoming increasingly cool to him because of his forthright stand on war at the Socialist International Congress, his attacks upon the AFL leadership and craft unionism and his espousal of industrial unionism. Many famous Socialists of that day had attended the 1910 gathering of the Second International, including Jean Jaurès from France, Rosa Luxemburg from Germany, Keir Hardie and Ramsey McDonald of England, and Victor Berger and Morris Hillquit from the United States. It was here that Lenin led the "Lefts" in the Congress to take a strong position against war. The Congress decided that all Socialists in parliament should vote against war credits and carry on propaganda that workers must not kill one another in a capitalist war for markets, to increase profits. When war actually came in 1914, the German, French, Belgian and British Socialists betrayed this resolution and the Socialist International was split asunder.

The Socialist Party had arranged no welcome meeting for Haywood on his return. He planned to make a nation-wide tour under the auspices of the *International Socialist Review,* an independent left-wing magazine, published by Charles H. Kerr Company in Chicago. The price of admission was a subscription to the monthly and its circulation soared.

Haywood needed to earn more than most of us at that time. His wife was a permanently paralyzed invalid in a wheel chair and he had two young daughters. He had to hire a nurse and housekeeper in his home while he was away. St. John had apparently contacted Haywood while he was abroad and suggested that his first return appearance be under IWW auspices, which Haywood accepted. It was an enthusiastic overflow meeting at Yorkville Casino in New York. The rank and file of both the Socialist Party and IWW as well as many other workers were there to greet him. I felt honored indeed to be chairman of this meeting, especially when he said: "I would rather speak for the IWW with Gurley Flynn on one side of me and Joe Ettor on the other than from a place between Sam Gompers and some other Civic Federation union official." (The National Civic Federation was an organization set up in 1900 by the employers to "bring about better relations between capital and labor." Senator Mark Hanna was its chairman. He was the owner of big coal companies, street railways, and other industrial holdings. Samuel Gompers was its vice-chairman. John Mitchell, leader of the United Mine Workers, was forced to resign from this organization by action of a union convention, which rejected its fake brotherhood of capital and labor in the midst of antiunion drives, open shops, injunctions, violence against strikers in the very plants and mines of these cooing vultures of capitalism.)

This was my first personal contact with this heroic giant of the American working class, William D. Haywood. He was over six feet, a big man, strong and vigorous. He was then 42 years of age. He had lost the sight of one eye, as a child, which gave him a misleading sinister appearance. He was born in Salt Lake City. At the age of nine he worked on a farm, and went into the mines in Nevada at the age of fifteen. He joined the Western Federation of Miners in 1896 at 25, when its organizer came to Silver City, Idaho, where he was then working. He became president of the local union. When he was 31, he became secretary-treasurer of the Western Federation of Miners, with its headquarters in Denver, Colorado.

In the succeeding eleven years he had shown bold leadership and courage in the epic struggles of that organization, had been framed and tried for his life and had been defended by the American working class. His speech was like a sledge-hammer blow, simple and direct— on the class struggle and the necessity for the widest possible political and industrial unity along class lines. He was the living symbol of that unity. When he walked through the streets of New York, he towered over other men. Workers would turn to look at him and say: "Why, that's Bill Haywood!" After this meeting, I was associated with Bill Haywood for years—and in some of the great strikes in the East.

A few weeks later, in the Summer of 1911, I had the privilege of meeting the other great Socialist leader of that generation. I made a speaking trip to the anthracite area around Pottsville at the invitation of a local Socialist barber, Con Foley, who wanted me to speak to a group of women and girls on strike in nearby Minersville. They were employed by the Coombe Garment Company making underwear, and were resisting a wage cut of eight cents to ten cents per dozen garments. Their menfolk were miners who gave their hall for a meeting. Just as I started speaking the fire whistle on the roof of the factory let out with a long and piercing series of blasts.

One morning when I came into Foley's barber shop a tall thin man rose out of one of the chairs and took both my hands in his. It was Eugene V. Debs. He was speaking that night in nearby Shamokin and had dropped in to see us. The word was spread in Minersville: "Debs will speak!" It was a unique experience to see this great orator of the people, who filled main auditoriums in all cities of the country, standing on an old wagon for a platform in a small town that afternoon. He was surrounded by the miners in their working clothes, begrimed as they came from work, the enthusiastic and determined women strikers, and the children just out of school, who gazed at him spellbound. I had heard Debs speak once in New York with Daniel De Leon at one of the first IWW meetings. I heard him many times after that. But that little mining town audience inspired him to eloquence such as I had never heard. His burning rage at the wrongs they suffered, his praise for their fighting spirt, his scorn for the mining companies and those "cockroach" small-shop capitalists who exploit workingmen and their families in these forlorn and isolated places, his contempt for the Coal and Iron Constabulary, patrolling the main street as he spoke—are unforgettable memories of the first time I met Debs. Later, Con Foley was arrested, charged with inciting to riot, but it caused such protest that the company gave in and the charge was dismissed, as the girls returned to work, gaining higher wages.

Born in Indiana in 1855, Debs was then 56 years old—at the zenith of his power as a "tribune of the people." He, too, had gone to work at the early age of 15, because of poverty. He became a railroad worker, was a brakeman at 19, and at 25 was secretary-treasurer of the

Brotherhood of Locomotive Firemen. During the American Railway Union Strike of 1894, he served a six-month sentence for contempt of court, for violation of an injunction. It was in jail that he first read a socialist book, brought to him by Victor Berger. These two—Haywood and Debs—were the real leaders of the American socialist movement in 1910.

I GET ARRESTED SOME MORE

While I was in the anthracite area in the Spring of 1911, the IWW local of Philadelphia sent for me. A critical situation had arisen among the workers in the plant of the Baldwin Locomotive Works, occupying a large area in the center of the city. It has long since moved to Chester, Pennsylvania. Twelve hundred employees, among whom were some IWW members, had been suddenly laid off by the company without reason. They were gathered around the plant in protest. It was our plan to try to organize them all into the IWW and fight for reinstatement. So we held a street meeting at the corner of 15th and Buttonwood Streets. The first few speakers were not molested, but when I spoke, I was arrested. The cops said officials of the company had telephoned a complaint. I was taken by car downtown and lodged in the jail in City Hall, under the statue of William Penn.

The police magistrate before whom I appeared was a squat politician who growled at me: "These people don't want you there!"— meaning the bosses, of course. The workers had hooted and booed the cops for arresting me and demonstrated that they *did* want to hear me. He sneered at our efforts to organize the men and called it "a money-making scheme." He was the first to call me "an outside agitator," a name I heard often in the next few years. I was fined $10 for "disturbing the peace."

The next week, after passing the word quietly around the plant, we returned to the widest streets bordering on it—Broad and Spring Garden, where we attempted to hold another meeting. Again no one else was arrested until I spoke. I was ordered to stop and "move on" and when I refused I was arrested. The police said they "had orders from higher up," though they acted reluctantly in face of the angry workers. Again the charge was "obstructing the highway and breach of the peace." I was taken before the same irate Irish judge who again fined me $10. We held a protest meeting on City Hall Plaza, which was generally used as a forum for Sunday meetings in those days, and enlisted much popular support.

On the occasion of one of these arrests, I believe it was the first, a very provocative act was committed by the police. A Negro policeman, and there were very few at that time, was thrust forward by the white cops to make the arrest and face the jeers and catcalls of over a thousand workers, predominantly Irish. The contemptible meanness of forcing him to arrest a white woman—and an Irish one at that—was clear to me. I felt the man trembling when he grasped my arm. "Don't worry, I'll see that they don't hurt you!" I assured him. He smiled down at me, at my naïveté and size, too, I presume. I was greatly relieved when we reached the local police station, followed by hundreds of workers. I felt I had delivered him safely. Usually I had scant sympathy for a policeman, but from this instance I began to realize that a special persecution of the Negro people extended to all walks of life, and no Negro was exempt, not even a policeman.

My mother and the whole family took care of my son while I was away. I had previously received $19 a week salary from the IWW plus railroad fares and expenses, which were very little. This was raised to $21 after Fred was born. Our rent at home was $18 a month. Anyone of the family who worked chipped in to help out. My sister Kathie worked in Macy's in the summer vacation months to keep herself in college. She was determined to be a teacher. It was hard sailing, but we were no different from hundreds of families around us in the South Bronx and those whom I met in my travels. I stayed in homes wherever I went. I knew the lives of working people at first hand. In those days no traveling Socialist or IWW speaker went to a hotel. It was customary to stay at a local comrade's house. This was partly a matter of economy, to save expenses for the local people, and partly a matter of security for the speaker in many outright strongholds of reaction, like one-plant company towns.

But, more than all else, it was a comradeship, even if you slept with one of the children or on a couch in the dining room. It would have been considered cold and unfriendly to allow a speaker to go off alone to a hotel. It was a great event when a speaker came to town. They wanted to see you as much as possible. People came from all around to socialize at the house where the speaker stayed. They heard about other parts of the country while the speaker could learn all about the conditions in that area. It was hard on the older speakers, but while I was young and vigorous I did not mind. Only many years later did it become customary for speakers to be put up in hotels. By then, I enjoyed it.

THE MCNAMARAS PLEAD "GUILTY"

In October 1910 the building of the open-shop anti-labor Los Angeles *Times* was blown up and 21 nonunion workers employed there were killed. At first it was believed that a gas explosion had occurred but later evidence indicated dynamite. Organized labor was accused of the crime by Harrison Gray Otis, the publisher. In April 1911, J. J. McNamara, secretary of the Structural Iron Workers Union was arrested at the headquarters in Indianapolis with his brother, J. B. McNamara. They were charged with murder and rushed to the Los Angeles jail, in a manner reminiscent of the Colorado kidnapping of the labor leaders in 1907.

Clarence Darrow became chief counsel in their defense. Debs and Haywood, who were speaking around the country, and the entire Socialist and labor press came to their defense. The Socialist Party nominated one of its lawyers, Job Harriman, as its candidate for mayor of Los Angeles, making their case the central issue of his campaign. The AFL helped defray the legal expenses of the defense. The IWW paper, the *Industrial Worker,* called for a general strike of protest. Like a bolt out of the blue, after a lot of secret negotiation between the prominent businessmen of the city, the lawyers on both sides, and Lincoln Steffens, then well-known as "a muckraking" newspaper man, the trial of J. B. McNamara was suddenly halted. Both prisoners were brought into court and changed their pleas from "Not Guilty" to "Guilty." It was a stunning blow to the labor movement of the country.

They had been prompted to take this action by the advice of their lawyers, labor officials, a Catholic priest and misguided friends like Lincoln Steffens, who had a notion he could settle the class struggle by the "Golden Rule." It was a selfless, courageous action on the McNamaras' part. They did not confess, they gave no information involving others, they named no names. Each brother was anxious to save the other and both to save the labor movement from further attack. J. B. McNamara was willing to accept hanging, if necessary, to win the conditions agreed upon, which were: a short sentence for his brother, J. J., no more arrests, a labor-capital conference to be held in

Los Angeles to settle the issues at stake for organized labor. All the parties agreed to these terms, none of which were carried out, except the life-sentence for J. B. McNamara. He died in 1939 in San Quentin, after 28 years in prison.

This agreement was treated like a scrap of paper. Three years later two more unionists were sentenced in Los Angeles as dynamiters—Matthew Schmidt to life imprisonment and David Kaplan to 15 years. A large group of trade unionists, including Olaf Tweitmoe of the San Francisco Building Trades Council, served terms in Leavenworth for complicity in dynamiting. No conference was ever held. The employing class was out for blood! Steffens spent years trying to secure the release of the McNamaras, but to no avail.

The unexpected turn of events shattered the Socialist campaign for mayor. The gutters of Los Angeles were full of Harriman buttons. Darrow was tried twice in Los Angeles on the charge of attempted bribery of a juror. The prosecutor said it was his life's ambition "to put Darrow where the McNamaras now are" and he nearly succeeded. The hostility to organized labor increased. The AFL was under heavy attack. Some newspapers commented: "The IWW talks direct action but the AFL practiced it." There was a great deal of criticism of both Darrow and Steffens for the "Guilty" plea, but not of the McNamaras. They were the tragic victims of this chapter of American labor history. J. B. McNamara was considered, as Foster says: "One of the bravest and most loyal fighters developed by the American labor movement."

While all this was happening on the Pacific Coast, we of the IWW held meetings to discuss labor problems in the East. One night, I recall, we arranged a debate on the organization of the clothing workers —should they go into the AFL or the IWW? The speakers were Joe Ettor and August Bellanca, later an official of the Amalgamated Clothing Workers. It was held on the lower East Side. As we came out of the hall, we saw a strange sight, a uniformed policeman stumbling along the street weeping. We gathered around him to ask what was wrong. He said he had just come from a most horrible sight—a fire in the Triangle Shirtwaist factory, high up in a loft building off Washington Square. The doors were locked and jammed. Young girls leaped from the windows, their bodies aflame like torches, and were dashed to death on the pavement below. One hundred and forty-six workers, mostly women and girls, died that day—March 25, 1911—in the heart of New York City. The reasons the door was locked, we heard later, were to search the girls as they left, lest they take a shirtwaist, and to keep union organizers out. No one went to prison, there was no newspaper clamor for punishment of the guilty after this holocaust—a striking contrast to what happened in Los Angeles. This terrible lesson was not lost on the workers, either—the great concern for property losses and the lives of "scabs" in California, as compared to the indifference to union girls struggling to better their lot in new York City, who were murdered by greed in that firetrap shop.

The Los Angeles *Times* never did become a union shop—and to this day is an open shop. It manages to hold out by paying more on all jobs than the union scale requires.

THREE

The Lawrence Textile Strike

◆◆◆◆◆◆◆◆◆◆◆◆◆◆

THE STRIKE OF 1912

In 1912 textile mills stretched along many miles of the Merrimac River—in Manchester and Nashua, New Hampshire, and in Lowell and Lawrence, Massachusetts. Lawrence was a major center. Here 30,000 workers were employed in its woolen mills, largely owned by the American Woolen Company whose president was William M. Wood. I had been in Lawrence on a speaking trip in the summer of 1911, and had visited Concord—my birthplace. A small IWW local had been organized by James P. Thompson, and held its meetings in the Franco-Belgian Hall in Lawrence. For the first time I saw sabots, the European wooden shoe, worn here by the Belgian weavers. The clatter on the stairs reminded me of what Voltaire (I believe it was) said: "Ever the velvet slippers coming down the stairs of history and the wooden shoes going up!"

The strike broke with dramatic suddenness on January 11, 1912, the first payday of the year. A law reducing the hours of women and children under 18, from 56 hours a week to 54 had been passed by the Massachusetts legislature. It affected the majority of the employees. The employers had strongly resisted the passage of this law. Now they cut the pay proportionately in the first pay envelope. Wages were *already* at the starvation point. The highest paid weavers received $10.50 weekly. Spinners, carders, spoolers and others averaged $6 to $7 weekly. Whole families worked in the mills to eke out a bare existence. Pregnant women worked at the machines until a few hours before their babies were born. Sometimes a baby came right there in the mill, between the looms. The small pittance taken from the workers by the rich corporations, which were protected by a high tariff from foreign competition, was the spark that ignited the general strike. "Better to starve fighting than to starve working!" became their battle-cry. It spread from mill to mill. In a few hours of that cold, snowy day in January, 14,000 workers poured out of the mills. In a few days the mills were empty and still—and remained so for nearly three months.

It was estimated that there were at least 25 different nationalities in Lawrence. The largest groups among the strikers were: Italians, 7,000; Germans, 6,000; French Canadians, 5,000; all English speaking, 5,000; Poles, 2,500; Lithuanians, 2,000; Franco-Belgians, 1,100; Syrians, 1,000—with a sprinkling of Russians, Jews, Greeks, Letts and Turks. The local IWW became the organizing core of the strike. They were overwhelmed by the magnitude of the job they had on their hands and sent a telegram for help to Ettor in New York City. He and his friend, Arturo Giovannitti, responded to the call on the promise of Haywood, James P. Thompson, myself and others to come as soon as possible, which we did. Ettor and Giovannitti were young—26 and 27 respectively.

They could speak eloquently in both English and Italian. Giovannitti, who as the editor of the Italian labor paper *Il Proletario,* was a poet and a magnificent orator. Ettor was an able organizer, a smiling, confident, calm man, who moved quickly and decisively. He selected interpreters to bring order out of this veritable tower of Babel. They organized mass meetings in various localities of the different language groups and had them elect a strike committee of men and women which represented every mill, every department and every nationality. They held meetings of all the strikers together on the Lawrence Common (New England's term for park or square), so that the workers could realize their oneness and strength. It was here one day that Giovannitti delivered his beautiful "Sermon on the Common." When Haywood finished his current lecture tour, he came to Lawrence on January 21, 1912, and was greeted at the railroad station by 15,000 strikers, who escorted him to the Common where he addressed them. There were 1,400 state militiamen in Lawrence, which was like an armed camp. Clashes occurred daily between the strikers and the police and state troopers.

The period of activity for Ettor and Giovannitti was cut short by their arrest on January 30, 1912. A tragedy on the picket line gave the authorities the excuse to get rid of Ettor and Giovannitti. In a fracas between police and pickets, a woman striker, Anna La Pizza, was killed. The two strike leaders, along with a striker, Joseph Caruso, were lodged in the county jail. Caruso, who had been on the picket line, was charged with murder, and the strike leaders were charged with being accessory to murder because of their speeches advocating picketing. It was the same theory of constructive conspiracy which had sent speakers at the Haymarket protest meeting in Chicago to their deaths on the gallows 25 years bfore. The first day they were in jail they received a telegram of support from Debs. It said: "Congratulations. Victory is in sight. The working class will back you up to a finish in your fight against peonage and starvation. The slave-pens of Lawrence under protection of America's Cossacks are a disgrace to American manhood and a crime against civilization."

William Yates of New Bedford, Massachusetts, and Francis Miller of Providence, Rhode Island, both textile workers and IWW leaders, took charge of the strike in place of Ettor and Giovannitti. They sent for Haywood and for me to come to Lawrence at once. The militiamen were mostly native-born "white-collar" workers and professionals from other parts of the state who openly showed their contempt for the foreign-born strikers. Colonel Sweetzer, their commander, banned a mass funeral for Anna La Pizza. He ordered the militia *not* to salute the American flag when it was carried by strikers. His orders were "Shoot to kill. We are not looking for peace now." Many acts of brutal violence were committed by these arrogant youths on horseback, such as riding into crowds and clubbing the people on foot. When they marched afoot, they carried rifles with long bayonets. On the same day Ettor and Giovannitti were arrested, an 18 year-old Syrian boy striker, John Rami, was bayonetted through the lung, from the back, and died. In the course of the strike several persons were injured with bayonets. The orders were to strike the women on the arms and breasts and the men on the head. This was actually reported in a Boston paper.

January 29, 1912, was also marked by the sensational arrest of John J. Breen, a member of the local school board and son of a former mayor, for planting dynamite in three different places, one next-door to where Ettor received his mail. The charge was conspiracy "to mar, deface and destroy property." Nothing was said of the lives placed in danger. He was released on $1,000 bail and subsequently fined $500. This was a dastardly plot to discredit the strikers and frame Ettor. The Ministers Association and the Central Labor Union started a recall movement against Breen which resulted in his replacement in October 1912. William N. Wood, head of the American Woolen Company, son of a poor Portuguese immigrant who climbed out of poverty by marrying the boss' daughter, along with Frederick H. Atteaux, a Boston businessman, and two others, were later indicted for complicity in the dynamite conspiracy. The jury disagreed on Atteaux when a trial finally took place in June 1913. William Wood was exonerated, but D. J. Collins, the man accused of transporting the dynamite, and Breen, were convicted. The *Outlook* of June 21, 1913, commented on the proceedings:

> Two things are perfectly plain, first in this strike there was an attempt to discredit the strikers by making it appear that they and their sympathizers were harboring dynamite; second, it was made clear that large sums of money were paid by the mill owners to Atteaux without an accounting to show for what purposes that money would be spent.

BILL HAYWOOD IN LAWRENCE

When Haywood came to Lawrence in February 1912 to assume the leadership of the textile strike it created a national sensation. Ettor and Giovannitti, who had been the leaders up to then, had just been jailed, charged with murder. Haywood had been tried for murder five years before, due to his labor activities. His whole life had been identified with the hard-fought battles of the rough and ready miners in the copper, silver and gold mines of the far West. Now he had become "a menace" in the East. "That two-fisted thug!" a Boston editor called him as he hurled a story about Bill into the waste basket. It was written by a young woman reporter, Gertrude Marvin, who resigned as a result of the editor's action and came to do publicity work for the strike. The press pounced upon and distorted every detail of Haywood's life and work. Articles were written about "Haywoodism," which was defined as violence.

But the more he was attacked the more the strikers loved "Big Bill." The strike committee elected him its chairman in place of Ettor. The strikers were denied the use of the Common, after the arrest of Ettor and Giovannitti, and we had to trudge from one hall to another in various parts of the city to address as many as ten meetings in a day. We brought them the reports from the strike committee, the news of outside support and protests, and we spoke on the American labor movement and what the strike meant. We were followed from place to place by the troopers. Sometimes they rode their horses right up on the steps of the hall, shoving the strikers through the narrow doors. The horses would try not to step on people and became very unruly. The people would laugh at the arrogant riders and say: "You see—horse IWW."

In addition to these daily meetings, Haywood introduced special meetings of women and children. It was amazing how this native-born American, who had worked primarily among English-speaking men, quickly adapted his way of speaking to the foreign-born, to the women and to the children. They all understood his down-to-earth language, which was a lesson to all of us. I was then 21 years old and I learned how to speak to workers from Bill Haywood in Lawrence, to use short words and short sentences, to repeat the same thought in different words if I saw that the audience did not understand. I learned never to reach for a three-syllable word if one or two would do. This is not vulgarizing. Words are tools and not everybody has access to a whole tool chest. The foreign-born usually learned English from their children who finished school after the lower grades. Many workers began to learn English during these strike meetings. The average American-born worker does not go to college, in fact the majority do not even finish high school. Therefore the vocabulary they have at their command is limited. Unfortunately many read very little after they leave school. The spread of pictorial newspapers, the radio and TV has accentuated this. Workers know scientific terms connected with their occupations in industry and are more and more scientifically minded. I have met many American workers who are highly intelligent, better thinkers by far than the average Congressman, but they are handicapped by their meager vocabularies from communicating their thoughts to others in speech and are even more limited in writing. I have tried all my life to write simply enough to be understood by the average American. If I have succeeded I can thank my early strike experience. I noticed that writers of advertisements and radio and television programs follow much the same approach to language. Our content differs, however, which bars me from their mediums.

Wherever Bill Haywood went, the workers followed him with glad greetings. They roared with laughter and applause when he said: "The AFL organizes like this!"—separating his fingers, as far apart as they would go, and naming them—"Weavers, loom-fixers, dyers, spinners."

Then he would say: "The IWW organizes like this!"—tightly clench-
ing his big fist, shaking it at the bosses. Workers invited him to their
houses and shared their simple food with him—Italian spaghetti and
Syrian shashlik. Once, when his life was threatened, the Syrians took
him to a tenement house built around a courtyard. They said they had
every family alerted an could muster 100 men if need be, by a signal
in the yard. They kept him there for several nights. They brought out
their national pipe—a hookah, I believe it is called. It stood on the
floor, like a tall flower vase, with long tubes for several smokers. The
smoke passed through water and was cooled. Suddenly, after a few
puffs, Bill turned green and rushed out sick. "You're lucky, Gurley,
they don't expect ladies to smoke!" he said when he returned. They
laughed and joked with Bill about it. "Big man and little pipe!"

Bill was very particular about having all the reports and the gist of
our speeches translated into all languages. It was a slow process, but it
guaranteed understanding on the part of everybody present. He had
the translators carefully checked by others, to be sure they did it correctly. Some who were not strikers were unceremoniously kicked out
when it was discovered that they were deceiving the people—and
some were provocateurs, who were advocating violence and stirring up
dissension.

We held special meetings for the women at which Haywood and I
spoke. The women worked in the mills for lower pay and in addition had
all the housework and care of the children. The old-world attitude of
man as the "lord and master" was strong. At the end of the day's work
—or, now, of strike duty—the man went home and sat at ease while
his wife did all the work preparing the meal, cleaning the house, etc.
There was considerable male opposition to women going to meetings
and marching on the picket line. We resolutely set out to combat these
notions. The women wanted to picket. They were strikers as well as
wives and were valiant fighters. We knew that to leave them at home
alone, isolated from the strike activity, a prey to worry, affected by
the complaints of tradespeople, landlords, priests and ministers, was
dangerous to the strike. We brought several Socialist women in as
speakers, and a girl organizer, Pearl McGill, who had helped organize
the button workers of Muscatine, Iowa. The AFL revoked her credentials for coming to Lawrence. We did not attack their religious ideas in
any way, but we said boldly that priests and ministers should stick to
their religion and not interfere in a workers' struggle for better condi-

tions, unless they wanted to help. We pointed out that if the workers had more money they would spend it in Lawrence—even put more in the church collections. The women laughed and told it to the priests and ministers the next Sunday.

We talked especially to the women about the high cost of living here —how they had been fooled when they first came here when they figured the dollars in their home money. They thought they were rich till they had to pay rent, buy groceries, clothes and shoes. Then they knew they were poor. We pointed out that the mill owners did not live in Lawrence. They did not spend their money in the local stores. All that the businessmen received came from the workers. If the workers get more, they will get more. The women conveyed these ideas to the small shopkeepers with emphasis, and we heard no more protest from them about the strike after that.

"THE MELTING POT BOILS OVER"

That's how one writer, Richard Washburn Childs, described Lawrence in 1912. (Later he was editor of *Colliers,* and American Ambassador to Italy in 1912, representing the United States at the Lausanne Conference.) Nobody knew or cared before the IWW came to lead the strike what happened to these ill-fed, ill-clothed, ill-housed foreign workers. The mills were owned by absentee capitalists, well protected against foreign competition by Schedule K of the tariff, which applied to woolen fabrics. The heat had been put under this melting pot, not by the IWW, but by the mill owners' cut in the starvation wages. The IWW was held up to scorn by John Golden, head of the United Textile Workers of America, because "it had only 287 members there" when the strike began. He had made no attempt to organize and defend the foreign workers against the wage cut of January 11, 1912. In fact, he had ordered the skilled workers to stay at work. A song had come out of the West, written by Joe Hill, called "A little talk with Golden makes it right—all right!" But Golden had not been able to hold the highly skilled weavers and loom-fixers in the mills. They came out with the others. They could not work alone even if they had wanted to, and they did not want to do so.

We talked to the strikers about One Big Union, regardless of skill or lack of it, foreign-born or native-born, color, religion or sex. We showed how all differences are used by the bosses to keep workers divided and pitted against each other. We spoke to nationalities who had been traditionally enemies for centuries in hostile European countries, like the Greeks and Turks and Armenians, yet they marched arm-in-arm on the picket line. There were Slavs and Italians, French and German, English and Irish. We said firmly: "You work together for the boss. You can stand together to fight for yourselves!" This was more than a union. It was a crusade for a united people—for "Bread and Roses."

Many of the foreign-born workers, especially Belgian, Italian, German and English, had been members of unions in the old countries. The message of socialism was not new to them either. We quoted the Bible: "He that doth not work, neither let him eat!" Our concepts as to how socialism would come about, were syndicalist to the core. There would be a general strike, the workers would lock out the bosses, take possession of the industries and declare the abolition of the capitalist system. It sounded very simple. Our attitude toward the state was sort of Thoreau-like—the right to ignore the state, civil disobedience to a bosses' state. For instance, Bill Haywood threatened to burn the books of the strike committee rather than turn them over to an investigation committee. He was arrested for contempt of court. However much or little the workers absorbed our syndicalist philosophy, they cheered Bill's defiance to the skies.

Mainly we carried on simple agitation. We talked of their own experiences, how they had come from Europe, leaving their native villages and fields, their old parents, sometimes wives and children. Why had they come to a faraway strange land where a different language was spoken and where all the ways of life were different? They had hopes of a new life in a new world, free from tyranny and oppression, from landlordism, from compulsory military service. They had hopes to educate their children, to be able to work, to save, to send for others to come to freedom. What freedom? Had they expected to be herded into great prison-like mills in New England, into slums in big cities, into tenements in these mill towns? Was it to be called "Greenhorns" and "Hunkies" and treated as inferiors and intruders? Heads nodded and tears shone in the eyes of the women. We reminded them of posters distributed by the woolen companies of Lawrence in small towns in Europe, with the picture of a mill on one side of the street and a bank on the other—and workers trooping from one to the other with bags of money under their arms. This was greeted with laughter and shouts of "Yes!Yes!" from those who had seen just such alluring travel ads.

"What freedom?" we asked again. To be wage-slaves, hired and fired at the will of a soulless corporation, paid low wages for long hours, driven by the speed of a machine? What freedom? To be clubbed, jailed, shot down—and while we spoke, the hoofs of the troopers' horses clattered by on the street. We spoke of how the American politicians had ignored their plight because they could not vote. "Just a bunch of foreigners," the politicians said. We reminded them how a legislative committee, headed by Calvin Coolidge, had walked into the strike committee with their hats on. "Take off your hats!" Ettor had ordered, and they cheered for Ettor and Giovannitti, their loved and lost leaders.

We spoke of their power, as workers, as the producers of all wealth, as the creators of profit. Here they could see it in Lawrence. Down tools, fold arms, stop the machinery, and production is dead—profits no longer flow. We ridiculed the police and militia in this situation. "Can they weave cloth with soldiers' bayonets or policemen's clubs?" we asked. "No," replied the confident workers. "Did they dig coal with bayonets in the miners' strikes or make steel or run trains with bayonets?" Again the crowds roared "No." We talked Marxism as we understood it—the class struggle, the exploitation of labor, the use of the state and armed forces of government against the workers. It was all there in Lawrence before our eyes. We did not need to go far for the lessons.

We talked of "Solidarity," a beautiful word in all the languages. Stick together! Workers, unite! One for all and all for one! An injury to one is an injury to all! The workers are all one family! It was internationalism. It was also real Americanism—the first they had heard. "One nation indivisible, with liberty and justice for all." They hadn't found it here, but they were willingly fighting to create it.

"SUFFER LITTLE CHILDREN"

The children's meetings, at which Haywood and I spoke, showed us mainly that there were two groups of workers' children in Lawrence, those who went to school and those who worked in the mills. The efforts of the church and schools were directed to driving a wedge between the school children and their striking parents. Often children in such towns become ashamed of their foreign-born, foreign-speaking parents, their old-country ways, their accents, their foreign newspapers, and even their strike and mass picketing. The up-to-date, well-dressed native-born teachers set a pattern. The working-class women were shabbily dressed, though they made the finest of woolen fabrics. Only a few American-born women wore hats in Lawrence. The others wore shawls, kerchiefs, or worsted knitted caps made at home. Some teachers called the strikers lazy, said they should go back to work or "back where they came from." We attempted to counteract all this at our children's meetings. Big Bill, with his Western hat and stories of cowboys and Indians, became an ideal of the kids. The parents were pathetically grateful to us as their children began to show real respect for them and their struggles.

As the terrible New England winter dragged along the terror and violence increased. On February 19, 200 policemen with drawn clubs routed 100 women pickets. A Boston newspaper described the scene: "A woman would be seen to shout from the crowd and run into a side street. Instantly two or three police would be after her. Usually a night-stick well aimed brought the woman to the ground like a shot and instantly the police would be on her, pulling her in as many ways as there were police." U.S. Senator Miles Poindexter made a personal investigated. He talked to a ten-year-old girl who had a black eye and many bruises. He saw women with nursing babies in jail. He made a strong statement to the United Press against the brutality.

Suffering increased among the strikers. They had no financial reserves. They needed fuel and food. Their houses, dilapidated wood-frame barracks, were hard to heat. Committees of strikers went to nearby cities to appeal for support. Labor unions, Socialist locals, and workers in Boston, Manchester, Nashua, Haverhill and other places responded generously. Eleven soup kitchens were opened. The workers of Lowell, a nearby textile town, led a cow garlanded with leaves, to the strikers of Lawrence. I felt sorry for her with her festive appearance and her mild eyes. But she had to be slaughtered to feed hungry children. Her head was mounted and hung up in the Franco-Belgian Hall.

All the strike leaders made weekend trips to tell the story of Lawrence and solicit funds in other places. I recall a trip I made to Pittsburgh. It took the local committee there hours to count the collection of several thousand dollars in small coins. I went to substitute for Bill Haywood at Wheeling, West Virginia. Fortunately the secretary of the miners' union took the cash and gave me a check for the collection. The train was held up that night near Piedmont, West Virginia, and I lost my purse. But I wired back to the union and they sent another check to Lawrence.

A proposal was made by some of the strikers that we adopt a method used successfully in Europe—to send the children out of Lawrence to be cared for in other cities. The parents accepted the idea and the children were wild to go. On February 17, 1912, the first group of 150 children were taken to New York City. A small group also left for Barre, Vermont. A New York committee, headed by Mrs. Margaret Sanger, then a trained nurse and chairman of the Women's Committee of the Socialist Party, came to Lawrence to escort them. (She has since become world renowned for her advocacy of birth control.) Five thousand people met them at Grand Central Station. People wept when they saw the poor clothes and thin shoes of these wide-eyed little children. They picked them up and carried them on their shoulders to the "El" Station. They were taken to the Labor Temple on East 84th Street, where they were fed, and examined by 15 volunteer doctors, then turned over to their eager hosts, all of whom had been carefully checked by the committee. There were not enough children and many New Yorkers left disappointed not to be able to have a Lawrence child. There was a long waiting list, until another group came later. One child was taken to a beautiful studio apartment. She looked it all over wide-eyed and then said: "I've seen it all now. Hadn't we better go home?"

The New York *Sun* described the children as follows:

The committee had no trouble looking after suitcases and extra parcels for the reason that the travelers wore all the personal belongings they had brought along. There were few overcoats in the crowd. For the most part the girls wore cotton dresses partly covered with jackets or shawls, and worsted caps. Fancy hair-ribbons and millinery were at a discount. It had been a long time since more than a few of the boys and girls had got a new pair of shoes.

The reporter described how the children looked a few days later, when, the committeeman said, he hardly knew them.

Concetta's dark hair was set off by a scarlet ribbon. Meta's fairer braids were tied with pale blue ribbon; the one wore a dark blue serge school dress brightened with touches of blue; the other a brand new frock of gay plaid finished with a white gimp. Both wore well-fitting, shiny new shoes.

For the street, each has a warm coat and for Sunday wear a wide-brimmed hat trimmed with ribbons. Meta's big brother and his friends, the two older boys, each had a substantial new dark gray suit, white collar and four-in-hand tie. One wore a flower in his button hole. Jimmy and Pietro had each been presented with a new top coat, shiny new shoes and warm underwear. Nearly everyone of the 250 visitors, by the way, has got a complete new outfit of underwear.

The letters the children wrote home glowed with accounts of their new warm clothes and how well they were treated. The Lawrence children were sent to school in New York, including those who had worked in the mills. Two homesick ones were sent back but most of them wanted to send for their families and stay in New York. When they finally returned to Lawrence at the end of the strike they were loaded down with clothing, toys, presents and clothes for their families from their New York friends. Correspondence went on for many years afterward between the children and "their New York families." It was a happy episode in a series of somber, tragic situations in the Lawrence strike of 1912.

WITH FORCE AND VIOLENCE

On February 24, 1912, a group of 40 strikers' children were to go from Lawrence to Philadelphia. A committee came from there to escort them, including a young Sunday School teacher, Miss Tina Committa. At the railroad station in Lawrence, where the children were assembled accompanied by their fathers and mothers, just as they were ready to board the train they were surrounded by police. Troopers surrounded the station outside to keep others out. Children were clubbed and torn away from their parents and a wild scene of brutal disorder took place. Thirty-five frantic women and children were arrested, thrown screaming and fighting into patrol wagons. They were beaten into submission and taken to the police station. There the women were charged with "neglect" and improper guardianship and ten frightened children were taken to the Lawrence Poor Farm. The police station was besieged by enraged strikers. Members of the Philadelphia committee were arrested and fined. It was a day without parallel in American labor history. A reign of terror prevailed in Lawrence, which literally shook America.

Statements were made by public-spirited, well-known Americans from coast to coast. Outstanding was one by William Dean Howells,

During the 1912 Lawrence, Mass. textile strike, the author *(right)* leads a group of strikers' children to New York City where they were cared for in workers' homes.

With love to Elizabeth from Buster Oct 2 - 1912

Joe Ettor and Arturo Giovanitti *(center figures, left and right)* leaving court. Lawrence October, 1912

The Lowell strikers march in 1912.

then 75 years old, dean of American writers, who said: "It is an out-rage—could anyone think it was anything else?" Senator William E. Borah of Idaho branded the act of the police in preventing the children from leaving Lawrence "an invasion of constitutional privileges." Judge Ben Lindsey of Colorado said it "shows the depravity of greed and the inhumanity of our industrial system." Samuel Gompers denounced the action of the police as "a crime," and Mayor Baker of Cleveland said: "America will not countenance such warfare against labor." Ed Nockels of the Chicago Federation of Labor said it was "military anarchy." Reverend Percy Stickney Grant of New York challenged the authority of Colonel Sweetzer to control the free travel of children he had personally offered to care for. Sweetzer had said the children were taken away for the purpose of raising funds. Frederick W. Lehman, who was solicitor-general of the U.S. government and legal advisor to President Taft made this statement: "What right did they have to do that? . . . It is the right of any parent to send his children anywhere if he is guided by parental forethought and is acting for their welfare. The action of the marshal in preventing them from being sent away from Lawrence was in violation of their constitutional rights." One of the few who criticized the strikers was John Golden, who said: "it was a desperate means to raise money for an unjustifiable strike."

Famous newspaper reporters and writers flocked to Lawrence. A searchlight of publicity was fixed on this desperately poor and struggling city. They were shocked at what they found in the heart of New England. Ray Stannard Baker, Mary Heaton Vorse, Joe O'Brien, George West, Marlen Pew, Mrs. Fremont Older and many others wrote scathingly of conditions in Lawrence. William Allen White said: "The demands were justified and there was no excuse for the violence by police and military." Years later, I visited him at Emporia, Kansas. He said in all his life he never saw more heart-rending sights than in that mill city. Demands were made for a Congressional investigation as an example, as the Cleveland *News* put it, of "an industry enjoying tariffs of 40 to 150% as a protection against the pauper labor of Europe, which pays only $6 to $8 per week for skilled American workers." Professors Vida Scudder and Ellen Hayes, of Wellesley College, spoke at a protest meeting in Lawrence and were threatened with loss of their posts, which they retained, however. Mrs. Glendower Evans of Boston, a stockholder of the American Woolen Company, went to one of the company's meetings to protest vigorously against their stand in the strike. She was a valiant defender of Sacco and Vanzetti in the 1920s.

At the insistent demand of Socialist Congressman Victor Berger of Milwaukee the House Rules Committee held a hearing in Washington, D.C. in March 1912. Senator Poindexter attempted to secure action by a similar Senate committee but was blocked by Senator Lodge of Massachusetts, father of the present ambassador. Congressman William B. Wilson, a member of the United Mine Workers of America, Chairman of the House Committee, made a strong statement to the press on the Lawrence conditions, particularly in reference to the 16 children who came to Washington to testify. *All of these children were strikers.* A 16-year-old boy testified that he worked for the American Woolen Company for $5.10 a week. He was the oldest of five children. A 15-year-old testified that he liked to go to school and got as far as the seventh grade. "Why did you leave?" a Congressman asked. "Well, we had to have bread and it was hard to get," the child answered. One striker explained the strike to the Congressman as follows: "The stomach telephoned to the head: I cannot stand molasses any longer for butter, and bananas for meat!"

Mrs. Sanger testified about the two groups of children who previously had been taken to New York City. Out of 119 children, only four wore underwear in bitter cold weather. "There was not a stitch of wool on their bodies," she said. "They were pale, emaciated, dejected children. They grabbed the food from the table in a way to bring tears to your eyes." An interested spectator at this hearing was Mrs. Taft, the wife of the President, who gasped at the testimony of pregnant women beaten by Lawrence cops. One of the witnesses was a striker, little Josephine Liss, who had been arrested for "assaulting a soldier." He had pushed her and swore at her. She hit him in the face with her muff, he lost his balance, fell over and dropped his gun. She helped him up. But two companies of soldiers came to his "rescue" and arrested her. On their way home to Lawrence, these children workers were guests of the New York *World,* and were taken to the Zoo, the Museum of Natural History and to a show at the Hippodrome.

More than 50 striker witnesses came from Lawrence to tell their stories and show their pay envelopes. The cause of the strike, extent of their poverty, the conditions of their lives, the violence of the authorities, were all revealed by them to the American people in this Congressional hearing. One child worker had been partially scalped in the mill. One hostile witness, a Lawrence minister, Reverend Carter, testified that "14 is not too young for children to work in the mill." There was no more interference with the children leaving Lawrence after that. On March 7, 50 children went to Philadelphia, where they were welcomed and fed at the Labor Lyceum. They were seven to ten years old, of Polish and Slavic descent. "Hungry like wolves," a spectator described them at the hall. The nation-wide protest had stopped further interference with the children.

On March 1, 1912, the American Woolen Company announced a 7.5 per cent increase in 33 cities. On March 6, 125,000 workers in cotton and woolen mills of six states were raised 5 to 7 per cent. On March 14, the Lawrence strike was settled with the American Woolen Company, the Atlantic Mill and other main mills. Twenty thousand workers assembled on the Common to hear the report of their committee. It was the first time in six weeks they were allowed to use the Common. Haywood presided at the meeting and introduced the delegates of all the nationalities. The demands which they had won secured an increase in wages from five to 20 per cent; increased compensation for overtime; the reduction of the premium period from four weeks to two weeks and no discrimination against any worker who had taken part in the strike. Telegrams of thanks were sent to the Socialist Party and to Congressman Victor Berger. The Arbitration Committee promised to help get Ettor and Giovannitti speedily released. The workers pledged to strike again if they were not freed. They had wrested millions from their employers. Yet their leaders, Ettor and Giovannitti, were still in danger of death, so they did not go back to work happy.

LOWELL AND NEW BEDFORD

The IWW textile strike in Lawrence was followed shortly afterwards by strikes in Lowell of 16,000 workers in its cottom mills and 25,000 in New Bedford. Their demands were higher wages and better working conditions. These strikes were less publicized. There were no state troopers and police interference was less. They were short in duration and spring weather was more favorable. But they were an aftermath of Lawrence and meant that thousands of workers had been encouraged and inspired by its example. Lowell was particularly noted in the history of New England's textile industry. It had once been called "the

Manchester of America." Here some of the first mills had been built a century before.

Thousands of apple-cheeked country girls had long ago flocked to the Spindle City from all the New England states to run looms and spindles. Their paper, the *Lowell Offering,* with stories and poems, attracted wide attention. Their "flare-ups" and "turn-outs," as the first strikes are described, were against wage-cuts. They had met in the basement of a nearby church. One Boston paper described their leader as "a veritable Mary Wollstonecraft." She had mounted a pump to speak to her sisters. One of the strikers, a Polish woman, Mary Kokoski, had been a modern prototype. It had taken six policemen to put her in a patrol wagon, because she was "ashamed to be seen in it!" She was charged with obstructing an officer and fined $45.

The workers on strike in 1912 were not the descendants of these earlier women workers of a century before, who had long since gone West or moved into other occupations—in stores, offices, professions. The 1912 workers were foreign-born immigrant workers—in fact, only about eight per cent in the mills were native born. Those earlier native women workers before the Civil War had been young and single, and at one time constituted 85 per cent of the city's population. They were supplanted by the Irish, who predominated around 1875. They, in turn, had been displaced by other foreign-born groups— French Canadians, Polish, Portuguese, Armenian and Greeks. There had been a strike in 1903, I was told, when the millowners refused a raise in wages. These millowners were old New England families. When the small union of the skilled native workers called a strike, the employers locked out all the workers. But the unorganized foreign-born supported the nine-week strike, even though they received no aid from the union. It showed that the immigrant workers were militant, could be organized and were staunch fighters.

There was still a high percentage of women employes in Lowell, except among the Greeks, who had a large colony, mostly single or married men whose families were still in Greece. There were very few Greek women in the community. The men still clung to the hope of making enough money to return to their native land and live in prosperity. They made no attempt at that time to bring their families here, as they did later. A whole street was given over to Greek coffee houses. I stayed at a local hotel when I first went to Lowell. I asked the clerk the first morning for directions to go to the IWW hall, which was also used for prize fights, and he warned me not to go through that "Greek" street. The leaders of the strike were Portuguese in both Lowell and New Bedford. When I arrived at the hall the chairman asked me "What language do you speak?" I said: "English, of course." He looked disappointed, and said: "They won't understand," but decided to take a chance, so I climbed up into the prize ring via a chair. On the picket line they played flutes and violins and carried a triangle frame, shaped like a Christmas tree, with all sorts of puppet figures strung on it. This they shook up and down as they shouted slogans. It was supposed to bring good luck to the strikers and bad luck to the bosses. It helped to mobilize a good picket line and drew many spectators.

The Greeks were slow to join the strike. Once it was called off and everyone returned to work. Suddenly it was on again when the bosses did not live up to what had been agreed. Now we were told the Greeks were to come out, too. We contacted leaders in their community. A meeting was arranged in the Greek Catholic Church. The bells were rung to call them to the meeting. A translator was ready to convey to them what the IWW had to say. Then we struck a snag. I was the only English-speaking organizer there and therefore the one designated to speak. The priest said: "A woman cannot speak in the church." We finally convinced him that I spoke as an organizer, not as a women. So it was agreed. It was a unique experience. I can still see those young eager faces with clear-cut classical features like an Apollo or Hermes in a museum, with dark eyes and curly hair. The intensity with which they listened was touching. It was their first experience of an American taking the trouble to explain everything to them and asking for their support. They gave it with enthusiasm and became the backbone of the second strike, which was speedily won.

I recall an interesting experience while I was in Lowell. I went with some strike organizers to a Chinese restaurant. It was decorated with new flags which we had never seen before, and signs in Chinese. It looked like a very special occasion. The smiling Chinese workers there told us that the Republic of China had been proclaimed by Dr. Sun Yat-sen. This was late March or early April 1912. We rejoiced with them though we little knew the full significance of what was stirring in far-off Asia. But we were for freedom—everywhere—and their happiness looked good to us. They liked the IWW too. So we were all friends.

My sojourn in New Bedford was short, as the strike was over quickly. Originally it was a seaport town, chief center of the American whale fisheries. As many as 400 whaling vessels a year left this port and as many as 60,000 barrels of sperm and 120,000 barrels of whale oil were brought back in a year. This romantic and adventurous past was but a haunting memory, however. By 1912 it was a textile town, with giant cotton mills. There were many English weavers in New Bedford then, as well as many Portuguese. The town stretches like a long narrow ribbon along the water. It had the same typical barracks-like tenement houses built for workers, found in all textile towns. Fifteen thousand workers were out again in July, against a fining system which the state legislature had declared illegal. Their average wage was $6.50 a week at this time. I was very tired and anxious to get home after the first round of strikes finished. But Lawrence called again.

THE ETTOR-GIOVANNITTI TRIAL

On May 1, 1912, we held IWW mass meetings everywhere. But those of us who had been in Lawrence during the strike became very uneasy and conscience-stricken about the fate of the three men in jail. It was now the third month since the strike had ended. It was the fifth month since they had been arrested. There was no sign of a trial. As soon as the other textile strikes came to an end and Haywood's current tour closed, we were summoned to Lawrence. A Defense Committee, consisting of Haywood, Trautman, Yates, Miller and myself, was set up. Fred Heslewood, who had run the defense office for the Spokane Free Speech Fight in Coeur d'Alene, Idaho, was brought in to take charge of the defense office here, so the rest of us could travel and speak for the defense. Mrs. Heslewood came with him. It was good to see these old friends again.

We hired several leading Massachusetts lawyers to supplement the local counsel and placed the IWW's chief counsel, Fred H. Moore from Spokane, in charge of the legal defense team. During my stay in Spokane I had become well acquainted with this brilliant young lawyer. Our friendship endured for nearly 30 years. We worked together in Spokane, Lawrence, in Seattle in 1917, in the trial that grew out of the Everett massacre, and in several important IWW cases, such as Wichita and the Kreiger case in Tulsa, Oklahoma, and finally in the

Sacco-Vanzetti case. He was a real labor lawyer, taking no other cases and devoting himself exclusively to this field. His fees were comparatively low. He was a determined fighter, tireless and resourceful in his preparation of a case and with a bulldog tenacity to follow a clue from one end of the country to another. He died from cancer in the 1930s at a young age—a real loss.

At the suggestion of Giovannitti, we brought a friend of his to Lawrence, an editor of an Italian anarcho-syndicalist paper in New Kensington, Pennsylvania, called *L'Avvenire* (Tomorrow). He had just been released from Blawnox jail in Western Pennsylvania, where he had served a sentence for a so-called libelous article against a local politician. He had fled from Italy a few years before as a political refugee and was an eloquent and dynamic speaker in Italian and a powerful agitator. He was an anarcho-syndicalist, but never a member of the IWW, nor was Giovannitti. We needed him to build a mass movement for the defense. His name was Carlo Tresca. I met him on May Day, 1912, on the street in Lawrence, a very dramatic event for me then and one destined to have far-reaching consequences in my life.

I went on a tour that summer on behalf of our imprisoned comrades, but returned to Lawrence around Labor Day to help. Once again we held mass meetings of all the nationalities. On September 29 we organized a memorial parade. Delegations came from other places, which fell into an impromptu parade *enroute* to the IWW hall. We had a permit for the planned parade from the hall to the cemetery to lay three wreaths on the grave of the dead woman striker, Anna La Pizza. A row of police lined up across the main street and tried to break up the march of the visiting delegations and the Lawrence workers who had welcomed them at the station, on the pretext that the permit did not cover this. Tresca was placed under arrest for refusing to order the people to disperse. A tussle ensued in which he was taken away from the police by the workers who formed a flying tackle as in a football game, and pushed him through the police line. Two policemen were injured. They never attempted to rearrest him. Tresca was very resourceful—a good strategist in struggles. He spoke very little English then. His favorite expression was "I fix!"

In the afternoon the memorial parade proceeded as per schedule except in one respect—it did not encircle the jail. The three prisoners, Ettor, Giovannitti and Caruso, had been secretly moved out of the Essex County Jail at 4 a.m. the day before by a heavily armed guard and taken to the Salem, Massachusetts, jail. Banners carried in the parade demanded a speedy trial, release on bail and a change of venue for the prisoners.

Agitation had been started in the summer by the Defense Committee, calling for a protest general strike on September 30, 1912, a demonstration of indignation at the delay and to demand their immediate release. On September 25 letters were received from both Ettor and Giovannitti, opposing the call to a general strike. It was a dangerous gamble they felt, never before attempted in this country as far as we knew—a political general strike with demands directed not to the employer but to the state. They felt that the risk of failure was too great on the one hand and the temper of the workers, particularly the Italians, too explosive on the other. We on the outside felt confident of success but tried to accede to their request at the eleventh hour. I read the letters to an overflow crowd gathered inside and outside of our hall. We had originally rented City Hall for this meeting, but were refused admission and were refunded the money. The workers as a whole apparently accepted the wishes of Ettor and Giovannitti. But the Italians, led by Tresca now, sent a committee to the jail to see them and check on the letters. Ettor gave them a second letter to the same effect. They (the Italians) rejected the advice and proceeded to action.

The strike broke out on September 27, when 3,000 men and women came out of the Washington Mill. By the next day 12,000 workers were out. "Strikers Refuse Pleas of IWW Leaders to Go Back," was the headline that day in the Lawrence press. The Boston *Telegram* estimated there were 4,000 out of Ayer Mill; 4,000 out of Wood Mill; 2,000 out at the Washington Mill; and lesser numbers at the Everett, Arlington, Pacific and Prospect. It was evident that the Italian workers believed since Ettor and Giovannitti were in prison they could not safely encourage a general strike, and it is likely that their foreign language orators managed to convey this idea to them. We all said that it was up to the workers to make the final decision, which they did in the action of striking by the thousands. The workers were logical. They had won their strike. They were back at work. They knew Ettor and Giovannitti were innocent. They should be free. It was really a demand for amnesty.

We had sent for Haywood, who had set September 30 as the date for a general strike. The Defense Committee proposed as a compromise, and to help the IWW local union get control of the situation, that a 24-hour protest strike be held instead on that date. In spite of misgivings, it succeeded beyond our wildest dreams and brought order out of chaos. The trial of Ettor and Giovannitti started on the same day in Salem, so the threat of strike had apparently succeeded in two objectives—a speedy trial and a change of venue—and thereby satisfied the determined workers. On September 30, the Lawrence Mills were dead. It was as if time had stood still between the springtime and that day in late fall, and that this was another day in the big strike.

The general strike idea to free Ettor and Giovannitti spread to other places. In Lynn, Massachusetts, two shoe factories closed and 500 workers paraded. In Quincy, Massachusetts, 1,200 quarry workers quit for the day and paraded. In the Belle Vernon, Pennsylvania area (Washington county) 14 coal mines were tied up for 24 hours and 5,000 miners marched. In St. Clairsville, Ohio, 3,000 coal miners were out. In South Barre, Vermont, 500 workers in Barre Wool Company quit. All this news came to Lawrence and enthusiasm was high. We rented a huge sand lot and held our mass meeting there on September 30. Haywood did not arrive until October 1. He had stopped over at Akron and New York—whether by accident or design. The 24-hour strike was over when he came. He was greatly pleased with our strategy.

The trial proceeded in the ancient town of Salem, where the notorious witchcraft trials had taken place in 1692 when 19 victims were hanged. We moved our agitation to Salem, spoke on its Common, and pleaded that this shameful history should not be repeated. A barbaric hangover of the past was still visible in the courtroom—the prisoners sat in a barred iron cage, yet were "presumed innocent." Ettor and Giovannitti both spoke eloquently on their own behalf. The verdict was an acquittal for all three defendants. Caruso rushed home to his young wife and their baby, born while he was in jail. Ettor and Giovannitti made a more formal return to Lawrence and were greeted at the railroad station as conquering heroes by thousands of cheering textile workers. A great victory meeting was held just before Thanksgiving Day at which they were the principal speakers. Giovannitti's prison poems were subsequently published as *Arrows in the Gale,* with an introduction by Helen Keller. "The Walker" is included today in many anthologies of the best American poetry. One, which we did not circulate until after their release, was addressed to Joe Ettor on his 27th birthday, in a gay and flippant mood. It said, "Since I am the older and you are the bolder, here's hoping they hang me the first!"

"NO GOD! NO MASTER!"

The Ettor-Giovannitti victory of 1912 paradoxically was like a swan song for the IWW in Lawrence. The local union had long faced a serious crisis. It was unable to hold the workers as dues-paying members. Most of us were wonderful agitators but poor union organizers. All the outsiders who had been active and dynamic leaders of the strike and defense struggles left Lawrence when they ended. Ettor went on a nation-wide speaking trip and to Tacoma to see his sick father. Haywood resumed his lectures for the *International Socialist Review* and I returned home. I had been away almost continuously during the year. I had brought my mother and two-year-old son, Fred, to Lawrence to stay for about two months. Mother was not well and worried less about me if she was there and saw me every night. Some days she sat in the sun on the Common with the baby, while a few blocks away a violent fracas occurred. He was fat and healthy and did not seem to mind the change. I was happy to see him daily.

One of the weaknesses of the IWW was the lack of any central authority to control situations, which made possible an incident in Lawrence fraught with far-reaching consequences. During one of the protest parades in connection with the Ettor-Giovannitti case a banner was unfurled by a group of Boston anarchists with the words: *"No God! No Master!"* It gave the Lawrence police a pretext to break up the parade. A few days later it caused a riot in Quincy. That banner was worth a million dollars to the employers and may have been a deliberate act of provocation. Some of us believed that it was.

The majority of the workers in Lawrence were Catholic. We had pursued a correct labor policy during the strike of confining our remarks to answering Father Reilly and others only on strike issues. We did not discuss religion and warned all speakers, regardless of their personal views, not to offend the religious feelings of the people. Now came this banner in an IWW parade, unsigned and with no reference to the IWW on its face. But the full impact of its appearance was used against the IWW in Lawrence. A committee in charge should have had the authority to yank it out of the line of march, as would happen in any other labor parade. But the IWW carried "rank-and-file-ism" to excess, and this was one unfortunate manifestation of it.

The churches, religious organizations, professional "patriots" and others, who had long awaited such an opportunity, seized upon it. They stretched a banner across Essex Street, the main street of Lawrence, which read: "For God and country! The Red flag never!" They organized a religious parade on Columbus Day, October 12, 1912, and the churches called on all their people to participate. It was a dangerous, divisive issue. Dissensions grew, threats were made against the IWW and one worker was killed in a fight that day. He was a Polish Catholic mill worker, a member of the IWW. We held a mass funeral for him, and his family succeeded in obtaining religious services at the church as well—after a struggle.

We fought back valiantly. We issued a leaflet called: *"Under the Folds of Old Glory,"* mentioning Mayor Scanlon, the chief clubber; John S. Breen, the dynamiter; William Wood, indicted for dynamite conspiracy; William Jewett, the local bank wrecker; and asking: "Working men and women, are you going to pull the chestnuts out of the fire for this bunch?" But disunity spread over the banner episode. It was a terrible climax to a great victory. The IWW slowly bled to death in Lawrence. In a comparatively short time practically nothing was left of it there as an organized union. Of course, the militancy and fighting spirit it engendered remained among the textile workers. At least three large strikes have taken place in the intervening years —all conducted by independent industrial union movements, such as the Amalgamated Textile Workers in 1919, the National Industrial Union of Textile Workers in the 30s, and later the Textile Union affiliated with the Congress of Industrial Organizations.

Today Lawrence, once a flourishing textile center, is practically a ghost town. The determination of the capitalists who own the industry to have cheap, plentiful, unorganized labor caused them, a half-century ago, to induce thousands to come from Europe. Now they are moving their mills to the South. Let us hope the modern labor movement will be as alert to follow them as was the IWW in 1912 with the foreign-born. "Be swift, my soul, to answer them and be jubilant, my feet," could be truthfully said of us in the IWW of that long-ago day.

FOUR

The Paterson Silk Strike

◆◆◆◆◆◆◆◆◆◆◆◆◆◆

NEW YORK COOKS AND WAITERS STRIKE

Carlo Tresca moved his paper to New York City in 1913. He was then a tall, slender, handsome man in his mid-thirties and I was deeply in love with him. A beard covered a bad scar on the side of his face, where one of his innumerable enemies had attacked him in Pittsburgh. I was still legally married to Jones and Tresca was separated but not divorced from his wife. We lived and worked together for the next 13 years—until 1925. This was according to our code at that time—not to remain with someone you did not love, but to honestly and openly avow a real attachment.

Almost immediately we became involved in a spectacular strike of hotel workers in midtown New York. It was organized by an independent union which had broken away from the AFL International of Hotel and Restaurant Workers. There were IWW sympathizers, especially among the Italians. They contacted the national office of the IWW in Chicago and asked for help. They really wanted Ettor and Giovannitti. St. John wired to us to go to their aid—which we did—and they accepted us.

They held their strike meetings in Bryant Hall, on 6th Avenue near 42nd Street, the same hall at which I had spoken for Hugh O. Pentecost seven years before. Now it was full of chefs, waiters and kitchen workers from all the fashionable hotels in the area—the Astor, Knickerbocker, McAlpin, Waldorf-Astoria, Belmont and others. They were Italians, French, Germans, Greeks. Upstairs, rehearsals were going on of Broadway shows in preparation, especially of musical comedies, with choruses of beautiful singing and dancing girls. It was a lively atmosphere, quite different from austere New England.

The mass picket lines encircled all the hotels and fashionable restaurants. Crowds gathered, especially to see the resplendent French chefs, who carried canes and looked like bankers. The waiters and others were poor by comparison. Sometimes there were violent scuffles between the police and pickets in front of the hotels, while other pickets went swiftly to the back alleys leading to the kitchens and pulled out the workers still there. Well-dressed sympathizers, as diners, would go into the places not yet on strike and at an agreed moment blow a whistle which was a signal for all the cooks and waiters to walk out. I was never in such a hectic strike. Something was doing every minute.

One day, Jacob Panken (now Judge Panken), who was counsel for the union, was speaking. Suddenly there was a commotion at the back of the hall. Someone shouted "Scabs" and the whole crowd rose up and left the hall. Some of us speakers, including Tresca and me, followed, hoping to persuade them to return. Then the police came. We were caught between them. I had my hand on a striker's back and was struck when a cop brought a club down on it. Carlo was arrested and the strikers tried to take him away from the police, who drew their guns. His coat and vest were pulled apart in the tussle. We shouted "Let go! Let go!" Finally, cooler heads prevailed and the strikers let go.

But in the scuffle a little covered book, *Sonnets from the Portuguese* by Elizabeth Barrett Browning, with an affectionate greeting from me to Carlo, had dropped on the street. What was my embarrassment the next day to see our picture, with copies of the book cover, marked sonnets, dedication and all, reproduced in the New York papers as a hidden IWW romance! The mighty chefs and cosmopolitan waiters thought nothing of it, however. In fact, one said: "Don't you care. It helps to advertise our strike!"

One interesting situation developed during that strike. The sheriff of the county, usually a forgotten man, appeared with his deputies to help the police handle the crowds who gathered to see the battles. After one particularly brutal struggle between the police and the pickets, my father brought down over 50 canes he had whittled out of tree branches in Kentucky and various places where he had made maps. It was a hobby with him. The next day a group of pickets appeared with Pop's canes and the crowds cheered. College boys who offered to take the waiters' places were jeered, and customers objected to their inefficient service. The strike was soon over.

It caused the International to give more serious consideration to organizing the New York culinary workers who were more numerous here than in any other city in the country. It helped to lay a basis for industrial unionism in this industry, which expressed itself in the 1930s in the Food Workers Industrial Union, out of which the present union grew. It publicized the long split-hours, low wages, bad working conditions of the workers in the finest, most expensive eating establishments of New York City. The poor shoes, the ragged clothing of the waiters, under the false fronts, the pauperism of the tipping system—all were exposed, as well as the unsanitary kitchen conditions. I spoke to clubs of middle-class women on this aspect.

From this unusual and exciting short struggle in the heart of New York's Broadway district, we were called to Paterson, New Jersey, then the silk-weaving center of America. We found our selves involved at once in a major battle of the class struggle of 1913—a long, hard and brutal strike.

Paterson was long known in labor history. Its first recorded strike of women and children was in 1828. In 1830, a Protective Association of the Working Class struck to reduce hours from 11 to 9 and against a fines system. It was known as the turbulent "Red City." An Italian anarchist movement had long existed there around a small paper. Enrico Malatesta, famous anarchist leader of Italy, who toured this country, had been shot at during a speech in Paterson. Luigi Galleani, editor of an anarchist paper, had led a strike there a few years before. (He skipped bail, went to Barre, Vermont, and was deported in 1920.) But the event that blazoned the city of Paterson as a Red center was that the man named Bresci, who killed King Humbert I of Italy in 1900, hailed from Paterson. Neighbors told how he target practiced in the backyard till he could shoot the top off a bottle. Then he demanded that the anarchist paper return to him a substantial sum of money he had loaned it. His comrades were very indignant and denounced him as selfish and a disrupter. He told no one of his purpose. Years later I met his wife and children at a mass meeting in San Francisco. Life had not been easy for them with all the publicity and questioning that grew out of his deed, which was not understood or approved even by his closest associates. But it helped to label Paterson as "a hotbed of anarchy."

In 1902, during a strike in the tempestuous city of Paterson, an Englishman named William McQueen had been arrested and sentenced to five years for "inciting to riot" and "malicious mischief" in connection with picketing. A Professor Wychoff of Princeton interested himself in an effort to secure McQueen's release, after he contracted tuberculosis in prison. This was granted in 1907 on condiiton that he leave the country immediately. He went to Leeds, England, where Joseph Fels, a wealthy soap manufacturer and single taxer, guaranteed him employment.

THE STRIKE OF 1913

Paterson, called the "Lyons of America," is the seat of Passaic County. It is about 15 miles from New York City on the Erie railroad. In 1913 it hummed with silk factories. The dye works were located in nearby Lodi. This was long before the development of rayon or nylon or any of the artificial substitutes for silk which abound today. Arthur Brisbane, editorial writer for the New York Hearst papers, once charged that Japanese raw silk importers had heavy interests in the Paterson mills. The IWW (Local 152) had a good sized organization there, a local membership and leadership known to the workers. There had already been one strike there in 1907 under IWW auspices, and a series of strikes in 1912 under the leadership of Rudolph Katz and the Detroit IWW (Local 25) against the 3- and 4-loom system. Before the 1913 strike I spoke there at Helvetia Hall to the Shirtmakers and 300 girls joined the IWW. Years before there had been silk weavers assemblies of the Knights of Labor and before that silk weavers were in the National Labor Union.

Coming as we did with the aura of the Lawrence victories and the publicity of the hotel workers strike, we were very welcome to the workers. But we were set upon by the city authorities with vicious fury. They attacked us as "outside agitators," ordered us to leave town, and arrested Tresca, Patrick L. Quinlan of the Socialist Party, and myself on our very first appearnace at a mass meeting. This was on February 25, 1913. Tresca and I had spoken at the meeting but Quinlan was late and was arrested as he came down the aisle of the hall toward the platform. One advantage of having outside speakers was that they were immune from the local blacklist and could speak fearlessly about the conditions which the workers primed us about. We were released on heavy bail and rearrested shortly afterward at the Paterson railroad station as we came off the train from New York, after we were indicted for conspiracy to cause an unlawful assemblage of persons, as well as to raucously and riotously and tumultuously disturb the peace of New Jersey." It was quite a charge. The station (not elevated as it is now) was then about level with the street, and thousands of workers who got wind of the arrests met us at the station and escorted us to the jail. We were again released on bail and continued our daily meetings for six months, while the strike lasted.

The strike was caused by the speedup system. It was precipitated by the attempts of the employers to increase the number of looms for the broad-silk weavers to three and four, which would increase output per loom weaver, decrease the number of workers employed, and not increase the pay. Further demands were made—for an eight-hour day for all—hard silk and ribbon weavers, dyers and dyers' helpers, etc. —a minimum wage of $12 per week for dyers' helpers; a flat increase of $1 for all hard silk weavers and the 1894 schedule for ribbon weavers. In addition, there was a demand of no discrimination because of union activities. It was estimated that 25,000 workers—men, women and children—were involved in this strike. There were Italians, Germans and other nationalities, though not as varied as at Lawrence. A general strike committee was set up and mass meetings were held in various halls, our usual procedure.

The city was a typical textile town with the same poor shabby firetrap wooden houses for the workers, dreary old mills built along the canal. The people were poorly dressed, pale and undernourished. From pay envelopes collected at various strike meetings and in the possession of the strike committee, I gathered the following figures which I used in my speeches. Girl, 16 years old, employed at Ramford's Ribbon Mill 32 weeks, average wage per week $1.85; girl employed same place, 42 weeks, average per week $1.25; woman employed at broad silk, 2 looms, 40 weeks, average per week $7.17; man weaver, 1 loom, 10 weeks, average $10.59; man weaver, 2 looms, $9.48; dyer's helper, 52 weeks, $10.71; miscellaneous, 22 envelopes, average per week, $6.17. One little girl made 66,528 yards of ribbon at Bamford's for $64.45. According to a series of statements which began in the Paterson press of March 11, 1913, by the "Press Committee representing the Silk Industry of Paterson," 25,000 were employed in silk manufacture with a total weekly wage of $240,000 or one million a month, which sounded very impressive but averaged $9.60 a week or $38.40 a month. This average included highly-paid foremen,

The Patterson, N. J. textile strike of 1913. The author at a workers rally.

Again, at closer view, the legendary platform style of Elizabeth Gurley Flynn.

A more formal portrait at Patterson.

Beloved comrade and friend, Carlo Tresca

superintendents, designers, etc. In the same series of articles they branded our statement of $10 a week average to dyers' helpers as "misleading, an instrument to inflame passion, unfair criticism of mill owners," and the like.

They stated that the monthly output of the mills was four million dollars, of which wages were a million. It was easy for even the strikers to figure the surplus value there. The 25,000 workers produce $4 million. They get back one million and the bosses—a few hundred men at the most—get the three million. There was no four million a month in March or April or through August of 1913—because, as we said, the workers stopped being "hands" and became "heads." Knotted color-stained hands came out of the dye boxes, women's slender hands turned away from the looms, children's little hands ceased to wind silk, and the mills were dead.

The bosses' ads said that "the entire fabric of the city's business interests and the Commonwealth itself is menaced to a point that should cause widespread alarm." This was calculated to stir up the businessmen against the strikers, which was usually easily done. I have before me notes of a speech I made at the time directed to this problem, which was typical of our "agitation." I said:

How do the employers spend their share of the three millions? Do they spend it in Paterson? Does the Silk Association have its banquets here? No, they dine in the Waldorf-Astoria in New York City. Have they their spacious offices here? No, their address is 354 Fourth Avenue, New York City. Do their wives and daughters buy their gowns (silk or otherwise), their furs, jewels or automobiles in Paterson? Do they attend the opera in Paterson? Whenever were Caruso or Tetrazini in Paterson, though there are thousands of their countrymen who would go without food to hear them once. Do the employers build their homes, attend church or send their children to school here? How many grocery, clothing, shoe, drygoods or drug stores, meat markets, coal dealers or doctors and dentists could exist if they depended on the mill owners for patronage? We address these plain words to the businessmen of Paterson. The manufacturers and stockholders are not your customers. The workers are!

Pressure was brought to bear on the owners of both the Turn Hall and Helvetia Hall with warnings that their liquor licenses would be revoked if they continued to allow us to hold our strike meetings there. So we were compelled in the Spring to rent a house with a big lot around it to use for a headquarters.

JERSEY JUSTICE

The strikers were harrassed continually by police brutality, arrests and trials. Over 1,000 strikers were arrested, including all the leaders and several casual speakers, all charged with "unlawful assemblage" and "inciting to riot"—stock charges in American strikes. The first trial was of Patrick Quinlan. Here we saw a frame-up unfold before our eyes. Scores of strikers testified that he had not spoken, and 2,500 people present in Turn Hall knew he did not speak. They now heard a half dozen cops and detectives brazenly commit perjury and swear as to his "exact words." They even pretended to have "notes" taken at the time. They were lurid liars indeed.

He was convicted at the heat of the strike by a businessmen's jury. We should have fought for delay until the strike was over, or for a change of venue. But unfortunately, knowing the facts, everyone was confident of his release. Instead he was sentenced to two to seven years in Trenton State Prison. He was released on bail, pending appeal. The New Jersey Supreme Court upheld his conviction and he was taken to prison. It was a striking lesson in capitalist law and order.

Another local New Jersey Socialist who was tried and convicted was Alexander Scott, editor of a Socialist paper, the Passaic *Issue.* His indictment was a clear violation of free press. He had written an editorial criticizing the Paterson police in his paper. Part of it read as follows:

Paterson was once famous as the City of the Reds. Now Paterson has become infamous as the City of the Blues, the hot-bed of brass-buttoned anarchists. These police anarchists, headed by the boss anarchist, Bimson, not only believe in lawlessness but they practice it. They don't waste words with workingmen—they simply crack their heads. With them, might is right. They swing the mighty club in the right hand and if you don't like it you can get to hell out of Paterson. This is anarchism of the worst sort.

For these words of protest against police brutality he was indicted under the New Jersey Criminal Anarchy Law for printing matter "with intent to incite, promote or encourage hostility or opposition to or the subversion or destruction of any or all government."

Scott was also convicted by a small businessmen's jury and sentenced to from one to 15 years in the State's Prison in Trenton. In both of these trials it was evident that a fair trial was impossible in Paterson for anyone connected with the workers' side of the silk strike. Grand juries and trial juries were carefully handpicked and loaded with men connected with the silk industry. After one more trial—that of another outside speaker, a Socialist and IWW from New York City, Frederick Sumner Boyd—our lawyers went to the New Jersey Supreme Court and moved in the cases of Tresca, Haywood and myself for what is called in that state a "foreign jury." Instead of a change of venue to another county, which meant moving the whole trial, a panel is brought in from another county and a jury selected. Supreme Court Justice Minturn granted our motions. Tresca and I were tried later in the summer under this arrangement and the juries disagreed. In 1915, in subsequent trials, we were both acquitted by juries from Hudson County. Quinlan was released in December 1916.

Big Bill Haywood spent as much time as possible in Paterson. There was a large IWW strike going on at the same time in Akron, Ohio, and he shuttled back and forth between these two struggles. He was arrested several times in Paterson. As in Lawrence, he was idolized by the strikers of all nationalities. Chief of Police Bimson, who looked like a stupid moustached walrus, could not understand Haywood and me. He would shake his head and say: "What are you two doing with all these foreigners?" Once when Bill Haywood had been arrested, he found John Reed in jail. "Jack," as everyone called him, was a young journalist not long out of Harvard, who had come to report the strike for the *Metropolitan Magazine,* of which Theodore Roosevelt was one of the editors. The police were extremely brutal that day. They beat pickets and spectators. Reed was ordered to move on by a cop. He stepped inside a yard and asked a woman standing on the porch if he could stay there. She said: "Yes." The enraged cop arrested him.

When he landed in the jail, which was full of strikers, no one knew him, and they were suspicious of this handsome big American until Haywood was brought in and identified him. The strikers gladly made him one of them, shared the food and smokes their wives had brought and his role changed to an active participant not only in the strike but in the class struggle from then on. He wrote a scathing article about the jail in the *Metropolitan Magazine* called "Chief Bimson's Hotel." He taught the strikers to sing songs of the French Revolution and organized that extraordinary event called "The Pageant," which I will describe later.

One of Haywood's arrests was on the humorous side. He went to speak at a baseball park when the police interferred. The crowd shouted, "Let's go to Haledon!" and with Bill at the head they started to walk toward this little Socialist oasis of free speech in a desert of suppression. A patrol wagon pulled up and Haywood was arrested. Some quick legal procedure—*habeas corpus,* I believe—brought it before Justice Minturn of the higher court. Haywood pointed out to the judge that he had once been arrested for coming to Paterson and now had been arrested for attempting to leave Paterson. The policeman complained that "a great crowd had followed him." The judge said: "Crowds follow many prominent people. Do you arrest them? Crowds follow a circus. Do you arrest the circus?" He dismissed the case—one of the few breaks we got in Paterson. Haywood was never tried there again.

THE SABOTAGE ISSUE

During the strike, the IWW was again plagued, as it had been in Lawrence, with the appearance of volunteer speakers on the strike platform over whom it could exercise no control. Once the damage was done, the IWW reaped the blame and felt compelled to defend these embarrassing friends of the strike. This happened in the case of Frederick Summer Boyd, a Socialist and IWW member from New York City. The particular issue his speech injected into the strike was "sabotage." He had made various speeches in his marked British accent, one a violent anti-American flag speech which the strikers did not like and other speakers had to correct. But this one on sabotage caused his arrest on the charge of "advising destruction of property." His appeal to the highest court in New Jersey failed and he was sent to Trenton State Prison to serve a sentence of two to seven years. While there, he signed a petition for a pardon, renouncing the advocacy of sabotage and all "other subversive ideas." He was released and disappeared out of the labor movement. Whether he was simply an irresponsible extremist or a provocateur, is hard for me to say.

The Socialist Party repudiated him and his speeches right at the start. The strike committee had a lengthy discussion as to whether such speeches should be permitted. But our IWW conceptions of free speech were very broad and, since we did not think that he had actually violated any law, we felt bound to defend him. It was in attempting to defend him that I made a speech on the subject of sabotage, which the IWW published as a pamphlet in 1915 and discontinued at my request and by order of the General Executive Board in 1917. After a few years, I no longer agreed with much of what I had said there on the desirability of advocating sabotage. I was greatly troubled that the pamphlet was being used effectively as so-called "evidence" by the prosecution in several IWW trials. I saw it so used in Seattle, Washington, in 1917. And it has bobbed up like a bad penny from time to time, even in the Subversive Activities Control Board hearing in July 1952, when I was a defense witness for the Communist Party. It was certainly highly immaterial there, since the Communist Party did not exist when I wrote it and I had repudiated it long ago. The IWW had ceased to circulate it before the Party was born. But any stick serves in a witch hunt, even a tattered and torn pamphlet, long since out of print, dug up by some sleuth in a secondhand bookstore, nearly 40 years after its publication.

Many of the practices I referred to in this pamphlet were not "sabotage" at all, but simply old-fashioned working class practices from time immemorial—such as the Scotch system of "ca' canny" or slow-down on the job. Another was the "Open Mouth" practice of workers in restaurants, stores, etc., telling the customer the exact truth about the quality of foods or goods. Another was the railroad workers' practice of "following the Book of Rules," which is an instrument devised to protect the companies against damage suits by placing blame for accidents on workers. It was never intended by the company that it should be obeyed to the letter for if it were, chaos would ensue. So it was used occasionally by European workers as a method of striking on the job. A few years ago when Michael Quill, the head of the Transport Workers Union in New York City, threatened the company with a strict enforcement of the Book of Rules, he was accused of having read this obscure pamphlet of mine, of which he had undoubtedly never heard. Very few copies are around today and most of them are in the government's files.

The discussion of the particular advice given to the dye workers by Boyd—to use certain chemicals in the dyeing of the silk—brought forth some interesting revelations from the strikers as to the adulteration practices of the employers which actually involved the use of these very chemicals. In fact, the sabotage of silk fabrics was being done as a usual practise by the employers. Old-fashioned silk of years ago was pure and when it was dyed and woven it was durable and would last for several generations. But in Paterson in 1912 we discovered that the silk was unwound from the cocoons, worked into skeins and then dyed, after a preliminary process of weighting. This business was picturesquely called "dynamiting"—loading with adulterants of tin, zinc and lead.

One pound of pure silk would come out from three to 15 pounds heavier in weight. In the journals of the Silk Association we found advice to master dyers on the use of salts for weighting purposes. Ashley and Baily, a silk mill in Paterson up for auction at that time, was advertised as having an excellent weighting plant. Our exposé explained to the public why the modern silk fabrics cracked so easily. Part of our "sabotage" advice to the workers was to throw the adulterants down the drain and dye the beautiful silk pure and durable, pound for pound. This was better advice than Boyd's. But neither were acted upon, I'm sure. Professor Brissenden in his history of the IWW makes the correct comment that the IWW *talked* rather than applied these tactics.

There was a wave of advocating "sabotage" during this period. It originated in France with the syndicalist General Conference of Labor. Books and pamphlets appeared on it in Europe and some were translated here. It had been the subject of a heated discussion at the Socialist Party Convention in Indianapolis in May 1912, and an amendment added to its constitution barred from membership anyone "who opposes political action or advocates crime, sabotage or other methods of violence." This was carried by a large vote. As a result, William D. Haywood was recalled as a member of the Socialist Party's National Executive Committee. The very wording of this Article 2, Section 6, Socialist amendment was a forerunner of the infamous criminal syndicalist laws passed subsequently in many states. Its passage widened the chasm between the IWW and the SP. It forced us to explain "sabotage," as we understood it, far more than we ordinarily would have done, and caused many attacks on the IWW.

This loose talk about sabotage opened the door for the most vicious charges against the IWW, such as setting forest fires in California, which had to be proven untrue in the Criminal Syndicalist trials by producing the fire records of the State of California. It was a form of infantile Leftism in a big way, consisting largely of "sound and fury, signifying nothing." We came to realize that class action and not un-controlled individual actions is required on behalf of the workers.

THE LIFE OF A STRIKE

The life of a strike depends upon constant activities. In Paterson, as in all IWW strikes, there were mass picketing, daily mass meetings, children's meetings, the sending of many children to New York and New Jersey cities, and the unique Sunday gatherings. These were held in the afternoon in the little town of Haledon, just over the city line from Paterson. The mayor was a Socialist who welcomed us. A striker's family lived there in a two-story house. There was a balcony on the second floor, facing the street, opposite a large green field. It was a natural platform and amphitheatre. Sunday after Sunday, as the days became pleasanter, we spoke there to enormous crowds of thousands of people—the strikers and their families, workers from other Paterson industries, people from nearby New Jersey cities, delegations from New York of trade unionists, students and others. Visitors came from all over America and from foreign countries. People who saw these Haledon meetings never forgot them.

In spite of the unpleasant episode of Boyd's anti-flag speech, the attempt to use the American flag to lure the people back to work boomeranged completely. The employers hung flags up over every mill gate with signs calling upon all patriotic workers to return to work. We called attention to the fact that some of the flags were old, tattered and weatherbeaten and at least they should be patriotic enough to fly new flags, especially as the flag silk was made right there in Paterson. Then the strikers appeared each with a little flag on his coat and signs that said: "We wove the flag; we dyed the flag; we live under the flag; but we won't scab under the flag!"

A touching episode occurred in one of our children's meetings. I was speaking in simple language about the conditions of silk workers —why their parents had to strike. I spoke of how little they were paid for weaving the beautiful silk, like the Lawrence workers who made the fine warm woolen cloth. Yet the textile workers do not wear either woolen or silk, while the rich people wear both. I asked: "Do you wear silk?" They answered in a lively chorus, "No!" I asked: "Does your mother wear silk?" Again there was a loud "No!" But a child's voice interrupted, making a statement. This is what he said: "My mother has a silk dress. My father spoiled the cloth and had to bring it home." The silk worker had had to pay for the piece he spoiled and only then did his wife get a silk dress!

We had a women's meeting, too, in Paterson at which Haywood, Tresca and I spoke. When I told this story to the women clad in shoddy cotton dresses, there were murmurs of approval which confirmed that the child was right—all the silk they ever saw outside the mill was spoiled goods. Tresca made some remarks about shorter hours, people being less tired, more time to spend together and jokingly he said: "More babies." The women did not look amused. When Haywood interrupted and said: "No, Carlo, we believe in birth control—a few babies, well cared for!" they burst into laughter and applause. They gladly agreed to sending the children to other cities and, chastened by the Lawrence experience, the police did not interfere this time.

I had one quite unusual experience during the strike. I stayed over in Paterson quite often, usually at the home of A. Lessig, one of the local leaders (accused in a later strike of being a company agent). One morning Mrs. Lessig and I were having breakfast when the doorbell rang. A young man with his coat collar turned up was at the door. He asked to see Miss Flynn, whom he said he understood was staying with her. She was inclined to be suspicious, thought he might be the police, and said: "Who are you?" He turned down his overcoat collar and to her surprise she saw he was a priest. So she invited him to come in. He told me he was greatly disturbed about the strike. When he heard from one of his parishioners, who was a striker, that I was right there, a few hours away from the church, he decided to come to talk to me. He said he knew the people in his parish were very poor, that they were suffering a great deal on account of the strike, but he felt their demands were justified.

His main concern was to learn something about the IWW. Were we as bad as the newspapers said? Were we really trying to help the workers of Paterson? He saw that the people loved us very much and that impressed him. We had an interesting discussion—it was evident he was seeking the truth and his sympathy was with the workers. I heard later that he told his flock to stick to their union, not to scab, and to help win the strike, which surprised some of them very much. But the man who sent him to see me never gave him away, nor did I.

Once again, as in Lawrence, John Golden of the AFL United Textile Workers tried to intervene. They hired the Armory (which, needless to say, we were never able to get) and called on all textile workers to come to hear the truth about the IWW. We arranged for the hall to be filled and it was, with over 5,000 strikers and as many more outside. Every striker carried his IWW book to that meeting. When Mrs. Sarah Conboy was furiously attacking the IWW, a local IWW official, Ewald Koettgen, jumped on the platform and asked: "Will we who represent the IWW have a chance to reply to these remarks?" The lady grabbed the American flag and wrapped it around herself. The chairman pounded the gavel. Side doors opened and police appeared. Koettgen pulled out his IWW card, waved it in the air and said: "If we can't talk, let's go home!" He was answered by a waving sea of red cards.The whole audience got up and left. The AFL textile organizers who came to break up the IWW were left in their empty hall with the police. The strikers marched to the halls we still had at that time and held their own meetings. Bill Haywood said Mrs. Conboy was so mad she threatened to scratch his other eye out, and the strikers howled with laughter. Laughter is a great tonic and a safety valve in a strike.

Our forces were few. We spoke at night in other places to raise funds. I went to the anthracite mining region to speak to girls working in a local silk mill, who were doing Paterson work. The Miners Union gave us their hall and their officials spoke with us. Many of the girls were miners' daughters, so we were able to stop all work on Paterson orders in these outlying areas. We worked very hard, day and night, to try to keep the strike alive and moving.

The Pageant

As the strike began to drag through the summer months, the IWW leadership was hard put to keep up the drooping spirits and the waning interest of the strikers. Many sought jobs elsewhere. Although we had always advocated short strikes, we found it was not so easy to actually terminate a struggle. Some of the Socialists involved in the strike advocated a shop-by-shop settlement, which we vigorously opposed. Two workers, both Italian, had been killed and hundreds beaten and arrested. One of the dead was a striker who was shot on the picket line. Another was a Paterson worker, not a striker. He lived opposite one of the dye houses. One afternoon, after he returned from work, he was sitting on his steps with his young child in his arms. Deputies came out of the plant, escorting a few strikebreakers. Pickets assembled there began booing and hooting at the scabs. The deputies started shooting. The man on the stoop grabbed his child and started through his doorway, when he was shot in the back. His wife grabbed the child and her husband fell and died at her feet. The strikers had a plaintive song, commemorating these two martyred workers: "Madonna and Valentino gave up their lives for you!"

As usual in IWW strikes, we arranged mass funerals and, as usual, the police were conspicuous by their absence. I recall going with a committee of strikers to see the widow of a worker slain near the dye plant to ask if we could give her husband a union funeral. She was in bed, awaiting the birth of a second child. On the other side of a folding partition was the casket of her dead husband, parallel to the bed. The priest came in while we were there but he made no objection to our request. She was a simple grief-stricken woman, who expressed her sympathy with the strikers, many of whom were her neighbors. She placed the blame where it belonged—on the company thugs who murdered her husband. It was a tragic example of force and violence by the employers in the class struggle—a worker dead, a woman widowned, two children, one unborn, left orphans—a story repeated all too often in my experience.

At about this time a suggestion was made by a New York friend that a pageant be presented in which the strikers would themselves act out the highlights of the strike. It was organized by Jack Reed, assisted by a group of New York artists and stage folk. It was held in the old Madison Square Garden, and 1,200 strikers were involved in this gigantic enterprise. Night after night, to advertise it, the letters "I W W" gleamed in red lights on the top of the Garden tower, under Diana's statue. It was a unique form of proletarian art. Nothing like it had happened before in the American labor movement. Nor has it happened since, to my knowledge, until the recent moving-picture production, *Salt of the Earth,* in which Mexican-American mine workers and their families graphically portrayed what actually happened in their strike.

At the Pageant, a great curtain, representing a silk mill, covered the back of the stage. The aisle was used as the street. In the first scene, the noise of the mill suddenly ceased, the cry of "Strike! Strike!" was raised and the workers poured out of the mill. Scene two showed the mass picket line, encircling the mill—singing, shouting, enthusiasm. The police (portrayed by apologetic strikers) beat and arrested them by the dozen. Strikers resisted, the police fired into their ranks and a worker lay "dead" on the street. Scene three was the mass funeral. The coffin was carried down the middle aisle, the strike leaders marched behind, followed by a parade of the strikers, singing the "Funeral March of the Workers" which Reed had taught them. On the stage red carnations were piled high on the casket, as had been done in the cemetery at Paterson. The actual speeches which we had made at the graveside were repeated now by Big Bill Haywood, Carlo Tresca and myself. It moved the great audience tremendously.

Scene four was of the Paterson children leaving their parents to go to friends and sympathizers in other cities until the strike was over. The children were enthusiastic over the adventure, the parents sad but resolute, willing to part with them because they knew they would have loving care, food, clothes and security with their adopted families. Scene five was a strike meeting in Paterson in the Turn Hall, our largest hall. The strikers came to the meeting down the middle aisle, massing around a platform erected on the stage, with their backs to the audience, who thus became a part of the meeting. Haywood addressed this vast gathering on the causes and history of the strike and what the silk workers of Paterson were fighting for. The Pageant ended with the entire crowd singing "The Internationale."

The Pageant was acclaimed in New York as a great production and a new form of art. But in Paterson the effects were not all positive. Over a thousand of our best strikers were taken out of activity and their attention centered on a play. It was detrimental to our real picket line and meetings. Jealousies arose as to who could go to New York.

Funds were running low and expectations were high as to the financial results of the pageant. The expenses of one such performance were naturally enormous. The final proceeds were extremely meager. That it was run by a New York committee was exploited by the local press to create suspicion and criticism. The Paterson papers accused the strike leaders and the New York committee of raising a large sum and lining their own pockets. It was disastrous to solidarity during the last days of a losing strike. Those of us who had to hold the fort in Paterson to the bitter end had little enthusiasm left for the Pageant. Unfortunately, Bill Haywood became very ill with ulcers, lost over 80 pounds, and was taken to Europe by a friend after the strike ended. Jack Reed, a newspaper correspondent and organizer of the pageant, was assigned to a trip to Mexico and then went to Europe. But this was all exploited to the limit by the Paterson capitalist press. These trips to Europe seemed strange to them, especially when their doubts and suspicions were fanned by the daily papers. It was a tough period in which to bring a strike to a close and save a union.

Free Speech in New Jersey

When the strike ended in 1913, the authorities of many towns and cities in New Jersey made a determined effort to prevent prominent IWW organizers from speaking. I was involved in the defense campaigns on behalf of Quinlan and Boyd, who were convicted during the strike. Others of us were still under indictment and could be called for trial at any time. The Scott conviction was reversed by the New Jersey Supreme Court. He was the local Socialist editor. That encouraged us to fight for dismissals of all charges. My numerous speaking engagements in New Jersey brought me into direct conflict with many repressive measures. In Trenton I was scheduled to speak in the open air at Broad and Front Streets. But I lost this battle with the chief of police, one Cleary, because I was ill and unable to appear. (I was troubled considerably with chronic bronchitis after the long speaking ordeal of the strike.) This irked me considerably as the Central Labor Union was accused locally of being the moving factor behind the police dictum that I could not speak. Bishop McFaul of Trenton commended the chief of police and denounced both Quinlan and myself. Our greatest crime in his eyes seemed to be our "Irish names."

But in Jersey City, where Frank Hague was then a budding politician and serving as Commissioner of Public Safety, I was more successful. He announced that I would not be allowed to speak in any hall or public place. But I did speak, just as the CIO finally spoke years later when Hague was the notorious tsar-like mayor of Jersey City and issued a similar dictum against their right of assemblage. The People's Institute, which conducted a public forum every Sunday in the Dickerson High School, invited me to speak in 1914. The Board of Education, in a stormy meeting which lasted till after midnight on January 16, 1914, denied the use of the school to the forum for this meeting. One woman member, Miss Cornelia Bradford, held out on the grounds of free speech. She had read Giovannitti's poems, which she said were "tender and beautiful." The officers of the People's Institute were resolute and after being turned down by the manager of the Orpheum Theater, finally secured the Monticello Theater. No uniformed police appeared, only plainclothes detectives, to see "that Miss Flynn did not say anything to incite her hearers to commit acts of violence," said the Hudson *Dispatch* of January 19, 1914, which added: "There was nothing in her address that would offend anyone." A strong resolution, condemning the action of the Board of Education, was subsequently passed by the Holy Cross Forum of Jersey City (Protestant Episcopal).

In New York City, a Paterson Defense Conference was refused the use of Cooper Union on January 29, 1914, and the meeting had to be held at Arlington Hall. Mrs. J. Sargeant Cram, who was a granddaughter of Peter Cooper, made a vigorous protest against this action to the Board of Directors of Cooper Union. She later bought land and built the Peace House at 110th Street and 5th Avenue, in further protest. The directors of Cooper Union were reported to have said that neither Haywood nor any other IWW speaker could appear on the Cooper Union's platform.

Meantime, between trips elsewhere, those of us who lived in New York City continued to go regularly to Paterson. We felt it had been a serious error for all of us to leave Lawrence as we had done, and tried not to repeat the mistake there. Prosecutor Dunn was riled by hearings of the Federal Industrial Relations Commission held in Paterson at which someone asked why the outstanding strike indictments were not pressed. In June 1914 he suddenly called Tresca to trial again. Charged with inciting to riot, tried again by a "foreign" (Hudson County) jury, with only police witnesses against him, and many Italian-speaking strikers testifying on his behalf, he was acquitted in 20 minutes. He was accused of saying, in part: "This strike is the start of a great revolution." Arthur Brisbane, in the New York *Journal* of July 3, 1941, remarked editorially, commending his acquittal: "Any man has a right to say that he is beginning a revolution. It is just as well for our judges and district attorneys to remember that this country *began with a Revolution.*"

The Paterson workers were extremely dissatisfied with the conditions in the mill—especially the speedup—and by the Fall of 1915 there was considerable talk of strike again. In an effort to suppress discussion of their grievances and organized action, Chief of Police Bimson ordered that all IWW meetings be suppressed and particularly that we notorious "outside agitators" should not be allowed to speak.

This culminated in a free speech fight. I went to Paterson. Although I was disguised with glasses and fashionable clothes and escorted by a committee of distinguished well-dressed ladies from New York, I was spotted by the Paterson police and held on the hall steps while the meeting went on inside. This demonstration for my right to free speech was organized by a teacher in Wadleigh High School, Henrietta Rodman, a truly remarkable woman. She fought the school system on a dozen fronts—for the right of married women teachers to teach and to use their own names, for equal pay, for the right of married teachers to have children and continue to teach, and many other issues more or less accepted today. These women were all suffragists. They were not supporters of the IWW but were not scared off by the Red-baiting of the time.

The Free Speech League of New York City organized a protest meeting in late September in Paterson. Leonard Abbott and Lincoln Steffens were met at the train by a crowd of cheering workers, shouting 'Free Speech!" and "Hurrah for the IWW." A meeting they had arranged at the Auditorium was ordered prohibited by the chief of police. They went to the Socialist Party headquarters and spoke from the window to the crowd below. There was no interference until Tresca was introduced, said "Good evening," and was stopped by the police. The crowd was forcibly dispersed at that point by the police who clubbed right and left.

Then I was called to trial on the indictment of two and a half years earlier. A defense committee organized in New York City read like the Social Register. It included Mrs. O. H. P. Belmont, Mrs. Robert Bruere, Mrs. J. Sargent Cram, Mrs. Sumner Gerard, Mrs. Philip Lydig, Mrs. J. Borden Harriman, Miss Fola La Follette, Mrs. Willard Straight, Mrs. Leonard Thomas, Miss Lillian Wald, Miss Margaret Wycherley, and Allen Dawson, Reverend Percy S. Grant, Rev. John Hayes Holmes, Walter Lippmann, Reverend John Howard Melish, Benjamin Luska and Dr. Ira S. Wile. This committee employed lawyers for me. A woman lawyer, Jessie Ashley, volunteered her services. I was tried again on November 27, 1915, by a "foreign jury" from Hudson County. Many workers testified on my behalf and I testified for myself. The Paterson *News* of December 1, 1915, after I was acquitted in a few minutes, remarked bitterly that "the police witnesses displayed that superhuman perfection of memory which is always suspicious and the jury did not believe them." They were my only accusers. Our IWW meetings were unmolested in Paterson after that. Bimson was forced to accept defeat. Many years later, after a long absence, I returned to speak in Paterson. He had retired. He died a few days after my meeting and the workers said: "He couldn't stand the idea that you were back again!"

FIVE

The IWW, 1912-1914

◆◆◆◆◆◆◆◆◆◆◆◆◆◆

FOSTER AND TOM MANN, SYNDICALISTS

Foster had showed such exceptional organizational ability and skill in negotiations in the Spokane free speech fight that it attracted the attention of Vincent St. John. In 1910, with $100 for expenses and the Saint's blessing, Foster went to Europe to study the syndicalist movement. In August 1911, St. John notified him to go to Budapest, Hungary, to represent the IWW at an international trade union gathering. There he challenged the credentials of Vice-President Duncan of the AFL as not representing the American working class and precipitated a two day debate before he was voted down. That night he was arrested for sleeping in a moving van. The French delegates secured his release. Having no funds, he decided to return for the IWW convention in September 1911.

His report created a stirring debate at the convention and in the organization throughout the country. As a result of his survey of the trade union movement in Germany and France, Foster had come to the conclusion that the IWW was making a basic error in trying to build rival or "dual" unions to those already existing. He proposed that we send all our members who were eligible for membership in these unions back to the organizations to "bore from within" for class-conscious industrial union ideas and tactics, and to help the IWW organize the unorganized. He argued that it was a mistake to pull out all the most militant, active workers and leave the control of strong unions to reactionary leadership. He proposed as a start that the IWW dissolve its dual unions in mining, building, metal, printing and railroads and go to work inside the unions already existing in these industries.

I was at the 1911 convention and heard Foster make his report. But he failed to convince the leadership of the IWW, although he won over some delegates, including Jack Johnstone and Frank Little. Foster made a hobo trip of 6,000 miles that winter, visiting all the important IWW centers of the West. He froze his hands and feet and narrowly escaped death under the wheels. Local Syndicalist Leagues were set up, whose members went into AFL unions. Foster left the IWW in February 1912. He was working as a railroader at that time, and joined the Brotherhood of Railroad Car Men. Among those who went with Foster in his new venture were Jack Johnstone, Jay Fox, Joe Manley, Sam Hammersmark, my ex-husband J. A. Jones, Mrs. Lucy Parsons and Tom Mooney. The league had hard sledding because "dual unionism" was so deeply embedded in the Left-wing movement and the IWW was at the very peak of its growth at that time, in 1912 and 1913, with Lawrence, Paterson, Akron and other strikes placing it in the forefront of the class struggle. We were "dizzy with success" and had no time for sober estimates or criticisms. Vincent St. John was disappointed in the loss of Foster and he expressed his pride and satisfaction when he became nationally known after he organized the stockyard workers of Chicago in 1918 and led the steel workers of the United States in a great strike in 1919. "A good organizer—worth a hundred soap-boxers!" Saint said of Bill.

Foster's campaign against dual unionism was aided by Tom Mann of England, who came over on a speaking trip in 1913. It was arranged originally by a Pittsburgh Left-wing Socialist paper, *Justice*. But they were unable to make a success of it outside their own area and it was taken over by the Syndicalist League and some of the IWW locals. The Socialist Party would do nothing—Mann was far too much of a Syndicalist for them. He was then nearly 60, a leader of the left-wing labor movement in England for many years. He was one of the organizers of the Dockers Union there, a leader of their big strike in 1889, and an active Socialist. He was an orator and agitator of great power. Fiery words poured from him in a torrent, as from a volc' no. He was lively and gay-hearted and won his audiences completely ırom the start.

He told how he had come here at the age of 27, in 1883, as a member of the Amalgamated Engineers Union to "sample the New World for myself." What shocked him was that in England he never worked on Saturday afternoon, but here he did. On his 1913 trip he was amazed to find that the workers in the steel industry were not organized and that they worked seven days a week, 12 hours a day. "The town of Gary," he wrote later in England, "named after the President of the U. S. Steel Trust, is run under conditions that are almost unbelievable by those without knowledge of the methods of this giant trust." His conclusion from his earlier personal experiences here as a worker and his present speaking trip was this: "There is no earthly hope for the cure of economic and social troubles by following in the wake of America."

He took issue with the leaders of the IWW on "dual unionism," but many of us helped arrange his meetings just the same. He was particularly pleased with one arranged in Salt Lake City by Sam Scarlett, who was at one time a fellow member of the Amalgamated Engineers and hailed from Glasgow. In New York City we arranged to take him to Paterson to address the silk workers. We boarded an Erie train at about 7:30 p.m. "Isn't that very late?" he said. As it meandered along, stopping at every station, he said anxiously: "Aren't we going a long way?" He was sure nobody would be there, "way out in the country, in the middle of the night!" But there were at least 5,000 people, gathered tightly-packed in our lot, their faces lit up with gas flares.

He was so impressed he outdid himself that night. Never had I heard such a flow of fast-spoken, picturesque and colorful oratory, charged with tremendous fervor and fighting spirit. It was a hot night and after he finished some English weavers took him away with them, promising to bring him to the railroad station to make an eleven-thirty train back. They came rushing him along at the very last minute, bubbling with reminiscences of where they knew him and had heard him speak before. We asked: "What did you do, Tom?" and he said cheerily, "They took me for warm ale. There's nothing like it after a speech." He was a living example of joy in struggle and proved that a light heart makes the road shorter and the load easier. He lived to be over 80— oratorical, exuberant and vital—a great agitator to the end.

It is idle to speculate on what might have happened if the IWW had followed what now impresses me as the correct advice of these two top labor organizers. Possibly a permanent industrial union movement could have been built a quarter of a century earlier than the CIO. But our incurable "infantile Leftism" blinded us to its wisdom at that time.

FREE SPEECH IN SAN DIEGO

While the two great IWW textile strikes were taking place in Lawrence and Paterson, and we were involved in the aftermath defense of strike leaders in both places, the IWW was busy elsewhere. In 1912 there was a textile strike in Little Falls, New York, where two strike leaders, Legere and Boccini, were imprisoned and a very capable little woman IWW organizer—Matilda Robbins—gave leadership which brought the strike to a successful conclusion.

There was a strike also in 1912 in Grabow, Louisiana, against the Long Bell Lumber Company. This was an abominable company town, where Negro and white workers worked for "scrip" money issued by the company, which owned all the houses and the stores. The whole town was enclosed, like a stockade, behind a high wooden fence. The strike spread to other camps and revealed conditions of virtual peonage in the turpentine and lumber camps of that state. The IWW launched its campaign in Grabow in 1911, when Bill Haywood spoke at a convention of the IWW Lumber Workers at the Alexandria Opera House. He insisted that segregation of Negro and white be ignored in IWW gatherings, law or no law, which was accepted willingly by all. Negro and white workers sat together wherever they pleased, in all parts of the hall, at the mass meeting and at their convention. This company finally "ran away" to Vancouver, Washington, but they found to their sorrow the IWW was there before them.

Also during the Lawrence strike, a long and brutal free speech fight took place in San Diego, California. Following the usual pattern, an anti-free speech ordinance was passed. On February 8, 1912, 41 participants in a street meeting were arrested, including two lawyers who were there as observers for a Free Speech League. Within a month over 200 were in jail, under horrible conditions. This continued until June when smallpox finally emptied the jail. The San Diego *Tribune* advocated taking the IWW prisoners out and shooting or hanging them. The hose was turned against meetings with such force that speakers were knocked off their feet. Self-appointed vigilantes took men out of prison and assaulted them with guns and clubs, sometimes torturing them indescribably. One old man, Michael Hoey, died from assaults in prison and another, Joe Micholash, was killed outside the IWW hall.

A Memorial Day parade was held unmolested, at the same time we held one in distant Lawrence for our dead strikers. Finally, protests to

Governor Johnson mounted throughout the state. He sent Commissioner Harris Weinstock to investigate conditions in San Diego. His report was a stinging condemnation of the authorities and vigilantes. The governor ordered the State's attorney-general to "afford redress to any who have suffered wrong and to mete out equal and exact justice to all." But nothing much came of his visit. Finally, a weak face-saving compromise was made by the police that "each case (or meeting) would hereafter be decided separately." The IWW continued to be molested although others were finally allowed to speak.

Among the last of the IWWs to be arrested was Jack Whyte, who was sentenced to six months and a $300 fine for conspiracy to violate the unconstitutional free speech ordinance. He made a remarkable speech to the judge which is today a part of labor and legal history. He said, in part, as follows:

There are only a few words that I care to say, and this court will not mistake them for a legal argument, for I am not acquainted with the phraseology of the bar, nor the language common to the courtroom.

There are two points which I want to touch upon—the indictment itself and the misstatement of the prosecuting attorney. The indictment reads: *"The people of the State of California against J. W. Whyte and others."* It's a hideous lie. The people of this courtroom know that it is a lie, and I know that it is a lie. If the people of the State are to blame for this persecution, then the people are to blame for the murder of Michael Hoey and the assassination of Joseph Micholash. They are to blame and responsible for every bruise, every insult and injury inflicted upon the members of the working class by the vigilantes of this city. The people deny it, and have so emphatically denied it that Governor Johnson sent Harris Weinstock down here to make an investigation and clear the reputation of the State of California from the odor that you would attach to it. You cowards throw the blame upon the people, but I know who is to blame and I name them—it is Spreckels and his partners in business, and this court is the lackey of that class, defending the property of that class against the advancing horde of starving American workers.

The prosecuting attorney, in his plea to the jury, accused me of saying on a public platform at a public meeting: "To hell with the courts; we know what justice is." He told a great truth when he lied, for if he had searched the innermost recesses of my mind he could have found that thought, never expressed by me before, but which I express now: "To hell with your courts, I know what justice is," for I have sat in your courtroom day after day and have seen members of my class pass before this, the so-called bar of justice. I have seen you, Judge Sloane, and others of your kind, send them to prison because they dared to infringe upon the sacred right of property. You have become blind and deaf to the rights of men to pursue life and happiness, and you have crushed those rights so that the sacred rights of property should be preserved. Then you tell me to respect "the law". . . . My right to life is far more sacred than the sacred right of property that you and your kind so ably defend.

I don't tell you this with the expectation of getting justice, but to show my contempt for the whole machinery of law and justice as represented by this court. The prosecutor lied, but I will accept it as truth and say again, so that you, Judge Sloane, may not be mistaken as to my attitude: "To hell with your courts; I know what justice is."

FORD AND SUHR

I was in Seattle in 1943, to speak on May Day. At the meeting I received a pathetic little note, as follows:

In Harbor View (Hospital) 9th Floor N. is a man by the name of Richard (Dick) "Forbes." He served 14 years in Folsom Prison out of Wheatland hop-yard trouble, 1913. He has known Gurley Flynn since he was a young boy and she knows him well and he is going to die in a week or two. Says he was visited by E. G. Flynn when he was in prison. He grew up where Flynn did and has always been a true rebel. He begged to see her if at all possible.

I hastened to the hospital and found an old man, partly paralyzed and crippled, weak and hardly able to speak, but still full of fighting spirit. "Keep it up, Gurley. Give 'em hell!" he said to me in parting. He died shortly thereafter. He was one of labor's forgotten heroes— Richard Ford. It was hard to believe this was the once handsome, black-haired youth who had so boldly led 2,000 men, women and children in a strike 30 years before—in August 1913. It was on the Durst hop ranch, the largest in the state, outside of Marysville, California.

The story of what happened on that hot day, with the temperature up to 120, is told in *Harper's Magazine,* April 4, 1914, in "The Marysville Strike," by Inez Haynes Gilmore. She tells the all-too-familiar story of frame-up against two volunteer labor organizers which resulted in life-imprisonment for Richard Ford and Herman Suhr. At the Durst ranch a few tents and wooden shanties were provided for housing; there were only eight toilets, and no drinking water, which had to be bought from a concessionaire. Irrigation ditches were used for garbage dumps. Women were expected to carry heavy bundles of hops to the wagons. Migratory workers, more than were needed, were lured by advertisements in cities, mining camps and farm areas as far away as

Oregon and Nevada. There were Mexican, Chinese, Puerto Rican, Cuban, Italian, Swedish and other national groups, 27 in all. Ford and Suhr became the leaders in presenting demands to Durst, who struck Ford across the face with his gloves. The workers then held a meeting at a dance pavilion and after someone sang "Mr. Block" (one of Joe Hill's songs), Ford reported to the striking workers. He held a child in his arms and said: "We are fighting for these children!" At that moment a group of deputy sheriffs appeared on the scene, accompanied by Prosecuting Attorney Manville from Marysville.

They ordered the meeting dispersed and advanced on Ford with drawn guns. When a Swedish girl intervened, the deputy aimed at her. He was shot dead by a Puerto Rican worker, who also killed Manville, and was himself killed by the deputies. An English boy carrying a bucket of water was killed. Ford and Suhr, who had wired a San Francisco paper to send a reporter there, were arrested, tried for murder and convicted, although neither had a gun. Mrs. Gilmore says: "Manville wanted to teach the IWW to stay away from Yuba County." The IWW put a boycott on the hop fields, and threw a picket line around them. Millions of dollars worth of hops rotted on the ground in 1914. Richard Ford was released by the parole board in October 1925, he was re-arrested at the door of Folsom Prison on a second murder charge. The warrant was issued by Manville's son, then district attorney in Marysville. Ford was tried in January 1926, and was acquitted; Suhr was paroled shortly afterward—with 14 years taken out of their lives for protesting against intolerable conditions of labor.

MAGON AND CLINE

In 1913, a tense struggle developed over the right of Mexican and American workers to join the Mexican revolution. American troops patrolled the border to prevent Mexicans from escaping as political refugees or getting any aid from here. Hundreds were turned back to Mexico and certain persecution or death. Charles H. Kerr Company had published a book, *Barbarous Mexico* by John Kenneth Turner, an American newspaper man. In the guise of an American investor he had been able to see the appalling treatment of the Mexican workers, who were virtually slaves—starved, beaten and murdered with impunity. From 1906 to 1914, he estimated that 150,000 Mexicans had perished in struggle—"by bullet, sword or bayonet." The brutal regime of Diaz had finally ended, to be replaced (after the assassination of Madero) by a provisional government of the equally tyrannical General Huerta.

In the South the famous Zapata was leading the revolution and ex-propriating the big landed estates. The Mexican Liberal Party, led by Ricardo Flores Magón and his brother, advocated the expropriation of all wealth and the expulsion of foreign exploiters, such as Standard Oil. These two men were heroic fighters. Out of twelve years' intermit-tent residence in the United States, Ricardo spent six years in Ameri-can jails, charged with violating the neutrality law, publishing a paper, etc. He and his brother, Enrique, were sent to Leavenworth during World War I under the Espionage Act—forerunner of today's Smith Act. Ricardo died in Leavenworth in the early 1920s. His public fu-neral in Mexico was attended by 250,000 people. Many American IWWs and Socialists, in the tradition of Lafayette and Kosciusko, crossed the border to join the Mexican revolution.

In 1913 a group of 14 Mexican workers, accompanied by one American IWW lumber worker, Charles Cline, secretly left Carizo Springs, Texas, to cross the border. The Mexicans were members of the Magón party. They were followed by Texas deputies who shot at them from the hills, killing an old man, Lemas. The workers captured two of the deputies and signed an agreement to release them at the border. One deputy, Ortiz, a Mexican renegade, attacked his guard, Guarra, in the night. Guarra killed him and fled and was never found. Later the little band was surrounded by vigilantes who kicked a wound-ed man, Ricon, till he died. His body was carried through the streets, jeered at and spit upon. A banner, *Terra y Libertad* (Land and Liber-ty), was in his hands.

The prisoners were marched to jail, chained together by their necks. Buck, the captured deputy, was on the Grand Jury and the principal witness against them. He also produced a moving picture called *Bor-der Bandits,* giving his version of the affair. All those on trial were found guilty and sentenced to 25 years to life. Nationwide meetings of protest were held, one in Union Square, New York City, in June 1914. The Standard Oil Company was deeply implicated in Mexican politics. Especially after the burning of the strikers' tent colony and the deaths of women and children in Trinidad, Colorado, in a hard-fought strug-gle against a mining company owned by the Rockefeller interests which controlled Standard Oil, feeling ran doubly high against it in this country.

In August 1926, after thirteen years in a Texas prison, Charles

Cline and his companions were given a full pardon by Governor "Ma" Ferguson, who said: "The record shows that there never was any designated plan to kill anybody and the killing of the deputy sheriff was merely an incident of a war period. In a war area in our state." She said further, it was no crime to overthrow the Mexican government any more than it was for those who defended the Alamo in 1836, in the war with Mexico. Charles Cline spoke at the second Convention of the International Labor Defense in Chicago in September 1926, toured later under its auspices for Sacco and Vanzetti, and exhibited a small replica of an electric chair he had made while in prison.

UNEMPLOYMENT DEMONSTRATIONS

The winter of 1913-1914 was a long one. It snowed continuously and was bitter cold. Unemployment had struck America. There were growing breadlines, homeless men were sleeping in doorways and cellars, families were in dire distress. New York City had set up a Mayor's Committee on Unemployment. Bill Haywood was in New York that winter, far from well, but able to consult with the local IWW members. He had interested a group of liberals of all shades of opinion to set up a Labor Defense Conference. Lincoln Steffens, Mary Heaton Vorse and her reporter husband, Joe O'Brien, Amos Pinchot, John Fitch, Heber Blankenhorn and Paul Kennedy were among them.

Meanwhile, a group of 200 unemployed hungry men had been gathered together by a thin, emaciated young member of the IWW, Frank Tannenbaum, who led them to St. Alphonsus' Catholic Church on lower West Street the night of March 4, 1914. He asked the priest in charge if these weary and homeless men who had no place to lay their heads might find shelter there and sleep in the house of the Lord. Father Schneider refused, saying that it would be a sacrilege. While Tannenbaum was talking to the priest, some of the unemployed men entered the church and sat down in the back pews. The police were called, reporters and photographers flocked there and all of the men were arrested. Tannenbaum was charged with inciting to riot and bail was set at $7,500. Justus Sheffield acted as their attorney, hired by the newly organized Defense Conference. One frail youth was sentenced to 60 days, four men to 30 days, three men to 15 days—the others were released.

Frank Tannenbaum, as their leader, was dealt with most severely. He was sentenced to a year on Blackwell's Island and a $500 fine, with the proviso that if the fine was not paid the sentence was to be increased by another year and a half. He served the year, the fine was paid and that ended the labor career of Frank Tannenbaum. Some philanthropic-minded people aided him to complete his education and he ultimately became a professor at Columbia University, where he now is. The poor and lowly remained with us.

In the Spring of 1914 we organized an IWW. Unemployed Union of New York (membership free) with a headquarters and reading room at 64 East 4th Street. A committee of ten was placed in charge. It published a program:

The Mayor's Committee has been investigating us for weeks and has done nothing. The CITY says it can do nothing. The STATE can do but little. The BOSSES say they have no work for us. LET'S GET TOGETHER AND SEE IF WE CAN DO SOMETHING FOR OURSELVES!

In order to force immediate and serious consideration of the Unemployed Problem, the I.W.W. Unemployed Union of New York advocates the following measures:

1. Organization of the Unemployed. (In Union there is Strength.)
2. A Rent Strike. (No wages, no rent.)
3. A Workers' Moratorium. (Don't pay your debts till the jobs come around.)
4. Refusal to Work at Scab Wages. (Don't let the boss use your misery to pull down the workers' standard of life.)
5. A Demand for Work or Bread. (If the bosses won't let you earn a decent livelihood then they must foot the bill for your keep.) The workers make the wealth of the world. It's up to us to get our share!

On the reverse side of the red card on which this program was printed were four pertinent quotations under the caption: "Unemployed: Attention!" They read as follows:

Cardinal Manning said: "Necessity knows no law and a starving man has a natural right to a share of his neighbor's bread."

Father Vaughn said: "The Catholic Church teaches that a man who is in extreme need of the means of subsistence may take from whatsoever sources, what is necessary for him to keep from actual starvation. . . ."

Oscar Wilde said: "Man should not be ready to show that he can live like a badly fed animal. He should decline to live like that and either steal or go on the rates. As for begging, it is better to beg than to take, but it is finer to take than to beg."

Jesus said (*Matthew,* Chapter X Verse 2): "And into whatsoever city or town you shall enter inquire who in it is worthy and there abide till you go hence. And into whatsoever house you enter, remain—eating, drinking such things as they have. For the laborer is worthy of his hire."

The Mayor's Committee instituted a clothing collection drive throughout the city. The IWW sent volunteers to help sort the clothing, some of which were filthy rags, fit only to be thrown away. But most of it was durable and useful. Our volunteers togged themselves out each day in a new overcoat, shirts, shoes, even suits, and thus brought them out to share with their fellow-workers of the IWW. In due time these unemployed at least were well dressed and we knew that much of the clothing served its purpose. Many stunts were played by this IWW committee to attract attention to the plight of the unemployed. They printed about 1,000 tickets—"Good for one meal. Charge to Mayor's Committee on Unemployment" and sent groups into good restaurants all over the city. It took several days before the hoax was discovered and the newspapers warned the restaurant keepers. But hundreds of hungry men were by then one or two meals to the good.

The police were viciously brutal to the unemployed whenever a street meeting was held or groups of them gathered anywhere. At every opportunity the so-called Bomb Squad, led by Lieutenant Gegen with officers Brown and Gildea, would club, kick and punch arrested men into insensibility. Two who suffered horrible beatings were Joe O'Carroll and Arthur Caron after an attempt to hold a meeting in Union Square while the Central Labor Council was holding one there. The anarchists, led by Berkman, were attempting to take over the leadership of the unemployed movement and in this case unfortunately gave the police a convenient pretext to interfere. A grim tragic end came to Caron later that summer.

MAY DAY IN TAMPA

After the Paterson strike I had a long siege with chronic bronchitis, which I could not shake off. That Spring, Carlo and I were invited to spend a week or ten days at Tampa, Florida, and to speak there at May Day celebrations. We went by boat most of the way. It was a restful and lovely trip. When we arrived it was as hot as midsummer in New York City. Tampa and its environs, especially Ybor City, were cigar-making centers. Men and women—Cuban, Italian, Mexican, Spanish—worked in factories. They were highly skilled workers who made the finest and most expensive cigars by hand. In the evening they sat on their porches smoking. The women smoked small cigars, especially made for them in these factories.

We were taken to visit a factory where there was a platform, like a pulpit, five or six feet above the ground, up over the heads of the workers. A man called a "reader" sat up there, employed by the workers with the employers consent and cooperation because it was conducive to quiet and concentration. He read papers, pamphlets and books in Spanish and Italian. The workers decided what he should read and the contents were usually extremely radical. The day we were there he was reading a pamphlet on birth control. We were introduced to the workers as the leaders of the Paterson silk strike and received a big round of applause. We said a few words.

We spoke on the public square of Tampa at noon of May Day and in the afternoon at a picnic of cigar workers. It was crowded and gay —with food, drink and music of the many nationalities present. The accents were odd, foreign such as we had heard in the North, but softened and blurred by the Southern accent acquired from the natives. I remember one young boy asking me about snow, which he had never seen, and he asked could I send him some the next winter. Carlo and I spoke with local people in the afternoon on the dance platform. Suddenly I realized there were no Negroes in the audience but outside the high wire fences I saw dark faces, lit with interest and eagerness to hear "the IWW from the North." I felt ashamed to see them excluded on May Day.

Carlo and I went over the fence after we finished and talked to them. They clustered around tightly to hear our words. We told them of the hundreds of Negro longshoremen who belonged to the IWW in Philadelphia and of the militant Negro dye workers we knew in the Paterson strike. But while we talked we saw the foreign-born committee was nervous and fearful lest the picnic be broken up by the police, as they had threatened to do. It was my first experience with the horrible Jim Crow system of the South and marred the pleasure I had in the trip. The warm climate helped my throat a great deal and I was ready for work again when I returned.

JIM LARKIN COMES TO THE UNITED STATES

One day in the Spring of 1914 a knock came on our door at 511 East 134th Street in the Bronx. We lived up three flights of stairs and the bell was usually out of order. There stood a gaunt man, with a rough-hewn face and a shock of graying hair, who spoke with an Irish accent. He asked for Mrs. Flynn. When my mother went to the door, he said simply: "I'm Jim Larkin. James Connolly sent me." He came regularly after that to drink tea with my mother, whom he called "my countrywoman." He had come to raise funds for the Irish Citizens' Army and the labor movement there. He had been a founder, with Connolly, of the Irish Transport Workers Union and a fiery leader of its great strike in 1913. Once he was out of Ireland, the British government did everything in its power to prevent his return. He remained throughout World War I, was jailed here during the Palmer raids and finally deported.

He was very poor and while in New York he lived in one room in a small alley in Greenwich Village, called Milligan Place. It ran diagonally from Sixth Avenue through to 11th Street and faced the old Jefferson Market Court. He had a small open fireplace and a tea kettle was ever simmering on the hearth. The tea was so strong that it tasted like medicine to us. His way of life was frugal and austere. He was bitterly opposed to drink and denounced it as a curse of the Irish. Once he was with a group of us at John's Restaurant on East 12th Street, which we frequented from 1913 on. He asked for tea. They had none, but out of respect for him they sent out for tea and a teapot, and he taught them how to make it.

He was a magnificent orator and an agitator without equal. He spoke at anti-war meetings, where he thundered against British imperialism's attempts to drag us into war. My mother gave him the green banner of the Irish Socialist Federation and he spoke under it innumerable times, especially on the New York waterfront. It finally was lost somewhere on the West Side by an old Irish cobbler who used to take care of it in his shop—but visited taverns *en route*. When Connolly and his comrades were shot down in the 1916 uprising, Larkin aroused a tremendous wrath of protest here, especially when he roared against the professional Irish, mostly politicians, who tried to explain away an actual armed uprising of the Irish people. He went to Paterson with us after we won our free speech fight, and spoke to a large gathering of silk workers who contributed a pathetic collection of pennies, nickels and dimes to help the Irish, in response to Jim's appeal "for bread and guns." Many an Irish cop turned the other way and pretended not to hear when Jim made this appeal. He joined the American Socialist Party's Left-wing movement after his arrival here and was a delegate to a founding convention of the Communist Party five years later in Chicago, in 1919.

Larkin's record as a fighting labor leader in Ireland was well known in America. He had cemented bonds of solidarity between Irish and British workers while leading the 1913 strike against William Murphy, an Irish super-capitalist, owner of the Dublin streetcar and lighting systems, railroads, hotels, steamships and two newspapers. A strike meeting was prohibited as "seditious" and Larkin burned the prohibition order, announcing the meeting would be held. Thousands waited patiently at the appointed hour and place. An old man with a long beard entered the Hotel Imperial. A few minutes later he appeared on a balcony, tore off the beard and said: "I am Larkin. I said I would be here and here I am." Then the police charged the crowd. That day, August 31, 1913, was marked as "the bloodiest day in Dublin"—up to that time. Five hundred were injured by the police attack and one man, Nolan, killed. A mass funeral, two miles long, was arranged by Connolly and Larkin. As they had with us in Lawrence and Paterson, the police remained away during the strike funeral.

James Larkin was the nephew of one of the Manchester martyrs, hanged by the British government in 1867. He boasted of his family tree, amid cheers of approval from Irish audiences, that "a man was hung in every one of four generations, as a rebel." Connolly and Larkin represented a remarkably effective combination in the struggle for Irish freedom, the building of an Irish labor movement and the establishment of a socialist movement. They complemented each other and were loved and respected in Ireland—and respected each other. I am proud I had the opportunity to count both of these truly great sons of Erin as my comrades and friends.

Murder Strikes at Children

When Spring came in 1913 the army of the unemployed melted with the snows. By the next winter, World War I had been declared and war-order jobs were on the increase. Our 1914 Eastern unemployed agitation was due to sink away into insignificance beside the bitter struggles of the copper miners in Michigan and the coal miners in Colorado. The right to organize into the Western Federation of Miners and the United Mine Workers of America, was at stake in these two areas. And as usual, employer-supplied brutality was rampant. Twice within a few months, miners' children were struck down by death. Cold-blooded murder was the verdict of the entire country, swept by new waves of horror and indignation.

The first tragedy occurred in Calumet, Michigan, on Christmas

Day, 1913. The women's auxiliary had arranged a party for the strikers' children, who were thrown into a wild panic by a fake cry of "Fire!" They rushed down the narrow stairs and 73 were smothered to death in the entryway when the door jammed shut. Charles H. Moyer, president of the Western Federation of Miners was beaten and deported out of the district when he refused $1,500 as "blood money," collected by the anti-labor Citizens' Alliance "to help the children."

Colorado was a scene of intense labor struggle since the turn of the century. A unique episode of force and violence occurred in the Cripple Creek area during the strike in 1893–1894. The governor, David Waite, was a Populist. He sent the militia to guard the miners and restore order against the company gunmen. A group of vigilantes, organized by the mine owners, took T. J. Tarney, adjutant-general of the militia, from the Antler Hotel at Colorado Springs, and tarred and feathered him.

The next big strike was in 1914, and extended into 1915, culminating in the Ludlow Massacre. The striking miners had been evicted from their homes by the Colorado Fuel and Iron Company, a Rockefeller subsidiary. They were living in a tent colony, surrounded by the militia. The women were fearful of the militia and had dug a deep cave under one tent where they put the children to sleep. On April 29, 1914, the militia set fire to the tent colony with kerosene. Two women, one pregnant, and 13 children were smothered to death in the cave. Two of the tent colonies, Forbes and Ludlow, were destroyed. The pretext for the massacre was that "a fugitive from arrest" was there. One woman, Mrs. Petrucci, lost three children, but no one was ever arrested for their murder. Louis Tikas, a Greek union organizer, was shot in the back trying to rescue a child. Over 30 miners were killed in the battle that ensued. Demonstrations of protest and sympathy started all over the country, particularly directed against the Standard Oil Company.

John D. Rockefeller, Jr., had testified before the House Mines Committee on April 6 (New York *World,* April 7, 1914) that the strike had become a fight for "the principles of freedom of labor" and that he and his associates "would rather that the present violence continue and that they all lose all of their millions invested in the coal fields than that American working men should be deprived of the right under the Constitution to work for whom they please." He expressed his confidence in the competent men he had placed in authority over the mines of Colorado, but admitted that for all his professed interest in "welfare work," he had never investigated the conditions in the Colorado coal fields. A group of miners' wives came East to testify before the Industrial Relations Commission and to speak at meetings. In the end not a single member of the National Guard was punished for the wholesale murder of women and children. Rockefeller did not lose his millions and the miners lost that battle for recognition of their union, which came years later. But the Standard Oil Company and the Rockefellers never regained the respect of the masses of American people, no matter how great their philanthropies from their ill-gotten gains.

John Lawson, the organizer of the United Mine Workers, was arrested for murder. He was tried in April 1915, charged with furnishing arms to the Ludlow tent colony and, since he was in charge of the colony and directed the strikers, with a responsibility for the death of a mine guard, John Mimms, who had been killed in a struggle on October 25, 1913. He was sentenced to life imprisonment. There was tremendous resentment all over the country and strong feeling against the Rockefellers. All unions and many public-spirited leading citizens joined in the campaign for Lawson's release. The Supreme Court allowed his release on bail in October 1917. Finally, in April 1918 the attorney-general of Colorado "confessed error" in the conviction of Lawson and the case was dismissed.

In New York City in 1914 Upton Sinclair, the writer, and Elizabeth Freeman, suffrage leader, led a group of pickets dressed in deep mourning, one wrapped in a shroud, in a parade before 26 Broadway, the Standard Oil offices. The Rockefeller estate at Tarrytown, New York, was picketed. A free speech fight started there when a protest meeting on Aqueduct property was broken up and a dozen speakers arrested, including Alexander Berkman. They were due to be tried for disorderly conduct on July 5, 1914. Three of those to be tried were killed on July 4 by a bomb explosion in the house where they lived on Lexington Avenue near 103rd Street. "DYNAMITE FOR ROCKEFELLER ESTATE," "DOUBLE ROCKEFELLER GUARDS," were the scare headlines in the day's newspapers.

There were reasons for grave doubt as to whether the dead men were responsible for the bomb which caused their deaths. The mystery was never solved. Louise Berger, a young woman in whose house the tragedy occurred, had left her half brother, Charles Berg, and his companions asleep that morning. She swore that there was no dynamite or mechanical devices in the house. She daily cleaned the small apartment herself and knew everything in it. One of those who was killed, Arthur Caron, had been an active participant in the unemployed demonstrations of the winter before. A huge memorial meeting was held on Union Square, July 10, 1914, at which I spoke. I felt a deep sorrow for Caron, who was a textile worker of French descent from Massachusetts. I said, in part, at this meeting:

Arthur Caron was a typical unemployed working man, not the "professional unemployed" nor one of the intellectual dilettanti so numerous during last winter's agitation. He worked many years as a weaver in Fall River, but was interested in architecture and longed for a chance to study. He lost his wife and baby a short time ago. Grief and loneliness drove him to the "Mecca of America," only to find thousands out of work, to tramp the streets hungry and cold and without success. Finally he drifted into Tannenbaum's unemployed group, in the hope of some solution for his pressing problem. He was arrested in the church raid, arrested again with O'Carroll while going home after a meeting, thrown into an automobile and frightfully beaten by two detectives, while two others held him. His nose was broken and he was sent to a hospital. Again in Tarrytown, where a meeting to protest against the Colorado outrages was attempted, he was hooted and jeered at when he said: "I am an American," and pelted with rocks and mud by the law-and-order element. He asked for bread. He received the blackjack. He asked to be heard. He received a volley of stones.

If this young man did turn to violence as the last resort, *who is responsible? Who taught it to him?* The psychology of violence is a very natural result of police brutality and mob lawlessness. This young man was denied any outlet for his protest against his misery, and left to brood over it. Coupled with this was his bitter indignation at the indifference of the latest Nero, who scattered Sunday school tracts while Ludlow burned.*

We should not spit on the mangled corpses of dead workingmen, whose lips are stilled and who may be the victims of a gigantic conspiracy. We need not accept their ideas, or deeds; yet *if we believe them guilty* we may extend to them sympathy for their intense suffering that found an outlet only in this desperate futile way; sympathy for the foolish shortsightedness that carried explosives into a crowded tenement house. We may realize that violence against an individual will not change conditions nor will it restore the babies of Colorado. But let us fix our condemnation on the brutality that produced such a psychology, a hate as quenchless as our wrongs, on the society that drives her children to such desperate retaliation.

That year, 1914, was indeed a barbarous and bloody year in the class struggle in America. It ushered in the holocaust of World War I, in which millions laid down their lives.

* The reference is to John D. Rockefeller, Jr., who taught Sunday school.—*Ed.*

By 1914 I had been in daily contact with workers and their struggles for eight years. I saw their honesty, modesty, decency, their devotion to their families and their unions, their helpfulness to fellows,
their courage, their willingness to sacrifice. I hated those who exploited
them, patronized them, lied to them, cheated them and betrayed them.
I hated those who lived in idleness and luxury on *their* sweat and toil.
More and more the iron was driven into my soul. In my youth I lived
through a long period of ruthless brutal force, of terror and violence
against workers. Private guards, armed thugs, sheriffs, police, state
troopers, militia and judges from justice of the peace to the Supreme
Court, were at the command of the employers—North, South, East
and West. I heard stories of all this wherever I went. I became more
and more strong in my hatred of all these evil things. I became in my
youth and I remain now, at 64, "a mortal enemy of capitalism"—to
paraphrase Karl Marx's description of himself.

Joe Hill—Martyred Troubador of Labor

After the gruesome year of 1914, relieved only by a trip to Tampa, I
was glad to go on a cross-country speaking trip in 1915, my first to
California. I visited many cities I had never seen—Denver, a mile high
in the Rockies, Salt Lake City, with its windswept wide streets and
long blocks, Los Angeles, and last but not least in my memory—the
fairest of them all—San Francisco.

The outstanding event on this trip was my visit to Joe Hill in the
County Jail in Salt Lake City. He was a troubador of the IWW, who
wrote songs "to fan the flames of discontent." Some were written to
popular tunes, some to religious airs and some to his own musical
composition. They were very catchy and were heard at IWW street
and hall meetings, on picket lines and in jails from coast to coast.
Sometimes he played the piano in meetings to accompany his songs.
Among his most famous songs are "Casey Jones," "Mr. Block,"
"Long Haired Preachers" or "Pie in the Sky," "Workers of the World
Awaken," "Hallelujah, I'm a Bum," and two anti-war songs, "Don't
Take My Papa Away from Me" and "Should I Ever Be a Soldier."
While in prison he sent me a copy of "The Rebel Girl" which he wrote
there and dedicated to me.

Joe Hill's full name was Joseph Hillstrom. He was an immigrant
from Sweden who had drifted to the West and become a migratory

worker. What caused him to stand out and to become a target for employers' special attacks were his songs. He had been active in the San Diego free speech fight. The IWW had been trying in 1914 to organize the copper mines owned by the Guggenheim interests. Joe went there and was active in an IWW strike at Tucker, Utah, involving 1,500 miners. In January 1914 a holdup and murder of a grocery man occurred in Salt Lake City. The police looked for IWWs to fasten the crime upon, and a crude frame-up was created against Joe Hill. It was built around his refusal to give an alibi and the fact that he had been shot that night. The story was that he had had a love affair with a married woman and to the day of his execution he refused to name her or her husband who presumably had shot him. The legal case was the flimsiest imaginable, but so great was the fear and prejudice against the IWW that it was made to stick.

I had never met Joe Hill before I went to see him in jail. He was tall, slender, very blond, with deep blue eyes. He was 31 years old— "the age when Jesus was crucified," he said to me. We sat in the sheriff's office, looking out the open barred door at the wide expanse of a beautiful lawn. It was spring in the garden city of Salt Lake, encircled by great mountains, crowned with eternal snows. In springtime its green shimmer, high altitude, and clear pure air were like wine. But the familiar fetid jail odor assailed the nostrils, the clang of the keys, the surly permission to enter, the damp air loaded with the sickening smell of disinfectants, all marked the prison abode. It was the first time Joe had been allowed to receive a visitor in the office and to shake hands with a visitor. The head jailer was one of the detectives who made up the case and they hoped that Joe would "talk." He was expected to prove himself innocent.

He had little to say to me about his case. I knew his appeal—taken over at the eleventh hour by Judge O. N. Hilton, long the chief counsel of the Western Federation of Miners—was pending. The case was a legal mess because his first lawyer, a local Socialist, was timid and inept and had made no real defense, had registered no proper objections and exceptions to "protest the record," as the lawyers put it. Joe finally stood up in court and fired him, telling the judge he did not need two prosecutors. The judge reappointed the same lawyer forthwith and Joe refused to participate further in the case. Joe had questioned at one time the advisability of an appeal because of the expense involved but we had persuaded him otherwise. In spite of all the legal difficulties, we were optimistic as to the outcome, with the victories of Moyer, Haywood and Pettibone, and Ettor and Giovannitti behind us.

Joe Hill did not share our optimism but he did not oppose our efforts. He said to me: *"I am not afraid of death, but I'd like to be in the fight a little longer."* He saw I was downcast as I left. A feeling of foreboding clutched my heart as I said good-bye to him. He joked about a bearded old man mowing the lawn outside. "He's lucky, Gurley. He's a Mormon and he's had two wives and I haven't even had one yet!" I can see him standing behind the barred door, "smiling with his eyes" as the modern song describes. Many young people of today may think Joe Hill is a mythical figure, like Paul Bunyan. They know him only through the song with its haunting refrain, "I never died, said he." The real story of this martyred troubador of the IWW is a tragic chapter of the infamous frame-up system against workers.

Judge Hilton came East and laid all the information before the Swedish Minister, W.A.F. Ekengren, who had heard from Sweden of tremendous protests there. He interceded with President Wilson, who had no power in a state case. However, he sent a request to Governor Spry of Utah, and the execution which was set for October 1 was postponed to allow the Swedish Minister to present his views to the governor. While Judge Hilton was in New York City, I introduced him to Mr. and Mrs. J. Sargent Cram. Mrs. Cram was a liberal, an avowed pacifist. Prior to World War I she rented stores in various parts of the city for neighborhood exhibitions of Robert Minor's magnificent antiwar cartoons. She made all her appointments at the swanky Colony Club in New York and occasionally took me to her summer home in Old Westbury, Long Island. She introduced me to Judge Lovett, president of the Union Pacific Railroad, who lived in a palatial home nearby and who was "amazed" that I thought he had "influence" with the governor of Utah. She also introduced me to one of the Guggenheims, owners of the mines in Utah. For me it was like talking to creatures from another planet!

Judge Hilton and I went to Long Island to see Mr. Cram. He was a portly, bald-headed, shrewd Democratic politician who thought we were all slightly goofy. But he was impressed with Judge Hilton's presentation of the case and he liked me as "a sensible woman," particularly because I enjoyed the rare wines from his cellar. So he agreed to arrange an interview with President Woodrow Wilson for Mrs. Cram and me. We had gone once before on September 28, 1915, to try to see him, but had been referred then to Acting Secretary of State Polk. Mr. Cram had led the New York delegation to vote for Wilson at the nominating convention and had easy access to the White House.

We went down on November 11, 1915. We had breakfast with Gifford Pinchot, Mrs. Cram's Republican brother-in-law, who escorted us to the White House. Mr. Tumulty, the President's Secretary, was friendly. He knew of me from the Paterson strike of 1913. When the President came in he greeted us cordially, in fact he held Mrs. Cram's hand. He listened attentively while we presented our appeal. He said he had once intervened at the request of the Swedish Minister. He wondered if further insistence might do more harm than good. Not knowing the etiquette of talking to the President, I interrupted: "But he's sentenced to death. You can't make it worse, Mr. President." He smiled and said: "Well, that's true!" and promised to consider the matter.

As the days passed we felt that our mission had failed. But fortunately the American Federation of Labor, meeting in San Francisco, wired a plea on November 17 to the President, signed by Samuel Gompers. President Wilson, under pressure, sent a second message to Governor Spry as follows: "With unaffected hesitation but with a very earnest consideration of the importance of the case, I again venture to urge upon Your Excellency the justice and advisability of a thorough reconsideration of the case of Joseph Hillstrom." Governor Spry curtly rejected this message from the President of the United States as "unwarranted interference."

In Utah a condemned man had the right to choice—to be hanged or to be shot by a firing squad. It was a remnant of the old West. Joe chose to be shot. On November 19, 1915, five masked men, one with a blank in his gun, were brought to the prison in a carriage with all the curtains drawn so the identities of those who fired the fatal shots would be unknown. Joe's last words were: *"Don't mourn, organize."* His wish "not to be found dead in the state of Utah," was respected and the IWW took his body to Chicago for cremation. I was unable to attend because of my pending trial in Paterson. Judge Hilton was the principal speaker at the services in Ashland Auditorium and because of his speech he was disbarred in the state of Utah from further practice there. This is the first labor case I know of where a lawyer was penalized for defending his client. It was a forerunner of such a procedure against similar attorneys over three decades later in Smith Act cases.

OUT BY THE GOLDEN GATE

On this trip I spoke on the Joe Hill case in Salt Lake City at a large mass meeting of over 400, and then went on to California. My first stop was Los Angeles, where I stayed at the home of our IWW chief counsel, my old friend, Fred Moore.

My outstanding experience in Los Angeles, which he arranged, was a visit to Dave Caplan and Matt Schmidt, lodged in the Los Angeles jail high up over a court building. They had been arrested in 1914 in the aftermath of the famous McNamara case of 1911, a further proof that Lincoln Steffens' "Golden Rule" contract with the prosecution had miscarried. A secret reward of $25,000 had not been canceled. A young man in the employ of the Burns detective agency, son of an anarchist woman from Howe Colony, near Tacoma, Washington, had wormed his way into a party at Emma Goldman's house, and there had met Schmidt and reported it to the police. Caplan got 15 years and Schmidt a life sentence. I did not know either of these men but considered it my duty to visit all the class war prisoners, as we then called them. Labor felt highly indignant that they should be arrested after the agreement which Steffens had so widely publicized, and meetings were held for their defense. I spoke at several such meetings on this trip.

In May 1915 I saw for the first time the American city which I love the best, that white city seated by the blue sea, which I felt then—and ever after—to be the most beautiful in our country, San Francisco. The IWW had a large hall at 3345 17th Street. I spoke there and at Carpenters Hall on Valencia Street alternately for about a week on the Joe Hill case, the Caplan-Schmidt case, on "Violence and the Labor Movement" and on "The Role of Women in Strikes." I also spoke in Oakland, where "Red" Doran was chairman. Many odd and amusing things happened in the IWW. At this meeting the double doors of the hall, at the end of a wide aisle, opened suddenly and a well-dressed young man entered with an enormous bouquet of flowers in one hand and a bottle of wine in the other. "Greetings and welcome to California, Gurley!" he sang out. He stopped the meeting till I accepted both.

The last time I had seen Howard Shaeffer he had been ordered to leave New York City or go to jail. He had hurled rotten eggs at the screen of a Broadway theater when the anti-Negro, pro-Confederacy film "The Birth of a Nation" was being shown, and then he popped up over 3,000 miles away. The days of my youth were full of such odd adventures! He became a successful businessman in California.

In San Francisco drinking coffee after the first meeting, I again met Tom Mooney and was introduced to his wife Rena, who taught music to children. They were not members of the IWW, but came to hear me speak. Tom was the same as when I had met him in Idaho— dark-haired, rosy-cheeked and jolly. He recalled that he had met me first at an IWW meeting in Chicago, when he bought a pamphlet from me he could not afford but was ashamed to say "No." In 1915 Tom was a member of the Molders Union, AFL, but was busy trying to organize the streetcar workers of San Francisco.

At the same time, I first met a "native daughter" of California, a slender beautiful woman in her forties, soft-spoken but firm and courageous in her ideas, Anita Whitney. As president of the College Equal Suffrage League, she had led her forces to victory in 1911, when California became the sixth state in the union to grant women suffrage. She was second vice-president of the American Equal Suffrage Association, of which Dr. Anna Shaw was president and Jane Addams first vice-president. She was a member of the executive committee of the National Association for the Advancement of Colored People (NAACP). In 1914 Anita Whitney had joined the Socialist Party. After graduating from Wellesley College in the 1890s, she had spent three months in a New York College Settlement on Rivington St. The sights and smells of the squalid slums, the sweat shops, child labor, the crowded living quarters of the poor with rats and roaches, the prostitution, crime and terrible fires were appalling revelations. Such mockery of the promise of life, liberty and the pursuit of happiness haunted her on her return to her pleasant California home.

She was a charity worker in Alameda County, California for 15 years. She fought for juvenile courts and became the first probation officer. She worked as a relief worker in the San Francisco earthquake and fire of 1906. She finally resigned from her profession because she felt a fundamental change of a political character was necessary to affect poverty. If "Miss Whitney of California," as she was known at suffrage conventions, had not been a Socialist she could have been elected to any office, even the Senate, by the women's vote of her state. But she set her feet on "freedom's road" and was ready to go all the way.

While I was in San Francisco, an Exposition was in progress, of a very colorful and interesting character. I went there with George Speed, who was even then a veteran of the labor movement. He was born near where we lived in the South Bronx and apprenticed in his youth to make high silk hats. Later, he had become a sailor and was one of the pioneers in organizing this group of exploited workers.

I visited San Quentin Prison for the first time during this stay in San Francisco. Fremont Older, the editor of a San Francisco paper, gave me a note of introduction to the warden. It is a few miles out from the city on the mainland, a forbidding, dreary place, like all prisons. I went to see Albert Ryan, a member of the Western Federation of Miners and an old friend of St. John. He was in prison for life for shooting a deputy sheriff. The Saint had asked me to see him. I also saw J. B. McNamara, secretary of the Bridge and Structural Iron Workers Union, who was serving a 15-year sentence. His hair was white, yet he was a comparatively young man. The other brother, J. J. McNamara, would not see any visitors at that time. J. B. expressed his gratitude that a stranger, a member of the IWW with which he had had no contact while on the outside, took the trouble to come to see him, while Samuel Gompers, president of the AFL, was in San Francisco at that very time and made no effort to come over to the prison. He dropped his gray prison cap on the floor as he rose to leave and I picked it up for him. He smiled and his deep blue eyes filled with tears. "That's the first thing a woman has done for me in four years," he said.

From San Francisco I went to Portland, Oregon, another beautiful city of hills, with the Willamette and wide Columbia Rivers, fir trees and roses, with resplendent Mount Hood on the eastern horizon. Here I met a stormy petrel of the Northwest, Dr. Marie D. Equi, a successful woman doctor, who put me up at the swanky Hotel Multnomah. She entertained all the women speakers who passed through the City of Roses—Anita Whitney and Sara Bard Field, suffrage workers, Hanna Skeffington and Katherine O'Brennan, Irish nationalists, Margaret Sanger and myself. We all appreciated the unusual comfort.

Dr. Marie D. Equi, then in her forties of Italian and Irish parentage, was a fiery personality. She was born in New Bedford, Massa-

chusetts, but had been sent out to eastern Oregon as a young girl to
live with an older New Bedford woman who was a school teacher at
The Dalles. She suffered from a tubercular condition, which the sun
and mild dry air of that area helped to heal. She attended medical
school in California and graduated in Oregon. During the 1906 earthquake and fire in San Francisco she organized a trainload of doctors,
nurses and supplies to go from Oregon and so distinguished herself
during the catastrophe that she was honored with a military rank by
the U.S. Army. No consideration was given to this service, however,
when she later became a political prisoner because of her opposition to
World War I.

She early identified herself with the IWW in the Northwest. Her
father has been a stonemason and a member of the Knights of Labor.
During her girlhood in Massachusetts she had aided in the fight for an
eight-hour day. In the West she carried on campaigns against the horrible, unsanitary conditions in the lumber camps and, although not a
member of the IWW, gave them medical attention, spoke for them and
defended them. During a cannery strike in 1913, involving women and
girls, she was arrested and so badly abused physically in the Portland
County jail, that she had to go East for medical examination and treatment. She helped to secure a law in Oregon limiting the hours of women
and child workers, and to place Oregon in the ranks of the first states
that granted women suffrage. She was among the most feared and hated women in the Northwest because of her outspoken criticisms of
politicians, industrialists, so-called civic leaders and all who oppressed
the poor. She was loved and cherished by masses of plain people.

"He Kept Us Out of War"

At the time that war was declared in Europe in 1914 there was a
strong anti-war feeling in this country which grew during the next
three years. A sense of complete isolation from Europe and the quar-
rels of its various dynasties prevailed. There was criticism of the German Socialists who had capitulated to their country's war program.
Anti-British feeling reached a high point after the Easter Week uprising and the executions in Ireland in 1916. Many peace organizations
came into existence such as the Emergency Peace Federation in 1914,
and the National Women's Peace Party in 1915, in both of which Jane
Addams of Chicago was a leading spirit. A large group of American

women delegates which she led and which included Emily Green Balch, Dr. Alice Hamilton and Leonora O'Reilly went to an International Peace Conference at the Hague in 1915.

One of the strangest demonstrations for peace at that time was the Ford Peace Party which chartered a ship, the *Oscar II,* known as the Peace Ship. It sailed on December 4, 1915 and its slogan was: "Get the boys out of the trenches by Christmas." Henry Ford paid all the expenses of the trip, it was rumored. The pilgrims for peace numbered about 30 determined souls, including Miss Addams, Miss Balch, Miss Beckenridge of Chicago and—amazingly enough—William C. Bullit of Philadelphia. The roster of prominent, honest Americans who stood squarely for peace and for keeping us out of war was impressive, including statesmen, ministers, professors, labor leaders, women leaders, writers, editors and even capitalists. However, we of the IWW took no part in any of these pacifist activities. To us it was a grim joke to see an anti-union exploiter like Ford a participant in a peace movement. We were suspicious of non-working-class elements of all sorts and held ourselves aloof from them. Yet, it was the IWW that bore the full impact of wartime prosecution as soon as war was declared.

While war raged abroad and President Wilson campaigned in 1916 on the slogan, "He Kept Us Out of War," we in the IWW doggedly stuck to our knitting. Our self-appointed task was to organize the unorganized workers and lead them in struggles for better wages, shorter hours and decent working conditions. Our concentration was bound to be in basic industries, where the war profits were soaring. It was not long before we were accused of being pro-German because the material produced in these industries was for war purposes.

The IWW was opposed to militarism and war. We were internationalists in our outlook. It was not accidental, though it may have appeared presumptuous, that we were called Industrial Workers of the *World.* There were actually IWW groups in England, South Africa and Australia, probably a result of our reputation and our visiting seamen. Haywood wrote at one time to Frank Little, who was pressing for an out-and-out stand against conscription: "Many of the members feel as you do, but *regard the present war between the capitalist nations as of small importance when compared to the great class war in which we are engaged.*" As a matter of fact, outside of a resolution passed in the 1914 and 1916 conventions against war in general, the IWW never did officially take a stand before or after April 1917 against American participation in the war or against conscription. It was left, as Haywood said on the witness stand in the famous IWW trial in Chicago, "to the conscience of the individual." The IWW stood aside even from the People's Council, a powerful mass political pressure movement of that period.

Of course, there was enough happening on the class struggle front right here in our own country to keep us busy during the years 1915 and 1916. It all unavoidably dovetailed with the anti-war struggle. Foremost was the Mooney case.

In July 1916 the open-shop forces of San Francisco staged a "Preparedness Day" parade. The entire labor movement of the city had gone on record against their membership participating in any way in this affair because of its anti-labor character and because they were against beating the drums for war. A bomb was thrown at the marchers, it was charged, that killed a number of people. There has always been a doubt as to whether it was a bomb or whether dynamite in a suitcase exploded. Tom Mooney and his wife Rena, Warren K. Billings, Ed Nolen and Israel Weinberg were arrested. One of the most infamous frame-ups in the history of the American labor movement began to unfold. The labor movement finally recognized the whole business as a frame-up and rallied to the defense of those accused. The theory of the defense, in which I believe there was validity, was that German agents, later convicted of blowing up bridges in Canada, were responsible for the explosion.

I was personally not in a position to become active immediately in the Mooney case because I was involved in the strike in the Mesabi Range in Minnesota. Carlo Tresca had been on a speaking tour as far as California in the late Spring of 1916 and at the request of Haywood, who was now general secretary of the IWW, had gone to the Mesabi Range in Minnesota to speak. He was arrested there in July with a group of speakers, organizers and strikers, who were loaded on a special train at Virginia and taken to Duluth County Jail. At this time the IWW also had considerable activity among the anthracite coal miners and a strike was on in Old Forge, Pennsylvania. I went there to speak at a picnic arranged by Joe Ettor, who was in charge in that area. We received a wire from Haywood to proceed at once to Chicago, prepared to go to the Mesabi Range to take charge of the strike and the defense of those in prison. Joe and I were off for Minnesota the next day.

HARVEST STIFFS ORGANIZE

In 1915, ten years after the IWW came into existence, there began to develop a self-critical attitude in the organization. Articles appeared on "Why doesn't the IWW Grow?" Debates grew on why we failed to hold our membership. The cold fact was that 300,000 membership cards had been issued during the decade. Workers passed through the IWW—but they did not stay. The most glowing figure set our membership at 50,000 in 1915. There was a growing demand by then to get out of the purely agitational state and build constructive and permanent organization. The first try at this was the setting up of the Agricultural Workers Organization, known as the AWO, in April 1915. It opened its own headquarters in Kanas City, Missouri. It drew up a plan to organize the farm laborers and harvest hands in a belt of mid-western states—"the breadbasket of America" and during the war years a producer of food for many other lands.

The soap box approach was abandoned. Skid row was no longer the forum of the IWW, a situation which had precipitated so many of the free speech fights. (One of the last of these was in Aberdeen, South Dakota, in 1914, the second struggle in that town in two years.) A job delegate system was organized, a mobile setup of men who worked on the jobs and followed the harvest, starting at the Mexican border in early Spring and finishing up in late fall at the Canadian border and beyond it. It functioned as a union, with a schedule of work and wages it was able to enforce, because of the highly seasonal nature of the work and perishable quality of the crops harvested. It moved its headquarters to Minneapolis, with Walter Nef as secretary, and by 1915 it numbered 18,000 members.

The AWO came into the 1916 IWW convention as the strongest group there. This stimulated similar plans among the lumber workers and metal miners, with concentration on wages, hours and working conditions. The lumber workers planned an industry-wide campaign for the eight-hour day and set May 1, 1917, as "bundle burning day"—all rolls of blankets, which the men carried on their backs, were to be burned and the camps forced to furnish clean bedding. This was considered a most revolutionary demand on the part of the "bindle stiffs." In 1916 the IWW made a real turn in the West toward job organization and union demands. If there had not been a war it might still have been able to anticipate the CIO by two decades, at least in building strong industrial unions in agriculture, mining, lumber and maritime. The attacks on the IWW were for this reason—not because it was particularly "anti-war," but because it challenged the war profit-eers at the "point of production."

The strike of 1916 on the Mesabi Range involved some 16,000 iron-ore miners, employed by the Oliver Iron Mining Company. It was a vital spot, the raw material supply for the U.S. Steel Trust. A thousand plug-uglies from Duluth and other places were deputized as marshals and had virtually taken over the Range, which swarmed with them and with gunmen of the companies. Fortunately some of the towns had progressive mayors—like Powers of Hibbings, and Boylon of Virginia—who kept them out of the towns. The Finnish organizations owned excellent halls, even opera houses in some places, which the strikers used as headquarters and where we held mass meetings.

The strike had started in June. Joe and I went there in July, and it wasn't easy to assemble a new core of leaders after all the known local leaders had been arrested. But they were good fighters. Many of them then on strike had been brought in from the Baltic states ten years before to break a strike of the Western Federation of Miners. Conditions had then driven them to revolt, as happened in Lawrence and in most IWW strikes—retributive justice for the employers. They were demanding an eight-hour day, a minimum wage of $3.00 for underground mining, $3.50 in wet places and $2.75 on the open-pit surface, abolition of the contract system and payday twice a month. Men were working on the open-pit surface for $2.60 for a ten-hour day. A system of graft on the part of the mine captains, where those who paid for them got the better jobs, and abuses such as "raffles"—held by the captains and paid for on a compulsory basis by the miners for non-existing prizes—aggravated the conditions. The miners had to pay for powder, fuses, tools, etc., but no proper accountings were given to them.

While the Range towns were clean and quite attractive, a great many of the miners lived in isolated settlements called "locations," with tumble-down shacks, outhouses, and no sidewalks. These were unincorporated company towns. Water was from a community pump or well, owned by the company, where the water was sometimes shut off in reprisal for the strike. Brutal clashes occurred between deputies and strikers on the desolate locations, often involving women and children of strikers as well. Mary Heaton Vorse describes one of the locations and the gunmen in her book, *Footnote to Folly,* as follows:

Carson Lake sits under the shadow of a great mine. There were no streets and the irregular spaces between the row of houses were full of blackened stumps and boulders, strayed pigs and a few lamentable chickens—and children. The whole place was so terrible, life was so stripped of all beauty, that the sight of children there shocked one. It did not seem possible that here women bore children and reared families.

It was a place so forbidding that it seemed incredible ambition should ever enter here. One expected a sodden and brutal population to match the brutal conditions. Instead, the women who stared at us with interest were serious and strong-looking and neatly dressed.

Above the door of one tar-paper shanty shone a bit of stained glass. There were white curtains at the windows, the bareness was thrown in relief by flowers blooming in the windows.

The men were standing moodily about their doorways. They were silent and quiet, and they seemed not unlike Provincetown men, for they also contended with the forces of nature.

We would have been very glad to talk with the women at Carson Lake, especially the woman whose house was ornamented with stained glass, for she smiled at us from her doorway, but we could not because of the drunken gunman who came at us bellowing obscenely.

So there remains to me only a picture without words—the silent and powerful men, the desolate location, the friendly women and their gallant attempts at beauty, and the gunman, at once absurd and menacing, reeling along the streets.

I had read of gunmen and I had been ready for tough-looking customers but seldom has life so magnificently lived up to expectation as there in Carson Lake—bloated, unshaven, toddy blossoms on noses, they looked like motion-picture plug-uglies. They were too exaggerated to be real.

The Saint Turns Prospector

Vincent St. John came to Chicago in 1907 after he had been shot in Goldfield. On his recovery, he became general organizer of the IWW and then its secretary. He remained at this post until July 1915. He was one of the clearest thinkers in the IWW and fought consistently to save it from becoming a tail to the kites of Daniel De Leon and the Socialist Labor Party on the one hand and what he contemptuously called "the anarchist freaks" on the other. He tried hard to make it a militant industrial union. Most of the big and dramatic struggles led by the organization occurred in this period—the steel strike at McKees Rocks, the Spokane and San Diego free speech fights, the lumber strikes in Louisiana and the Northwest, the textile strikes of Lawrence, Little Falls and Paterson, the Akron rubber strike, the struggle to free Ettor and Giovannitti. At the helm in the Chicago national office was this quiet, rather obscure man who wrestled with irksome financial crises and wearisome office details.

He felt frustrated and dissatisfied because permanent organization failed to materialize from all of these heroic efforts. He had been an organizer and a strike leader, identified closely with the rank and file of the militant Western Federation of Miners. Now he felt he was on the side lines. He disliked the East and big cities; he longed for the wide open spaces of the West, and cast around for a successor. William D. Haywood, still far from well, had indicated his desire to take over the office. St. John came East to testify before the Industrial Relations Commission, of which Frank P. Walsh, a progressive lawyer, was co-chairman with ex-President William Howard Taft. The change-over to Haywood was discussed by all of us, then St. John resigned and Bill Haywood was proposed and accepted at the next IWW convention. Joe Ettor was elected general organizer.

St. John was weary of the routine of indoor work and decided to become a prospector. He went to Jicarilla in Lincoln County, New Mexico, to take up the development of a copper mining property there. As a self-employer, he automatically ceased to be a member of the IWW.

He knew Haywood was "touchy" as to his authority and resentful of the hold "the Saint" had on the love and loyalty of the members. Therefore his correspondence with me and a few others was personal and casual. A stockholding company had been set up around Saint's project, many old-time ex-miners became interested and some went down there to work with the Saint. He made trips to stockholders' meetings in Chicago, one in 1917, and naturally paid a friendly visit to the IWW office. But when he came he was careful to keep it on that basis. He had once advised me on lawyers for the Mesabi Range and we both incurred the wrath of Haywood in consequence.

"Prospecting" was the dream of every hard-rock miner in those days. Tucked away in their memories were likely locations and untapped veins, which might spell striking it rich. Many old-timers who had worked in rich mines of big corporations would struggle for years like this in the hope of hitting the "mother lode" in some other areas. Saint had one spot called "Red Mountain," where they worked hard for several years, but unsuccessfully, on such a project. His hope was to make enough money to finance the revolutionary movement. He had no personal ambitions. He and his wife had separated and she remained in Chicago and eventually remarried. His one weakness was a good hat—a common trait in male Westerners then. They wore their hats like Walt Whitman, "indoors and out."

When the IWW campaign among the copper miners began many of them urged the Saint to become an organizer, but he refused. Haywood did not consult him on any of the new policies and the only link between St. John and the IWW was that Haywood placed his name on the list of persons who could take over the office of secretary in case the incumbents were arrested. Saint did not know of this. To prevent the possibility of Saint resuming leadership of the IWW in the event of Haywood's arrest, he was included in the Chicago indictment of 1917 and arrested on October 31, at Jicarilla, New Mexico, where he was working in the shaft. He was held in jail in that state until December 13, when he was taken to the Cook County jail in Chicago. We raised his bail by March 23, 1918, and he was at liberty until the trial ended and he was convicted. They were taken in a special train to Leavenworth Prison.

The charge was "seditious conspiracy," under the wartime emergency law. I tried very hard to persuade him to do what we had done in New York—move for a severance of his case on the legal ground of non-membership and inactivity during the entire period of the indictment. But he was confident that his case would be dismissed without a trial or that a trial would result in his acquittal. He vainly hoped that his "good case" would help focus attention on the flimsy nature of the whole conspiracy charge. He testified during the trial as a defense witness. In an atmosphere of wild hysteria, before a sadistic and erratic judge, Vincent St. John was not tried for any words or deeds after the United States entered World War I. He had simply worked in his mine, and he could hardly be tried for that. But this man, who was modest to a fault, his name unheralded by any halo of heroes, was called in the press "the brains of the IWW." Even more sinister hatreds operated against him, especially among the mine owners of the West, than against any other of the defendants. The head hunters were out to get him.

He was tried solely for his activities and reputation as an organizer in former years and as the ex-secretary of the IWW. He was sentenced to ten years and a $30,000 fine by Judge Kenesaw M. Landis. (Thirty-four years later a nephew of Judge Landis was on the jury that convicted me under the Smith Act at Foley Square.) Saint was in Cook County jail for five months before trial. He was eight months in Leavenworth after conviction, before bail was raised.

While he was at liberty he helped raise bail for the ones still in prison, making a trip East for this purpose. He stopped off at Pittsburgh to visit Foster who was then leading the nation-wide steel strike. I knew his visit to the Iron City pleased him very much but I heard the details from Foster years later. Saint said: "You've got a bunch of AFL organizers here. They must all own war bonds. Let's tackle them for bail." Foster introduced Saint to them and he collected a substantial amount while there, but it was all "sub rosa" at that time.

His mining project was ruined by this interruption and his two years of hard labor were wasted. When the Supreme Court rejected the appeal, he returned to Leavenworth in 1921. He was extremely bitter, as were many of the IWW prisoners, when "the Big fellow," as he called Haywood, left for Russia, especially after Haywood had insisted on all the men surrendering for trial in 1917. Big Bill had a 20-year sentence, was sick with diabetes and wanted to die in freedom. He died in the Soviet Union in 1928.

In retrospect, many of them felt that our course in New York had been more sensible and effective. Because of the particularly outrageous aspects of St. John's case and my personal devotion to him, I made a special campaign on his behalf. I had tried to get Judge Hilton to handle his appeal. But no motions for severance and other necessary legal moves had been made to protect the rights of individual defendants and there was no peg to hang an appeal on. But I secured the services of Clarence Darrow to make a try at it. He presented a special brief to the Supreme Court on Saint John's behalf. After the Saint went to Prison, I arranged for Harry Weinberger of New York to handle further legal efforts on his behalf. We were greatly disappointed when he was not released at Christmas, 1921. Sydney Lanier had written a letter to the President characterizing Saint's imprisonment as "a gross miscarriage of justice and an outrage that every consideration of right and the peace and good order of society demand should be corrected." Later, in 1922, the good news came through that St. John's application for a commutation of sentence had been signed by the President. A few days later Carlo called me at my office and said: "Guess who's here? The Saint." We took him to the beach with us for a few weeks, where he began to recuperate from the effects of prison.

But he was restless and anxious about the "boys in the Big House."
"It's a nice place," he said, "if it only had a mine in the back yard!"

BLOOD ON THE RANGE

No strike passed in those days without bloodshed, caused by vicious
attacks on strikers. "Force and violence" was not advocated by the
IWW. It was frankly advocated and freely used by the employers. This
was true on the Mesabi Range. When the striker John Alar was shot
by the deputies feeling ran high. At the funeral, strikers carried banners which read: "Murdered by the Oliver Iron Mining Company."
This was the company dominant on the Range—named after Henry
W. Oliver, who had squeezed out the original local owners in the panic
of 1893, shortly after the ore beds were discovered. Bitter speeches
advocating self-defense against attack were made at the graveside.
Deputies, who lounged nearby in menacing attitudes, were reminded
of the Biblical proverb: "An eye for an eye." Pictures were taken by a
self-styled "IWW photographer" from New Castle, Pennsylvania,
named Dawson. These pictures were later used in a preliminary hearing against the strike leaders. The photographer was subsequently
revealed as a stool pigeon for the U.S. Steel Company.

Shortly after the funeral a group of four deputies raided the home
of a striker, Nick Masonovich, in Biwabik. In a letter I wrote on July
21, 1916, to my friend Mary Heaton Vorse, after my arrival on the
Range, I described what had happened as it was reported to us by the
strikers.

Four deputies entered a striker's home without a warrant and attempted
to arrest him. His wife objected and they clubbed her into insensibility.
The husband and three boarders (Montenegrins) jumped to her defense
and in the fracas a deputy, Myron, and a strikers' sympathizer, sitting on a
pop wagon outside the door, were killed. No guns were in the crowd but
the deputies, and an eleven-year-old son testified that he saw the mine
guard, Nick Dillon (ex-bouncer of a disorderly house), fire directly at the
man on the wagon. The boarders were all shot and lay in jail wounded
for days. The woman had to be taken to a hospital. The strike speakers
were at once arrested, charged with murder on the theory that their
speeches had incited violence. It is like the Ettor-Giovannitti case—except
that in this state, accessories are guilty in the first degree and are liable to
life imprisonment. No arrests were made for the murder of the popman;
the death of the deputy is the only one the state concerns itself with.

The ranks are unbroken, and the ore production is crippled. Of course, relief is becoming a pressing problem and we hope the East will realize this and help financially.

When Joe Ettor and I arrived in Duluth we found that Mr. and Mrs. Masonovich and the baby, the three boarders and 15 organizers and local IWW leaders—all they could round up—were in the county jail in Duluth. I went to see Sheriff Meining in his office to get permission to see Carlo Tresca. He was a much worried man, not too bright, as is usual with sheriffs. But he gave me the desired consent to go to the jail. When I was leaving he asked: "Do you plan to go up to the Range?" and I replied: "I was there in 1909 and in 1915 and I plan to go now. That's what I'm here for and I demand protection from you against any attacks." He seemed astounded at my audacity—an IWW organizer demanding protection—and he growled: "Nothing will happen to you there."

That evening I took a train to the Range, escorted by a local co-worker. But not trusting the sheriff, I got off at a siding near Virginia, where the train made a short stop. Devastated by lumber companies and the steel corporation, it is a stark, bleak country, relieved by the red earth and the evergreen trees. We were met by a strikers' committee who took me directly to a Finnish striker's home. For quite a few days I stayed first in one home and then in another. I was not welcome at the local hotels. Finally, during the hot days of July and August, I slept the weary sleep of exhaustion at an Italian boarding house. The wife of the family was a fat, jolly, perspiring woman who cooked and cleaned for a group of boarders—12 or 14 men—who slept, barracks fashion, in one big attic room upstairs. She banished her husband to this masculine retreat and took me in with her in a little bedroom off the dining room. There was not much air, the room was festooned with their clothes, working and Sunday best. The men sat up late, playing cards, drinking wine and talking about the strike. Finally they clumped off to bed. It seemed no time at all until they were cheerily making coffee and starting out for the picket line in the gray dawn. When Mary Heaton Vorse came, I sneaked into a hotel room with her, without registering, and enjoyed some quiet and the luxury of regular baths.

I considered it my first task to secure the release on bail of Mrs. Masonovich. I made a trip to Minneapolis, where I contacted some prominent club women who became interested in her plight. One, Mrs. Hamlin, was the daughter of former Governor Austin of Minnesota

Mrs. Masonovich
and child. Arrested
for murder. Mesabi
Range 1916.

Judge O. N. Hilton. Courageous
defender of Joe Hill. 1914.

Mary Heaton Vorse

and through their efforts we finally secured her release on a nominal amount of bail. After the preliminary hearing, Tresca, Schmidt and Scarlett, the three leading organizers, were held as accessories to murder, and all of the Montenegrin workers and Mrs. Masonovich were charged with murder. The other organizers and local leaders, except two, were released. When the Grand Jury indicted for first-degree murder in August, these two were also released. An additional charge of assault with intent to kill was made against Mrs. Masonovich and the four strikers.

All that summer the strike dragged out a dogged existence. We raced up and down the Range from one end to the other in an old bakery truck driven by a couple of young Italian strikers, who often forgot we were not bread and bounced us unmercifully over the unpaved rocky roads. The deputies came to know the truck and took pot shots at us, so we had to stop using it, much to our relief. There were about 14 towns from one end to the other, which we covered. Several times the strikers marched the length of the Range, holding meetings in each town. On one occasion some towns shut off the drinking water while they were there.

Mrs. Hamlin accompanied me on one trip to Crosby, Minnesota, on the Cuyuna Iron Range, adjoining the Mesabi. No sooner were we settled in a hotel than an anonymous message was shoved under my door threatening bodily violence if I did not leave town at once. A few minutes later I was informed the sheriff of that county wanted to see me. With Mrs. Hamlin by my side we went downstairs to find the parlor full of deputies. The sheriff started very belligerently—if I had come to make trouble, he would arrest me forthwith, he threatened. But when Mrs. Hamlin told him who she was and that she had come from St. Paul, delegated by a group of women's clubs, to see that I was not assaulted as other women had been while picketing, and insisted that I had the right to speak and that no harm must come to me, he quieted down very quickly and was quite apologetic. We had a large, enthusiastic meeting of local workers that night who supported the Mesabi strike generously.

On another occasion, Mrs. Vorse accompanied me on a trip to the iron mining county of Michigan, where all male organizers who went there, including Frank Little, had been deported. But we got by without incident and held a very good meeting at Iron Mountain, raising considerable funds. Our only concern, as she humorously described in her book, *Footnote to Folly,* was that our bodyguards, a group of spirited young Italians, were so anxious to demonstrate how well they could defend us that we were alarmed that they, and not the deputies, would start something. We were relieved to get on the train and depart without incident. I made one quite long trip among the midwestern cities to raise funds.

On this trip, in the local IWW hall at Des Moines, Iowa, Kate Richards O'Hare was also speaking for the Socialist Party and we not only visited each other but she came to speak with me at one of my meetings and I reciprocated at one of hers. She was a tall, slender woman, not yet 40, who was born in Kansas, had been a school teacher and social worker, and was at this time associated with her husband in the editorship of a Socialist paper, *The Ripsaw,* of St. Louis, Missouri. Kate had been the American Party's secretary to the Socialist International. She was an active Socialist for 17 years and had the reputation of having covered more territory and delivered more socialist lectures than any other person in the country. She had four children, whose pictures covered her bureau top in the hotel room.

Kate told me of her experiences in Socialist "Chautauquas" in Oklahoma and Arkansas, where the farmers came from miles around, camped out for three or four days, and listened to a continuous round of speeches and entertainment provided under a big tent by the local Socialist Party. Kate was their star attraction, sometimes speaking three and four times a day. She spoke with such fervor that she would be wringing wet with perspiration at the end of each performance. She loved to dress in white and her laundry bills caused the committee to remark she should buy stock in a laundry. So she started to wash and iron all her garments herself. This was before the days of nylon, and women wore a lot more clothes—petticoats, corset covers, etc. She had a clothesline up in her room and an ironingboard which fitted into her suitcase, and she worked at her chores as she talked to me. She was a splendid orator and a militant Socialist. She made a big hit with the IWW men in my audience. They sang for her all the Joe Hill songs that had any reference to women, like: *"One little girl, fair as a pearl, Worked everyday in a laundry."*

A SOLOMON'S DECISION

Finally, fall was upon us, with a knife-like chill in the air that forewarned of the regular sub-zero winter soon to grip that area. Its tenacious cold settles early and clings late into the spring. Our financial difficulties increased. Funds came to us in such meager amounts we could not meet the relief situation. Families were hungry all around us. Haywood refused to come to the Range to discuss our problems or to speak to the strikers. He had inaugurated a new system that all funds, both for the strike and defense, be addressed to him in Chicago. This was a radical departure from all previous procedure in IWW strikes. When funds came directly to a local strike committee they were bound to participate much more actively in raising them. They knew exactly what there was to dole out. But when they come from a national office far away, they create illusions and distrust. The local people always expect more and suspect there is more, no matter how much or how little they get.

The AWO, after I told their officers all our problems on a visit to Minneapolis, sent us several large sums directly, which saved the strike from collapse, but Haywood objected. At least twice I made trips to Chicago to argue the matter out with him and demand more funds. Finally the strike committee, consisting of 15 miners from the different towns on the Range—of Italian, Finish and Slavic nationalities—decided it was impossible to keep the strike going any longer. It would peter out as the men left for other parts. We organizers did not have the heart to urge prolonging a losing struggle into the bitter Minnesota winter. So the miners finally returned to work.

This is always a sad and bitter time in the class struggle, to see brave workers who had suffered and sacrificed compelled to accept defeat. Later, however, due to war conditions, the employers were forced to grant many of the demands. I loved the people on the Range and did not mind staying on, as we did for several months. But it made me very lonely for my little son to see the blond children of the Finnish workers, with their rosy cheeks, playing around the halls during our meetings. Maybe one of them was Gus Hall, whose father was one of the strikers then. And there were dark-eyed Italian children, trying to be friends. The young people, so fair and so dark, were now dancing together on Saturday nights. The Italian young men had complained to me that the Finnish girls didn't dance with them, until we persuaded the girls and their Finnish boy friends that solidarity required more socializing. The Finns, whom I met there for the first time, are a wonderful people. So quiet and reserved that, as Debs said: "They never applaud. You only know they like what you say if they come back the next time." They are one people among whom the women are truly equal, participating in plays, meetings and all affairs, side by side with their menfolk, an example for all others.

We set up a defense office in the Finnish Opera House in Virginia and Joe Ettor and I remained to carry on the defense of those in jail. However, we found no such enthusiasm or will to action in support of the prisoners as there had been in Lawrence four years before, after a real victory. Ettor and I both spoke up and down the Range, again and again. Ugly rumors had been spread that it was not a strike arrest but a bootlegging fracas that occurred at the Masonovich house. I traveled as far as New York City and back several times. Fred was now six years old and I welcomed those trips so I could spend a few days with him. He looked upon Carlo as a father and would ask when he was coming home, too. I promised, as mothers do in these situations: "Soon, very soon."

Our big job was to create interest and collect funds to hire lawyers. We had a splendid local lawyer in the person of John Keyes of Duluth, who had worn himself out defending dozens of strikers, month in and month out, during the strike. He was greatly respected in local legal and labor circles. We added Arthur Le Sueur, a well-known midwest Socialist, father of the present-day writer, Meridel Le Sueur, and Judge O. N. Hilton, who had defended Joe Hill in the last days and had been general counsel of the Western Federation of Miners for many years. I had met St. John on one of my trips and he told me Joe and I could get the judge if we asked him directly, but not through Chicago. This aggravated our relations with Haywood, who had decided to send an unknown local Chicago lawyer to the Range. He insisted Ettor confine his attention to defense and not "interfere" with organizers he sent up there. It was a very unpleasant situation. Ettor and I suggested we step out and turn the defense over to some other IWW organizers. But the men in jail insisted we remain there. For their sakes, we did.

Unfortunately, we were caught in the middle of several conflicting currents within the organization. Friction developed between Joe Ettor and Bill Haywood, until at one time early in 1916 Joe sent in his resignation as general organizer. From the extreme of anarchistic decentralization, from which the IWW had long suffered, Haywood began now to develop a degree of bureaucratic centralism that was equally dangerous. He rented a three-story building at 1001 West Madison Street, bought an expensive printing outfit, and proceeded to move all the IWW papers to Chicago. These included *Solidarity,* the English paper then in Cleveland, and 13 language papers from all over the country, regardless of national composition or the support they had in the communities where they were located or the opinions of the staffs, several of whom quit in consequence. He attempted to move some of the industrial unions as well, but there was much protest by those who felt they belonged in the areas where the industries predominated and who felt that this was a dangerous tendency at that particular time. It was a mistake to put all our eggs in one basket for the government to scoop up at one blow, which was just what happened after war was declared in 1917. Ettor had not been consulted on any of these grandiose plans nor given information on those given credentials as organizers or made editors of papers. St. John, who might have acted as peacemaker, was now far away, completely out of all IWW activities.

In late December 1916 the lawyers called us to Duluth for a conference. They arranged it in a large room in the courthouse, with all the defendants present. We knew they had been holding pre-trial conferences with the state's attorney but their proposal was a complete surprise to all of us. It was that three of the four Montenegrin defendants should plead guilty to manslaughter and serve one to three years; the woman and one of the workers were to be dismissed unconditionally and the three organizers were to be set free without trial. "You mean my wife will not go to prison?" Phillip Masonovich asked incredulously and with great joy. He shook hands with Tresca and patted him on the back, saying: "Carlo, you go out and do more good work." Each of the four insisted another go out and he remain. It was left to them to decide who was to be freed. It was not strange that they so readily greeted the idea with satisfaction since they had resigned themselves to the fate of life imprisonment for all concerned.

The organizers demanded further explanation from the lawyers, who said the state was willing to agree to this in view of the fact that the strike was over and they did not want to enter into a series of long and expensive trials. But since two men had been actually killed in the fracas, and it was agreed by all witnesses that the woman and one man were inside the house and could not have been involved in the actual shooting, this was the best they could propose. If the proposal was rejected they would proceed to try the Montenegrin workers first and felt sure they could get a verdict of guilty from a handpicked, English-speaking, middle-class jury in that area. We had no illusions on this score. We knew they could. Mr. Keyes felt confident he could secure their release by the Parole Board at the end of one year. The defendants discussed it alone and decided to accept. All present concurred. It was a Solomon's decision. We all believed we were doing the very best for all concerned. Then everything started to happen.

The next day in court the judge sentenced the three workers to five to twenty years for manslaughter. The organizers protested: "This was not the agreement." We were stunned. The lawyers insisted: "It's all right; it was agreed; they will get out before the three years are up." Mr. Keyes, who was the one we most depended upon to see us through, died of pneumonia within a few weeks. The prosecutor went to France in World War I and his successor denied any knowledge of the agreement. Haywood blasted us publicly without even waiting for our explanations, which complicated the problem. We put some money in a local relief fund for Mrs. Masonovich and her family for one year and $2,000 in a trust fund to carry on further legal efforts for their release, and for further relief to the family if necessary. We sent a lawyer before the parole board twice.

Considering that it was wartime, with ferocious attacks then being made on the IWW, plus our later arrests and other obstacles (which even involved the bank holding up the funds temporarily because they were "IWW"), it was a great relief to all of us concerned when these heroic workers were finally freed, just a little over three years after their imprisonment. The whole episode terminated the official relations of Ettor and Tresca with the IWW. I stuck for a while longer, determined to prove to my fellow-workers that my loyalty and devotion could not be shaken by my relations with Haywood. But it wasn't easy, and became increasingly difficult in the next few years after 1916.

SIX

World War I and its Aftermath

◆◆◆◆◆◆◆◆◆◆◆◆◆◆◆◆

THE MOONEY FRAME-UP

Developments on the labor front in other parts of the country had weighed heavily with all of the IWW organizers involved in accepting the settlement of the case on the Mesabi Range. Foremost was the Mooney-Billings case, as it came to be known later—a notorious frame-up exceeding anything that the employers had attempted since 1886. When we came to our decision in Minnesota, four men and a woman were in jail in San Francisco charged with murder. This grew out of the anti-labor, open-shop "Preparedness Parade" on July 22, 1916, when an explosion caused the death of ten people and injured many others. The ones arrested were my friend, Tom Mooney and his wife Rena; Warren Billings, who had been president of a Shoe Workers Union and active in various strikes; Edward D. Nolan of the International Association of Machinists; and Israel Weinberg, a member of the executive board of the Jitney Operators Union. ("Jitneys," a nickname for nickels, were automobiles carrying passengers along regular routes for a five-cent fare. They were forerunners of buses and popular competitors to the streetcar system, which finally succeeded in outlawing them.)

At the time of which I write, December 1916, one prisoner, Warren K. Billings, had already been convicted and sentenced to life imprisonment in Folsom Penitentiary on one indictment. Others were held over him. Tom Mooney was facing trial in January 1917, under indictment for eight murder charges. That was the number of victims who had died up to the date of the Grand Jury hearing. A spirit of mob hysteria had been created in the area by the prosecution. But a bold, fearless and able defender appeared for Tom Mooney and the others—Robert Minor, a great artist and valiant fighter for human rights.

At this time, Minor, who was then 32 years old, was well known as a cartoonist and political writer. Born in Texas in 1884, he had worked as a painter, carpenter and railroad worker before he became one of the most famed and talented cartoonists in America, employed on the St. Louis *Post Dispatch* and the New York *World*. He was fired for making cover designs for Emma Goldman's monthly, *Mother Earth*. He was a member of the central committee of the Socialist Party in St. Louis in 1910 and a member of the Press Writers Union. When Mooney and his co-workers were arrested Minor plunged fearlessly into their defense. He aided in the organization of the International Workers Defense League of San Francisco in 1916, and became its publicity director. He wrote the first two pamphlets on this case and worked tirelessly to bring their cause before the American labor movement.

He was finally able, with the assistance of a young New Jersey Lawyer, Leon Josephson, to persuade John McDonald, a star witness, to confess his perjury and his dealings with the prosecution. But this was later, in the 1920s. At the period of which I write, Bob Minor was engaged in organizing protest meetings, speaking to labor unions and labor conventions, exposing the frame-up, piece by piece, as new revelations of perjury came to light. He was a tower of strength in saving the lives of Mooney and his comrades. Out of this experience, Minor became one of the most skillful strategists and one of the most able organizers of labor defense cases.

His pamphlet revealed the first bold outlines of the frame-up—the attempts by detective Martin Swanson, employed by the United States Railways, to bribe both Billings and Weinberg to testify against Mooney; and the fact, provable by the famous accidental photograph of a street clock, that Tom and Rena Mooney were watching the parade a mile and a quarter away from the scene of the crime at the precise moment he was supposed to be at the scene with the bomb. It exposed the professional jury system under which Billings had been convicted in September 1916 by 12 old men, hangers-on around the courtroom, some of whom had sat on juries for nine years at $2 per day. Afterwards they said they had sent the young man to prison for life on the chance that he might "help find the guilty parties." Eight of the 12 had no other occupation than serving on juries. The Billings case, however, ended this shocking system.

Labor slowly rallied to the defense as the frame-up began to be exposed. In opening the case, Assistant Prosecutor James Brennon shouted: "This is a labor union conspiracy." The San Francisco Building Trades Council, the California State Federation of Labor, and the Chicago Federation of Labor denounced the conviction of Billings as a hideous miscarriage of justice. The characters of the most important witnesses against Billings were revealed in Minor's pamphlet as underworld figures and perjurers, bought and paid for. Later, the whole frame-up fell apart like a house of cards. But as I have said, it was made to stick in the Mooney trial, bolstered by two star witnesses—a so-called "honest old cattleman from Oregon," Frank Oxman; and John McDonald, who purported to be an eyewitness to the presence of Mooney and Billings at the crime scene. Mooney was found guilty and on February 24 he was sentenced to be hanged on May 17, 1917. Thirty Bay City labor bodies, including the San Francisco Labor Council, on a motion of the Machinists, in February 1917 belatedly affirmed their belief in the innocence of Mooney and branded the case a "trumped-up charge on the most brazen and contradictory evidence."

Before the year 1917 was over, Oxman was exposed as a "suborner of perjury," because not only had he lied but he had attempted to persuade a friend of his to do likewise. As a result, Mrs. Mooney and Israel Weinberg were both acquitted by juries and Nolan was never brought to trial. The execution of Mooney was delayed and finally, in 1918, commuted by the governor to life imprisonment. This followed mass demonstrations throughout the world, particularly in Russia after the revolution. It followed the report of a Mediation Commission sent in by President Wilson—headed by the Secretary of Labor and Professor Felix Frankfurter—which said the Commission lacked confidence in the justice of the conviction due to "the dubious character of the witnesses," and pointed out that "when Oxman was discredited, the verdict against Mooney was discredited." President Wilson thereupon urged postponment of the execution and a new trial for Mooney. The new trial was denied.

Although we were isolated in the northern section of Minnesota and unable to confer with others, we felt the terrible seriousness of the Mooney case and the necessity to smash this vicious and ugly plot against all organized labor to send four labor men and women to the gallows. For us it took priority over all other struggles. Little did we realize it would be a 23-year struggle until Mooney and Billings were free men again!

Undoubtedly, I would have plunged immediately into the Eastern agitation over the Mooney case had not another call come to me after my return home. Christmas was approaching and I wanted so much to be at home with my son. I was exhausted after the long, gruelling six months in Minnesota. The physical and emotional strain was very great. When we got back to 511 East 134 Street in the Bronx and opened the street door to go upstairs, my son Fred stood on the stairs with a loaf of bread in one hand and a can of condensed milk in the other. He was going on seven years old, curly-haired but thin for his age. He looked at us in amazement, then dropped the groceries and shouted: "Oh! Carlo! Carlo!" and jumped into Carlo's arms. He had seen me quite regularly during the year, so my greeting could be deferred. All the anxiety pent up during Carlo's long imprisonment was now released and he was very happy. He ran upstairs to call my mother: "Mama! Mama! Carlo and my mother are here!"

It was always a great joy to come home and a terrible tug on my heart strings when I had to leave again. Fred was now a frail child with a tendency to a bronchial condition, which worried me a great deal. This time, once we were reunited, I planned to stay home for quite a while and so assured my son and Carlo and all the rest of the family.

The holidays passed pleasantly enough, with Mama cooking a big turkey and pumpkin pies and Carlo cooking his famous spaghetti and preparing a marvelous antipasto to go with his gallon of wine. Fred hung up his stocking as usual, although his faith in Santa was wavering. It was a standing joke which amused me greatly to find a piece of coal and a cake of soap in the bottom of the stocking—under the little gifts. And then, around New Years I was confronted with one of the hardest decisions I ever had to make, one which caused me a lot of heartaches.

THE EVERETT MASSACRE

I received a telegram from Seattle, signed "Everett Prisoners' Defense Committee," urging me to come out there to speak and help raise funds. Another factor which had weighed heavily with us in trying to bring the Mesabi Range case to a quick and satisfactory conclusion was the very serious struggle which the IWW faced in the Northwest. As a result of the Everett massacre on November 5, 1916, over 100 members of the organization were in jail in Seattle, charged with murder. I was no longer needed on the Mesabi Range. Joe Ettor planned to return there for a few weeks to have the books of the defense committee audited by the local union, to set up a relief and trust fund to which I have referred and then close up the defense office. Joe had said definitely he was through. His father had died, leaving him about $10,000, which started Joe in the wine business in California. Carlo had returned to the editorship of his newspaper, which was his personal organ, and a pleasant round of festive occasions started among his Italian friends and readers to celebrate his release.

I wanted to remain with the IWW, though Haywood and I were completely at odds by now. In fact, he protested aginst the organization inviting me to the Northwest. This contributed to making me all the more determined to go. Carlo was shocked and amazed that I would even consider leaving him after he had been in jail since July. "But you are out now," I protested, "and all these men are in jail!" I felt I was right, hard as it was to go. I had never yet heard of a "professional revolutionist," but this was a real test of my devotion to my principles and I tried hard to meet it. Carlo was so angry that he did not write to me for six weeks after I arrived in Seattle. But my mother and my sister Kathie both sympathized with my problem and wrote me regularly, so I had news of Fred. I suffered a great deal from loneliness and worry.

Fred Moore (from Spokane and Lawrence) and Charles Ashleigh, with whom I had worked in 1914 in the New York unemployed movement, were there. Both were close friends of mine and understood I was having a bad time. Caroline Lowe, a Socialist woman lawyer, was busy on the case. My old friend, Edith Frenette who had been with me in Missoula in 1909 before Fred was born, lived in a small hotel up a hill on a side street in Seattle. I moved into the same place. She was helping to organize the defense and was an important witness. She had been arrested innumerable times during the prolonged struggle in Everett and gave me a graphic eyewitness account of the events of November 5 and before.

Dr. Marie D. Equi, my friend from Portland, came over to help. I went with her to see the men in jail and the wounded at the hospital. It made me feel a lot better—and ashamed of my doubts and misgivings about coming—when I heard their welcoming shouts of greeting to "Doc" and "Gurley." Harry Golden, a youth of 22, was lying there in a high fever from a festering leg wound. On Dr. Equi's demand, he was removed immediately to a private hospital, but only an amputation saved his life. He had come to this country at 16 from Poland, seeking "liberty." Now, six years later, he was a cripple. He had been shot on November 5.

It was on Sunday when the Everett massacre happened. A simple flyer had been distributed in Everett, calling for an IWW open-air meeting at 2 p.m. at Hewett and Westmore Streets. It said: "Come and help maintain your own and our Constitutional privileges." This was part of the prewar campaign of the IWW to organize the lumber industry, which centered there. The Shingle Weavers Union, not IWW but an independent union, had carried on a successful strike in the Northwest. Only one mill, the Jameson Mill, held out. The IWW cooperated on the picket line and through their street meetings which had not been molested up to August 1916. Then a reign of terror, led by drunken Sheriff McRae and an employers' outfit, the Commercial Club, was let loose on Everett. Meetings were broken up, speakers arrested and beaten. Roads were guarded by deputy sheriffs against IWW entering the city. Groups of IWWs were deported out of the city, in a condition which sent many to the hospitals with broken limbs and internal injuries. Citizens of Everett rallied against these outrages and held one meeting in September. Over 2,000 people came to the public park to hear James P. Thompson of the IWW speak.

On November 5, 1916, a delegation of 250 IWWs left Seattle for Everett on a regular passenger boat, the *Verona*. The overflow, and many regular passengers, took another boat, the *Calista*. The Everett authorities were tipped off by two Pinkerton detectives who were stool pigeon passengers on the *Verona,* pretending to be IWWs. As it proceeded, one of them raised his hand in a signal and the little boat was ambushed from three sides in a deadly fusillade from the dock and the adjoining piers. It listed and some men fell overboard. It then backed out into the stream and, bullet-scarred and bloody, with a grim load of dead, dying and wounded men, returned to Seattle. En route they warned the *Calista* to turn back.

The known IWW death toll was five—Felix Baron, Hugo Gerlot, Gustav Johnson, John Looney and Abraham Rabinowitz. They were French, German, Swedish, Irish and Russian-Jewish. Two bodies were later found on a nearby beach and six who were checked onto the *Verona* were missing, probably wounded and swept overboard. When the two boats docked in Seattle, 38 IWWs were arrested from the *Calista* and 236 from the *Verona*. The men arrested were surprisingly young. Thirty were severely wounded. A passenger, not an IWW, was shot nine times and one of the Pinkerton stool pigeons had a scalp wound. In Everett there were two dead, C. O. Curtis, an office manager of the Canyon Lumber Company, who was armed and shooting at the boat, and Jefferson Beard, a deputy sheriff. About 16 were injured, including Sheriff McCrae. They were hooted and jeered at by Everett citizens as they were taken to the hospital.

Mayor Gill of Seattle, who was criticized in the Everett and Seattle papers for allowing the IWW to board the two boats, replied heatedly: "In the final analysis it will be found these cowards in Everett, who without right or justification shot into a crowd on the boat, were a bunch of cowards. They outnumbered the IWWs five to one and in spite of this they stood there on the dock and fired into the boat—IWWs, innocent passengers and all. McRae and his deputies had no legal right to tell the IWWs or anyone else that they could not land there." Efforts to start a recall movement against Mayor McGill fell flat. He ordered that decent food, blankets and tobacco be furnished to the IWWs in the city jail.

Tom Tracy Aquitted

Nine days after the arrests, all but 74 men were released. These were charged with the murder of Jefferson Beard and C. O. Curtis. They had been picked out by the two Pinkertons. The prisoners were secretly taken out of the jail, heavily handcuffed and taken to the Snohomish County jail in Everett. The others were released quietly in small groups, in an effort to avoid public interest. Thirty-eight IWWs, taken from the *Calista,* were charged with unlawful assemblage.

Conditions in the Everett jail under Sheriff McCrae were frightful, and only a little better after January 8, 1917, when a new Sheriff, McCullogh, took over. The IWWs cleaned the place from top to bottom and finally gained food demands, blankets, etc., by "battleship" methods—literally hammering the jail apart. Committees of women were allowed to bring cooked food to the prisoners in Seattle and later in Everett. I was at one of the "banquets" served on tables set the full length of the jail corridor—a full meal topped off with cigars and flowers. Finally, as the date of trial drew near, Judge Ronald from Seattle was appointed by the governor for the trial, and on January 26 a change of venue was granted on the ground of prejudice in Snohomish County. The trial was moved to Seattle. This was a real victory. On March 5 the first defendant, Thomas H. Tracy, was brought to trial in the King County Courthouse.

Meanwhile, I had spoken in every city and hamlet in King County and vicinity and in many throughout the state—as far north as Bellingham and Port Angeles, west to Gray's Harbor, east to Spokane and south to Vancouver and Portland, Oregon. One of the most impressive meetings at which I spoke was held in Everett during the month of February, on a Sunday afteroon in a large hall. I said in opening: "We are here this afternoon to present to you the workers' side of the Everett situation." I spoke of it as "a segment, a miniature of what labor is enduring everywhere, all the time," and instanced the women and men shot and killed in the year 1916 in Bayonne, New Jersey, Standard Oil Company stronghold, "where the Statue of Liberty out in the bay casts her gleaming light into the very windows of the workers' homes," and where gunmen shot a young Polish girl through the forehead as she was looking out the window, killing her instantly. A worker, not a striker, who ran in fear had 42 bullets shot into his fleeing body. I spoke of those beaten, shot, arrested on the Mesabi Range. I spoke of what I had seen in Lawrence and finally of what had happened right here in Everett. The working-class audience listened attentively, with profound sympathy and then gave a large collection for the defense.

Wherever I spoke the reaction of the people was the same, especially in labor circles. We told the story of what had really happened—the deputies had killed their own men in the crossfire. Because this was true, the murder charge against the IWWs involving Curtis' death was dropped after the body of Curtis was exhumed and examined. In the course of my work on this case I sometimes had an escort, as a sort of bodyguard, although I had no trouble anywhere. One was a tall, lean, young lumberjack, who was greatly embarrassed at this assignment, "riding the cushions with a lady organizer." He wouldn't talk, and finally in desperation, I looked out the car window at the majestic Olympic Mountains in the distance and remarked: "The scenery around here is certainly beautiful." He answered me laconically: "Can't enjoy the scenery under the capitalist system!" I had an amusing experience with another escort—this time self-appointed, a wiry little fellow who carried my suitcase to the train in Spokane. Next morning when I got off at Seattle, there he was waiting to carry the suitcase. When I asked in surprise: "How did you get here?" he laughed and said: "Rode the rods, Gurley." He followed me to Portland and several other places in a similar manner, bobbing up smiling to meet me and carry my bag.

I made a trip to California in the Spring of 1917 to speak at the State Building Trades Convention, which was held at Marysville. This sleepy little town was where Ford and Suhr had been tried three years before. Minor was there, representing the Mooney defense. A most repulsive misleader of labor, P. H. McCarthy, was chairman of the convention. Our friends there, including Anton Johannsen, had to fight to get us the floor, but they succeeded and the delegates gave both of us a rousing welcome and passed resolutions supporting our appeal.

I went on to San Francisco and spoke with George Speed at an IWW meeting for Mooney's defense. This meeting was held at the Moose Temple and was one of the first public gatherings held in San Francisco in defense of Mooney and Billings. I went to see them in jail where they were held pending court proceedings. Billings was very young-looking, red-haired and spirited. Tom looked much older and paler than the rosy-cheeked youth I had met in Idaho eight years before, but was full of fighting spirit. At his request I went to see his mother and met his devoted brother John. I also went to see Rena Mooney who was in a women's jail far out of the city—a long trolley-car ride across flat marsh country. I could not persuade any women I knew in San Francisco to accompany me, so great was the terror of being connected with this case. She had pleaded with the authorities for a piano—she could keep occupied and soothe and entertain all the miserable inmates if she had her beloved piano. But they ridiculed the idea. So she was very restless and unhappy and worried about Tom when I arrived. She was both surprised and glad to see me but shocked that I had been allowed to come alone.

I returned to Seattle. I did not attend the two-month trial but continued to travel around the state and speak on the case. War was declared while the trial was going on—in April 1917—less than six months after Woodrow Wilson had been reelected on the slogan, "He kept us out of war!" The IWW had been carrying on a steady organizational campaign in the lumber and copper mining industries. Long before the declaration of war, the IWW had announced their demands for an eight-hour day in both industries. Aside from general declarations against war, the IWW had concentrated on the struggle for the right to organize and for shorter hours and better job conditions. It was in this connection that May Day was celebrated by the Seattle IWW in 1917. Strangely enough, the women on the Tracy jury, of which there were six, had decorated the courtroom with green flowering branches. Some of us (eternal optimists!) dared to take it for a good augury in the case. We held a memorial at the graves of those who had been killed on the *Verona*. Then the crowd returned to surround the city jail and sing songs from *The Little Red Song Book,* which were answered with other songs from inside the walls.

In the evening a great mass meeting was held at which Mrs. Kate Sadler, a local Socialist and a wonderful speaker, spoke with me. She had been at the St. Louis Convention of the Socialist Party held April 7, 1917, one day after war was declared. There, a resolution on war was passed, which read as follows: "The Socialist Party of the United States in the present grave crisis, solemnly re-affirms its allegiance to the principle of internationalism and working-class solidarity the world over, and proclaims its unalterable opposition to the war just declared by the Government of the United States." Mrs. Sadler spoke along this line and in this spirit. We of the IWW, as I recall, spoke more specifically of the class struggle in the United States, which we considered our main concern.

The trial drew to a close. I went to speak at Cle Elum, a mining area where there were a large number of Italians who knew me from the East. It was agreed I was to proceed homeward from there. What was my joy to receive a wire on the train on May 5 from Herbert Mahler, Secretary of the Defense Committee, that Tom Tracy had been acquitted and expressing appreciation for my work. (All the other cases were dismissed and all prisoners freed.) The railroad conductor who delivered it to me said: "Well, it must be good news. You look so pleased." I told him what it was. He looked astounded and then asked, probably thinking I was a relative of Tracy: "What's your interest in it?" He would not believe I was an IWW organizer. He said they always rode the rods, not the cushions.

ARRESTED FOR VAGRANCY

On my way home from Seattle, I stopped at Chicago and visited the IWW headquarters. This was the last time I was there. I remarked at an informal meeting with the editors and others that I thought certain IWW pamphlets should be revised and some should be taken out of circulation. The reasons I gave were valid; loose phrases or bad formulations like "Right or wrong does not concern us!" in St. John's pamphlet, taken out of context, were misleading and could easily be distorted. I had seen in Seattle how they could be used in trials against our members, and I said I was going to request the general executive board not to reprint my pamphlet on "sabotage."

The new orientation of the IWW toward job organization and mass action and away from individual action, like sabotage, I felt was correct. I no longer agreed with the contents of the pamphlet and felt it had served its purpose to defend Boyd, arrested in Paterson four years before. "Why put ammunition in the hands of the enemy?" I asked. After the discussion, Haywood, in an unfriendly tone, said: "What's the matter, Gurley? Are you losing your nerve?" He ordered a new edition printed with a lurid cover, designed by Ralph Chaplin, of black cats and wooden shoes. But the executive board stepped in and ordered that it should not be published. Other pamphlets were later either discarded or reedited to fit the new position of the organization, which was becoming more and more a labor union setup.

When I came home to our crowded way of life in the Bronx flat, I felt ashamed of the burden my mother carried so uncomplainingly and I decided I must stay home a while and relieve her. Carlo was showing the reaction from his imprisonment and the hectic pace he had kept up since his release. I was really tired after ten years of continuous intensive activity and the nervous strain of strikes and trials. In spite of a state of war in the world, I longed for a quiet and peaceful summer with my loved ones. Carlo had some Italian friends who lived at South Beach, Staten Island. We decided to take a small bungalow there and all try to rest, relax and recuperate. We found one in a pleasant camp, on top of a green hill with beautiful trees looking out over the Lower Bay, opposite Coney Island. We could see all the ocean liners, freighters, troop ships. It was a thrilling sight to see the great ship of that day, the *Leviathan,* come into view. The camp had its own beach and in no time Fred began to flourish and became an excellent swimmer.

Most of the people around us were Italian workers, nice friendly people who feasted on spaghetti and wine out under the trees. We joined them. I began to put on weight at that time. Italian food was my nemesis. Next door were two brothers and their families, German acrobats who practiced their stunts in the back yard. The owner of the place was Irish-American, a strong nationalist who was delighted to meet Nora Connolly, the daughter of James Connolly, James Larkin and other Irish who visited us. We went there every summer in late June and stayed until mid-September for nine years through 1925, when Carlo and I separated. Staten Island is a large and beautiful island in New York Harbor, facing both the lower and upper bays. Then it was even more inaccessible than today, as there were no bridges. The ferry ride of about 20 minutes past the Statue of Liberty was pleasant. The cares of the city seemed to fall away on this trip. I stayed home with Fred, cooked and did a little gardening, went in the water daily and had a real vacation for the first time in my life. The family came and went as they liked and we all enjoyed it immensely. But there were bound to be interruptions in our kind of life.

There came an invitation to me from the Mesabi Range for the big annual picnic of the Finnish Socialists in July, when workers came from all over the mining area and from the lumber camps. If it had been from anywhere else in the country I probably would have refused. But my heart was enlisted in that area and I felt a responsibility to it. Over the protest of Carlo and my family, off I went again. I consoled myself that it should only take a few days of travel up and back, and one day to speak. I decided not to stop in Chicago, to save time and to avoid further friction with Big Bill. I really loved and respected Bill Haywood and hated to fight with him.

When I arrived in Duluth I went to the Holland Hotel where I had stayed innumerable times the year before, during the strike and after. The clerks welcomed me. I went a couple of blocks to the local IWW hall and found they were worried about my coming back to the Range; they thought the Finns should not have asked me to come. They were planning to take me there by car right away so I could stay safely in Virginia in somebody's home until the meeting hour at the picnic. The hot breath of war hysteria was in the air. They said there was a lot of agitation against the IWW and if I were questioned I should make it clear I had come for the Socialist picnic which had been a respected annual event there for many years.

I returned to the hotel to check out, but almost immediately Sheriff Meining and a couple of federal men came to interview me about my plans, especially how long I was staying. This was seven years before

J. Edgar Hoover headed the FBI and they were not as well publicized then as they became later. In fact, we identified GM as they were then called, more with enforcing the Mann Act than with any other activity. Later, prohibition became their special job. They asked me if I was going to advise anyone to evade the draft. I assured them I was not and that my visit was limited to this picnic. They left, apparently satisfied.

But while they were there—and probably with their knowledge— the City Council of Duluth was holding a special meeting at which they passed a so-called wartime emergency ordinance to the effect that anyone in the city who did not have a visible means of support could be arrested for "vagrancy." Within a few minutes the police raided the IWW hall and arrested everyone there. A couple of them came to the hotel and arrested me, much to the surprise of the hotel people. This was on a Saturday. The picnic was to take place Sunday. We were held over the weekend in a jail overlooking beautiful Lake Superior. We were refused bail, and after the picnic was over I was released on condition I leave town. I had nothing else to do. My speaking date was ruined and I returned home. Later, Scott Nearing went there to speak at a Socialist peace meeting and the same thing happened to him. A month later the Duluth IWW office was wrecked by a mob of soldiers. I returned to the Range a few years later to speak in defense of Sacco and Vanzetti and had no trouble.

"Safe for Democracy"

After war was declared a mounting wave of hysteria and mob violence swept the country. It was not shared by the vast majority of American people who became increasingly intimidated. Printed signs were tacked up in public places: "Obey the law and keep your mouth shut!" signed by Attorney General Gregory. The victims of mob violence were varied—Christian ministers, Negro and white, advocates of peace on religious, moral or political grounds; Socialists, IWWs, members of the Non-Partisan League, which was strong among farmers in the Middle West; friends of Irish freedom, and others. Some individuals, both men and women, who made chance remarks on war, conscription or the sale of bonds were tarred and feathered, beaten sometimes to insensibility, forced to kiss the flag, driven out of town, forced to buy bonds, threatened with lynching.

In mob raids on halls, newspapers, headquarters of organizations and printing plants, uniformed soldiers took part without rebuke from the government. Inoffensive Germans, residents of this country for years, parents of American-born children, were suspected as potential "spies" and attacked merely for being German, even though they said or did nothing. This spirit of mob violence was one of the most dangerous and shameful manifestations in our country, all in the name of making the world "Safe for Democracy." From April 1917, to March 1919, the American Civil Liberties Bureau listed nearly 500 such acts of mob violence against individuals. Undoubtedly there were many more which were not recorded.

The IWW had long planned a struggle for the eight-hour day in the lumber industry and for the end of notorious abuses, both there and in the copper industry. The price of copper and lumber went up with the war demand, but accidents and speedup increased on the jobs. The cost of living soared skyward. Among the miners, a blacklist system prevailed, known as "the rustling card." All over the country the IWW became increasingly the main target of mob violence. Its organizers were beaten, tarred and feathered, and deported. Its halls were attacked and wrecked in Oakland, Seattle, Yakima, Aberdeen, Duluth and other places. The press screamed "German gold" at the IWW. The government did nothing to repress violence, which was spread on a mass scale by the employers whose fat war profits were threatened by the demands of the workers exploited in their industries. Some 50,000 lumber workers in the Northwest and 40,000 copper miners in Montana, Arizona and New Mexico were on strike at one time during 1917, under the leadership of the IWW. That it was effective as a union in wartime was the real reason for the ferocious attacks on the organization.

On June 8, 1917, a fire broke out in the Speculator mine in Butte, Montana. One hundred and seventy-eight men were burned to death 2,400 feet below the surface of the earth. A sympathetic strike was called by an independent union. Among the demands was union supervision of safety appliances. Meanwhile the speedup practices and the blacklist system had caused a strike in Jerome, Arizona. On July 10, 1917, 80 copper miners involved in this struggle were loaded in cattle cars and deported to California by gunmen of the United Vedde Copper Company. They were turned back at the California state line and lodged in jail in Prescott.

On July 12, 1917, in Bisbee, Arizona, 1,200 striking miners were rounded up by 2,000 armed gunmen masquerading as a Loyalty League, organized by the Phelps Dodge Corporation. At the point of machine guns they were locked into cattle cars, filthy with manure, with only a little water and taken into the state of New Mexico and left in the hot desert. After 48 hours without food, U.S. troops at Columbus, New Mexico, gave shelter and food. They were held there and not allowed to return to their homes for three months. When the government discontinued rations in September, 300 Mexicans returned to Mexico, and 600 other strikers returned to Bisbee where the majority were again driven out of town. Finally, a settlement of a sort was made by the U. S. Labor Commission. An increase in wages was granted in Butte but the miners held out until December in an attempt to abolish the "rustling card" system.

In the Northwest, the demands of the lumberjacks were finally realized. The Washington Lumbermen's Association granted the eight-hour day on January 1, 1918. In Oregon, Colonel Disque, supervising all lumber production in the Northwest for the U. S. Government, after a conference in Washington, D. C., declared an eight-hour day in the lumber industry. A government-sponsored company union was set up to counteract the IWW, called the Four L's (Loyal Legion of Loggers and Lumberjacks).

Not only in the lumber and copper industry but also in the oil industry the IWW was on the job organizing workers, especially in Oklahoma. Their work centered in Tulsa. Tulsa businessmen organized the Knights of Liberty, which countered with a campaign of terrorism. Posters appeared: "Mr. I. W. W. Don't Let the Sun Shine on You in Tulsa," which were signed "Vigilance Committee." On November 5, 1917, eleven men were arrested and charged with vagrancy. The case ended with the judge stating: "You are not guilty. But I will fine you $100. These are no ordinary times." The men were taken out of their cells by a masked mob, away from the police, who made no resistance, and their hands tied. They were whipped, tarred and feathered, "in the name of the women and children of Belgium." The police were furnished with masks and clubs to participate in the outrage. Both local newspapers, the Tulsa *Daily World* and the Tulsa *Democrat,* approved the mob's action. More than $500 in currency belonging to the victims was burned when the mob set fire to their clothing.

Our summer at the beach became increasingly unhappy as so much horrible news poured in from all over the country. But the worst trage-dy—striking home most sharply, causing us the greatest personal grief —occurred on August 1, 1917. I was cooking supper the day after it happened. My young brother Tom and a friend of his, a German-American youth who lived across the street from us in the Bronx, had spent the day at the beach. Johnny had just been drafted and he had come down to say goodbye to all of us. Carlo came home with the day's papers. There was no radio in every room in those days. He said: "Elizabeth, I have bad news for you. Frank was killed yesterday in Butte." "You mean Frank Little?" I asked. "Yes," he said, "he was lynched."

Frank Little Lynched

When Carlo told me the terrible news I left the stove, sat down and began to cry. Our friend Johnny, soon to be in uniform, asked in sur-prise: "What's wrong?" As Carlo told us the horrible details—of how six masked men came to the hotel at night, broke down the door, dragged Frank from his bed, took him to a railroad trestle on the out-skirts of the town and there hanged him—this simple working-class youth said sorrowfully: "So that's what I'm going to fight for?"

Frank Little had been with us in the Mesabi Range in 1916, in jail with Carlo. Before that I had known him both in Missoula and in Spo-kane in 1909 and 1910. He was tall and dark, with black hair and black eyes, a slender, gentle and soft-spoken man. His one eye gave him a misleadingly sinister appearance. He was part Indian and spoke of himself as "a real American" and "a real Red." "The rest of you are immigrants," he said. He was dependable in all situations. He had been in Arizona when the miners were on strike and had an automo-bile accident there in which one leg was broken.

He came to Chicago for an executive board meeting on crutches, with the leg in a cast. When he announced he was going to Butte, some of his fellow-workers tried to dissuade him. They knew Butte was a rough and tumble place and were fearful he could not take care of himself in his crippled condition. But he went and made several fiery speeches to the miners. When his dead body was found, it had a card pinned to it with the names of several men prominent among the striking miners and electrical workers, with a threat: "First and Last Warning 3-7-77." The numbers were those of a grave measurement.

Frank Little was the first friend of mine to meet such a dreadful, violent death. Whenever I visited Butte in later years I went to his grave out in the flats. It is adorned by a stone erected by the workers of Butte, surrounded by the graves of copper miners, victims also of greed and violence in the copper city. On the day of his funeral, the largest ever seen in Montana, the line of the procession of marching thousands covered the entire horizon. Many grim-faced and sorrowing workers asked, with our friend Johnny: "Is this what we are fighting for?" The following month in Chicago, a 61-page federal indictment charged 168 men and women with conspiring *with one Frank Little, now deceased,* to hinder and delay the execution of certain laws of the United States." Even in death they did not let him rest in peace.

Fall came and we were just as well satisfied to return to the city, not knowing what to expect but realizing anything could happen in the prevailing political climate. We were anxious to have Fred back home with the family and in school. He had started the year before. But he had been sick with an attack of appendicitis. There had been a widespread epidemic of infantile paralysis in 1916, and my mother and sister Kathie kept him out of school. We lived on the top floor and during the summer of that year, while I was away in Minnesota, he had played on the roof and was kept off the streets. After the summer at the beach, he was sunburned and had gained weight. He was fortified to tackle school again. He entered P. S. 43 on Brown Place and 135th Street. Then things began to happen.

On September 29, 1917, Carlo and I were arrested on the Chicago indictment of 168 persons. I was the only woman named. Ben Fletcher of Philadelphia was the only Negro. The local cop on our corner for many years, Harry Hand, had been promoted. But because we had known him since we were children, he came with two federal men to identify and arrest me. He apologized to my mother: "I haven't got anything to do with it, Mrs. Flynn." They asked, seeing some Irish literature, "Is your daughter a Sinn Fein too?" My mother answered proudly, "No, I'm the Sinn Fein here!" Fred, who was playing on the street, came running to me, disturbed by the presence of the three strange men. I said: "It's all right, dear, I have to go to a meeting. You go upstairs to Mama." We went to the 134th Street Elevated Station, and while we were waiting on the double platform for a train, Carlo got off on the uptown side. I tried to ignore him and to shoo him off. But he rushed up to me and asked what was wrong. Harry Hand said to the Federal men: "This is Carlo Tresca," so they arrested him.

They took us to the City Hall station and then to the nearby offices of the Department of Justice for questioning. But we refused to talk until we secured a lawyer, so we were taken to the Tombs which was within walking distance. It was a Saturday and we were locked up over Sunday. Bail was announced from Chicago, in the Sunday papers, as $25,000 and the report said that anyone who gave bail for us would be investigated. From the Sunday papers I also knew that Ettor and Giovannitti and another Italian IWW organizer, Baldazzi, had been arrested. The old Tombs, built in 1838 and now torn down, was a massive structure. It looked like a dungeon and was connected with a city court building by a passageway up in the air, across a street called the "Bridge of Sighs." The windows were narrow and high above our heads.

The womens' section was on one side and not very large. The matron and the male doctor were both Irish, and after they discovered I knew James Connolly and Tom Mooney they were very kind to me. They told me that Liam Mellows, an Irish patriot who was later killed in Ireland, was in jail there at the time. That I knew Mrs. Cram, who was mentioned in the press as a possible bondsman for me, so impressed the matrons that they brought me an extra pillow and gave me a cell to myself. It was a damp, evil-smelling place, the food was unspeakably awful and the atmosphere dreary and full of human sorrow. A bright old lady, who was accused of major fraud in stock speculation, wrote letters for the illiterate, gave out free legal advice and was generally helpful. A weeping woman, who had killed her husband with a butcher knife, was getting ready for trial. All the inmates were coaching her on how to behave and what to say. Her sister brought her a black dress and a new black hat to wear in court. The matrons, as they were then called, and prisoners all became involved in making her look presentable and pathetic. Somebody brought a mirror and she looked at her reflection. We all gasped when she burst out crying again and said: "Oh, if my husband could only see how nice I look." We felt a terrible tragedy could have been averted by a few new clothes and kind words.

For our appearance before the commissioner, we were brought to the old post office, then south of City Hall Park. Carlo and I were confronted by an unusual and interesting situation. The U. S. attorney for this district was a man we both knew personally, Mr. Harold Content. He was as surprised as we were, since the case had not originated here. He had worked in the office of George Gordon Battle, the lawyer, and on several occasions had been assigned by Mr. Battle to represent Carlo in his regular tussles with the postoffice department over violations of a minor character. The type of radical paper published by Carlo operated on a shoestring basis; it sometimes skipped an issue for lack of money or advertised a raffle which brought them into trouble with the post office and jeopardized their second-class mailing privileges. When I was brought in by the federal marshal, Mr. Content said: "Bring her into my office." Then he told the marshal to wait outside. His first question was: "Did you have any breakfast, Elizabeth?" I answered: "Well, not worth speaking of," so he sent the marshal across the street to bring "breakfast for one." The marshal assumed it was for Mr. Content and did himself proud in his selection, which I enjoyed.

"Seditious Conspiracy"

While I was eating my breakfast, Mr. Content asked me: "What is this all about?" Although he was the U.S. attorney it was not his case. I told him as much as I knew, which was very little. He had read the scare headlines in the press and said he could help on bail, at least. He assured people that it was all right to put up bail for me and he accepted it without consulting Chicago—so I was the first one out and was able to get bondsmen and real estate for the others, which he also readily accepted. He advised me as to lawyers. My sister had contacted Mr. Louis Boudin. Mr. Content said he knew Mr. Boudin and held him in high esteem, and that I should consult with him on the advisability of getting a non-Socialist lawyer to make a legal fight for severance in our case. Mr. Boudin agreed it was a good idea after he heard my strange story. I tried to get George Gordon Battle but he could not accept because he was chairman of a draft board. He referred me to George W. Whiteside, who agreed to see me.

At this point the men were all still in jail. I was shabbily dressed and had hardly enough money in my purse to pay carfares. But my list of bondsmen was at least impressive—Mrs. Cram, Dr. William J. Robinson, Amos Pinchot, Alice and Irene Lewisohn (who later owned the Grand Street Theatre) and others. Mr. Whiteside listened to me courteously. Undoubtedly he had never met one of those notorious IWWs before and he looked dubious and curious as he listened. He asked how I happened to come to him and I told him of Mr. Battle's recommendation. I suggested he call Mr. Battle, who in turn suggested he call Mr. Content—which he did. Apparently he was satisfied we were not traitors to our country and decided to accept our case for a moderate fee. He represented Tresca, Giovannitti and myself. Baldazzi's friends had secured a lawyer for him and Ettor had a Boston lawyer, a personal friend of his, John Feeney. Charles Recht also represented Giovannitti in the bail issue. It was far easier to secure lawyers then than it is now.

Our next problem was to raise a defense fund to pay our lawyers and our fares to Chicago when we were called there for arraignment. We were all very poor. There was no type of defense organization then in existence. A group of women organized a special committee for me, and we also set up a general defense fund for ourselves. We raised and spent about $5,000. I recall a conversation I had the first day I was out on bail with Fola La Follette, the daughter of Senator La Follette, who said: "I have no money for bail. But here's a little for your expenses." She never knew, I am sure, how much I appreciated that $5.00!

Ettor, Giovannitti, Tresca and I discussed our legal strategy. Arturo was no pacifist, in fact he was pro-Ally. He said: "Elizabeth, if you don't get me out of this, I'll come to court in a uniform!" I said: "Well, that won't hurt us!" I had to laugh. I said: "All my life men have demanded I get them out of jail!" Many of those indicted had already been arrested in various parts of the country, but others on the indictment had not been arrested. Suddenly Haywood sent out word from the Cook County jail that all those named in the indictment should surrender to the nearest federal marshal and all arrested should waive extradition and come into Chicago. We completely disagreed with such tactics, which were calculated to aid the government in expediting the trial. We argued that time was our greatest asset. The war hysteria was at its height. A trial was tantamount to a lynching. Delay, we felt, was our only reasonable strategy. We proposed that our IWW friends in Philadelphia and New England pursue a similar course and that we would set an example for all others around the country whom we could not reach directly. Our plan was to tie this dragnet case up in legal knots—in a dozen places—by a fight against extradition and for severance.

Strangely enough, two lawyers came from Chicago—George W. Vanderveer, the IWW lawyer, to persuade us to abandon our course, and U. S. Attorney General Clyne from that district to oppose our motion in court. Apparently we had substantial legal grounds—three of those arrested here were known not to be members of the IWW; none of us had been involved in IWW activity during the short indictment period of April 17 to September 17, 1917; none of us had been in the IWW headquarters in Chicago during the indictment period and not a single overt act was alleged in the indictment against any one of us. Mr. Content turned the case over to Mr. Clyne and did not participate in the arguments. Ettor, Giovannitti, Tresca and I won our severance motions, and we were never tried. Unfortunately, we were the only ones who pursued this course; the government's attack could have been stymied at the outset in legal arguments all over the country. Baldazzi followed Haywood's instructions, discharged his lawyer and went to Chicago—and to prison. After several years, he was deported to Italy following a commutation of sentence.

It was a tragedy—and I believe an avoidable one—that all of these splendid workingmen should have been sewed up in this manner in one case, without even a fight. Especially is this true because apparently there was a period when the government "higher-ups" were divided on the wisdom of such mass prosecution. Vanderveer sent two telegrams from New York City to Chicago, on January 29 and 30, 1918. The first one said: "If all other cases can be dismissed and raids stopped do boys prefer dismissal or trial Chicago case." In reply to a query as to "conditions" from E. F. Doree, the second wire said: "No conditions but government would give out its version. I have taken position here I would rather fight if other abuses can be eliminated. Am confident of outcome and think case presents publicity opportunities which may never return. Principles involved are fundamental. Why not fight? People here timid. Cannot understand my optimism, but like defense plans and may help on trial publicity." Vanderveer was apparently carried away by his Seattle victory in the Tracy case. Ed Doree wired back: "If dismissal is absolutely unconditional General Defense Committee unanimously in favor. Not interested in any version issued. What fundamental principles involved do you refer to?"

Haywood, however, wired to Vanderveer: "Trial or dismissal may be left to government. We cannot compromise." This apparently ended the negotiations. At the time, I did not see these telegrams or know of these discussions. After the trial was over, Fred Moore sent them to me in January 1919 to check with Roger Baldwin, who said that those "interested" were finally told the IWW "preferred trial." Mr. Baldwin said that Mr. Brooks of their organization (the National Civil Liberties Bureau) had tried to secure an indefinite postponement until the war was over. Fred Moore, who had not been consulted at the time of these negotiations, was very indignant. He said: "Certainly, a mere desire to carry on propaganda would not warrant the assumption of the enormous expenses of the trial of the case and the danger of a war-hysteria verdict." This was correct. But the IWW was gripped by leftism of the most extreme type. Moore's opinion was a year too late.

Ninety-three men were convicted in Judge Landis' court and received brutal sentences of 20, ten and five years. They were taken to Leavenworth prison in chains on a special train. To secure their release on bail, to carry an appeal to the U. S. Supreme Court and then to fight for their release from prison, were the tremendous tasks now ahead of us. The prisoners were of a heroic mold. Several died, many came out ill and their health was permanently injured. Some died soon after. Many died in the prime of life. Prison could not kill their spirits. But prison can kill and does maim the human body. Let those outside never forget that.

The War Year of 1918

The repercussions of political arrests are very hard on the children of those thus singled out. It is not easy to explain to them and there is sometimes prejudice in the neighborhood and in the schools. Fred's stay in P. S. 43 was of short duration due to this. He had not been told by the family that Carlo and I had both been arrested. He was accustomed to us coming and going to speak in different cities and being away for varied periods. It was easy to keep the papers out of sight. But the teacher in school made it her business to tell this small boy that his mother was in jail and that "only people who lie and steal and kill are put in jail." He came home in tears to my sister Kathie, who explained to him as best she could and assured him we would be back in a few days.

At the suggestion of Mrs. Vorse, whose children had gone there, she placed him in the Friends' Seminary, a Quaker school on Stuyvesant Park at East 16th Street. Later, Carlo or I would take him down in the mornings and put him on the El to go home in the afternoon. He was very happy there. Many children of the people who opposed the war were his fellow-students at the time, including those of Scott Nearing, Rabbi Judah Magnes, Jacob Panken, Norman Thomas and others. He remained there until he graduated from grammar school. Then he went to Stuyvesant High School nearby. Quaker school had a profound effect on Fred. A few years later, when Congressman LaGuardia asked him if he would like to go to West Point, he said: "Oh, no! I do not believe in war!"

Mob violence and legal terror mounted in the country. It did not stem from the masses of people, but from big employers and the loud-mouthed professional patriots and witch-hunters of that period, most of whom are long since forgotten. It was directed against labor and all who opposed war in general or this war in particular, or profiteering on war. The lists of victims grew, especially among those who were indiscriminately classified as "Reds"—anarchists, socialists, IWWs and progressive trade unionists. After the revolution in Russia in 1917, the details of which we knew very little here but which was greeted with great enthusiasm by Americans generally, a drive began against anyone who could be called a "Bolshevik." Fear of "revolution" swept the reactionaries of this land.

A wholesale attack was directed against the IWW. The Chicago indictment was followed by similar ones on Omaha, Sacramento, Wichita and Spokane. Several hundreds of IWW men were sent to prison, with sentences up to 20 years. The leaders of the Socialist Party were also singled out for attack. Congressman Victor L. Berger of Wisconsin was excluded from his seat in Congress after a Chicago conviction under the Espionage and Sedition Act, along with Reverend Irwin St. John Tucker, J. Louis Engdahl and William F. Kruse. They were sentenced to 20 years, which was later reversed by the Supreme Court. Victor Berger was later reinstated in Congress and his back pay refunded.

Eugene V. Debs, the great Socialist orator and many times candidate for President, was convicted in Cleveland under the Espionage Act, and sentenced to ten years. He had spoken in Canton, Ohio, outside the jail where Ohio Socialist leaders Charles E. Ruthenberg, C. Baker and Alfred Wagenknecht (father of Mrs. Helen Winter, one of the present-day Smith Act victims), were sentenced to one year for "their anti-war speeches." The charge against them was "inducing men not to register." Debs said in Canton: "I would rather a thousand times be a free soul in jail than be a coward or sycophant on the streets." He said: "Our hearts are with the Bolsheviki of Russia," and noted the fact that "the very first act of the triumphant Russian revolution was to proclaim a state of peace with all mankind." He said: "There are few men who have the courage to say a word in favor of the IWW. I have. Let me say here that I have great respect for the IWW, far greater than I have for their infamous detractors." He concluded his ringing and brave speech with the words: "The world is daily changing before our eyes. The sun of capitalism is setting. The sun of Socialism is rising." These fighting words from a peace-loving prophet landed him in Atlanta Federal Penitentiary.

Kate Richards O'Hare, Socialist woman speaker—only woman member of the Socialist Party's national committee—was sentenced in Fargo, North Dakota, to five years "for discouraging enlistment." Rose Pastor Stokes, who had temporarily gone along with her millionaire husband and others in supporting the war and withdrawing from the Socialist Party, had returned after the Russian Revolution and had resumed speaking for the party. She was sentenced to ten years in Kansas City for a letter she wrote to the Kansas City *Star,* correcting a report of what she had said in a speech on the government and profiteering. Emma Goldman and Alexander Berkman, who organized a No-Conscription League, were sentenced to two years for conspiracy to violate the Conscription Law, and on the expiration of their sentences were both deported to Russia.

Mollie Steimer, 19 years old, and three young men were sentenced to 20 years for publishing a leaflet denouncing intervention in Russia and calling for a general strike among munition workers against the use of arms against Russia. This is the case in which Supreme Court Justice Holmes gave his famous "clear and present danger" minority opinion and in which Justice Brandeis concurred. They did not believe that any such danger existed in this case and expressed their conviction that the defendants had been deprived of their rights under the Constitution of the United States.

Dr. Marie D. Equi of Portland, Oregon, suffragist and sympathizer with the IWW, was sentenced to three years under the Espionage Act over a month after the Armistice had ended the war. Irish nationalists were sent to prison in New York and Hindu nationalists were jailed in California. These are only a few of literally hundreds of cases all over the country in which men and women suffered long prison terms. There were comparatively few actual pro-Germans arrested. A few Germans accused of espionage were deported.

In addition to political and labor objectors to war there was a large number of religious objectors—followers of Judge Rutherford, members of the International Bible Association, Amish people and Mennonites. Some refused to register, others to accept combat service or to work in prison. "Thou shalt not kill," became subversive doctrine. There were several hundred conscientious objectors of various sorts confined in U.S. military prison on March 1, 1919—four months after Armistice Day. Fifty-four foreign-born members of the IWW were ordered deported on Lincoln's Birthday, 1919, under a new Deportation of Act of October 1918. I had been associated with the American Civil Liberties Bureau during the year 1918. The IWW had recommended that I act as liaison between the IWW and the Bureau, since I was so thoroughly familiar with its problems. I felt personally dedicated to the task of freeing my comrades and fellow-workers and spent the next six years at it.

CAME ARMISTICE DAY

European countries had been at war on their own soil for over four years when the Armistice arrived on November 11, 1918. The people there were war weary and in revolutionary motion. Royal dynasties had collapsed in Russia, Germany and Austria-Hungary. The Russian Socialist Revolution, with its slogan of "Peace and Bread," hastened the general peace, although the Allies, including the United States, attempted by armed intervention to force the Russians to stay in the war. When it became known in the United States that American armed forces were actually on Russian soil, in Siberia, this met with widespread opposition. Particularly in Detroit and Seattle, from whence came the American soldiers who were in this expeditionary force, there were protest demonstrations demanding their return. The soldiers and even their commander, General Graves, were accused by the war forces here of being "pro-Bolsheviks" because they attempted to maintain a neutral attitude and confine their efforts to guarding allied military supplies. Their stand was universally supported in this country.

The United States had been in the war in an active military capacity only a year and seven months when the Armistice was declared. It had suffered less, so far removed from the battlefront, than other participants. But peace was welcomed here, too, in a delirium of joy. The killing was over. Impromptu parades, dancing and singing in the streets, occurred on 5th Avenue in New York and on the main streets of all cities and towns from coast to coast. Strangers clasped hands and hugged and kissed each other. Factories, stores and offices shut down, schools were dismissed, churches were opened for prayer. A spontaneous holiday was declared in which everybody joined. It was beautiful to behold.

For the peace-loving forces of America, Armistice Day was saddened, however, by the thought of thousands of American youths who would not return and hundreds of Americans in prison for their religious, labor or political opposition to the war. Over 8,000 had been convicted for violating the draft alone. But their sentences were generally of short duration. The majority of those whom we called "political prisoners" were in federal prisons under wartime free speech convictions for long sentences up to 20 years. The conscientious objectors, who had refused to register, were in military prisons and numbered nearly 400. They were both religious and political. Their sentences too, were severe—up to 35 years.

In round figures, our estimate of those in all prisons, or convicted and soon to go, totaled approximately 1,500 cases at the war's end. For us in the left-wing Socialist and labor movement the Armistice cleared the decks for a campaign for *Amnesty for all wartime political prisoners,* which we immediately launched. We demanded the cessation of further prosecutions under these wartime laws which had restricted freedom of speech and assemblage. But we were not alone. Liberals, pacifists, church leaders, professionals and many conservative labor leaders, even congressmen and senators, participated for the next five years in the Amnesty movement, until President Coolidge freed the last 31 political prisoners at Christmas of 1923. The freeing of all the men and women who were political prisoners of World War I was a notable achievement. It represented the hard work of hundreds of devoted people throughout the land, constant agitation and demonstrations, and unremitting demands upon all government agencies— addressed to the President, to congress, and to all the various officials and departments involved.

We had fought as best we could, even during the war, and continued throughout the Armnesty campaign, to demand the status of "political prisoners" for Debs, the IWWs and all others. Such a status had long been recognized in other countries, even in the most backward and tyrannical absolute monarchies, as in tsarist

Russia. As time passed we called attention to political amnesties granted in Allied countries: in France, March 1920; in Italy, by a series of royal decrees beginning a month after the Armistice, December 19, 1918; in Great Britain all conscientious objectors were released in 1919 and the few politicals freed, too, although there was no sentence there which exceeded six months. Wartime political prisoners were freed in Canada in 1919, and in Belgium in the same year.

In England a committee to help us here was organized. It was called Class War Prisoners Release Committee, and had as members George Lansbury, editor of the *Daily Herald,* Tom Mann of the Engineers Union, Robert Williams and Ben Smith of the Transport Workers, and Harry Pollitt, representing the Boilermakers. Their leaflet read in part as follows:

We have had some little experience in this country of individuals being prosecuted and imprisoned by the authorities for expressing ideas that the dominant class consider harmful to their interests. The most recent case is that of Albert Inkpin, the Secretary of the British Communist Party, who has been sent to prison for six months. But persecution here has been nothing compared to what our American brothers have suffered.

It is hard for the British worker, who is used to some pretense of justice, to understand the conditions in the U.S. There, the class war is fought nakedly and with brutal ferocity; trustified capital uses ALL means and methods, legal or illegal, to prevent the workers from organizing and so gaining power.

Union men have been deliberately murdered in cold blood, they have been cruelly beaten up, branded, tarred and feathered, kidnapped, driven insane by the fiendish punishment and torture of the hired gunmen and thugs of Big Business.

The infamous, labor-hating Judge Landis sentenced 93 men to a total of 807 years and 21 days imprisonment, and fines amounting to 2,570,000 dollars!!!

What was their crime?

They were educating and organizing the workers on the industrial field, they were fighting for a better standard of living, they were loyal and unselfish in their efforts on behalf of the working class!

Ideals and ideas were on trial as the prosecution conclusively showed during the whole proceedings. The Government of the U.S.A., representing Trustified Capital, took advantage of their Espionage Act and the war fever to put out of the way men who were likely to prevent the unrestricted exploitation of the workers and the amassing of fabulous profits by the employing class.

Twelve of these men are Britishers.

Sam Scarlett of Glasgow, an old member of the A.S.E., and one of the finest orators in the movement, is serving 20 years. Richard Brazier of Bir-mingham, a metal worker, and Charles Lambert, also suffer this ferocious sentence.

Each and all of these victims showed a splendid spirit, they took their sentences without flinching, even the capitalist press had to admit their cool and dignified bearing. One who was sent down for ten years smiled as he said: "Judge Landis is using bad English today, his sentences are too long."

They recommended that protests go to the Foreign Office, to the American Ambassador, to President Harding and to the Labor Party.

Amnesty for All Political Prisoners, 1918 to 1923

Besides the hundreds of men and women, wartime labor and political prisoners who were already serving long terms on Armistice Day 1918, the untried wartime cases and those still on appeal at various court levels included an even greater number. To secure the release of all of these—some 1,500 Socialists, IWWs, radical individuals and re-ligious opponents of war—was the purpose of our amnesty campaign. The Communist Party did not come into existence until a year later, although many of the Socialists involved were attached to the left-wing movement in the Socialist Party, a forerunner of the Communist Party. Little did we anticipate that the tasks we assumed after Armistice Day would become multiplied a hundred-fold by a whole host of new at-tacks during the next two years—with the Palmer raids which precipi-tated state cases all over the country under criminal anarchy and syndi-calist laws; with the struggles against the deportation of foreign-born workers and finally seven long and tragic years of tireless efforts to save the lives of Sacco and Vanzetti from a dastardly frame-up that fin-ally took their innocent lives in the electric chair at Charlestown, Mas-sachusetts. However, we tackled our immediate job with spirit and de-termination. It prepared us for the stormy days ahead, which came upon us in 1919.

The only organization then in existence which attempted to cope with these problems was the National Civil Liberties Bureau, led by Albert De Silver and Roger Baldwin. But it had been set up as a com-mittee of individuals to deal with wartime problems of free opinion and conscience. They were all busy people and served as volunteers. It was not staffed or equipped to handle a large-scale fund-raising job nor to mobilize the labor movement. It had attempted to set up a Liberty

Defense Union of similar progressive individuals but they were all too busy in other fields and it dissolved, leaving its assets in the hands of a subcommittee of the Civil Liberties Bureau headed by Charles Ervin, editor of the New York *Call,* and Scott Nearing of the Rand School. They felt strongly the urgency of reaching the unions if we were to get the Amnesty campaign off the ground. They gave me a credential on November 8, 1918, to organize a delegate body—a Workers Liberty Defense Union. The emphasis was on *workers.* They advanced $250 in funds left by the defunct organization to pay my salary for nine weeks. By that time we were a going concern.

We had a founding conference on December 18, 1918, at the Forwards Hall, with delegates coming from 163 organizations. Among these were locals from the Amalgamated Clothing Workers, the Brotherhood of Painters, Decorators and Paperhangers; the Furriers Union, the International Ladies Garment Workers, the Socialist Party, the Teachers Union, the Brotherhood of Carpenters and Joiners, the IWW, the Young Socialist League, the Workmen's Circle and many others. It was a representative gathering—far more than we had expected. On January 5, 1919, at our next meeting, we adopted a working program of "Objects" and "Means"—with a resolution defining the range of our activities. Fred Biedenkapp, an officer of the Brotherhood of Metal Workers, was elected treasurer, Simon Schachter, who represented the Furriers Joint Board, was elected secretary, and I officially became the organizer. Later, Ella Bloor became our field organizer.

Fred Biedenkapp was a German-American; his father had been a friend and associate of Albert Parsons and of the German workers hung in Chicago in 1887. One hand had been badly crippled at work in a machine shop. His union was an offshoot from the International Association of Machinists. Fred was a picturesque figure. He and Luigi Antonini, who was also one of our delegates from the ILGWU, both wore black flowing ties, called "anarchist ties." Fred signed his name on all our checks in red ink, to the amusement of the bank tellers.

He gave us the use of a small back room in his union offices at the Rand School, 7 East 15th Street, and there we functioned for four years. There were bars on the windows, it was dark and gloomy, facing a small closed airshaft. We had the electric lights on all day. Fumes of nearby factories polluted the air. I often felt I, too, was in jail and when the others came out I, too, would be freed. We moved in

1922 to 80 East 10th Street, along with the Brotherhood of Metal Workers, when the Rand School had labor trouble with the cafeteria workers and a picket line of food workers marched outside.

Our relationship with the National Civil Liberties Bureau remained close and friendly. Albert De Silver, its director, wrote to Biedenkapp on January 14, 1919, regretting that they could no longer pay my salary because the funds ran out: "The work she has done has been most admirable. I should like to express my satisfaction at the successful organization of the Workers Defense Union and to wish you all success." A year later, in finally closing up all the accounts of the old Liberty Defense Union, Roger Baldwin sent us $227.17 to be used for defense purposes. We were like a godchild of the Civil Liberties Bureau.

In 1920 the National Civil Liberties Bureau dissolved and the Civil Liberties Union succeeded it as a permanent organization to deal with the postwar civil liberties issues. On their invitation the Workers Defense Union became a local affiliate and we continued as such until we dissolved in 1923. I became a founding member of the National Committee of the American Civil Liberties Union in January 1920, by invitation of L. Hollingsworth Wood, Norman Thomas, Albert De Silver and Roger Baldwin. In its earlier days this organization did yeoman service for civil liberties and for amnesty, and it also participated in the defense of Tom Mooney, the IWWs, Sacco and Vanzetti, and countless deportees. Courageous and notable liberals of that day were on its national committee, such as Jane Addams, John Lovejoy Elliott, James Weldon Johnson, Oswald Garrison Villard, Father John A. Ryan, Frank P. Walsh, Helen Keller, Vida Scudder, Frederic C. Howe, Robert Morse Lovett, Judah L. Magnes, Dr. Harry F. Ward, Mary McDowell, Rose Schneiderman and many others. My name on their early listing was followed by William Z. Foster of Pittsburgh and his name was followed by Felix Frankfurter of Cambridge, Massachusetts.

I remained a member there for 20 years and treasured my association with many wonderful people. Then I was expelled in 1940 because of my membership in the Communist Party.

FREE YOUR FELLOW-WORKERS!

When we launched the Workers Defense Union in December 1918 we set forth our purposes very specifically. We knew otherwise we might not be able to hold together. We planned to work for the release of all industrial and political prisoners convicted during the war and also for all unjustly imprisoned prior to the war for reasons due to their participation in the labor movement. This covered Mooney and Billings, Ford and Suhr, Rangel and Cline, and similar older labor cases. Thus, we gave Amnesty wide meaning, to cover both federal and state cases. Secondly, we planned to cooperate in the defense of political and labor defendants under indictment or appeal, and to defend such as might be prosecuted in the future.

We pledged to agitate against the policy of deportation for political opinions. One of our main tasks was to work for the establishment of a recognized status for "political prisoners"—for all categories—such as was accorded to their counterparts in European countries. We demanded, finally, that the U.S. Government respect the rights of free press, free speech and free assemblage, which was supposed to be guaranteed by the Constitution of the United States. Our Slogan "Free Your Fellow-workers" was printed on a magnificent cartoon made especially for us by Robert Minor.

The means we set forth included news publicity to papers, mass meetings, visits to unions, leaflets, raising of defense funds and bail, and the development of an organization looking toward a permanent national workers defense council, consolidating all existing committees. This was realized in 1925 with the organization of the International Labor Defense, which did splendid work throughout the balance of the 1920s and throughout the 30s. We suggested tentatively in our statement of purposes that if all else should fail, the desirability of a general strike of protest be considered. However, we decided to exclude from our deliberations and activities all extraneous subjects not directly connected with our immediate objects, because of the widely divergent views on political and economic subjects held by members of our delegate body. This went a long way to cementing our ranks, because everybody—from extreme anarchists on the left to conservative trade unionists on the right—felt strongly about the injustice of wartime prosecutions of fellow Americans and was willing to fight for their release. The imprisoned comrades, of whatever persuasions, were a bond of unity. It wasn't always easy to keep all other issues out in those turbulent times, but we did succeed to a remarkable degree in all pulling together for a common purpose.

One of our first undertakings was to publicize the facts of each case, as well as who the prisoners were, and their past services in the cause of labor. We organized outside correspondents to write to the prisoners—in fact several happy marriages resulted from this activity. We had local lawyers in cities near the prisons who visited the prisoners regularly and kept tabs on how they were treated. Through these channels we soon became very familiar with the conditions inside the gray, forbidding walls of federal penitentiaries. In some ways, strange as it may seem, there was more recognition of the existence of "political prisoners" then—in the 1920s—than there is now, over 30 years later. For one thing, the prison wardens were not all in slavish fear of attacks by the then unheard of "columnists"—the Walter Winchells and Westbrook Peglers—for "coddling" the politicals. Present-day political prisoners (who are accused, not of criminal acts but of "teaching and advocating" ideas—as were the political prisoners then) are denied rights and privileges extended to all the ordinary prisoners, let alone rights accorded to politicals over three decades ago. A comparison of the 1920s and the 1950s is truly an astonishing one.

In those far-off days, the prisoners were allowed to write to many people outside. I have a stack of letters from the prisoners of that time. I was allowed to reply officially, as organizer of the Workers Defense Union, and to do many chores for them. We published their letters, including poems and literary products. Today, the imprisoned Communist leaders are restricted to correspondence with their families only. All others are screened out by the Department of Justice. Even the subject matter to and from their families is severely censored and these prisoners are threatened with punishment if any part of their letters is published or read in public.

In the twenties an organization like ours was allowed to send the prisoners money, books, Christmas presents and other articles, such as games, small looms for hand-weaving and musical instruments. At Christmas, we sent large packages with underwear, sweaters, nuts, candy, etc. Today no relief committee is allowed direct contact with the Communist political prisoners. All dealings are limited to families, and what they are allowed to do is much more circumscribed. Lawyers are allowed to visit them today only if litigation is pending. In the twenties, through the regular visits of lawyers, we were able to secure special diets for some, to fight to remove others from "the hole," to protest work assignments that were unsuitable for the age and physical condition of the prisoners, and to some extent, to alleviate bad prison conditions. The IWWs at Leavenworth were allowed to assemble in the chapel, without guards, to hold a meeting in conference with lawyers and others. I do not mean that conditions were good in the twenties—far from it. But there was an acknowledgement of their status as prisoners of opinion and conscience and not ordinary or dangerous criminals. There was some recognition of their need for a mental life.

During the Harding Administration, when Attorney General Dougherty desired to interrogate Debs he sent for him to be brought to Washington. Debs refused to travel under guard and he was allowed to come up from Atlanta by himself and return to the prison in the same manner. Rumor had it that he had had a long talk with the President. Today's political prisoners in transit are chained like animals.

Many prominent people, including Samuel Gompers, president of the American Federation of Labor, were allowed to see Debs. A Socialist Party convention committee was permitted to notify him of his nomination as their candidate for President in 1920, and he was allowed to give out an acceptance statement to the press. Silenced in prison, he received 920,000 votes. I was allowed to see a whole group of IWW prisoners with a lawyer in the warden's office at Leavenworth prison. We were seeking some information that we hoped would be helpful to Sacco and Vanzetti. The second day I was permitted to see Vincent St. John alone in the office. Ella Reeve Bloor, as field organizer for the Workers Defense Union, visited prisons all over the country. Today, only members of families are allowed as visitors. I was able to consult with Eugene Dennis in 1952, on an order from a Federal Judge, on legal defense problems only. It created a sensation in the prison because it is so out of the ordinary today.

WOMEN WHO OPPOSED WORLD WAR I

When congress adopted a resolution on April 6, 1917, which authorized President Wilson to declare war, over 50 members of Congress voted against it. Among them were Senator La Follette, Socialist Congressman Meyer London, and the first and only woman member of Congress at that time—Jeanette Rankin of Montana. Whatever her subsequent political shortcomings may have been, progressive women were very proud of her at that time. The Espionage Act, passed in July 1917, had many women among its targets. Mob violence, too, was meted out to woman victims. The records of the Civil Liberties

Bureau give many such instances, some extremely brutal. Mrs. Frances Bergen of Benton, Illinois, was ridden out of town on a rail by Loyal Leaguers. Mrs. Margaret Selby of Omaha, Nebraska, was severely beaten. Mrs. Hanely Stafford of Montrose, Michigan, was tarred and feathered. Two Negro women in Vicksburg, Mississippi, whose names were not recorded, were tarred and feathered, and Elizabeth and Margaret Paine of Trenton, New Jersey, were mobbed and forced to kiss the flag. These women were accused of seditious remarks.

There were at least nine women who served terms of varying length under the Federal Wartime Emergency laws. They were brave women who suffered greatly—arrests, imprisonment without bail or release on exorbitant bail, long and bitterly fought trials, public prejudice, imprisonment in vile places, and for some, finally, deportation. One of the most obscure cases was that of a very young and beautiful anarchist girl, Ella Antolini, who had been sentenced in New England for alleged activities against the war. Other women politicals found her in Jefferson City, Missouri, in the women's state prison, and due to their efforts she was released after serving about two years.

In the twenties there were no federal penitentiaries for women, so the women political prisoners were farmed out to women's state prisons scattered around the country. Three were sent to Jefferson City —Kate Richards O'Hare for five years, Emma Goldman for two years, and Mollie Steimer for 15 years. Emma Goldman's sentence was less because she was not charged under the Espionage Act, as were the others. She was charged with obstructing the draft in speaking under the auspices of the No Conscription League. The meeting at Hunts Point Palace in the Bronx drew an overflow of several thousand sympathizers.

Kate Richards O'Hare, as I have described, was a prominent and extremely effective Socialist speaker. She was arrested in North Dakota, on July 29, 1917, for a speech which she had already delivered all over the country in 70 places. She had been indicted by a Federal Grand Jury on complaints originating in Bowman, North Dakota, for alleged violation of the Espionage Act. This was a small town where a bitter political feud was in progress between the Non-Partisan League (farmers) and the two entrenched old parties. In a state whose population was 80 per cent farmers, the jury was 80 per cent businessmen, all bitter opponents of farm organizations. There were several bankers on the jury.

Mrs. O'Hare was convicted in December 1917 and sentenced to prison. She entered prison in April 1919, when all appeals were exhausted and the war had been over for five months. In sentencing her to prison, Judge Wade read a letter from the St. Louis office of the Department of Justice, as follows: "We have been unable to obtain anything specific against her that would be a violation of federal law. Nothing would please this office more than to hear she got life." She served over half her sentence before she was released. She was a mother of four children, three boys and a girl, whose ages ranged from nine to fourteen. One of her sons came to see her at the prison and played his violin outside the walls for all the inmates to hear.

Louise Olivereau was a librarian and Socialist in Seattle, also an IWW sympathizer. She was sentenced to ten years for "interference with the draft," for printing a small leaflet advising young men of their legal rights in relation to claiming exemption. She was sent to Colorado Springs State Prison. She served two years. Another western woman, Mrs. Flora Foreman, was a schoolteacher and a Socialist in Oregon. Her house was burned down by so-called "patriotic" neighbors. She was tubercular and went South to visit relatives in Texas. She was arrested there and held in communicado all the summer of 1918 in the county jail at Amarillo, Texas, for lack of $10,000 bail. The excessive heat, bad food and solitary confinement nearly drove her insane. She had said in a private conversation that she "did not belong to the Red Cross, had not contributed to it, and they could tell the little schoolteacher in Washington that, if they liked." She was found guilty under the Espionage Act, sentenced to five years in the Women's Prison at McAllister, Oklahoma. She was released at the end of two years by Presidential order and was a physical wreck. One of the jury said later that they did not really believe all the accusations, "but she is one of those 'radical Socialists,' so we just thought we ought to lock her up until after the war!"

In Minnesota, Elizabeth Ford, co-editor of a Socialist Labor Party paper in Fairhault was sentenced to one year and a $500 fine for "discussing enlistment." In Philadelphia another Socialist woman, Dr. Elizabeth Baer, served 90 days in prison for a leaflet against conscription which began: "Long live the Constitution of the United States." Dr. Baer neither wrote nor distributed the leaflet but was held responsible for it as a Socialist Party official. The arguments advanced were those of Champ Clark, the Speaker of the House, when he opposed the passage of the Draft Act. Dr. Baer lost her license to practice medicine and was virtually driven out of Philadelphia.

On the Pacific coast, in Portland, my friend Dr. Marie D. Equi, was arrested in June 1918 after a speech in the IWW hall. She was tried in December under the Espionage Act, after the Armistice was signed. Her speech dealt with defense of the IWW prisoners and conditions in the lumber camps. Two operatives of Army Intelligence admitted they were coached, did not recall her exact words, but finally wrote down several lines and "agreed to stick to it." The prosecutor appealed to the jury: "The red flag is floating over Russia, Germany, and a great part of Europe. *Unless you put this woman in jail,* I tell you it will float over the world!" She was sentenced to three years and a $500 fine. On her way out of the courtroom, she was called a foul name by a Department of Justice detective named Byron, who struck her and a woman spectator who interfered. His action was severely condemned by a resolution of the Oregon State Federation of Labor, who called for his removal. She served ten months in San Quentin Prison.

Mollie Steimer and Emma Goldman were deported to Russia. Many of these women, if not all, are now dead. But in a great crisis they stood staunch and true in defense of peace and democracy.

"LIFE BEHIND BARS"

For many years I have been in contact with labor prisoners within the stone walls that do "a prison make." My first was a visit to a poor, desperate shoe worker, Buccafori, who had killed an attacking foreman in self-defense during a Brooklyn strike and who was sentenced to 15 years in Sing Sing Prison. From that long-ago day in 1911 to the last visit I have made to a prison—to Atlanta Penitentiary in the summer of 1952, when I saw tall, smiling Eugene Dennis walk as serenely as if he were at home down a prison corridor to greet me—my heart has been enlisted in the cause of their freedom. Many of my best friends, great Americans I have loved and admired, have been in prison. It has truthfully been said: "All roads to human liberty pass through prison!" Of those who have gone to prison for their political and labor views and activities, only an infinitesimal percentage wilted under the pressure and eventually became stool pigeons and informers —like Paul Crouch and Ben Gitlow—both of whom I visited in prison. All the others remain staunch and true in their principles and loyalties, even under the hardest conditions and during long years of waiting for release. Such a hero was Tom Mooney.

But it is wishful thinking and an evasion of reality to think for a moment that prison does not affect the political prisoner. It is designed, not to assert but to destroy human dignity. The health of all the political prisoners in the twenties was adversely affected by the confinement, crowded living conditions, food, types of work, lack of opportunity for mental life, etc. "Every day is like a year—a year whose days are long!" a poet wrote in prison. Men died in prison, like the great Mexican patriot, Magón. Others, like Tony Martinez and William Wejh, contracted tuberculosis and were released just in time to die. J. B. McNamara died in prison. Tom Mooney's robust health and sturdy frame wore out, so that he lived only a few years after his release, and spent a large part of those years in a hospital. The lives of many IWW young men were shortened and they died in their prime —as did Doree, St. John, Doran—and many others. So great was the fear of the administration that Debs, who was frail and sickly at his advanced age, would die in prison that he was kept in the hospital ward at Atlanta Penitentiary during his stay there.

Poor food, lack of food and lack of variety, were the burning grievances in both the civil and military federal prisons. Shortages were caused by graft and selling prison food supplies outside. Coming away from Leavenworth on the old-fashioned street car I saw that guards going off duty were loaded down. Each had several loaves of sweet-smelling, freshly-baked bread. One wondered if the prisoners fared as well! Riots occurred in federal prisons over food, as for instance when the men were fed parsnips day in and day out at Leavenworth. What can be a tasty dish outside became anathema to these prisoners. I heard four of them say: "No, thank you!" when offered parsnips by my mother at a Thanksgiving dinner after they were freed. She was much surprised until one explained why they could not bear to look at parsnips. She said: "I understand," and took them away.

Riots also occurred over mean and hard jobs handed out to men unfit to do them. Race riots were fomented by the guards, a horrible pitting of race against race, which would be much more difficult today. In Fort Leavenworth, vicious Southerners were encouraged to attack the comparatively few helpless Negroes. They broke arms, knocked out teeth, and left their victims beaten unconscious. In Leavenworth civil prison, on the other hand, a group of Negro prisoners were armed by the guards and forced to attack IWW prisoners. In June 1920 we received a letter from a released IWW prisoner on "Life Behind the Bars," which described brutalities inflicted in Leavenworth, after several riots in the mess hall during 1919 had been blamed on the IWWs.

The writer, E. J. Coshen, was held in solitary confinement from November 25, 1919 to May 28, 1920, forty-one days of which he was on a bread and water diet. He was strung up by the wrists to the bars of the inner door of the dungeon. He was denied reading, writing and smoking, and held strictly incommunicado. "All of the time I was in isolation," he said, "six months and a few days—the electric light in the dungeon into which I had been cast, continued day and night to flood the otherwise dark and damp inclosure with its rays—no rest for the eyes, the object being that the light bring about a nervous collapse. My eyes—as is my stomach to food and my lungs to fresh air—are fast reaccustoming themselves to humans and to the rays of the sun."

Many years later, during World War II—a different kind of war, a just war against fascism—I was speaking at a Communist Party mass meeting in a Pacific Coast city. Two tall, handsome blond girls in war workers' outfits came up to speak to me before they left for work in a nearby shipyard. They were the daughters of this same man. They said he was now old and not too well, but very spirited and he sent his love "to Gurley."

In January 1919 the 3,700 men at Fort Leavenworth went on strike on account of the food shortage and the poor quality. They folded their arms and refused to work. Their demands were presented to the commandant by two conscientious objectors, one a newspaperman from Chicago. The commandant agreed to go to Washington to present their demands, especially their amnesty demands that all sentences be reduced to peacetime levels. He agreed to improve the food, to reduce the number of men in each cell, to increase letter-writing privileges, enlarge the visiting hours, the right to walk and play in the prison yard, and to exterminate the bedbugs. (This was before the days of DDT.) Men were released from "the hole." The commandant did go to Washington and material reduction of sentences, as well as a large number of releases, were the result, not only for conscientious objectors but for many ordinary military prisoners who were there for small offenses in the army.

Pathetic stories of conscientious objectors had to do with religious sects, such as the Mennonites, some of whom were sentenced to 20

years for their uncompromising opposition to warfare. When they refused to wear uniforms they were manacled to bars so high they could
barely touch the ground. They slept on a cold concrete floor without
blankets. Two, Joseph and Michael Hofer, died as a result of the inhuman treatment they suffered in Leavenworth. The Mennonite colony
to which they belonged in South Dakota left in a body for Canada after the imprisonment and death of these young men. The bodies had
been returned home dressed in the uniforms which they had rejected
in life. This caused considerable protest, especially in religious circles,
even among those where "Thou shalt not kill!" was not taken as literally as by the simple Mennonite people.

THE PALMER RAIDS

In October 1918 Congress passed the Deportation Act. It is the gran-
daddy of all present repressive legislation—the Smith Act, the Mc-
Carran Act and the McCarran-Walter Act. It provided for the deportation of aliens who are anarchists or who do not believe in organized
government, and of aliens who believe in or advocate the overthrow
by force and violence of the U. S. Government, or who are members
of any organization which so advocates. At that time, as now, we had
an attorney general who saw "reds" in schools, at dances, in plays, in
unions, under the bed—just everywhere. (In those days all reds were
called "Bolsheviks.") He is dead now. His name was A. Mitchell Palmer. Let us hope no red roses grow near his grave to disturb his slum-
ber. He would be entirely forgotten except for one thing—a shameful
happening in American history is named after him, the Palmer Raids.

He had a young assistant, a roundfaced, bullnecked, eager beaver
by the name of J. Edgar Hoover, who not only suffered from the same
disease as his superior, but became violently afflicted with it for life.

A new outfit was created at this time by the Department of Justice's
Bureau of Investigation, then headed by William J. Flynn. It was a
Radical Division run by this young, unknown but aspiring red-hunter,
Mr. Hoover. It took over an established index system which they
claimed numbered 200,000 cards, on all persons connected directly or
remotely with the "ultra-radical movement."

He stepped up and widened the index so that rumor has it when
Franklin D. Roosevelt was elected Hoover had to quickly pull out
cards on Eleanor Roosevelt, Frances Perkins, Harry Hopkins and oth-

er New Dealers, many of which probably went back into the card files during a Republican administration. Some day a real progressive people's government will open up the archives and lay bare for public scrutiny this police-state, stool-pigeon work that has gone on so long in our country. Many surprised people will find themselves there. You can't compile a list of hundreds of thousands that are just "Communists"—that's clear. Later, they boasted that they had sent spying operatives into all organizations and gatherings of workers to collect data and to keep track of what men and women said and did, especially in strikes, in preparation for a series of "experimental raids" which took place on November 7, 1919, when the second anniversary of the Russian revolution was celebrated in many meetings.

These raids, conducted in cities, were especially directed against the Union of Russian Workers. Speakers, teachers, students, diners in restaurants, men playing pool, were herded to jail, with bandaged heads, black eyes and blood-spattered clothes. The *New York Times* called these injuries "souvenirs of the new attitude of aggressiveness which had been assumed by the Federal agents against Reds or suspected Reds." Typewriters, pianos, desks, bookcases, files were smashed, as well. This was Mr. Palmer's dress rehearsal.

The 1919 climax was the deportation of 249 persons who were loaded on the transport, *Buford*. They included Emma Goldman and Alexander Berkman. The majority belonged to the Union of Russian workers. The *Buford* sailed just before Christmas 1919, under sealed orders to be opened at sea by the captain. Families were torn apart and wives and children left destitute. After this brutal and inhuman deed, Palmer and Hoover were ready for a really big job—what came to be known as the "Palmer Raids."

On January 2, 1920 their master plan was carried out. Brutal raids were conducted, without warning or warrants, on meetings, headquarters and homes in about 70 cities from coast to coast. Some 10,000 men and women were reported arrested that night. About 700 were arrested in New York City. Some were dragged from their beds. Undercover agents had been instructed to arrange meetings of clubs on the night set "to facilitate making arrests." As soon as a raid was made the agents were instructed to telegraph to J. Edgar Hoover, assistant to the attorney general, to give the number of arrests, to telephone about any special seizures, and to mail in detailed reports. Aliens were to be held for deportation, citizens were turned over to state authorities for prosecution. Again the dragnet swept in musicians playing for dances, bowlers, diners in restaurants of workers halls. There were many members of the Amalgamated Clothing Workers and the International Ladies Garment Workers Union among the victims. The prisoners were held by the hundreds on Ellis Island in New York, on Deer Island in Boston, at Fort Wayne, Michigan, and elsewhere.

Before the deportation delirium let loose by Palmer ran its course and was finally stopped by the pressure of public opinion, over 500 so-called "aliens," foreign-born workers, were torn from their homes and families and deported—some to certain death in their homelands. Louis F. Post, Assistant Secretary of the Department of Labor, cancelled 1,547 deportation warrants and made a principled stand against Palmer's lawlessness, when impeachment proceedings were lodged against him. Nothing came of the proceedings.

There was tremendous protest against the Palmer raids. Francis Fisher Kane, U.S. Attorney of Philadelphia, resigned in protest. Federal Judge George W. Anderson spoke out strongly in Boston against the invasion of civil rights. A brochure entitled "Report on the Illegal Practices of the Department of Justice," signed by 12 eminent lawyers, was issued in May 1920. It was addressed "To the American People." Among those who signed were Professors Frankfurter, Pound, Freund and Chafee, Mr. Kane, Frank P. Walsh and Jackson H. Ralston, general counsel of the AFL. It was a scathing exposé of how these raids flouted the Constitution and all legal procedure.

In 1924 when Attorney General Harlan F. Stone reorganized the Department of Justice, he criticized these raids and ruled that the FBI should not concern itself with political opinion. At that time, Hoover said to save his face and his job: *"The activities of Communists and ultra-radicals have not up to the present time constituted a violation of federal law, and consequently the Department of Justice, theoretically, has no right to investigate such activities, as there has been no violation of law."* Thus he confessed the Palmer Raids were illegal in every respect.

RUTHENBERG—"MOST ARRESTED MAN IN AMERICA"

As I have already indicated there was sharp cleavage in the ranks of the Socialist Party from its earliest days. The "left wing" was primarily the working-class element, builders of industrial unions, the followers of Haywood, Debs and Ruthenberg. I first met Charles E. Ruthenberg when he was a leading figure in the Socialist Party of Ohio. A tall, slender, blond, blue-eyed young man in his thirties, he was soft spoken and courteous in private conversation but a powerful, hard-hitting orator in meetings, especially effective in outdoor rallies. He was born in Cleveland, in a working-class family of German Lutherans. He joined the Socialist Party there in 1909 and immediately became very active. He lost his job as an accountant for the Prince & Biderman Company because he participated in an organizational drive for the International Ladies Garment Workers Union.

He was recording secretary and organizer for the Cleveland Socialist Party central committee for the next ten years, as well as a vigorous campaigner and an annual Socialist candidate. In 1910 he ran for state treasurer; in 1911, 1915, 1917 and 1919 he was candidate for mayor of Cleveland, and a candidate for Congress in 1916 and 1918. In 1913 he became editor of the *Cleveland Socialist*. He was an exceptionally capable organizer and built the Socialist Party of Cleveland up so that it was numerically stronger than the whole Socialist Party after the 1919 split.

Ruthenberg's identification with the left-wing forces began in 1912. He defended Haywood at the Socialist Party convention, when he vigorously opposed and voted against Haywood's expulsion from the national committee. When World War I began, Ruthenberg assumed the leadership of the anti-war forces in the Middle West. It was around this issue that the left wing—long a tendency in the Socialist Party—took organizational shape. Ruthenberg led the anti-war forces at the St. Louis convention in 1917. The anti-war resolution was the subject of sharp struggle. On her return to Seattle, while I was there during the Everett case, Kate Sadler, a Socialist speaker in the Northwest, told me that she and Ruthenberg were on the resolutions committee and fought for a strong position of outright opposition to the war as imperialist in character. Only five delegates finally supported John Spargo's pro-war position; 172 delegates voted against it. After war was declared a whole flock of pro-war "Socialists" left the party, including Spargo, J. G. Phelps Stokes, William Walling, Robert Hunter and others.

After War was declared, the official leadership of the Socialist Party did nothing to implement the resolution. Debs, Kate O'Hare and

Ruthenberg salvaged it and blew the breath of life into it, while the Hillquit-Berger leadership did their best to smother it. Ruthenberg spoke throughout Ohio at anti-war meetings which drew enormous crowds. Finally, he was arrested in 1918 with Alfred Wagenknecht and sentenced to ten months in the Canton, Ohio, Workhouse. While they were in jail, their wives edited the paper.

The end of World War I ushered in a period of militant struggle on the part of American workers, and of intense reaction and repression on the part of the employers. Over a million workers were engaged in strikes—in steel, coal, on the railroads, in textiles and clothing. There was a sensational general strike in Seattle which tied up the city. A policemen's strike in Boston was broken by Governor Calvin Coolidge. May Day, 1919, was the occasion for brutal police onslaughts in many cities—notably New York, Cleveland and Boston. Ruthenberg, then the Socialist Party's chairman in Ohio, was the speaker on Cleveland's Public Square. Thugs broke up the parade, police clubbed the marchers and troops and armored cars were on call. Three people were killed, including a child. Ruthenberg, Tom Clifford, veteran Ohio Socialist, and others were arrested, charged with murder, on the Haymarket "constructive conspiracy" charge, which was later dismissed. For the next eight years, until his death in 1927, Ruthenberg was one of the most persecuted and arrested men in this country.

Ruthenberg was fearless and clear in his understanding and defense of the Bolshevik Revolution of 1917 in Russia, which had overturned capitalism and ended the war for the Russian people. A referendum vote was initiated in the Socialist Party in the spring of 1919 to send delegates to the first Congress of the Third International in Moscow. It was carried overwhelmingly but was deliberately sidetracked by the officials of the Socialist Party. A left-wing conference was called in June 1919 in New York City, which Ruthenberg attended. While this conference was in progress, a raid was perpetrated against the left-wing headquarters on West 29th Street in New York City by what was called the "Lusk Committee"—a forerunner of the rash of Velde, Jenner, McCarthy un-American red-hunting committees of today.

Headed by State Senator Lusk, this committee was officially designated as a "New York State Joint Legislative Committee Investigating Seditious Activities." Fearful lest the Federal red-hunters would get all the publicity, they started a series of raids in June 1919 against the Rand School, the left-wing Socialist headquarters and the IWW office.

They also raided the offices of the Soviet Government Bureau, headed by Ludwig C. A. K. Martens, who was the unofficial Soviet envoy here, having presented his credentials to the State Department in March 1919.

Ruthenberg was a member of the Manifesto and Program Committe of the Left-Wing Conference and was elected to its national council. The Manifesto was published in its new paper, which appeared in July 1919 as *The Revolutionary Age*. Meantime, Ruthenberg had left New York City. Evidence at his trial later showed he had not seen the final draft of the Manifesto. But he and Isaac Ferguson, a lawyer, were indicted under the Criminal Anarchy Law of New York State at the instigation of the Lusk Committee, and arrested in Chicago. They were returned to New York in December 1919.

In September 1919 the Socialist Party convention was held in Chicago. It was immediately apparent that the left wing had the majority of the delegates. But the officials of the national office in charge of the convention refused to seat them, called the police and ejected a large group from the premises. They went to the IWW hall and organized the Communist Party. Later, another group withdrew and organized the Communist Labor Party. These two joined together early in 1920 as the United Communist Party, with Ruthenberg as its secretary.

A large group of those who had participated in the June 1919 left-wing conference, or in the Chicago conventions, were indicted in New York State, including James Larkin, Harry Winitsky and Benjamin Gitlow (of present unsavory fame as an informer and stool pigeon). The law under which they were tried was passed in 1902 after the assassination of President McKinley, and is still on the statute books. It proscribed the advocacy of force and violence, of the overthrow of government and of the assassination of public officials. All were found guilty and sentenced to from five to ten years in Sing Sing Prison. Ruthenberg and Ferguson served two years. They were released on bail by Judge Cardozo on a writ of error which Ferguson prepared and argued. During the trials, District Attorney O'Rourke appealed to the jury: "These men intend to take our fair America and transform it into a Red Ruby to be placed in the crown of the Bolshevik Lenin." Gitlow was defended by Clarence Darrow, Winitsky by a prominent New York criminal lawyer, William O'Fallon, and Larkin defended himself. But the results—convictions—were identical. In addition to the Communist leaders, two IWWs, both Finns, one of whom was secretary of the Finnish IWW local in the Bronx—Gus Alonen and Carl Paivo—were sent to prison. This local had been torn by an anti-Communist feud. Alonen and Paivo were brought up on charges as "Communists," trying to disrupt it. A lengthy document was prepared by their accusers, giving all the "evidence" of their Communist sympathies and attachments. This was turned over to a higher body—a central committee of all IWW locals, with offices downtown. When the Lusk Committee raided these offices, the document fell into their possession. The prosecution built their case on it and the two men were sentenced to four to eight years in prison. Paul Marko, who was sent to prison for distributing Communist leaflets, went insane while there. Two Lettish women, Anna Leisman and Minnie Kolnin, went to the women's prison in Auburn for distributing May Day leaflets. Mrs. Leisman was turned out of prison in the freezing cold of January 1923, in clothing she had worn to prison in July weather. She was not allowed to wait till her family arrived with heavier clothing. As a result, she contracted pneumonia and died. Carl Paivo later became a Communist, was held for deportation under the McCarran Law and kept on Ellis Island for many months. He died shortly after his release in 1954.

All of these New York State cases, except Gitlow's, were terminated by pardons granted by Governor Al Smith when he assumed office in 1923. He said: "I believe the safety of the state is affirmatively impaired by the imposition of such a sentence for such a cause." Gitlow's case was made the test of the constitutionality of the law and when the U.S. Supreme Court upheld it in 1927, he too was pardoned by Governor Smith. The cases of Ruthenberg and Ferguson, who were out on bail, were settled by the Governor's action. But Ruthenberg was by this time already involved in another arrest at Bridgeman, Michigan, in August 1922, as the result of a raid on a Communist conference held there.

CENTRALIA, 1919

After the war ended, lawless force and violence continued, now led by ex-soldiers, fomented by stay-at-home patriots, employers and their hirelings. Many violent scenes had occurred in 1918 and 1919. The Rand School in New York City was attacked by a mob of soldiers and sailors who tore down the American flag flying from the building. The

Socialist daily paper, the New York *Call,* was raided and wrecked. Employees were driven out and beaten as they were forced to run the gauntlet of armed men.

On Memorial Day in 1918, the IWW hall was raided by paraders in Centralia, Washington, its records and literature burned in the street, its furniture wrecked or stolen. All who were found in the hall were beaten, arrested and driven out of town. The governor, the mayor, the chief of police and a company of National Guard were in the parade. The mob action was led by the president of the Employers Association. The hall looked like a war ruin. But the undaunted IWW opened another hall. They determined to defend themselves and their headquarters from further lawless attacks.

Many attempts had been made to smash the Lumber Workers Industrial Union of the IWW during the war, especially during and after the great strike of 1917 for the eight-hour day. Men had been beaten and jailed for long periods in Yakima, Ellensburg and other lumber towns. Rope, tar and feathers, and clubs were used time and time again. The Eastern Railway and Lumber Company controlled much of the lumber land, sawmills, railroads and banks around Centralia. The head of this outfit, F. B. Hubbard, was also president of the Employers Association of Washington. The American Legion had been organized in Centralia after the war and was in the forefront of the campaign to smash the IWW and imprison its members.

A blind man, Tom Lassiter, made his living at a little newsstand in Centralia. Among the papers he sold were the Seattle *Union Record* and the IWW paper, *The Industrial Worker.* In June 1919 the newsstand was broken into and everything there taken out and burned. He was warned to leave town in a note signed "U.S. Soldiers, Sailors and Marines." Later, when he refused to leave, he was seized, beaten and dropped in a ditch over the county line. When he returned to Centralia, he was arrested under the criminal syndicalist law. All attempts of his lawyer, Elmer Smith, failed to bring the perpetrators of these outrages to justice, which emboldened the lawless elements in Centralia.

The Employers Association continually incited its members to action by regular bulletins, proclaiming such slogans as "active prosecution of the IWW; hang the Bolsheviks; deport Russians from this community; deport the radicals or use the rope in Centralia," and similar sentiments. A Citizens Protective League was organized which called meetings to discuss how to handle "the IWW problem." The police, the

Elks and the Legion participated in these discussions. A secret committee, similar to the vigilante committees of the old West, was set up. The news leaked out that a raid was being planned on the IWW hall, and was discussed at the Lewis County Trades Council. Some members from there warned the IWW of the threats. The IWW issued a leaflet, "To the Citizens of Centralia We Must Appeal," in which they recited the threats and accusations against them. It closed by saying: "Our only crime is solidarity, loyalty to the working class and justice for the oppressed."

At a Legion meeting on November 6, the line of march for the Armistice Day parade was changed to pass the IWW hall and it was agreed that they would halt in front of it, make a swift attack and proceed with the parade. They voted also to wear their uniforms. The line of march was publicized. Walter Grimms, in charge of the Legion, replaced Commander William Scales who did not favor raiding the hall. Grimms was a veteran of the Siberian Expedition of the American army. He had attacked "the American Bolsheviki—the IWW" in a Labor Day Speech. Elmer Smith, the IWW's lawyer, advised his clients: "Defend the hall if you choose to do so—the law gives you the right." For this remark he was subsequently charged with murder.

Armistice Day, November 11, 1919, was the day of the parade. Some of the marchers carried coils of rope. At the words, "Let's Go!" the Centralia Legionnaries raided the hall, led by Grimms. Shots were fired from inside the hall as the invaders smashed doors and windows. Shots came also from a nearby hillside. Grimms was shot, at the head of the invaders. He died later in the hospital. A Centralia druggist, Arthur McElfresh, was killed. Wesley Everest, an IWW member and veteran of World War I, had done the shooting. Five of the IWWs left in the hall took refuge in an unused icebox at the rear, where they remained until they were arrested.

Everest escaped from the back door, chased by the mob. He fired again as they closed in on him and killed Dan Hubbard, a veteran and nephew of the lumber baron who had instigated the plot and then planned "to let the men in uniform do it." Everest was kicked and beaten, a rope put around his neck and he was dragged senseless to the jail. In the night he was taken out, castrated and lynched, his swinging body used as a target for shot after shot. The next day the body was brought back to the jail and thrown in among the prisoners, then taken out and surreptitiously buried in an unknown grave—so the IWW could not take pictures of it, the authorities said. The men in jail were tortured and third-degreed to make them "confess." One, Lorens Robert, went insane as a result. A reign of terror against workers prevailed in Centralia. A newspaper reporter from the Associated Press was compelled to leave town hurriedly, without his suitcase or typewriter, because he had sent out a report containing a damning remark made by a Dr. Bickford that the hall had been raided before the shooting started. This was the first statement of the shootings to reach the outside world.

Lumber trust lawyers appeared as special prosecutors at the trial in Montesano, seat of Gray's Harbor County. A change of venue had been granted but it made little difference. Threats were made that the defendants would never get out of that county alive—if they were acquitted. The men on trial were ably defended by labor lawyer George W. Vanderveer. Two defendants, Elmer Smith and Mike Sheehan, were acquitted. Loren Roberts was declared insane. Britt Smith, O. C. Bland, James McInery, Bert Bland, Ray Becker, Eugene Barnett and John Lamb were found guilty of second degree murder. They were sentenced to from 25 to 40 years in Walla Walla penitentiary. Not one of the mob who attacked the hall, who murdered Wesley Everest and drove Roberts insane were ever punished. A "labor jury" of six workingmen of AFL unions from Tacoma, Washington, met on March 15, 1920, in the Labor Temple there and gave their verdict. It was that the defendants were not guilty; that there had been a conspiracy to raid the hall on the part of the business interests of Centralia; that the hall had been unlawfully raided and that Warren Grimms had participated in that raid.

During the trial, the courthouse was surrounded by soldiers who camped on the lawn, and jurors admitted later that they were intimidated by the atmosphere. The court was full of Legionnaires in uniform from all the surrounding towns. They were now private citizens but they had an armed camp set up under command of former army officers. Two years later, six jurors gave affidavits to Elmer Smith, who worked on the case until his death in the early 30s, stating their fears and asserting that if they had known the full story of the raid they would have voted to acquit the defendants. As it was, the jury recommended leniency, which the judge ignored.

Some law-abiding elements in the Legion spoke out. Edward Bassett, an overseas veteran and commander of the Butte, Montana, post, issued a public statement before the trial, stating that the IWW were justified in defending their hall and that the Legionnaires disgraced themselves by becoming party to a mob. Ten years later, in 1929, the Centralia Publicity Committee issued a four-page leaflet called "The Centralia Case," by an American Legionnaire of the Hoquiam, Washington, post of the Legion—a former captain of the U. S. Army, Edward Patrick Call—urging people to "rectify a great wrong" by writing to the governor to release the "innocent workers beginning their tenth year of imprisonment." He said: "A short résumé of the Centralia case shows Centralia Legionnaires were used by local business interests to eject the IWW. On Armistice Day, 1919, the workers' hall was raided before a shot was fired in self-defense. A gigantic frame-up followed, and the trial at Montesano bears all the earmarks of being an attempt at 'lynching'."

Meetings were held on behalf of the Centralia victims for years. Leaflets in 1919 were issued by our Workers Defense Union in New York City and funds raised to help the Centralia defense. One donation of $500 came from the Joint Board of the Amalgamated Clothing Workers. I spoke with Elmer Smith in March 1929 at the Seattle Civic Auditorium. I recall saying: "If the IWW had raided a Legion Hall, imagine what heroes the Legion would be to shoot them down!" Elmer Smith died of cancer shortly afterward. The legal struggle was taken over by Attorney Irwin Goodman of Portland, a valiant civil liberties lawyer. Five were paroled in 1936, after 17 years of unjust imprisonment, and the others, who refused parole, were released a short time later. The Legion defiantly erected a statue to Grimms but the truth has prevailed, and what happened in Centralia is now known as the murder of Wesley Everest, ex-soldier, and the frame-up of seven innocent workingmen.

CRIMINAL SYNDICALIST LAWS

It is hard to recreate a picture of the long years of intense brutal reaction which lasted from 1917 to 1927. Literally hundreds of workers —men and women—were arrested, beaten, abused, jailed or deported. It seemed then like hideous nightmare amidst the hurry and horror of it all, working day and night in a defense office. I lived in the Bronx, came down early to our office, and stayed late or spoke at night. I saw little of my family, my child or my husband. I recall

Christmas Eve, 1919, walking through Union Square, white with snow, with Isaac Shorr, the attorney who represented many of the Russian deportees, and realizing suddenly that I should be home, filling my child's stocking instead of attending a meeting. Another Christmas Day, possibly a year later, I was at our family dinner, a festive occasion even though none of us were religious. The phone rang and I was asked by the wife of one of the IWWs then at Leavenworth to come downtown right away. She had a message that her husband, William Wehl, was in a serious condition from tuberculosis and would be released next day. She needed money to go to him at once.

I took a long breath before I returned to the dining room to announce that I had to leave. "This is outrageous!" boomed Carlo and they all agreed, except my gentle mother who said: "No, Elizabeth can't help it. This is her work!" So I went with a feeling of great concern lest such an episode would antagonize my son and cause him to resent my outside affairs. But my sister Kathie and my mother explained everything to him, so that he always felt I was a good and useful person and was increasingly proud of me as he grew older. My friend Elsa needed money, which we secured. She took her husband to Arizona where he died shortly afterward.

In retrospect a definite pattern emerges, the result of world revolution and a capitalist class either mad with fear (of which A. Mitchell Palmer was the outstanding example) or cold-bloodedly using the bugaboo of revolution to smash the American labor movement. The term "revolution" was used to cover a barbers' strike in Brooklyn, the organizational efforts of the Amalgamated Clothing Workers in Rochester, N. Y., and the great steel strike in Pittsburgh. The Chicago Federation of Labor correctly said at that time: "The Red Raids are a part of a gigantic plot to destroy organized labor by the employers."

These raids and their aftermath of deportations and trials were nationwide. Prosecutions in many states were under criminal syndicalist laws, although some laws, as in New York State, antedated these. In Tennessee, a sedition law was used that had been passed during the Civil War period. In New Jersey, a similar law was passed in 1908. In 1916 during World War I, Australia passed an "Unlawful Association Act," aimed specifically at the IWW and its anti-war campaign. This was seized upon immediately as a model in the Western states of this country. Idaho and Minnesota passed criminal syndicalist laws in 1917, following the strike on the Mesabi Range and in the lumber camps. Montana, North Dakota and Washington came next in 1918, following the Everett massacre; California passed one in 1919. A total of 36 states finally had similar laws on their statute books.

Washington repealed the law in 1937, but most of them are still on the books and while generally inoperative they are coiled like sleeping serpents, capable of striking whenever reaction is in the saddle. During the war, and even afterward, until peace was formally declared, the federal Espionage Act was used to prosecute large numbers of Socialists and IWWs. But after the advent of "peace," vicious nationwide onslaughts continued under these new state laws, designed to rivet the spirit of the Espionage Act upon the American people. The IWWs were the first victims of the criminal syndicalist laws, but membership in this particular organization was not specified, as it was in the Australian law, which made possible the wholesale prosecution of Communists as well, after 1919. These laws were the forerunners of the Smith Act of today. They were actually anti-free speech legislation. Like the Smith Act, they were directed primarily against utterances— teaching and advocacy, verbal or written—and organizations disseminating *ideas* on political or social changes. The "by force and violence" then—as now—was read by stool pigeons' interpretations into the articles and books, though there were not so many to quote from in the 20s as there were in the 50s. The prosecution was not concerned with the actual use of force and violence, which would have required evidence of actual overt acts.

From a legal standpoint, there were plenty of laws on the statute books dealing with the use of force and violence which made such laws as the original criminal syndicalist laws superfluous. The real purpose was to prevent political and trade union organization, and the discussion of vital problems of the people. These laws caused the arrest of eleven hundred people. It would be hard to convey the human suffering, the mental torture, the loss of liberty, the broken homes, the cost in dollars for defense, inflicted upon militant American workers in this decade.

The state of California alone spent a million dollars on criminal syndicalist prosecution. In the IWW cases they had a team of paid stool pigeon witnesses, Diamond and Couts, who traveled from place to place testifying against workers. The Sacramento *Bee* said of the IWW in 1919: "It would be waste of time to have them arrested and tried. The best thing is to shoot them and not wait for sunrise either.

The sooner, the better, even if there is no time to permit them counsel or benefit of clergy." One IWW case in California was strangely dramatic. The defendant, W. I. Fruit, was drafted and went to France early in the war. He sent contributions regularly to the Workers Defense Union office "to defend the fellow-workers." He was in the army of occupation in Germany. On his return he marched in the Victory Parade that honored General Pershing's homecoming. Then he came to our office, a friendly, eager young man who promptly divested himself of all his equipment and accoutrements of battle, left them there with us and went off to look up the IWW.

On his return to California, he found so many of his former co-workers in jail that he became secretary of the Defense Committee. He was soon arrested under the infamous Busick injunction which made IWW membership sufficient ground for imprisonment without trial (also a forerunner of modern anti-Red procedure). The next letter I received from this veteran, who had fought "to make the world safe for democracy," was from San Quentin Prison, in a humorous vein: "Well, here I am, Gurley, home at last!"

Another California criminal syndicalist prosecution was that of Anita Whitney. She had been a member of the Oakland Socialist Party and her local, part of the left wing, had voted to go into the Communist Party in 1919. She spoke at a meeting under the auspices of the new organization. An American flag was draped over the piano in the hall. When she was prosecuted, a big to-do was made over this to the jury and it was called "desecrating the flag." She was convicted and sentenced under the law. Her case, along with the Gitlow case in New York, became test cases before the U. S. Supreme Court on the constitutionality of this type of law. The cases dragged until 1927 when the Supreme Court upheld the laws. Miss Whitney was pardoned by the governor of California. Another group was similarly pardoned by the governor of Illinois. By this time, the laws were becoming null and void through the pressure of public opinion and the campaign against them. But in 1924 there were 105 members of the IWW in San Quentin and Folsom prisons and 53 awaiting trial. In this year a brutal raid on the IWW hall in San Pedro brought indignation to a high point. Men were tarred and feathered and women and children scalded with boiling coffee. These state laws flared up again in the class struggle of the 30s in California and elsewhere.

"511"—MEETING PLACE OF MANY MINDS

Our family had widely varied interests which, however, were not basically antagonistic. Our house at "511" was the meeting place of many interesting people, active in many political and social fields. My father was still a Socialist Party member, my mother was connected with the Irish Progressive League, an ardent supporter of the Irish Republic and of women's suffrage. Carlo was an anarchist. My sister Kathie, two years younger than I, was by dint of perseverance and hard work a public schoolteacher. She was studying at Columbia for her master's degree in Fine Arts, though it was a miracle that she was able to study in such a mad household. My brother Tom had learned the trade of optician and was a member of the union. My younger sister Bina had left school and joined the Celtic Players, who were giving a repertoire of Synge, Yeats and Lady Gregory's plays. And Fred was still a pupil at the Quaker School.

I had been a devoted IWW, but my activities in the Workers Defense Union also brought me into contact with Socialists, anarchists, trade unionists, Communists, suffragists, pacifists, liberals, Indian and Irish nationalists and official representatives of both the Soviet and Irish Republics. Many groups met in our office, among them the Friends of Freedom for India, a Society for Technical Aid to the Soviet Union, and others. Later they moved to offices of their own.

The Hindus were anxious to make contact with the Irish movement. I sent them to Dr. Gertrude Kelly, a surgeon of great skill and a supporter of the Irish Republic. (There is a little park on the West Side which Mayor LaGuardia named for her.) I heard nothing further of my Hindu friends until lo and behold! on St. Patrick's Day they marched as a contingent in the parade down 5th Avenue. Their colorful turbans and picturesque appearance attracted a great deal of interest. It is unheard of for anyone but the Irish to participate in this sacred event, but feeling ran high against England and Dr. Kelly had been able to arrange it.

Because I was an IWW my relations with the American Irish were sometimes strained. But the Irish from the old country were not so narrow-minded. I had many friends among them. Kathleen O'Brennan was a peppy little Irish woman who came here to speak on behalf of the Irish freedom cause, but took up the cudgels while she was in Portland for Dr. Equi, whose mother was Irish. Dr. Equi had done much to help the cause financially. Miss O'Brennan did not allow the conservative Irish to dissuade her from defending "Doc," and she worked valiantly with a woman lawyer, Helen Hay Greeley.

Mrs. Hannah Sheey Skeffington came here with her young son who was about Fred's age. Her husband had been killed during the Easter week uprising in Dublin in 1916. He was a Socialist and a pacifist, and was shot down while caring for the wounded. She was not allowed to leave Ireland until the war was over, when she made a speaking trip around this country. Sometimes she left her son Owen in my mother's care. Judge Daniel F. Cohalan, a bigwig leader in Irish circles, warned her against associating with Margaret Sanger (whose maiden name was Higgins) and me. Dr. Patrick McCarten, who was the official envoy of the Irish Republic in the United States from 1917 to 1920, came to visit us in the Bronx. Our friendship with James Connolly was well known in Ireland, and the Irish from over there sought us out. James Larkin first brought Dr. McCarten to see my mother. He had entered the country disguised as a sailor.

When Larkin was arrested, I took a particular interest in his case, helping to raise bail and defense funds. Although he was one of the founding delegates of the Communist Party in Chicago in 1919, he was a citizen of the Irish Republic, held here against his will and desirous of returning to his own country. A special Irish-American committee was organized on his behalf. I went on a delegation with them to the old Waldorf-Astoria where the President of the Irish Republic, Eamon De Valera, had his headquarters. We reminded his representative of the respect and admiration the Irish workers had for Jim Larkin and that there would be severe criticism of De Valera if Larkin were allowed to remain in an American jail for lack of a few thousand dollars in bail. John Devoy, editor of the *Gaelic American,* was also contacted by this committee.

Larkin insisted from prison that he was as much entitled to legal aid from the Irish Republicans as Liam Mellows or Dr. McCarten, both of whom had been arrested and bailed out in 1917. The charge against them was illegal entry. As a result of this pressure, Irish funds were made available through a friendly saloon keeper, Barney O'Toole, to secure Larkin's release on bail. But this was kept sub rosa because the smug Irish-American politicians who swarmed around the Irish Republican cause would heartily disapprove of any aid to the agitator

Mrs. Hannah Sheey Skeffington. Irish Socialist.

Fanny Sellins

Tom Flynn's Socialist Party membership card.

TRANSFER RECORD.

Date Admitted _____
Date Withdrawn _____
Local _____
Financial Sec'y _____

Date Admitted _____
Date Withdrawn _____
Local _____
Financial Sec'y _____

Date Admitted _____
Date Withdrawn _____
Local _____
Financial Sec'y _____

Date Admitted _____
Date Withdrawn _____
Local _____
Financial Sec'y _____

Date Admitted _____
Date Withdrawn _____
Local _____
Financial Sec'y _____

Socialist Party of America.

State _Penna_

Local _Lacka_

Branch _Scranton_

MEMBERSHIP CARD.

Name _Thomas Flynn_

Address _418 Mulberry St_

Admitted _June_ 19_17_

No. _____ Page _____

JGBlack
Financial Secretary

Address _1230 Webster Ave_

ISSUED BY AUTHORITY OF THE
State Committee, Socialist Party.

Larkin who never spared them in his public speeches and expressed his contempt for them on all possible occasions.

One such event occurred later, in Sing Sing prison on St. Patrick's Day. It was decided to have a celebration and Jim was permitted to speak. He was a Catholic, attended church regularly, and spoke with great reverence of the good St. Patrick. The Irish guards standing around the hall were very pleased. Then he told how St. Patrick had driven all the snakes out of Ireland. "And where did they go?" thundered Larkin. "They came to America to become politicians, policemen, detectives—and prison guards!" The prisoners cheered to the rafters and the celebration was summarily dismissed.

I went with my sisters to an Irish house party for Liam Mellows, who had been in the Tombs while I was there. I was anxious to meet him. When I mentioned our common experience, one of the guests said in quite a shocked tone: "And what were *you* in jail for?" Before I could answer, Mellows replied: "Don't you know there is a struggle for peace and freedom here, too?" I had Fred with me that night. There were two frosty-looking middle-aged ladies, the Misses Kelley, who finally asked a $64 question: "To which of the Miss Flynns does the little boy belong?" My sister Bina answered: "Hush—don't tell anybody! But we really don't know!"

One of my first experiences with the Irish Nationalists had been a visit that Carlo Tresca and I paid in 1914 to the offices of the *Irish World,* where we met its famous editor, Patrick Ford. He was then quite an old man. Carlo wanted to borrow a cut of the Homestead strike scene which had appeared in its columns. When we introduced ourselves as leaders of the then recent Paterson strike, he said something about "IWWs—oh! anarchists—direct actionists, eh?" I had heard of him for years from my father, who was his great admirer. I could not contain myself and said: "Well, Mr. Ford, my father tells me how he collected money when he was a boy to send to your paper for a 'Dynamite Fund' to blow up the British Parliament." His eyes began to twinkle and he said: "All right! All right! Maybe you're right. You can have the cut."

THE IRISH AND SOVIET REPUBLICS

Strange as it may seem now, there was a strong natural affinity between the Irish Republic, which had been proclaimed first in the Easter

Week uprising of 1916, and the Soviet Republic of workers, soldiers and sailors which came into power in November 1917. James Connolly's last words to his daughter before he was executed in 1916 were: "The Socialists will never understand why I am here. They will all forget that I am an Irishman." This was true of some Socialists, who called the uprising a folly. But before two years had passed a mighty revolution overthrew Russian imperialism, an ally of the British imperialism which had executed Connolly and his comrades. The Socialist leader of that revolution, V. I. Lenin, understood Connolly. In the auumn of 1916 he wrote a sharp rebuke to Karl Radek, who had characterized the Irish rebellion as "a putsch," a term which Lenin said could not be applied to "the centuries-old Irish national movement." Lenin said further: "The misfortune of the Irish is that they arose prematurely when the European revolt of the proletariat had not yet matured." He recalled how Karl Marx, back in 1867, had called upon the British workers "to demonstrate in favor of Fenianism"—the Irish freedom movement of that day.

The Irish Republican Brotherhood, which was the governing power of the Irish Republic, decided to send an envoy to Russia to discuss mutual recognition. Dr. Patrick McCarten was selected for this mission and came to the United States in 1917 en route to Russia. But there were many interruptions and developments before he finally got there, three years later. Attempting to leave, he was arrested in Halifax in 1917 and returned to jail in this country. Once on bail, he was compelled to remain here. So he publicly assumed his post as Envoy of the Irish Republic and gave leadership to the Irish Republican movement here. One of his first official acts was to object to the conscription of Irish nationals residing in the United States, since England had been forced to eliminate Ireland from the operation of her Conscription Act.

As soon as war was declared in April 1917 the *Gaelic American, Irish World* and *Irish Press* were suppressed. Jeremiah O'Leary, fiery leader of the American Truth Society, was charged with treason and his satirical paper, *The Bull,* was also suppressed. Some of the older Irish societies, like the Ancient Order of Hibernians, suspended operation during the war. But new ones, like the Friends of Irish Freedom and the Irish Progressive League, came froward. Padraic Colum, distinguished Irish poet, was dropped by the American Poetry Society. In spite of all difficulties, the Irish circulated their press, held meetings against the war and demonstrated for the Irish Republic. Both the House and the Senate passed resolutions in 1919 urging the Peace Conference at Versailles to favorably consider Ireland's claim for self-determination. But this was ignored by Woodrow Wilson.

The secret arrival of Eamon De Valera in June 1919 electrified the Irish movement and its American sympathizers. Headquarters were set up at the old Waldorf Astoria on 34th Street and admirers gathered daily to see the tall form of the President of the Irish Republic stride down 5th Avenue. A ten-million-dollar bond issue of loans to the Irish Republic was an immediate success in a campaign headed by the labor lawyer, Frank P. Walsh. By 1920 the situation in Ireland was desperate. Lord Mayor McCurtain of Cork was murdered by British soldiers, 60,000 of whom were quartered in Ireland. To dramatize the situation, 60 Irish-American women picketed the British Embassy in Washington, denouncing the impending massacre and demanding that Congress abrogate all treaties with England and recognize the Irish Republic. Pickets were arrested by order of Secretary of State Bainbridge Colby for insulting the British Ambassador. Next day he backed down when quotations from his own speech of 1916, denouncing England for the Easter Week executions, were carried by pickets. These demonstrations helped to stay the hand of England in Ireland to some extent.

A Commission on British Atrocities was set up here of public spirited Americans, including Jane Addams, Senators Norris and Walsh, and James Maurer of the Pennsylvania State Federation of Labor. Witnesses came from Ireland, including Mrs. Terence McSweeney, widow of the Lord Mayor of Cork who had been arrested in August 1920 and died in Brixton Jail in England on October 25 while on a hunger strike. His death had caused world-wide indignation.

The plan to negotiate a treaty between the Soviet Government and the Republic of Ireland had not been abandoned. But President De Valera preferred to press for U. S. recognition first. After two years of fruitless effort, he authorized Dr. McCarten to discuss the matter with the Russian representatives here—L. A. K. Martens and S. Nuorteva. A proposed treaty was drafted by Nuorteva, which is in an appendix to Dr. McCarten's book, *With De Valera in America.* One provision was that the Soviet Government would entrust to a representative of the Republic of Ireland in the Soviet Union the interests of the Roman Catholic Church within its territory. Dr. McCarten was ready to sign the treaty, but De Valera delayed. Finally, the President left secretly for Dublin, sending Dr. McCarten to Russia in 1920, but without power to sign, an empty gesture in which the Russians were not interested.

Years later, in 1948, during an election contest between De Valera and Dr. McCarten, a startling piece of information came to light in regard to these Soviet-Irish negotiations. It was revealed that in 1920 the representatives of the Irish Republic in New York City had loaned the Soviet representatives (who sorely needed dollars) approximately $20,000. They had received as security precious Russian jewels worth many times the amount. The jewels were smuggled into the United States originally—and then out again, when they were taken to Dublin, Mr. De Valera stated. They were placed in the vault of the Bank of Ireland where they probably still remain. This is a dramatic variant of the "Moscow gold" legend.

Dr. McCarten broke with De Valera after 1921 over the truce and the treaty between De Valera and Lloyd George, which resulted in the shameful partition of Ireland into the Irish Free State and Northern Ireland and precipitated a horrible two years of civil war. Liam Mellows was shot in Mountjoy Jail in December 1922 by order of the Free State.

This came as a shock to his American friends who knew him as a valient fighter for Irish freedom. The fratricidal struggle between those who had been in prison and exile together gnawed like a cancer at the vitals of the Irish movement. Even when peace finally came, the British grip on the six Northern Counties belied national independence. The situation in Ireland then and since has not measured up to the expectations of the Irish people and their kinsfolk around the world. The population of this strangely sterile country has fallen alarmingly in the past three decades. Its development industrially and in rural areas has been retarded by its isolation from progressive countries. Censorship has stifled its press and literature. Creative mental life is limited, causing its best sons, like Sean O'Casey, to seek refuge in self-imposed exile. Large numbers of the younger generation have gone away to live in England and elsewhere. A dour and puritanical state, in the image of the fanatically Catholic professor of mathematics, De Valera, has curtailed human freedom and attempted to crush the joy of life. Equal rights for women, guaranteed by the earlier proclamations of Connolly, were stricken from the 1937 constitution, causing Mrs. Skeffington to campaign in protest. James Connolly would have scornfully repudiated De Valera's friendship with Franco and his act in sending official condolences on the death of Hitler. A free workers republic was Connolly's ideal.

WOODROW WILSON AND "VOTES FOR WOMEN"

It is not strange that Woodrow Wilson collapsed before his second term expired. He spoke fluently and freely on all subjects as a "liberal," but his sorry deeds belied his words. "Self-determination" and "make the world safe for democracy" were the most vulnerable. Demonstrations and delegations of advocates of peace, "Hands off Russia," freedom for Ireland, amnesty for political prisoners and last, but not least, "Votes for Women," confronted him at every turn. His administration was faced with the great steel strike of 1919–20. His plans to join the League of Nations were defeated by the Senate. Members of his administration resigned in protest over various issues —a secretary of state over war, a collector of the New York port over suffrage, the issue that perhaps plagued him most.

World War I made many radical changes in the lives of American women. It brought to an end the "lady" type. The labor shortage was great, the need of trained workers acute. At the end of 1918, nearly three million women were employed in food, textile and war industries. Occupations hitherto regarded as "men's work" were open to woman. They worked as conductors on street cars. For the first time they were trained as radio operators. Women volunteered for the motor corps in the army and wore uniforms for the first time. "Farmerettes," wearing bloomers, went from the cities to farms. Women did relief work, sold war bonds, organized canteens for the armed forces, joined nursing units. Thousands emerged from their homes into public life. Many remained in industry, either from necessity or choice, when the war ended.

Under the exigencies of war, the Department of Labor finally set up a Women in Industry division under Mary Van Kleeck, which became the Women's Bureau in 1920. The need for adequate labor standards and for protective legislation for women was pressing. A demand for equal opportunities at skilled trades and professions and resistance to pressure to go back to the home grew apace. Unions of women were growing. All of this added fuel to the increasing demand of women for the right to vote. Rich women and working women, professional women and women from the farms, Socialist and non-political women—all pressed for votes for women. It was truly a mass movement, especially after World War I, a unique solidarity around a single issue.

Brave women like Elizabeth Cady Stanton and Susan B. Anthony had been the early pioneers, facing abuse and ridicule, violence and even arrests for attempting to vote. Later, women like Dr. Anna Shaw and Carrie Chapman Catt headed the National American Women's Suffrage Association, which struggled against "the lethargy of women and the opposition of men." But by 1916 a younger, bolder and more militant group emerged, which was dissatisfied with the slower process of winning suffrage, state by state, and fought for a constitutional amendment. They organized the Women's Party in 1916, which planned to mobilize the women's vote in all suffrage states only for parties and candidates who would support national suffrage. That year a group of wealthy suffragists financed and toured in a Suffrage Special. They did not campaign directly for the Republican candidate, Charles Evans Hughes, but their slogan was anti-Wilson: "Vote against Wilson! He Kept Us Out of Suffrage!" Many voted for Eugene V. Debs, then in prison.

Wilson came to office indifferent to suffrage. On his first Inauguration Day, he was greeted by a suffrage parade of 10,000 women. His first address to Congress set off another women's demonstration. On that day, April 7, 1913, the 19th Amendment, known as the Susan B. Anthony Amendment, was introduced in both the House and Senate. It took seven years of organized struggle by the women before it was adopted and ratified. The women felt correctly that Wilson could have speeded it up.

The tactics of the Women's Party caused sharp differences in the suffrage ranks. The Golden Special, as the suffrage train was dubbed, caused rifts. Dr. Marie Equi, my Portland friend, and others there who helped win suffrage in Oregon, opposed such a display of wealth in the name of suffrage. She carried a banner when they arrived there, naming several wealthy sponsors and asking: "Which Goose Laid the Golden Egg?" They tried unsuccessfully to have her arrested. Wilson was extremely bitter against the women who campaigned against him. Yet he did not remember Dr. Equi's stand when appeals for executive clemency came to him on her behalf, and allowed her to go to San Quentin prison.

The Women's Party picketed almost continuously from January 1917 until March 19, 1919. They picketed the White House and Capitol, held military parades, return receptions for Wilson after his trips to Europe and receptions when he departed. They picketed him in Washington, Boston and New York. Only the Irish had attempted such tactics. Later, a Children's Crusade for Amnesty picketed President Harding. Suffrage banners were addressed to foreign visitors and President Wilson's speeches on "freedom" and "democracy" at home and abroad were burned by the suffragists in a "watch-fire of freedom" urn.

Large numbers of women, old and young, were arrested, refused to pay fines and were sent to an unspeakably vile workhouse, "Occoquan." Some were wives of government officials. Their husbands went to Wilson and raised hell. They had been dinner guests at the White House! Released, they returned to picket. Their banners were destroyed and they were beaten by hoodlums, including soldiers and sailors, while the police looked on. They fought for the status of political prisoners and resorted to a hunger strike as a protest against horrible conditions. Forcible feedings were attempted and they were threatened with insane asylums. Women were arrested on Boston Common as they burned Wilson's speeches there, and outside the Metropolitan Opera House in New York City, where he spoke. They all boarded a "Prison Special" on their release and toured the country. Public sympathy and support for the women grew.

It was some ordeal these plucky women endured. On May 19, 1919, President Wilson called a special session of Congress and the Amendment was carried by both houses and sent to the states for ratification, with the two long-needed votes finally mobilized by the reluctant President whose reputation as a statesman was tarnished by this long delay. Both parties now worked hard for ratification so the women could vote in the November 1920 elections. Our country trailed behind over 20 others in granting the right to vote to women. Australia, New Zealand, Finland, Russia, England and Sweden were among the first.

The suffrage forces did not unite after victory. About 51 per cent of the eligible women voters came to the polls in 1920. This went up to 61 per cent in the next election. Many of the suffragists joined the National League of Women Voters, founded by Mrs. Catt in 1919, an excellent organization which has since campaigned to educate women voters and get out their vote at the polls. Others remained with the Women's Party, which concentrated on a campaign for an "Equal Rights Amendment"—in some ways, a misleading misnomer. It is opposed by the Women's Bureau, all leading labor organizations and many women's organizations, like the Women's Trade Union League. So far it has not been successful because of the danger that it will nullify all protective labor legislation for women and other laws necessary for the safeguarding of mothers. Attempts to arrive at a compromise amendment, which will remove a multitude of existing legal inequalities and disabilities and yet preserve such necessary legislation as noted above, have so far not been successful. Once the right to vote was achieved, women did not remain united as women, but divided into the existing political parties and other organizations as their views and interests dictated. The one common denominator of *peace* could, I believe, unite women once again, with a few exceptions.

"UNITED FRONT" IN THE TWENTIES

I have no recollection of the term "united front" in the 1920s. It came into use considerably later. But the extent to which the radical and progressive movements operated then on such a principle is very apparent. Men and women who spoke out for suffrage would also sign appeals for financial aid to the IWW and appear on Irish and amnesty delegations and were in the peace movement. There were no hard and fast lines drawn between one good freedom cause and another and no such fears of reprisal as there are today. People were not afraid they would hurt one cause by identifying themselves with another. I marvel today at how wide and diffuse were my contacts and friendships in those days. For instance, I came to know many suffrage leaders during our struggle for free speech in Paterson, New Jersey, in 1915, which I have described, yet I was a "Leftist" of the left, then, as now.

I was invited to speak on the IWW and its activities in the organization of women workers in the textile industry before a unique group in New York City. It was a women's luncheon club which met fortnightly, called the "Heterodoxy." Marie Jenny Howe, whom I had met in Cleveland with Tom L. Johnson, was its chairman. It shunned publicity, but as its name implied had free and frank discussions on all subjects. I was invited to join after my speech. The speakers were always women, and included Helen Keller, Margaret Sanger, Mrs. Malmberg, the Finnish woman peace advocate, Bessie Beaty and Louise Bryant on their return from Russia, Mrs. Skeffington from Ireland, and other interesting foreign visitors.

The subjects mainly dealt with women and their accomplishments. All its members were ardent suffragists, some were quite extreme feminists. All were people in their own right in many and varied fields of endeavor. No one was there because her husband or father was famous. I met some of the foremost women of that time through "Heterodoxy." Among its members were Mary Shaw, Fola La Follette, Margaret Wycherly and Beatrice Forbes-Robertson—actresses; Mary Heaton Vorse, Alice Duer Miller, Zona Gale, Inez Haynes Irwin and Mary Austin—writers; scientists Elsie Clews Parsons and Leta Hollingsworth; educator Elizabeth Irwin; editor Katherine Leckie; interior decorator Amy Mali Hicks; artist Lou Rogers; suffrage leaders Doris Stevens, Paula Jacobi and others. One Negro woman, Grace Mayo Johnson (associated with her husband, James Weldon Johnson, in the many activities that distinguished Negro leader pursued on behalf of the Negro people), was a member. She was a co-worker with her husband in the National Association for Advancement of Colored People.

This club remained in existence until the late 30s, when its ranks were perceptibly thinned by the death of many of the older members. I recall only one unpleasant experience during World War I, when a few super-patriots were shocked at the anti-war sentiments freely expressed at our meetings. They demanded the expulsion of Rose Pastor Stokes and myself after we had been arrested. When the club refused, they resigned. I had worked almost exclusively with men up to this time and my IWW anti-political slant had kept me away from political movements. It was good for my education and a broadening influence for me to come to know all these splendid "Heterodoxy" members and to share in their enthusiasms. It made me conscious of women and their many accomplishments. My mother, who had great pride in women, was very pleased by my association with them.

During this same period I became an early "united front" sympathizer and co-worker with the American Communists. My interest grew out of my friendship with so many of their leaders and my cooperation with them as "left wingers" of the Socialist Party preceding the political conventions of 1919. I recall meeting Jack Reed and Jim Larkin immediately after their return from the Chicago convention that fall, when Jack said enthusiastically: "Gurley, we've got it—a real American working-class Socialist party, at last!" Many Socialists, who became charter members of the Communist Party, were delegates in the Workers Defense Union, which came to their defense after both the Lusk and Palmer raids. Delegates from both parties met in our office to confer on legal strategy in these cases. Among these early Communists with whom I worked were Ella Reeve Bloor, Rose Pastor Stokes, Robert Minor, John Ballam, Alfred Wagenknecht, Rose Baron, Carl Brodsky, Irving Potash, Harry Winitsky and Jim Larkin.

I was still an IWW in my convictions and hesitated to join a political party, although the Russian Revolution and association with the suffragists and the Communists were modifying my views considerably. I was busy at all times in defense of *all* political prisoners, regardless of their views. Each group appreciated our activity on its own behalf and I was often like a bridge, trying to build a united front for common defense. Sometimes I was drawn into the inner conflicts of various groups, even in prison. When Jim Larkin was shifted to Dannemora prison to stop a constant flow of visitors and much publicity around him, I secured permission to see him there.

It was a lonely place up near the Canadian border. But when I arrived I was refused permission to go in, without explanation. One of the guards told me that a young woman reporter had been there the day before. Not knowing her or that she came from the New York *Call,* they escorted her through the prison. She saw the men march in, among them James Larkin. Thereupon she had announced that she was Agnes Smedley, a personal friend of Larkin, and demanded to see him. She got a good story but I had a long hard trip in vain. The friendly guard promised me he would let Jim know that I had come. I heard from Jim later that he had gotten the message.

I visited Harry Winitsky in Sing Sing—a very fat, jolly young man, who had a romance in Sing Sing. He met a young lady, a concert singer, who came to entertain the inmates and married her on his release. I also made a trip to Auburn prison to see Benjamin Gitlow who had been transferred away from Sing Sing. He was a clothing cutter by trade and a Socialist from his youth. His mother, Kate Gitlow, was extremely active and devoted to him. He was a hard man to talk to—a silent, rather dour person. When Jim Larkin was released in 1922 by order of Governor Al Smith, who said his imprisonment was a violation of civil liberties, Jim came to see me in my office of the Workers Defense Union on East 10th St. We were to speak together that night in Bryant Hall. He said, "Elizabeth, I'm going to denounce that man Gitlow. He's no good in prison. He has no solidarity." I was appalled. I knew Jim was swayed by strong personal likes and dislikes and was very critical of the manners and morals of all Americans. Gitlow was then a respected Communist leader and remained such for quite a few years later. I urged Jim not to say any such thing, to go to his Party committee if he had any complaint, but to "remember Gitlow is a political prisoner." His parents would be in the front row at the meeting. I went there with fear and trepidation about what Jim would say. But, although he made a long speech, so long that I did not speak, he said nothing critical of Gitlow. I was greatly relieved that I had successfully dissuaded him. But when Gitlow became a star stool-pigeon witness against the Communists for the Dies Committee, the "Un-American Activities Committee" in the 30s, I recalled Jim Larkin's earlier estimate of him. Harry Winitsky died of a heart attack immediately after Gitlow testified, which was a strange coincidence, or it may have been a result. Who knows?

Our office was an interesting place. Many visitors dropped in. I recall a famous "infant prodigy," named Sidius, a mathematical genius but a lonely and rather forlorn and helpless human being. He had been arrested on Boston Common during a May Day demonstration in 1919, and his professor parents had disowned him. He found warmth and comradeship in our office and was pathetically grateful. He used to help my son Fred do his algebra and geometry at our work table. Another visitor was a gray-haired prosperous-looking, rotund, middle-aged man, later mayor of Massillion, Ohio, as I recall. He was General Jacob S. Coxey, leader of the famous Coxey's Army of 1894, who had assembled the unemployed of the Western states and marched them to Washington to bring their grievances before Congress. Attempting to demonstrate near the Capitol on May 1 he was arrested. While he was in jail he was nominated for Congress in Ohio.

Another visitor who dropped in occasionally was an IWW seaman friend of mine, "Jimmy." When he was in Russia, he told me, Jack Reed had taken him to see Lenin, who asked him how soon there would be a revolution in the United States. Jimmy said, "Not very soon," and Lenin eagerly questioned him about the reasons for his answer. He said to Jack, "I'm so glad to meet a real American worker." Jimmy said, "He's a smart man. He wants to know the truth—no nonsense for him."

When Americans First Heard of Lenin

When the news of the Russian Bolshevik Revolution of November 1917 burst upon the world, American workers learned for the first time of a man named Lenin—through this great event in human history, the beginning of socialism. We also learned some new words, which became part of the language in no time, "Bolshevik" and "Soviet," among them. Even those of us who were left-Socialists and IWWs knew practically nothing of the Russian Socialist movement, except that we had great sympathy with its long, agonizing struggle to overthrow the tsar's cruel and bloody regime. Overnight, "Bolshevik" became a household word, even to those who did not know it merely meant "majority," and referred to a political division in the Russian Social-Democratic Labor Party. "I am a Bolshevik from the crown of my head to the tip of my toes!" said Debs. "Damned Bolsheviks!" employers shouted at militant workers and union organizers. All strikers were "Bolsheviks," of course.

The Russian-speaking people in our midst knew the meaning of the word "Bolshevik," and also of "Soviet," which meant "council" in Russian. But it, too, was new to us, although it had originated in the unsuccessful 1905 Russian revolution. "Soviet (Councils) of Workers' Deputies" were elected by the workers in all mills and factories. They had started in St. Petersburg and Moscow, and spread to many cities. They created a strange and novel structure, which appealed enough to workers everywhere that they were eager to know all about it.

American newspaper correspondents flocked to revolutionary Russia from all war fronts in Europe. One, Isaac McBride, went across the border under a white flag, carrying a suitcase, in his eager zeal to see what a revolution looked like. Everything that we of the left-wing movement heard from there through the press fired us with enthusiasm. In the fourth year of the bloody European war the first act of the new Congress of Soviets was a Decree of Peace, calling for a "just and democratic peace—an immediate armistice, and the abolition of all secret treaties." Later they published all the secret treaties of the tsar's government. The second act of the Soviet Republic was to abolish private ownership of land, mineral resources, forests and waters. It would be hard to describe today the impact of this news on the outside world —the consternation of the militarists, the imperialists, the capitalists, in short, the ruling classes of the world—and the thrill of satisfaction among the poor and lowly, the downtrodden and heavily laden in all lands.

Curiosity and a burning desire to know what was going on in Russia swept through the Socialist and labor movement everywhere. I recall a little pamphlet, possibly the first one published here, called *The Soviets at Work,* by Lenin, Premier of the Russian Soviet Republic. It was issued in 1918 by the Rand School of Social Science. In the introduction, Alexander Trachtenberg, then director of research at this school, makes this significant comment on Lenin: "The Soviet revolution makes no romantic appeal to him. It is a matter of how ready and willing the workers are to understand the building of a new order which would not prove a house of cards but a formidable structure rooted in the very foundations of sound economics." Almost a million copies of this pamphlet were sold.

The flood of books started in 1918 with *Ten Days That Shook the World* by John Reed, followed by *Six Red Months in Red Russia* by his wife, Louise Bryant. An exposé of the corruption of the tsar's court and the influence of the dissolute monk, Rasputin—called *The Last of the Romanoffs*—was written by Mr. Rivet, the *Paris Temps* correspondent. The *Daily Herald* (London) correspondent, Henry Brailsford, wrote *Across the Blockade.* Albert Rhys Williams, who was European war correspondent for the *Outlook,* an American magazine, went into Russia in 1917. He wrote *Through the Russian Revolution,* and later *The Russian Land,* and *The Soviets,* also *Lenin—the Man and His Works,* and *76 Questions and Answers* on the Soviet system, all enthusiastic accounts of the new Russia. He lectured here all over the country on what he saw there. Richard Washburn Childs, American ambassador to Italy under President Wilson, wrote *Political Russia.* All these books came out under the imprint of well-known publishers.

A little later, Arthur Ransome, war correspondent of the *Manchester Guardian,* wrote *Russia in 1919* and *Crisis in Russia* (1921). William Z. Foster went to Russia in 1921 and wrote a series of articles for the labor press here, subsequently published as a book, *The Russian Revolution.* Journalists and others wrote interviews with Lenin—including H. G. Wells of London, Colonel Raymond Robbins of the American Red Cross, Bessie Beatty of the San Francisco *Chronicle,* and Lincoln Steffens, who said, "I have seen the future and it works." The trade union delegations went there from all countries and made elaborate reports. Russian-born Sidney Hillman, president of the

Amalgamated Clothing Workers, went to Russia in 1921, talked with Lenin and organized help to the new workers' country. Two hundred and fifty thousand dollars were collected among this union's members and an A.C.W.A. Relief Ship, the *S.S. Margus,* was sent carrying wheat, milk, clothing and drugs. Hillman organized a project to equip clothing factories in the Soviet Union. In return, the Soviet government gave the two banks of the Amalgamated the exclusive concession for the remittance of drafts to the Soviet Union. In five years, from 1923 to 1928, over 18 million dollars in remittances were handled by the Amalgamated banks. Needless to say, Hillman was not a Communist but he was impressed by Lenin's practical plans to build a new world.

An official British Trade Union Delegation of ten men went to Russia in 1924 and a delegation of six British union women went in 1925. Both made voluminous reports, stressing the need of recognition and cooperation. The women concluded as follows: "No honest observer of present-day Soviet Russia can doubt for a moment that a great and sincere experiment in working-class government is being carried out in Russia." A trade union delegation finally went from the United States in 1927. It consisted of James Maurer, president of the Pennsylvania State Federation of Labor; John Brophy, former president of District No. 2 of the United Mine Workers of America; James W. Fitzpatrick, president of the Actors and Artists; Frank Palmer, editor of the Colorado *Labor Advocate;* and Albert E. Coyle, of the Locomotive Engineers. On their advisory, technical and editorial staff were Stuart Chase, Robert Dunn and Rexford Tugwell, and Professors Arthur Fisher and Paul Douglas. They issued an exhaustive and quite favorable report on their return.

Later, the Vanguard Press issued a series of studies of the Soviet Union, edited by Professor Jerome Davis of Yale University, on such diverse topics as women, village life, religion, health, art and culture. One, by Roger Baldwin, was on *Civil Liberties in the Soviet Union.* (In my copy, given to me by the author in 1929, is the inscription, "To Elizabeth Flynn, who knows far better than I the meaning of liberty to the workers.") All of which goes to show the tremendous interest and eager desire for knowledge about the Soviet Union at that time. People were not afraid to express their sympathy and friendship for the new system, nor were they immediately labeled "foreign agents" for so doing. That came a long time later.

Some of the first translations of Lenin's writings came here from

Britain. I have a copy of his *April* (1917) *Theses,* from Glasgow, published by the Socialist Labor Press. Another pamphlet I received from a friend there was *The Proletarian Revolution* by V. I. Ulianov (Lenin), published by the British Socialist Party. In the early twenties Lenin's pamphlets began to appear here. I recall Robert Minor, with his pockets full of copies of *The State and Revolution,* passing them out enthusiastically to all of us. It was written in August and September 1917. Another that had a great effect on those of us who were called "syndicalists" was *"Left-Wing" Communism—an Infantile Disorder,* particularly the chapters "Should Revolutionaries Work in Reactionary Trade Unions?" and "Shall We Participate in Bourgeois Parliaments?" The answer Lenin gave to both questions was "Yes," which caused much debate here, especially in the IWW and left-wing Socialist circles, and led many to join the Communist Party.

A little later, an earlier pamphlet written in 1916, called *Imperialism—the Highest Stage of Capitalism,* was translated into English. It is here, in his introduction to the first Russian edition, that Lenin referred to the necessity of formulating his few observations on Russian politics "with extreme caution, by hints, in that Aesopian language—*in that cursed Aesopian language*—to which tsarism compelled all revolutionaries to have recourse." I gave no special thought to this at the time. I knew how Irish songs like "Dark Rosaleen" and "Kathleen-ni-Houlihan" referred to Ireland and "Spanish ale will give you hope!" meant help was coming to the revolutionaries from Spain. In all oppressed countries such figure of speech were necessary. Little did I think that this phrase, "Aesopian language," would be twisted and perverted 30 odd years later in a Federal Court in Foley Square in New York City by a renegade stool pigeon, Louis Budenz, to convict Communists, myself included, accused under the thought-control Smith Act.

FOSTER—LEADER OF LABOR

In recalling the onslaught of the Palmer Raids, the deportation drives and state syndicalist prosecutions after World War I, it would be a serious mistake not to see the other side of the picture—the magnificent fight-back spirit of the American workers at that time. In addition to the above repressive government efforts, there was a vicious drive against the trade unions by Big Business all over the country in a campaign to install the "open shop" and company unions. The employers resented the wartime gains of labor and were determined to destroy them. The cost of living was extremely high during and after the war, and the workers' grievances were aggravated. The years of 1919 and the early 20s saw American workers engaged in heroic struggles on a gigantic scale. There emerged in these epic battles a new leader of labor—a great organizer and strategist, William Z. Foster. He had advocated, as a delegate to the Chicago Federation of Labor, the utilization of the war period to bring the unorganized millions of basic industry into the American Federation of Labor, but the AFL leaders rejected his plans.

Aided by a few coworkers, among them Jack Johnstone, and supported by John R. Fitzpatrick, president of the Chicago Federation, Foster demonstrated in a most dramatic manner that it could be done. He had worked long hours in the car barns of Swift and Company, yet he could not afford an overcoat in 1915. He knew the lot of the stockyard workers. A vice-president of Armour's had recently insulted a workers' committee when they came to complain of low wages, long hours, dangerous and unsanitary working conditions in the slave pens of the yards. "Tell your union friends," he said, "that organized labor will never get anything from this company that it hasn't the power to take." Bill Foster, exploited worker from the stockyards turned labor organizer, never forgot those cynical words. He packed a deadly wallop for the Big Five—Armour, Swift, Morris, Cudahy and Wilson— who made 40 million dollars in 1917. He organized their plants.

Many of the workers were immigrants, many Negroes. For the first time 20,000 Negro workers were organized side by side with their white brothers. This was a unique historical accomplishment. The IWW had had no great success in organizing Negro workers, although they had organized some in the lumber camps of Louisiana and on the waterfront of Philadelphia. But in textiles and lumber in the North and mining in the West, where the IWW was strong, there were as yet few Negro workers. This therefore was the real beginning of organizing Negro and white workers together in basic industry. When workers were fired for joining the union, a national strike vote was carried 100 per cent. The workers were ready and willing to quit. With the huge wartime demand for foodstuffs, the packers could not stand a strike.

The Federal Mediation Commission stepped in and offered arbitration. For three weeks the unions exposed the conditions in that terrible industry. There had been no great changes in conditions from the days *The Jungle* was written by Upton Sinclair a decade before. The hearings were, as Foster described them, "a long recital of starvation, exhausting labor, sickness, mutilation, ignorance, drunkenness, insanity, despair and death." One woman worker testified that she had had a hat when she came from Poland, but it got worn out and she could never afford another. In December 1917 came the first victory. The Commission agreed to the right to organize, a 10 per cent wage increase, seniority, no discrimination. They also agreed to abolish arbitrary discharges and to establish sanitary lunchrooms, dressing rooms and washrooms.

This was followed in March 1918 by Judge Altschuler, wartime administrator of the packing industry, granting 85 per cent of their additional demands, which included 10 per cent to 25 per cent wage increases, an eight-hour day with ten hours' pay, extra pay for overtime, equal pay for men and women, a guarantee of five days' work a week, and lunch periods with pay. Even today, these would be substantial gains. To top it off, the awards were retroactive; 125,000 Chicago workers received six million dollars in back pay—and a few overcoats and hats were then possible for the packinghouse workers. This victory thrilled and encouraged the members of the entire labor movement. It prepared them for the postwar struggles, the greatest of which was led by Foster in 1919–20.

While Bill Foster was listening to the arbitration hearings on packing he had a plan in his pocket for organizing steel, citadel of the open shop. Representatives of 15 international unions were called together by the Chicago Federation of Labor. Samuel Gompers, president of the AFL said skeptically, "Well, Brother Foster, what do you propose?" The 15 unions grudgingly agreed to a federated campaign and pledged the ridiculous sum of $100 each. Foster was made the unpaid secretary of the National Committee for Organizing Iron and Steel Workers. Fortunately, his own union, the Railway Carmen, paid his salary as an organizer. He remarked with justifiable bitterness, "You would think we were setting out to organize a bunch of peanut stands instead of a half a million workers." Gompers never spoke at a steel workers' meeting. Finally, he resigned as chairman of the committee and appointed John Fitzpatrick in his place.

However, Foster was not easily discouraged. He had faith in the workers. He said many years later in his pamphlet on *Unionizing Steel*, written to help the CIO in this field: "I was never one of those who considered the organizing of workers such a huge task. The problem in any case is merely to develop the proper organization crews and systems, and the freedom-hungry workers, skilled or unskilled, men or women, black or white, will react almost as naturally and inevitably as water runs down a hill." He demonstrated the truth of his words in the greatest single key industry in the country, steel. The *New Republic* called it a "miracle of organization." The *Journal of Political Economy* commended "his remarkable ability."

THE GREAT STEEL STRIKE, 1919

Judge Gary, arrogant president of the U.S. Steel Corporation, tried to head off the organization drive among steel workers. He ordered a basic national eight-hour day, which he referred to contemptuously as, "Give them an extra cup of rice!" On October 1, 1918, Foster and his corps of organizers moved into the heart of steel—Pittsburgh, "The Iron City"—which is surrounded by a ring of what were then company towns, Aliquippa, Ambridge, Duquesne, McKeesport, Clairton, Homestead, Donora, Johnstown and others. The going was rough. In the course of the drive, 30,000 workers were fired. The KKK appeared and the spy system spread. Speech and assemblage were suppressed and the workers were held in a state of industrial peonage. Organizers were jailed and beaten up. Foster, Mother Jones and others were arrested and driven out of town. Mayor Crawford of Duquesne, called "The Toad" by the workers, remarked when he heard that Rabbi Stephen Wise of New York was to speak at a free speech protest meeting: "Jesus Christ himself could not speak here for the A. F. of L.!"

There were 33 nationality groups involved in the drive, many foreign-born, brought directly from Ellis Island to these industrial prisons. As in our IWW textile strikes a few years earlier, language was a tremendous problem for the organizers at meetings and in literature. Foster, like Haywood, trained the organizers to use simple nontechnical speech, and to speak slowly, and distinctly, repeating the main ideas. Many foreign-speaking workers began to learn English at these meetings, an "Americanization" by-product of the strike.

A barrage of redbaiting was let loose on Foster. A Senate Investigation Committee did not concern itself with the many just grievances and indescribably bad working and living conditions of the workers, some of whom were huddled in barracks. Nor did they concern themselves with the brutality of the Coal and Iron Constabulary (later abolished by Governor Pinchot), nor with the violations of all constitutional rights. No, their main concern was to picture Foster as the chief Red in America, who was using the strike to start a revolution. His previous activities as an IWW and a syndicalist and all his writings were featured in newspaper scareheads. He was charged with being a "Bolshevik"—then the last word in redbaiting.

But Foster proceeded on his determined path, in his characteristically quiet and systematic manner. By June 1919, over 100,000 workers were in the union, which made a demand on Judge Gary for collective bargaining. He ignored the letter. A strike vote registered 98 per cent in favor. On September 22, 1919, approximately 304,000 workers quit the steel mills. By September 30, there were 367,000 out on strike in 50 cities in ten states. The giant industry stopped; the fires went out, blast furnaces ceased to roar, the red glow that filled the skies for miles, faded; smoke and gas no longer polluted the atmosphere. The great life-giving force, the workers, had gone out of the vast plants.

A reign of terror was then let loose on the strikers. The steel areas were overrun by police, deputy sheriffs, state troopers and strike breakers who were brought in under their protection. Picketing was forbidden and strikers who attempted to picket were arrested and beaten. Twenty-two workers laid down their lives in this great struggle. No mass meetings or union meetings were permitted during the four months of the strike. The workers maintained a magnificent unity as long as humanly possible, and were supported in a spirit of solidarity by other workers all over the country. Outstanding were the contributions of the needle-trades workers of New York City, who sent their brothers in steel $180,000.

But terror and hunger, and the indifference, even sabotage, of the official Gompers machine of the AFL finally crushed the heroic effort. However, as often happens in what are called "lost strikes," it had cost the employers dearly and they were forced to abolish the 12-hour day and seven-day week and to make many changes in wages and working conditions, which the workers credited to their own battles. The great moral victory was in the proof that the octopus steel could be successfully organized. Fifteen years later the CIO finished the job that Bill Foster so courageously tackled back in 1919. Phillip Murray said when he was president of United Steel Workers, CIO, "There's one Communist my door is always open to—Bill Foster, for what he did for the steel workers!"

At the same time that the great steel strike was going on, in the year 1919, more than four million American workers were involved in other strike struggles. There was a general strike in Seattle and one in Winnipeg, Canada. There was what was called the "outlaw strike" of 200,000 railroad shopmen, unsanctioned by their officials. Despite a temporary injunction, over a million coal miners were on strike at the same time as the steel workers. The textile workers of Lawrence were out again, under the banner of the Amalgamated Textile Workers and won the 48-hour week. Clothing workers and maritime workers, were on the march in 1919. Labor was aggressive, stubborn and persistent in defense of its rights after World War I. Blood was shed in these great struggles. Heroic men and women died for the working class.

Such a one—a woman who gave her life—was Mrs. Fannie Sellins. Her maiden name was Mooney. She was a widow with four children when she began her labor organizing work for the garment workers of the AFL in St. Louis. She was very successful and was loaned to the United Mine Workers of America to go into the coal towns and work quietly in the homes, especially in places where men organizers had been beaten up and deported. On August 22, 1919, she was brutally murdered in Natrona, near Breckenridge, Pennsylvania, in Allegheny County. A strike of miners at the Allegheny Steel Company's mine was taking place there. A dozen armed men, called "deputies" but actually paid by the mining company, were stationed at that place. They tried to break up the picket lines of the miners by threats and brutality. Their hatred of Mrs. Sellins was fanned further by the fact that she was loaned by the miners to help organize the steel workers.

Foster referred to her as "one of the finest labor organizers I ever met." He said:

Fannie Sellins had a special distinction as an organizer during the great 1919 Steel Strike. She was one of the best of our whole corps of organizers. In New Kensington [Pennsylvania] she lined up 15,000 to 20,000 steel workers. Of the whole 80 centers, this was the only one which spontaneously organized itself. Fannie Sellins had an exceptional belief in the workers and she went out and organized them. She was killed because she organized these thousands of steel workers. She took the initiative and in the midst of terror went out to her work."

On a hot afternoon in August Mrs. Sellins received a call to come to Natrona. A striker, a young veteran, had been arrested. She found deputies flourishing guns at an excited group of men, women and children. She felt trouble brewing and tried to get the children away, into nearby yards behind a fence. The deputies opened fire and killed an unarmed striker, 60-year-old Joseph Starzeleski, and shot Mrs. Sellins in the back. After she fell, they pumped more bullets into her body. One deputy put her hat on his head and swaggered around shouting, "I am Fanny Sellins now!" The two victims are buried in a common grave under a beautiful monument erected by the union, with an inscription, "Faithful ever to the cause of Labor." It was dedicated by Phillip Murray and organizers of the United Mine Workers of America. Every year the workers of the area commemorate the death of Fannie Sellins, one of the many martyrs who died for labor.

THE CHILDREN'S CRUSADE

The dramatic climax of the movement for amnesty came unexpectedly out of small groups of friendless and poverty-stricken families in Oklahoma and Arkansas. They became the center of a Children's Crusade to the nation's capital, a long trek for backwoods folks who had never been but a few miles from their little farms. The idea of a living petition, one that could not be pigeonholed or thrown in a wastepaper basket, originated with resourceful and determined Kate Richards O'Hare. She had just finished serving two years in the Jefferson City, Missouri, prison for an anti-war speech.

A Women's Committee to Free Kate O'Hare had been set up in the Rand School building in New York City. A talented and eloquent young Negro woman Socialist, Helen Holman, was its secretary. Thanks to the tireless efforts of the Socialist women, the sentence had been cut from five to two years.

As a Socialist agitator, working out of St. Louis, Mrs. O'Hare had made many speaking trips into the Southwest and knew the barren, hard lives of the tenant farmers and their wives and children. Now a group of the leaders of these people were in Leavenworth prison for opposing the war and resisting the draft. Some were Socialists, all were members of an organization called The Working Class Unions, and their anti-war movement became known as The Green Corn Rebellion. With their shotguns in hand, they went up into the hills to barricade themselves against being drafted.

The families left behind by these political prisoners were in dire poverty, unable to visit their men in prison for lack of funds. Kate was aroused to great indignation by the story of the wife of Stanley Clark, a Socialist lawyer, whose only "crime" was that he had collected funds to help the families of the Bisbee miners who had been deported into the desert in 1917 during a strike. Mrs. Clark had gathered affidavits to prove that her husband was actually pro-war and had sent all the material to Washington but heard nothing of it. Kate decided to gather up all the families in that part of the country to make a tour on the way to Washington, and to tell their stories in every city. Several IWW families joined en route and there were 33 in the party when they reached New York City. They had visited Cincinnati and Detroit and had stopped off at Terre Haute, Indiana, to see Debs who was quite ill at that time. Their meetings collected over $4,000 for their expenses on the Crusade, a large sum in those days.

Everywhere, the Crusade was greeted with deep emotion and enthusiasm. Over three years had passed since the armistice and there had been great disappointment at Christmas, 1921. President Harding had pardoned only a few of the political prisoners and had then refused to see delegations to discuss the matter further. The families had expected a general amnesty. The vociferous opposition of the American Legion slowed the President down after he released Debs.

The Crusade left St. Louis on April 16, 1922, and arrived in Washington on April 29. They remained until after July 19. When they arrived in New York City from Buffalo on an early morning train, they were a forlorn yet valiant little band of eager, wide-eyed youngsters, sleepy babies and anxious, tired mothers. As they came off the train, they efficiently unfurled their signs and marched proudly through Grand Central Station. This extraordinary "Army with Banners" created an immediate sensation among all spectators. "A Little Child Shall Lead Them," was out in front. Then came "A Hundred and Thirteen Men Jailed for Their Opinions," and "My Daddy Didn't Want to Kill"; another said, "Is the Constitution Dead?" and another, "Eugene Debs Is Free—Why Not my Daddy?" A young girl, Irene Danley, carried a sign that read: "My Mother Died of Grief." A young mother walked with a three-year-old child carrying a banner:

"I Never Saw My Daddy." An elderly woman; Mrs. Hough, mother of an imprisoned IWW youth marched proudly along. Our first destination was the nearby headquarters of the Amalgamated Food Workers. The police asked me if I had a permit for a parade. I said, "No, it's not a parade. We intend to take these women and children to a place where they can eat and rest." They looked at them and gruffly acceded to our plan and we were soon there.

Here, at last, at the food workers' union, were not strange people, staring at them and their banners. Here were comrades and friends such as they had found in other cities. Few local people dared to speak to them or come near them at home. But now their circle of friends grew even stronger and wider. They were not alone on a bleak farm on a lonely hillside. Big handsome bearded French and Italian chefs from the most exclusive hotels and restaurants in New York were there, wearing their white cooks' hats a foot high. The most skilled waiters in the world, with tears in their eyes, tenderly served these hungry children. The tables were decked with flowers. Each child was given a souvenir, a small replica of the Statue of Liberty. The children sang "My Country, 'Tis of Thee," for their hosts. It was heart-rending to hear their childish voices sing of "Sweet land of liberty!" under the circumstances.

That afternoon the older children went to the circus at Madison Square Garden as the guests of Mrs. J. Sargent Cram, a granddaughter of Peter Cooper. It was a great event, as most of them had never seen a circus, certainly nothing comparable with the Garden's three-ringed wonders. The mothers and babies were taken for rest and tea to the Fifth Avenue mansion of Mrs. Willard Straight. Sympathetic friends came in to meet them. They sat erect in Mrs. Straight's beautiful drawing room, telling their stories. I recall a thin, stern-faced little woman, Mrs. Hicks, who had four children under seven. The baby, a beautiful child named Helen Keller, was born after her father was put in jail. Her husband was a preacher, William Madison Hicks, a descendant of Elias Hicks who founded the Quaker sect known as the "Hicksites." They were pacifists by religious conviction and politically were Socialists. He had been threatened with lynching before his arrest. We heard that day tales of heart-breaking poverty and labor, chopping cotton, of cruel discrimination by neighbors and townsfolk inflamed by war hysteria and of how these women became tired of petitions to Washington to which there were no answers. Then their "Kate" called them to go with her "to see the President."

That night we held a mass meeting at Webster Hall. Between events, however, we had quite a scare. Several of the boys had disappeared. We telephoned around frantically and finally located them at a local police precinct in what was called the "Tenderloin" area, not too far from the Garden. They had started out to see the "ocean," which they had heard was near by. It had a great fascination for these inland youngsters. We should have thought of that. But their odd appearance, in their denim overalls and their strange twang as they asked people "which way is it to the ocean?" caused the police to take them in tow. When the relieved committee arrived to claim them, they were the center of an audience of New York police listening to their description of life in their part of the country and their mission. One hard-boiled cop said: "These kids say they are going to Washington to see the President to get their 'Paws' out of jail! What are they talking about?" It was explained to the mystified cops who shook hands with them and wished them luck.

At the meeting the tired children sat on the floor of the platform and one by one curled up asleep. Among the many speakers was Clare Sheridan, a famous British sculptor and the cousin of Winston Churchill. She was here on a lecture tour. Clare Sheridan had been to Moscow in 1920, where she had made busts of all the leaders of the Russian revolution, including Lenin. Lenin had asked her about her relationship to the then much-hated Churchill. She replied, "I also have another cousin, who was in the Irish rebellion!" Lenin replied, "It must be interesting when you three get together!" Her diary, published as *Mayfair to Moscow,* had made a sensation in England and here because of her social position, her standing as an artist and her frank though non-political admiration of the Russian leaders. This was one of the few meetings outside her regular lectures she addressed, and she spoke with feeling and indignation about America's political prisoners.

But I remember most vividly Kate O'Hare, tall, gaunt, standing there speaking, while she held Helen Keller Hicks asleep in her arms. There were no loudspeakers then, but Kate's powerful ringing voice filled every part of the hall. "This," she said of the sleeping child, "is a petition they cannot throw away!" Two days later, after a stopover in Philadelphia, they reached the nation's capital. But the President was too busy to see them. He had an appointment with Lord and Lady Astor.

However, these strong women and solemn children from the Southwest were not easily rebuffed. They had come a long way. The Crusade rented a house, and one of the women, Mrs. Anna Pancner, a jolly, rosy-cheeked, Finnish woman from Detroit, whose husband was an IWW prisoner at Leavenworth, took over the cooking. The only trouble they had in the neighborhood was due to the older boys chewing snuff and spitting out the windows. Day after day they sought an audience with President Harding and were refused. They visited Congress, various departments of government, were interviewed by the press. Their presence in Washington created widespread interest in amnesty. The press was largely sympathetic. Finally, they decided to picket the White House, when all else failed to move the President. The little "Army with Banners" started their picket line on June 1, 1922, and continued daily, without a break, in the terrible heat of a Washington summer until July 19, when President Harding finally agreed to see a delegation on amnesty, the first delegation he had received since Christmas 1921.

While the children were picketing, Senator Carraway of Arkansas made a caustic attack on a federal pardon issued to the banker, Charles W. Morse, and on the President's refusal to see the Children's Crusade. The famous report, "Illegal Practices of the Department of Justice," signed by a group of the country's most prominent lawyers, was issued at this time by Senator Walsh of Montana. Twelve sentences of political prisoners were commuted, primarily including the tenant farmers. Seven families returned home in July with their men released. The President promised to review the remaining cases within 60 days. At that time it was reported he had said: "I can't stand seeing those kids out there any longer!"

There is no doubt that the Children's Crusade highlighted the human and just appeal for the remaining political prisoners and hastened their release. It accomplished its particular mission. The children did not see the President and they did not see the ocean. But they did "get their Paws out of jail!" It had been a hard job and they were happy to go home. One of the most difficult tasks of the Committee was to prevent sympathetic people from dressing the children up. But they returned triumphant heroes to their own countryside—dressed up at last in all their new finery, with boxes and bundles of gifts, and the light of victory and love in their faces, to greet their "Paws" on their return from prison.

SEVEN

Sacco and Vanzetti

◆◆◆◆◆◆◆◆◆◆◆◆◆◆

BOMB SCARE—PRELUDE TO MURDER

In April 1919 a bomb scare broke into the press. Some 30 mysterious packages, addressed to prominent people around the country, with a return address of Gimbel's, were allegedly picked up in the mail. By strange coincidence this happened on the eve of May Day. It was stated by the Department of Justice that they contained bombs. Again, in June 1919, a series of so-called "bomb" explosions took place in eight cities. The front porch of J. Mitchell Palmer's residence was damaged. No one was hurt. The whole thing was characterized as a frame-up by labor circles. It was a prologue to the Palmer raids. William J. Flynn was then in charge of the Bureau of Investigation, forerunner of the FBI. He claimed that a "pink leaflet" had been found near one of the spots under investigation, and in February 1920 arrested Roberto Elia, a Brooklyn printer, and Andrea Salsadeo, a typesetter in the same shop.

These two men, although threatened with deportation by the Department of Justice, were not turned over to the Department of Labor, then in charge of deportation matters. Nor were they booked in any police court or placed in jail. They were private prisoners, practically incommunicado, held secretly and mysteriously in the office of the Department of Justice on the 14th floor of 15 Park Row, a most unusual procedure. Only their closest friends and families knew of their imprisonment and helplessly accepted it. They hired a lawyer with offices in the same building, who did nothing.

Salsadeo had a group of anarchist comrades in Massachusetts who were troubled over his disappearance. Many of their group had been arrested and secretly deported as a result of the Palmer raids. They sent one of their number to New York City to investigate. His name was Bartolomeo Vanzetti. Italian workers from other places visiting New York City often came to the office of Carlo's paper at 208 East 12th St. I met a few, now and again, if I happened to know them personally. But I did not know of Vanzetti's visit; apparently it made little impression on the New York anarchists. A long time later he told me that he had tried to find time to visit the Statue of Liberty but missed the boat. His comrades laughed at his notion, but he wanted to see the Lady with the Lamp and was quite disappointed.

What he found out about Salsadeo shocked him very much. He felt that the lawyer that represented him was either scared or incompetent and decided they should raise funds to hire a better lawyer. They contacted Walter Nelles, a lawyer connected with the American Civil Liberties Union, who agreed to take the case. Salsadeo's lawyer was later branded as a Department of Justice accomplice. Vanzetti had heard that Salsadeo had been beaten and tortured by special agents there, especially one Francisco, that he had been threatened with death and was in a state of terror and collapse. Whether he jumped from the window or was pushed out, we will never know. Those who knew, never told. But early on the morning of May 3, 1920, his crushed body was found by passers-by on the street outside the building. The pavement was shattered by the force of his fall. Elia was quickly deported before his story could be told. But he left a sworn deposition telling of the torture of Salsadeo, in which he stated: "I am afraid of the agents of the Department of Justice and I do not want this statement made public until I leave the country."

Vanzetti, on his return to Massachusetts, with others began to arrange protest meetings. One such meeting was scheduled for Brockton, Massachusetts, on May 5. Leaflets were distributed. They had many friends among the shoe workers there, but by now the Department of Justice was under severe criticism. Meetings on this ghastly death were not welcome to them. They had to be stopped. So on the very day of the meeting, two days after the Salsadeo tragedy, Vanzetti and his comrade Sacco were arrested on a streetcar on their way to Brockton. For the next seven years a great point was made by the state about why these two radical foreign-born workers on their way to a meeting with other comrades of theirs, to protest the violence of a powerful government agency, *did not tell the truth about where they were going and whom they were going to meet.* It was very natural, especially in view of the fact that all the police asked them that night was, "Are you Reds?" They had every right to anticipate deportation proceedings, with possibly a similar fate to that of Salsadeo added. Many of their closest comrades, including Luigi Galleani, the brilliant editor of their paper, *Cronaca Sovversiva,* in Barre, Vermont, had been victims of the Palmer raids.

Nothing much was said or done about the arrests of Sacco and Vanzetti by anyone at first. They were very humble and obscure foreign-born workers. A small Italian committee of close associates was set up in Boston. But soon they were to realize that this was a different matter—not a political charge but a criminal one. Sacco and Vanzetti were bundled into cars and taken around from one town to another, where they were put on exhibition. Strange people were brought in to look at them while the police queried insistently, "Are these the men?" —and insisted: "Sure, these are the guys all right!" They were told to put on certain caps, to crouch down, which was very confusing to Sacco and Vanzetti. Then, for the first time they were told they were accused of two murders and a robbery in nearby towns.

Vanzetti was tried and quickly convicted for an attempted robbery in Bridgewater, Massachusetts, on December 24, 1919. All that saved Sacco from this trial was a time-book record in the shoe factory that showed he was at work at that hour. Sacco and Vanzetti were jointly charged with the holdup of a $15,000 payroll in the yard of the Slater and Morrill Shoe Company at South Braintree, Massachusetts, on April 15, 1920, where the paymaster and guard had both been killed. The charge was first-degree murder. This was another Mooney case, in New England. But it took time for the American people to realize it.

It was not until after this first trial of Vanzetti that I heard the names of Sacco and Vanzetti. I was then secretary of the Workers Defense Union in New York City. A woman in New England who occupied a similar post was Mrs. Marion Emerson of the New England Defense Conference. We were both busy with the struggles growing out of the Palmer raids—raising bail, feeding families, hiring lawyers. I went several times to Boston to speak on behalf of hundreds of deportees herded on Deer Island. Dr. George Galvin, a noted physician, was chairman of a huge meeting there.

Just before I left New York on one of these trips, Carlo said, "Elizabetta, there are two Italian comrades in big trouble in Massachusetts on account of Salsadeo. You investigate while you are there and maybe get the Americans to help." He gave me the address of A. Felicini who worked on a local Italian newspaper, *Le Notizia,* in South Boston. I asked Mrs. Emerson who I le irned on this trip was related to Ralph Waldo Emerson, if she knew about them. She had vaguely heard of them through the local press. She agreed to go with me to investigate their plight. We went into the turbulent but colorful, overcrowded slums of old Boston, now a little Italy, with its crooked streets and narrow houses, in search of this unknown man on an obscure paper. We found him, but he spoke so little English we had to wait until he found an interpreter. He was very glad to see us and eager to tell us everything. He called together the Italian committee, and for the first time two Americans heard the story of Sacco and Vanzetti. Thus began my seven years' labors to help save Sacco and Vanzetti.

THE ANATOMY OF A NEW ENGLAND FRAME-UP

The original Sacco-Vanzetti committee were all anarchists, authorized by the two prisoners to represent them. They were a close-knit group of friends who worked as volunteers for seven years, never taking any remuneration. They were workers, mostly highly skilled, and there was one building contractor among them. They were inclined to be suspicious of political Socialists, but they knew me because of my textile strike activities in New England eight years before; of my connection with the cases of Joe Hill and Ettor and Giovanitti and of my personal relationship with Carlo. Mrs. Emerson was a large motherly-looking woman, with mild eyes and a gentle manner, and they liked her at once. They knew of her untiring work for the many deportees on Deer Island. So they accepted us and told us all they knew of the developments so far.

They dealt mainly with Vanzetti's first trial, which was indeed a tragic travesty of due process, and they told us who he was. Bartolomeo Vanzetti, then 32 years old, had come to America in 1908, a strong individualist who hoped to find happiness in this great land of opportunity. One of his first jobs was as a steel worker in the mills of the American Steel and Wire Company in Pittsburgh, inferno of toil and sweat. After that he worked as a laborer in construction camps and later as a pastry cook in New York City at Moquin's restaurant. He learned at first hand the lot of the foreign-born worker in America

—the crowded boarding houses for single men, the back-breaking toil, the loss of identity as a man—workers in the mills, like in prison, carried numbers. The scornful epithets of "Hunky" and "Dago" were hurled at the immigrant workers.

Vanzetti lived at the time of his arrest in Plymouth, Massachusetts, site of the landing of the Mayflower and the famed Plymouth Rock. He had been employed in the Cordage Works there and had led a strike in 1916 against intolerable conditions. The demands were granted and all the 4,000 workers returned to work except Vanzetti, who was blacklisted by the company. He refused to let the workers make an issue of it. "I am a single man," he said. "Lonely man!" he called himself, "I'll get along!" So he bought a handcart and became a fish peddler. He remarked that many of Jesus' disciples were fishermen. It was a good occupation.

All the Italian people in the colony knew and loved him. Others, too, Jewish and Irish, were his customers, and spoke of him with warmth and respect. His philosophical remarks in his quaint broken English, his gentle good humor, his sad smile, endeared him to people. Eighteen people came to court to testify for him—that on the afternoon and evening of December 24, 1919, Christmas Eve, he was busy in Plymouth selling eels, which are a great holiday delicacy among Italian people. He could not have been in Bridgewater, 18 miles away. A 13-year old boy whom I met later, Beldrando Brini, helped Vanzetti deliver eels and thus made his Christmas money. He so testified, and good Italian Catholic housewives testified that they had bought eels from Vanzetti on that day. Seven years later, when Vanzetti faced the electric chair, Governor Fuller of Massachusetts said: "There has never been produced any document to show that Vanzetti was selling eels." An immediate search of the Boston Atlantic Avenue fish dealers' records by a defense lawyer produced an American Express Company receipt for a barrel of live eels shipped to Vanzetti in Plymouth two days before the Bridgewater crime. Neither Governor Fuller nor his so-called investigating committee ever acknowledged this fact, the eel receipt. I am writing now of 1920. But the terrible importance of this will unfold as the story develops.

Vanzetti's lawyer in this first case was apparently a run-of-the-mill criminal lawyer in a small town, recommended to him by a court runner. The papers had featured "Italian bandits" and "Italian holdup men" in sensational stories of the two crimes. Vague identifications of

a "foreigner with a mustache" were accepted. One youth testified that
he knew the holdup man was a foreigner "by the way he ran!" One
woman first identified a policeman as the bandit. Vanzetti had wanted
to testify but his lawyer refused to allow him to do so when he heard
he was "an anarchist." He said in a panic, "Just keep it quiet!" No
matter how much a judge instructs a jury that a defendant need not
testify, it is usually held against him just the same.

It would be hard to convey today the deep-seated distrust existing
then among the New England Yankees of all "foreigners," especially
the Italians. It was like the Dixicrat attitude in the South to the Negro
people today. They dismissed the testimony of Italian housewives and
children with "They all stick together!" Vanzetti was quickly convicted and the Bridgewater police collected the $1,000 reward. He was
sentenced to prison for 12–15 years by Judge Webster Thayer. This
happened in August 1920. He and Sacco were still to be tried on the
murder charge. The Italian committee earnestly pleaded with us to do
two things—arrange some protest meetings with English speakers to
reach American workers and help them get a labor lawyer who would
understand the radical viewpoint of the defendants and the possibility
of a frame-up against them. This we pledged to try to do.

We both reported to our committees who authorized us to proceed
with such meetings. In New York we hired the Forwards Hall on
East Broadway. Present at this first Sacco-Vanzetti meeting were
about 25 people, mostly our own delegates. One of the speakers was
Leonard Abbott, nephew of Lyman Abbott, editor of the *Outlook*.
Leonard Abbot was then or later editor of *Current Literature*. He was
president of a Free Speech League and connected with the Ferrer
School. The other speakers were veteran anarchist, Harry Kelly, and
myself. The caretaker of the hall, alarmed at the meagerness of our
audience, insisted we pay the rent in advance. "You'll never get it in a
collection tonight," he whispered to me.

In Boston the meeting was held in an old opera house on Washington Street, a dark and dismal place. But a large crowd turned out and
there was real interest in our story. Mrs. Emerson and I spoke with an
Italian trade union leader. Thus the agitation among the New England
and New York workers for Sacco and Vanzetti began as a small spark
at first. But it eventually spread around the world. When I returned to
New York City, Fred Moore, the IWW lawyer, was in town. He had
just successfully defended Charles Kreiger, an IWW, in Oklahoma. At

the moment he was not involved in any big case elsewhere. Carlo and I asked him to go to Boston, to meet with the Sacco-Vanzetti committee and investigate the case. We urged him favorably to consider undertaking their defense. He spent a few weeks there and finally decided to do so.

It was put up to Sacco and Vanzetti, who were delighted to accept him. They knew of his good work in Everett, Wichita and Chicago for the IWW, and felt correctly that Fred was more than a legal advocate. He was a defender of labor. For the next few years, Fred Moore worked tirelessly. He was determined and persistent in his preparation of his cases, overlooking not even the small details. He developed a fanatical zeal built on his absolute faith that these two men were innocent. He was determined to save them at all costs—regardless of money spent, investigators hired, publicity on a huge scale. None of us fully realized then the terrible load he would be forced to carry as "an outside lawyer" from the wilds of California in the staid New England courtroom. A local lawyer from Brockton, Mr. William J. Callahan, was also retained at the same time.

I Visit Sacco and Vanzetti

In October 1920 Mary Heaton Vorse and I visited Nicola Sacco in the Dedham Jail. Fred Moore arranged the interview so that we could give some publicity to their plight. Mary wrote a fine article for *The Nation* which began, "We drove through the sweet New England towns." It was autumn, the pungent smell of burning leaves was in the air. As jails go, it was not a bad place, Mary said—it looked like a library, with its large central rotunda; only men were put away on the shelves, not books. Then a handsome youth, slim, erect, with flashing eyes and a gay smile came rapidly toward us. This was Sacco. He was 30 years old. His blue shirt was clean and neat, open at the throat. He greeted me with enthusiasm. "Elizabetta—I know you. I heard you speak for Lawrence strikers!" he said. Then he greeted Fred Moore and met Mrs. Vorse who spoke a little Italian, which gladdened his heart. We all sat down. He told us of himself and his views—"The Idea," he called it, which to him meant social justice. No government, no police, no judges, no bosses, no authority; autonomous groups of people—the people own everything—work in cooperation—distribute by needs—equality, justice, comradeship—love each other; eager

words like this flowed in a torrent from his lips. He hated to be idle.
He wanted to be able to work—this bothered him.

He said he was ready to die for "The Idea"—for the people. But
not for "gunman job." He spoke of how he had worked all his life, his
hands were the skilled hands of a shoemaker, they were for work not
for killing. "To steal money, to kill a poor man for money! This is insult to me!" he said passionately. He threw back his head and explained: "I am innocent. I no do this thing. I swear it on the head of
my newborn child!" This vehement cry, *"Io innocente!* You are killing an innocent man!" were the words he shouted at the craven jury
months later. To Sacco, a cold-blooded murder of a factory employee
to carry out a mercenary holdup was unthinkable. He was hurt, deeply
hurt, to be accused of such a thing.

One hand had remained tightly clasped during our talk. But in his
anger he spread his fingers apart and a little piece of metal fell out, a
Catholic sacred heart medal. He smiled with embarrassment and explained, "Boss' wife, good Irish lady, she came, she cried, and she
said, 'Keep this Nick, it will save you!' " "I no believe," he said, "but
I no want to hurt her feelings, so I take." I was well acquainted with
this idealistic type of kind and good Italian anarchist, who might kill a
king as an act of "social justice"—but not a mouse. I believed Sacco
when he said, "Elizabetta, I am innocent." I believe it now, after 34
years. So confident was he of his innocence that sunny afternoon that
he had no fear. He was sure when he told his story in court he would
go free. He did not know that he was approaching the valley of the shadow of death. He feared no evil because the truth was with him. But
greed, corruption, prejudice, fear and hatred of radical foreign-born
workingmen were weaving a net around him. I remembered another
fair young man—Joe Hill—whom I had visited a few years before,
who had been put to death by executioners' rifles. My heart was
heavy, though I smiled and said "Be of good cheer. We will do our
best."

Then a few days later I went with Fred Moore to the dungeon-like
prison in Charlestown to see Bartolomeo Vanzetti. He was serving his
sentence there. He seemed very much older than Sacco, though he
really was not. He was 32 years old. He was heavier, slower in his
movements, very calm and controlled. He told me of his visit to New
York, and how he missed his date with Miss Liberty. He wondered if
he would ever see her again. He had a whimsical kind of humor—but

much of the same unworldliness as Sacco. He was anxious, however, he told Fred Moore, that we should fight for a separate trial for Nick because of the fact that he, Vanzetti, had already been convicted of a holdup. "And wouldn't that go against Nick?" It was a good legal point and Fred assured him that they had it in mind. Vanzetti's social philosophy was a belief in human freedom and the dignity of man. He was a lover of Galileo and Giordano Bruno, Dante, Garibaldi and Mazzini. He would have been at home with Emerson, Thoreau or Walt Whitman.

Fred Moore then arranged to take Mrs. Vorse and me to see Nick's wife, Rose Sacco. She lived in a pleasant little New England house owned by Mr. Kelley, the owner of the nearby shoe factory where Nick worked. Her little boy of seven was named Dante. Her newborn daughter, Inez, was sleeping in her little bed. We sat in her big kitchen, with a wood-burning stove, and discussed their little family and the tragedy that had befallen it. Mrs. Sacco was beautiful, quite fair, her hair a dark red. She told us of how she and Nick took part in plays to raise money for strikes and to help "educate the people." She told us that she had gone with Nick to Boston to the Italian consulate on April 15, 1920, the day the Braintree crime was committed. She felt sure that the employees there would remember them because they had brought a large family portrait instead of the regulation passport pictures. And they had lunch at Boni's restaurant, opposite the Paul Revere house. The people there would certainly remember them, especially as some knew Nick very well. So she reassured herself Nick would never be tried and convicted.

Of such human elements are great historical tragedies constructed —a frightened young woman, clinging to her children, smiling through her tears, visiting her young husband in jail in such a courageous spirit that warden, keepers and other prisoners turn away in embarrassment from her radiant face. The cold hand of fear was not yet on all these gallant young people who had around them the shining armor of consciousness of innocence.

THE CAMPAIGN STARTS

After my return from visiting Sacco and Vanzetti we began, through the Workers Defense Union, to arrange public meetings and to raise money on their behalf. On October 4, 1920, we sent out as complete a factual statement as was possible then—the first in English. We stated prophetically, "If convicted they will be sentenced to electrocution." We voted a contribution of $100, which I am quite sure was the first sizeable contribution from New York. Meantime, Mrs. Vorse had gone to the American Civil Liberties Union. The minutes of their November 22, 1920, meeting read as follows:

Mary Heaton Vorse reported on the cases of Sacco and Vanzetti, two young Italian anarchists on trial in Boston for highway robbery and murder, stating that they had been indicted on questionable circumstances and because of their activity on behalf of Andrea Salsadeo, a political prisoner who committed suicide by throwing himself from the Park Row Building, New York, while being held for deportation. It was agreed that the Union should do everything possible to secure publicity for this case.

At the next meeting of the ACLU on November 29, 1920, the minutes read as follows:

Mr. Baldwin reported that Miss Flynn, who is in Boston on the Sacco-Vanzetti case, had requested that the Union hold a New York meeting to present the facts of their prosecution. Tentative arrangements have been made for a meeting at the People's House Auditorium, on December 11th. The proposed meeting was approved.

Meantime, while I was there, I made a speaking trip in New England on their behalf, going to places with which I was long familiar, and on my return the minutes of our next Workers Defense Union meeting read as follows:

Comrades E. G. Flynn and Fred Biedenkapp reported that they had loaned $200 to the Sacco-Vanzetti defense fund, to help them over their great financial difficulties. Moved and carried to donate the $200. Moved we send out special appeals and speakers for this and help them to the best of our ability.

While I was in Boston on this trip, Art Shields, a young labor reporter, came there at my urgent request, seconded by Fred Moore, to write a popular pamphlet on the Sacco-Vanzetti case. He made a painstaking search of the whole story. He studied the transcript of Vanzetti's first trial and catalogued the innumerable discrepancies of government witnesses. He dug up the labor records of both men, their aid to the Lawrence strike and to the defense of Ettor and Giovanitti. He found that the only previous arrest of either of them was when Sacco was arrested in Milford, Massachusetts, for a speech at a mass meeting protesting against the arrest of Carlo Tresca in the Mesabi Range strike of 1916. Sacco, although he was a highly paid skilled worker, had aided the foundry workers of Hopedale in a strike and had participated in an insurgent shoecutters' strike in 1918. They were both supporters of the struggling Italian radical press, of which there were a half a dozen at least, each with a different line and quarreling with each other.

When the pamphlet was ready to go to press, the Boston Defense Committee asked the Workers Defense Union to publish it and undertake its distribution. They wrote that they deemed it advisable to have it printed outside of Massachusetts by an "English-speaking committee." We gladly accepted the task and it came off the press in March 1921. It was a 32-page pamphlet that sold for 10 cents a copy and we sold it in bundles of 100 for $7.50. It was published for us by the New York Call Printing Company, which printed the Socialist paper. We distributed 20,000 before the month was up and had to order a second edition of 25,000. It carried a financial appeal from the Sacco-Vanzetti Committee. Before the trial started we had issued at least 50,000.

The name of the pamphlet was *Are They Doomed?* The cover design was drawn by the great people's artist, Robert Minor, showing the Wall Street background, Trinity Church and the old Post Office Building opposite the tall Park Row Building. The body of Andrea Salsadeo was hurling from one of the top windows, portraying the tragedy of the cold gray dawn of May 3, 1920. It was the first analysis of the case and the grim forces behind it—which were the Department of Justice and the employing class of New England, determined to keep foreign-born workers inarticulate and unorganized. It showed the legal trickery resorted to in frame-up cases, involving workers and unions. It compared it to the Mooney-Billings prosecution, which was then in a state of collapse, due to the splendid work of Minor and others.

I left one Saturday night, March 5, 1921, to speak next morning at a Sacco-Vanzetti meeting in the Amalgamated Clothing hall in Philadelphia, to help popularize and sell the pamphlet. My friends with whom I stayed overnight, Walter Nef of the IWW and his wife, accompanied me to the meeting. Under the pretext that we had no permit for the use of the hall, we were hustled into a small anteroom and questioned by an elderly police sergeant, who was semi-hysterical with excitement. Why had I come to disturb the people of Philadelphia? Didn't I know that a real American (Harding) was now in the White House and would make short work of radicals like me? What business had I defending anarchist murderers? He found *The Nation, New Republic, World Tomorrow* (edited by Norman Thomas) and an *International Socialist Review* in my briefcase. He spotted an article on Karl Liebknecht. "For this," he shouted dramatically, "I will put you under arrest!"

Walter and I and several of the committee were arrested and the audience was driven out of the hall. I was locked up temporarily in Moyomansing Prison. We were finally released without trial, although it led to deportation proceedings against some of the Italians. When we were arraigned before a magistrate on the charge of disturbing the peace, a copy of Art Shields' pamphlet was produced as evidence.

Art Shields mentioned in his pamphlet that the New England Civil Liberties Committee (affiliated with the ACLU) had appointed three prominent attorneys to investigate the case. They also issued an appeal for funds to be sent to Mrs. Anna Davis, their treasurer, stating, "So far the bulk of the defense funds have been borne by Italian rank-and-file workers. Must they carry the whole burden?" Their appeal was captioned, "Shall There Be a Mooney Frame-Up in New England?" Finally, the case broke into all the Boston papers in a big way, causing the Boston *Post* to give a detailed history of it and of the Salsadeo death and Vanzetti's trial. It declared: "Many well-known local people have always doubted the guilt of Sacco and Vanzetti, while labor unions here and in the mill cities of Lawrence, Lowell and Fall River have declared that two men are being 'railroaded' by the Department of Justice." This arose out of a strange new episode, which occurred just as the pamphlet went to press, namely the De Falco affair.

THE DE FALCO AFFAIR

There came one of those queer problems that sometimes causes one anxiously to debate—later—did we do right? Many things in cases like this force you to be constantly on guard against frame-up. For instance, a spy, named Carbone, was placed in a cell next to Sacco in the Dedham jail, with the cooperation of the sheriff and the knowledge of Prosecutor Katzman, as he subsequently admitted when the story came to light. He said, "It was done by the Federal authorities who wanted to put a man there in the hope of getting information about the Wall Street explosion"—a terrible event that happened on September 10, over four months after the arrest of Sacco and Vanzetti. This is another of the great William J. Flynn's unsolved "mysteries."

We of the Workers Defense Union had Art Shields make a thorough investigation of what happened there, which we issued as a publicity statement. Shortly before the explosion, nearly a dozen witnesses saw a horse-drawn dynamite wagon with the customary red flag at the tail, an ordinary sight in those days. Thirty people were killed; 100 were injured and two million dollars' worth of damage was done by the subsequent explosion. The horse's body, which was important evidence, was carted away by the police and destroyed. Six excavating jobs in the neighborhood required dynamite, then in general use for such work. One was the New Stock Exchange extension, then being built. The foreman of the blasting work there, named Clark, told the New York *Post* reporter that he had talked to the driver three minutes before the explosion and since he (Clark) had not ordered the explosives, the man went to telephone his company and find out where to deliver them. Inspector Lahey of the New York Police Department said it was obviously an accident.

Then came the great red-hunter, William J. Flynn and his aide, William J. Burns, and it became an "anarchist plot." Of course, the powder company involved was not anxious to admit responsibility; the driver had either been killed or had disappeared. Millions of dollars in damages were saved for this outfit by Mr. Flynn's diagnosis. Incidentally, it helped Flynn and Palmer get bigger Congressional appropriations and put back to work some 50 operatives who had been laid off. A humorous by-product of this otherwise horrible tragedy were the headlines in the press, "Flynn Wants Tresca." When his lawyers called Flynn, after Carlo gave a press conference, Flynn denied the stories completely.

It was natural that everybody involved was suspicious when the De Falco affair developed in Boston. There was a young Italian tailor named Benny, who lived in Providence, Rhode Island, whom we all knew. A few years before, during an unemployed demonstration there, the hungry crowd had broken into a warehouse and helped themselves to its contents. Benny was identified as one of the leaders. He had escaped arrest by approaching a priest walking toward the railroad station and asking to accompany him there as he "did not know the way." Naturally, the police never suspected that an Italian Red would walk with a priest, so he safely left town. He went to the state of Washington and got a job in a custom tailor shop in Everett. (This was before the massacre which I have already described took place in 1916.) He heard many conversations among the county and company officials as they were being measured and fitted. When the IWW members were charged with murder he came to Seattle to see me and from then on he brought valuable information for the defense lawyers, reporting to Fred Moore.

Benny eventually returned to Providence when the old charge blew over. He was a relative of an Italian woman in Boston, who was an interpreter and runner in the Court House at Dedham, Massachusetts. Her name was Angelina De Falco. He spoke to her about his friends, Sacco and Vanzetti, and asked her for help. She offered to try. Subsequently he brought her to Felicani, the treasurer of the committee. She claimed she could secure an acquittal if they would fire their present lawyers and pay two others $50,000. The money was to be paid to Francis J. Squires, clerk of the police court in Dedham, and Percy Katzman, brother and law partner of Frederick Katzman, the district attorney. All evidence in the hands of the committee was to be surrendered to Percy Katzman, as the new defense lawyer. When the Committee members said $50,000 was impossible for them to raise, she reduced the figure to $40,000. She cited a recent case of an Italian woman charged with murder who was released, as an example of how successful her efforts were.

The committee finally communicated the matter to Fred Moore and William J. Callahan, who were greatly disturbed. It presented them with quite a dilemma. It also caused considerable disagreement with some of the anarchist group around the committee, who had no faith whatever in the courts and public officials, and were not surprised at the De Falco proposition. They knew such deals were made all the time in all sorts of Italian cases and were inclined to take a chance. But the attorneys acted quickly and swore out a warrant in Felicani's name, charging her with unlawfully soliciting law practice by pledging an acquittal. The Commonwealth permitted them to act as the lawyers to prosecute her. The trial lasted a week. Then Municipal Judge Murray acquitted Mrs. De Falco. There was considerable question as to why Benny was not tried too; it was because no one would make a complaint. The committee, Fred Moore and I all believed he had acted in good faith trying to help his comrades. Later he cried, telling me "You were all wrong about Angelina. She could have saved them!"

The lawyers insisted that their procedure was imperative, as they were fearful of charges of trying to bribe public officials against Felicani and others who had talked to the woman. But the issue rankled for a long time. Did they do right not to deal with her, since Sacco and Vanzetti were still obscure unknown prisoners? Was it a bona fide offer or a trap for the committee? Some of the extreme anarchists were critical of using government agencies to arrest and prosecute Mrs. De Falco. There was an undertone of criticism among them that Fred Moore wanted to make this the biggest labor case in history, regardless of the two men involved. It started friction that grew and festered throughout the case. But the De Falco story made the Sacco-Vanzetti case front-page news in every Boston paper and elsewhere. Some papers reviewed the connection of the case with the Salsadeo tragedy. Speculations as to the role of Mrs. De Falco as a possible entrapper of the committee were widespread. The trial came within a few weeks after this.

BEFORE THE TRIAL

The trial of Sacco and Vanzetti for murder was set for March 7, 1921. In preparation for it, Fred Moore had sent a man to Italy in November 1920 to search for four essential defense witnesses and to secure depositions from them. The man sent on this mission was Morris Gebelow, who wrote under the pen name of Eugene Lyons (and still does.) He had been introduced to me first by one of our Workers Defense Union delegates. They had been fellow students in college. A thin pale young man, he was in uniform at our first meeting in 1918. He had been drafted, but the Armistice had saved him from active service and he was seeking a job. He became the publicity man for the Workers Defense Union, although he told me frankly that his sole interest and ambition was to become a writer and he wanted the experience.

He went to Tulsa, Oklahoma, with Fred Moore to do publicity on the case of Charles Kreiger, an IWW charged with dynamiting. Kreiger was acquitted and when Fred Moore moved into Boston, he took Lyons there to help him. From Rome, Italy, Lyons sent a story dated December 27, 1920, in which he said: "There is scarcely a Socialist or labor paper in this country that has not lifted its voice for the two imprisoned men." He reported that Deputy Maililasso, spokesman for the Socialist group in the Chamber of Deputies, demanded "that the government intervene." Under-Secretary De Saluzzo, replying for the government, assured the deputies that "the Ministry of Foreign Affairs had already interested the American ambassador in the matter." The Socialist daily *Avanti,* published an article on its front page, "Justice in America." Lyons quoted a paragraph:

Although its prisons are filled with the best elements of the working class, the American bourgeoisie is still clamoring for proletarian blood. Against Comrades Nicola Sacco of Torre-Maggiore, Province of Foggia, and Bartolomeo Vanzetti, of Pedmonte, the American bourgeoisie has mobilized all its class hatred and its race prejudice.

A motion was made for a 90-day postponement to allow defense counsel to complete its search in Italy for the witnesses. Also, new counsel had come into the case, Thomas F. and Jeremiah J. McAnarney of Boston and Quincy, Massachusetts, conservative Catholic attorneys with reputations for great professional integrity. "If the McAnarneys are defending Sacco and Vanzetti," Bostonians said, "it means that they are certain they are innocent." Meantime the Italian Embassy in Washington, D. C., through the U. S. State Department, had transmitted to Governor Cox an appeal that he use his good offices to insure a fair trial.

Public interest was now beginning to stir on their behalf. U. S. Congressman Tinkham, E. M. Grella, owner of three large Italian newspapers, Fiorello LaGuardia, then president of the New York Board of Aldermen, the Central Labor Council of Boston, and Dr. Scudder of the Massachusetts Federation of Churches had all spoken out in support of the request for time. The 90-day delay was granted by Chief Justice Aiken of the Massachusetts Superior Court.

Meantime, many other struggles were going on, as I have indicated elsewhere. An item from our Workers Defense Union minutes of March 19, 1921, is of special interest. It reads:

Letters from the New York Italian Committee and Mr. Walter Nelles, read, requested the Defense Union to contribute $50 towards the expenses necessary to carry the suit of Mrs. Salsadeo for damages against Palmer, Flynn, etc. to a higher court. The Italian Committee agreed to contribute $50. Carried to comply with the request.

Mr. Nelles had told me of his great anxiety to interrogate Attorney General Palmer as a witness before he went out of office. He needed this money for railroad fare and a court stenographer. Mrs. Salsadeo's suit had been transferred from a state to a federal court at Palmer's request, where a U. S. Judge sustained his demurrer to the complaint. Mr. Nelles was appealing on behalf of the widow and her two children to the U. S. Appellate Court. Nothing ever came of his efforts.

And in the minutes of April 1921, is my report, as organizer, on the case of:

> Irving Potash, a young Brooklyn boy of 19 years, who was accused of being a Communist and had pleaded guilty to a charge of "criminal anarchy" as a misdemeanor, on the bad advice of his lawyer. He was then held for deportation. His brother requested us to take up his case. We secured bail and instructed Attorney Weinberger to proceed on his behalf. It was a difficult case, on account of the plea of guilty. But we were glad to report success.

(Almost 35 years later, in 1955, Irving Potash was deported to Poland after serving a prison sentence under the provisions of the fascist-like Smith Act.)

I reported on the increase of requests for speaking dates on Sacco and Vanzetti. I had letters from the Liberal Club of the University of Pennsylvania; from the Students Liberal Club of Harvard; also from Mrs. Elizabeth G. Evans of the League for Democratic Control and from the New England Committee, which planned a supper meeting to raise funds, as well as from many trade unions. By this time we were sending out from our New York office weekly publicity releases on Sacco and Vanzetti, written by John Beffel, to over 500 papers.

A most unusual meeting was held in Bridgewater, Massachusetts, in April 1921, at which I spoke. This was the town where the payroll robbery of the L. G. White Shoe Company truck had been attempted, for which Vanzetti was already convicted. It was Beffel's idea to hold this meeting, as good publicity. I admit it was with trepidation that I took the train to Bridgewater. We got off at the railroad station, which had figured in the testimony, and walked up the street which had been traversed by the pay truck.

It was a quiet little New England town with wide streets and a beautiful white inn on the square. This, the Bridgewater Inn, was our destination. Its proprietor, George Alcott, a local Socialist, sponsored the meeting, got a police permit, printed and personally distributed the handbills. After supper he drove his car around to the square in front of the Inn under the spreading trees. Slowly the townspeople gathered until we had an audience of about 500, including three policemen.

I was acutely aware that I was there to tell these New Englanders that Vanzetti, a foreigner and an anarchist, was an innocent man falsely accused and that townspeople witnesses who might be present were mistaken or had deliberately lied. I could feel the coolness as John introduced me. I knew this must go off all right, for if a meeting in Bridgewater was broken up by irate townspeople it would flash all over the country and be extremely injurious to Sacco and Vanzetti. So I strove with all my powers to tell Vanzetti's story to that stern New England audience. Finally, by that sixth sense of unity with an audience which speakers possess, I felt they were changing, melting, even becoming a little friendly as I spoke of the contradictions and inconsistencies in the evidence, such as the woman who identified a policeman as a bandit, and the boy who knew a foreigner by the way he ran. Chief of Police Stewart could not have been too popular, because they laughed uproariously at the fact that he had lost the number of the bandit's car. We took up a collection of $19—a remarkable achievement under the conditions. The crowd said, "Come again!"

Waiting for the streetcar in a drug store nearby, the clerk treated me to a drink of lemonade. Then we took the interurban to Brookline—the same route on which Sacco and Vanzetti had been arrested. We had an hour to wait for a train to Boston and seeing a light in Mr. Callahan's office, took a chance on going to see him. Rather a silent Irishman, when he heard where we had been, he said: "Quite an undertaking! Would you like a drink?" It was most welcome, I assured him. I don't think that the unimaginative Beffel ever realized the ordeal I had been through. He was concerned that I had made a mistake in pronouncing the name of the shoe factory, and did not get the exact caliber of the gun, and corrected me quite formally on the train on the way home. I said I'd remember next time.

THE TRIAL OF SACCO AND VANZETTI

For months prior to the trial, which started May 31, 1921, Norfolk County was the scene of a widespread whispering campaign against Sacco and Vanzetti and their friends as anarchists and bomb throwers, and it was prophesied that a reign of terror was likely to break loose during the trial. On the day the trial opened the Dedham County Courthouse was surrounded by armed officers and plain-clothes police. The two defendants were manacled and marched from the jail to the courthouse surrounded by eight officers. This was re-enacted during the entire 36 days of the trial. The defendants were placed in an iron "cage," a barbaric custom in Massachusetts, and four armed officers

February Ist.,1926

Ruth **Albert,**
     Executive Secretary League for Mutual Aid,
          New York City.

My dear Miss Albert:
     Please allow me to thank you for your **kindness** in writing me in
regard to the Dinner proposed to be given to our **loyal** and dearly
beloved comrade,Elizabeth Gurley Flynn,on the fourteenth instant.
The invitation to participate in the happy occasion honors me and
is appreciated accordingly,and were it at all **possible** I should be
happy indeed to present my personal compliments to the guest of hon-
or and to mingle with the good comrades who will honor themselves
in this **very beautiful** and fitting celebration.

     Elizabeth Gurley Flynn holds a proud and enviable position in
the American labor movement and yet she is one of the humblest and
most unpretentious of its members. Ever since I first heard of
this brave,dauntless leader of the working class she has been at the
forefront,one of its most eloquent spokesmen and one of its most
consecrated servants. She has espoused and championed the cause of
the weakest,lowliest,most despised and persecuted,even when she
stood almost alone,and in this she has never weakened or wavered a
moment but faced and fought the enemy without fear and without reference to consequences to herself.

     Elizabeth **Gurley Flynn** is a typical proletarian leader,an intrep-
id warrior of the **social revolution,**and after twenty years **of single-**
hearted **devotion** and unflinching service to the cause **she is** loved
and honored throughout the labor movement of the United States.

     And so I gladly join as do also my wife and my brother and his
wife in the loving and appreciative testimonial to Elizabeth Gurley
Flynn,our faithful friend and our high-souled comrade, and with all
cordial **greetings** to you all and wishing you a most joyous and in-
spiring **celebration** I am,

          Yours faithfully,

Letter from Eugene V. Debs, written Feb. 1, 1926, paying
tribute to the author as "an intrepid warrior of the social
revolution."

11 Feb., 1926.

To Elisabeth G. Flynn:—

Dear Comrade:—
I have heard that there will be a banquet in your honor — for your faithfulness and perseverance for the triumph of more and more true freedom and justice.

I would like to participate to this simposium — surely I would also honor the cooks and the baker because I have not yet lost completly that blessed appetite by which I gain a fair reputation.

If it is true that "man" means "bread-eater", I can surely boast my me a real, great man.

You know — I have not yet yeld — only my utter annihilation could bend my heart, crush my spirit, split my will.

I have still the heart of a lost vedetta at the outpost of "the eternal war between the tyranny and freedom"; as old Abe said. And consequently I can still partake to a festival in honor of a brave comrade: I will, in spirit I will be with you.

I am holding a tin-cup of water to drink and to toast at your good health and to your life,

Yes, Comrade, good health and long life to you; and long life the brave struggle for the triumph of liberty!

I drink.

To you and to the presenter Ones, my sincere regards and augural greeting Yours, Bartolomeo Vanzetti

Letter from Vanzetti.

Son Fred's picture (at six years of age) sent to Joe Hill in 1915 and acknowledged in a letter saying to Elizabeth he now "knew the reason why you felt so homesick when you made your trip to the Pacific Coast."

Jim Larkin, the Irish revolutionary leader. 1924

Woman's Conference Delegate Badge. Patterson 1926

The Author. Seattle 1926

surrounded it. It created an atmosphere of fear in the courtroom and made them appear like dangerous criminals.

The jury, going daily through the guarded doors of the courthouse, passed the spectators lined up to enter the courtroom as they were searched by officers for concealed weapons. Judge Thayer, during the examination of the jury panel and after the jury was sworn in, made unwarranted remarks on patriotism and loyalty to the government which were obviously directed against the defendants as radicals. Throughout the entire trial he made many prejudicial remarks, and by methods that do not appear in court records—tone of voice, facial expression and demeanor—conveyed his dislike of the defendants, in much the same manner as did Judge Medina years later in the Communist trial at Foley Square. Finally, in his charge to the jury, Judge Thayer went far afield from the regulation instructions on matters of law and called upon them to perform their duty as loyal citizens and to seek courage in their deliberations "such as was typified by the American soldier boy as he fought and gave up his life on the battlefields of France"—a covert attack upon the defendants as men who might use violence against the jury. Only one weapon was found on a spectator and that was a deputy sheriff from another county! Yet, a desperado atmosphere was created.

Harassments inside and outside the courtroom plagued the defense. It was necessary to raise $6,000 to pay for the stenographic minutes of the trial when Mr. Katzman, the prosecutor, refused to share the expenses, as was customarily done. An eleventh-hour attempt was made to speed the deportation of Frank Lopez, Spanish-born secretary of the Sacco-Vanzetti Defense Committee, a man with a family and an expert cabinetmaker who had been in this country since 1904 when he came here at the age of 19. He was a valuable witness for the defense, and the Department of Labor finally agreed to postpone his departure until after the trial.

The government's case, like that of the Mooney case, hinged on testimony of identification witnesses. No attempt was ever made to connect the $18,000 stolen in South Braintree on April 15, 1920, with either defendant or anyone connected with them. Seven witnesses attempted identifications. On May 18, 1920, in Judge Avery's lower court, Louis Wade had said, "I might be mistaken." Frances Devlin had said: "I do not say positively." Mary Splaine had said: "I do not think my opportunity afforded me the right to say he is the man."

Then, over a year later, they made more positive identifications which, after the trial, either fell apart or were exposed as perjury. Against the weak testimony of these persons, the defense was able to produce 28 persons who were at the scene of the crime, all of whom said they had not seen Sacco or Vanzetti. Some were close enough to the bandits to be shot at by them and had seen them clearly. Some of the state's witnesses were at the windows of the factory and a nearby factory. One woman said she knew the man she saw was a foreigner because "he had that blue look that foreigners have when they shave!"

The defense further proved that Sacco and Vanzetti were many miles from the scene of the crime. Sacco was in Boston at the office of the Italian consulate applying for passports. The clerk of the consulate was by then in Rome, but he went before the American consul general there and swore to Sacco's presence in Boston on that day. The clerk recalled the large family picture brought by Sacco, which Rose had described to Mrs. Vorse and me. Others testified they saw Sacco in a Boston restaurant. Eleven townspeople testified that Vanzetti was in Plymouth that day, 25 miles away, going about his regular work.

The lawyer for the Commonwealth (as Massachusetts is strangely called) relied primarily on psychological arguments, namely, "a consciousness of guilt." He argued this on the basis that Sacco and Vanzetti had lied on May 5, 1920, 20 days after the crime was committed. The state said they had gone with two other men, Boda and Ociani, to the house of a man named Johnson, where Boda kept his car, an Overland, in the garage. (The murder car was identified as a Buick). Mrs. Johnson, seeing four "foreigners," had called the police. Sacco and Vanzetti were arrested later on a streetcar. The other two men were not arrested. Because, as I have already described, Sacco and Vanzetti would not state where they had been and with whom, they were branded with "consciousness of guilt." By this crooked legal device, Katzman forced the defense to introduce the issue and evidence of the activities and radical views of Sacco and Vanzetti, and then he disclaimed all responsibility.

Both defendants testified at length. They said the reasons they did not tell the police the truth was, first, that during the war they had refused to register and had gone to Mexico. Secondly, when Vanzetti was in New York City in April 1920, the secretary of the Italian Defense Committee there, Luigi Quintiliano, had told him, on the advice of Attorney Walter Nelles, that if they had anarchist literature in their possession it should be destroyed or hidden in anticipation of further trouble. He so reported to his New England comrades and it was decided to take a car, gather up any literature in all comrades' homes and convey it to some safe place. On the night of their arrest, the police questioned them solely in reference to their radical views and associates and made no mention of the Braintree crime, therefore they were justified in assuming it was a political arrest. They said they were determined to protect themselves and their friends and therefore refused to give correct information, and that they had good grounds to be fearful because just two days before their comrade Salsadeo had been found dead.

The Commonwealth also made much of the fact that both men were armed at the time of their arrest. An investigation made by three reputable lawyers, one an ex-prosecutor, for the New England Civil Liberties Committee made this comment on that point: "It is safe to assume that seventy-five percent of all Italians go armed." Sacco's employer, Mr. Kelley, testified as a character witness that he employed Sacco for three years, knew that he was always armed, had employed him as a night watchman at the factory and that he could have stolen stock worth upward of $20,000 at any time. Carrying arms was much more prevalent among workers then than it is today.

An attempt was made by police testimony to connect Sacco's Colt with the murder through a fatal bullet. But experts from the U. S. Cartridge Company and the Colt Automatic Pistol Company flatly contradicted their statements. Captain Proctor of the state police was a strangely hesitating witness and later told Albert H. Hamilton, ballistic expert, that he was convinced the fatal bullet was not fired through Sacco's pistol. The jury was out five hours and found both men guilty of first-degree murder.

The verdict of the committee of the New England Civil Liberties Committee did not agree with the jury. It stated that they had been denied "the essential ingredients of a fair trial." They said:

Nothing has occurred up to this hour that has in any wise shaken our confidence in Nicola Sacco and Bartolomeo Vanzetti. In fact, our confidence is greater today than before they went on trial. Now we have their story, have seen them on the stand, and have heard the Commonwealth's case, we sincerely believe that they are innocent of the Braintree crime. . . . We are determined that someway, somehow, the wrong the twelve men composing the jury at Dedham did Sacco and Vanzetti shall be righted.

This was the verdict of millions.

THE WORLD AS JURY

Now began the long and difficult struggle for a new trial which for six years beat upon the ears of stone of the stiff-necked courts of the Commonwealth of Massachusetts. Those years were a long drawn-out torture for Sacco and Vanzetti, sustained only by the tremendous growth of the movement for their liberation. Vanzetti's days of waiting were relieved by work in a shop in Charlestown Prison. He found great solace in reading and writing. His English improved and his writings in the new language were very beautiful. A remarkable friendship grew between the austere, elderly liberal, Mrs. Glenower Evans, and Vanzetti, as their published letters revealed. Sacco was much more disturbed by his prison life. He longed for his wife and children, for his work in a shop and fellow-workers, for activity. Idleness tortured him. It was unfortunate that they could not have been together for those terrible years and sustained one another.

The verdict of guilty was received with shocked incredulity around the world. A wave of indignant protest engulfed American embassies in every capital, large and small. Demonstrations mounted until the American press was full of news of barricaded ambassadors, and embassies stormed, with troops turned out to guard them. The names of the once obscure Italian immigrants were on the protesting lips of shouting millions. Rome, Paris, Moscow, London, Barcelona, Milan, Genoa, Mexico City, Montevideo, Buenos Aires, Havana, Toyko, Berlin, Lisbon, were among the places heard from in the news. In Paris 20 workers were wounded by the police. Debs sent the $5 he received on his discharge from Atlanta Prison to the defense fund of Sacco and Vanzetti. Tom Mooney, who had then been in prison for five years and had been saved from the gallows almost by a hair's-breadth, linked his case with that of Sacco and Vanzetti, against the advice of many friends in California. He used his magazine, *Tom Mooney's* Monthly, to blast both frame-ups and to show how in both cases witnesses were being exposed as liars, perjurors, crooks—coerced or bought and paid for. In a most dramatic parallel, these two examples of the deadly frame-up system, eventually fell apart. Labor was fighting it with two fists—in San Francisco and in Boston. If Sacco and Vanzetti had been given life imprisonment, as was Tom Mooney, they, too, would eventually have been vindicated and liberated.

In the Mooney case, the star witnesses, Oxman and McDonald, and the two Edeau women were thoroughly discredited by 1921. The same process then began in Boston. Of course, this all took time and did not result in motions for a new trial, based on an exposure of the witnesses, until November 8, 1923. Meantime, an extensive appeal was prepared to go before the State Supreme Court. One of the strongest legal points in it was the one Vanzetti had raised on my first visit to him. It argued that Judge Thayer, in refusing to give the defendants separate trials, had thus prejudiced their chances for justice.

The defense attorneys, especially Fred Moore, did a heroic job in their tireless and devastating investigation of the State's witnesses. Four motions were finally made for a new trial, but unfortunately they had to be presented first to the trial judge, Webster Thayer, whose prejudice was publicly known. He had openly discussed the case on the golf links in Worcester, where he lived, and his contempt for the defendants was well known. He asked the newspaper men several times during the trial what they thought of his conduct of the trial, and finally demanded that they publish a statement "that this trial is being conducted in a fair and impartial manner." He turned to Frank P. Sibley, star reporter of the Boston *Globe* and dean of the reporters, and asked, "Sibley—you are the oldest—what do you think?" Sibley gave his classical answer: "Your Honor, I have never seen anything like it!"

For the next six years it was a horribly monotonous process of making the motions for a new trial, and having them ridiculed and denied by Judge Thayer, who became increasingly hysterical, practically maniacal on the subject of "those arnychistic bastards!" as he described them to Professor Richardson of Dartmouth College in 1924. His full remark was "Did you see what I did to those arnychistic bastards the other day?" (referring to a denial of new trial motions). "I guess that will hold them for a while! Let 'em go to the Supreme Court now and see what they can get out of them!"

Professor Felix Frankfurter of the Harvard Law School wrote an article for the *Atlantic Monthly,* reviewing the case and exposing the errors, distortions and prejudices of Judge Thayer. It showed that Thayer had falsified the record on Sacco's testimony, quoting bogus passages not actually in the record.

The four new motions for a new trial started with the exposure of the jury foreman, Ripley, a former chief of police, who had told a friend of his, Daly, a few days before the trial that he was going to serve on the jury trying those two "ginneys." Daly remarked that he did not believe they were guilty, whereupon Ripley said heatedly, "Damn them, they ought to hang anyway!" Felix Frankfurter remarked in his book on Sacco and Vanzetti, published in 1927: "The unfitness of a man in this frame of mind to serve on a jury needs no comment." (It is difficult to understand why years later Justice Frankfurter did not raise the same issue in relation to juror Russell Janney in the Dennis case, as did Justice Hugo Black.)

Louis Pelzer and Lola Andrews, state witnesses, retracted their identification. Carlo E. Goodridge, an alias, was exposed as a degenerate and a criminal named Whitney whose record was known to the prosecutor when he placed him on the witness stand. Motions for a new trial were made in each instance. There was yet another motion calling for an invalidation of the verdict because foreman Ripley had brought four bullets, not in evidence, into the jury room for purposes of comparison with the fatal bullet in evidence and had shown them to the jury. In addition to all this, the defense had succeeded in locating a salesman, Roy Gould, who had been shot at by the bandits, a bullet going through his overcoat. He had notified the authorities of this fact and had been willing to testify. But the state did not call him, undoubtedly because he stated definitely that he had seen neither defendant at that time.

"A GHASTLY MISCARRIAGE OF JUSTICE"

"Hope springs eternal in the human breast!" So it was with all who were defending Sacco and Vanzetti in the two years following the trial. The exposure of the three main witnesses as perjurors and liars, and of the outrageous conduct of the jury foreman, caused the Sacco and Vanzetti Committee to print a jubilant four-page leaflet, giving all the facts, headed *"Victory Is In Sight."* It had a cover design of four bent prison bars in front of Sacco and Vanzetti, grasped in a powerful hand marked "labor." The bars were labeled with the names of those exposed—Goodrich, Andrews, Pelsen and Ripley. These exposures also caused the American Federation of Labor in its 1922 convention at Cincinnati, Ohio, to demand "a new trial for Sacco and Vanzetti, convicted of murder in the first degree by a biased jury under the instructions of a prejudiced judge in the State of Massachusetts."

In its next convention at El Paso, Texas, in 1924, the AFL charac-

terized their prosecution as *"a ghastly miscarriage of justice,"* and re-
iterated its demand "for a new trial for these defenseless victims of race
and national prejudice and class hatred." The Locomotive Engineers
Journal said bluntly, "Must justice be so blind, judges so biased, that
men can be hanged when the evidence declares conclusively that they
are not guilty?" But Judge Thayer procrastinated, and months passed
before he ruled, and then he followed his set pattern of denial after denial. Meantime, it was hard to keep up a sustained interest while the
case dragged along without action. Other issues in the class struggle
pushed to the front for public attention. There were 53 wartime prisoners left in federal penitentiaries in February 1923. There were pending appeals on some wartime cases. There were a large number of deportation cases in the courts. In Pennsylvania 38 Communists were
indicted under the State Sedition Act and in Michigan 22 Communists
were held under the state Criminal Syndicalist Act for attending a convention at Bridgeman, Michigan, in the summer of 1922. In addition
to all of this, the United Mine Workers was confronted by trials for
murder and treason in West Virginia, growing out of the miners'
armed march of 1921 in Logan County, and the labor movement was
fighting injunction proceedings in a dozen places.

By November 1922, the Sacco-Vanzetti Committee had spent
$155,000 and was $8,000 in debt. It had printed hundreds of thousands of leaflets and pamphlets in English, Italian, Spanish, Portuguese, French and German. It had planned tours for Italian and English speakers, including Fred Biedenkapp, myself and others. It had
employed publicity men, lawyers and investigators. The trial transcript
was 10,000 pages long. It had called expert witnesses at heavy expense. It was quite desperate for funds. Unemployment was widespread in New England, especially in the shoe and textile industries,
and the miners were involved in a big strike. These workers had been
heavy contributors for over two years.

In 1922 there had been set up in New York City the American
Fund for Public Service. Norman Thomas was president; Roger Baldwin, secretary; and its board of directors were Harry F. Ward, William
Z. Foster, James Weldon Johnson, Sidney Hillman, Lewis Gannett
and Scott Nearing. Fred Moore made an application to them, through
me, asking for funds up to $5,000 to do "special investigation work." I
forwarded the application to the fund office. It was popularly called
"The Garland Fund" because it was set up with one million dollars by

a young man named Garland. Along with the application went a letter
from the Sacco-Vanzetti Defense Committee stating that they were familiar with the contents of the application, that their Committee "is
fully advised of the plan of investigation outlined by Mr. Moore and if
it can be carried into effect it will be with our entire approval." This
was signed by A. Felicani, F. Lopez and F. Guadagni, as Executive
Committee. In view of future developments, this document was extremely important.

It referred to a new line of investigation outside of the trial—an attempt to find out and prove who was actually guilty of the holdup and
robbery at South Braintree. Fred Moore was convinced by some clues
he ran across in Boston's underworld that a well-trained payroll robbery gang had not only committed this crime, but others before and
after. It opened up the task of pursuing endless leads which took defense investigators all over the country. On one of my innumerable
speaking trips for Sacco and Vanzetti, I gave and received information
from IWW prisoners in Leavenworth. But with the aid of the Garland
Fund and the waning approval of the defense committee, Fred fever-
ishly pursued every clue. Some of the anarchists began to question this
procedure. "It is the job of the government, not our job!" they would
say.

At the end of three long years, idle in a prison cell, taken into court
intermittently to be placed beside Vanzetti in the iron cage and to listen to futile legal arguments for a new trial scornfully ridiculed and rejected by the hateful Judge Thayer, Nicola Sacco took matters into his
own hands. He followed the example of the heroic McSweeney in Ireland and declared a hunger strike. For three days he refused to eat. By
March 17, 1923 we sent out an appeal to labor, "Nicola Sacco is
dying." His wife, lawyers, comrades, pleaded with him; his co-defend-
ant, Vanzetti, sent him a message—but Sacco was determined to register his protest.

Judge Thayer, at this juncture, after consultation with judges of the
Massachusetts Supreme Court, agreed to hear the long deferred motions for a new trial. Sacco was too weak to be brought into court. Alienists were appointed and he was transferred to the Boston Psycho-
pathic Hospital for two weeks' observation. To prove his sanity and
that his hunger strike was a protest weapon, Sacco accepted food in
the hospital after Judge Thayer acted. He was transferred to the Bridgewater Hospital for the Criminal Insane and finally back to Dedham

Jail, where he was allowed to do basket weaving to relieve the strain of idleness. But the fact that Fred Moore, as his attorney, had agreed to the examination as to his sanity by alienists was never forgiven by Sacco and, I believe, by Mrs. Sacco. It was a terrible decision for Fred Moore to have to make but he was determined to save Nick's life, at all costs.

THE DARK DAYS OF 1924

The year 1924 was marked by increasing dissatisfaction on the part of the Sacco-Vanzetti Committee with Fred Moore's spending money on "investigation." Money came in slowly in small amounts and went out in big checks. It was hard for these workers to understand it, particularly as there grew up an ideological objection to the whole business among the anarchists, in which Sacco emphatically joined. Vanzetti usually did not express any disagreement with Sacco on any issue. There was validity in Sacco's position, which was, "Must we prove somebody else guilty in order to prove our innocence?" He said it was a bad example and would be used against other workers falsely accused of crime in similar frame-ups. He pointed out that Mooney and Billings were not following this course. His position was, "It is the duty of the prosecution, of the state, to find the guilty parties. It is not our business."

On the other hand, the lawyers and all practical-minded supporters of the defense asked why Sacco and Vanzetti should go to the electric chair for a gang of murders who would not lift a finger to save them. They pointed out that Mooney and Billings were sentenced to prison, not to death. And after Fred Moore had been forced to withdraw from the case, mainly at the insistence of Sacco and Vanzetti, new lawyers later followed the very clues he had labored so hard, and against such bitter opposition, to uncover. It was this question of both policy and tactics in legal defense that caused the break between Fred Moore and the Sacco-Vanzetti Committee. His efforts were heroic and his labor tremendous. He was supposed to be paid $150 a week but often he spent it all on the case. His mistakes were magnified out of all proportion and his devotion and services overlooked when the break came.

The defense counted heavily on the "Proctor motion," following expert testimony that the mortal bullet could not possibly have come through Sacco's pistol. This was buttressed by photographs. But the state countered with other experts and it went beyond the comprehension of laymen. Judge Thayer, of course, always accepted the state's experts as the more authoritative. The Proctor affidavit from a sick old man, near death, whose conscience forced him to speak out for men he believed to be innocent, revealed his part in the frame-up. It showed how the prosecutor had put questions to him, by agreement, that he could answer so that the jury would believe he was saying something different from what he was really saying. He said in his affidavit that the district attorney had wanted to ask him the flat question—Was he convinced that the murder bullet had been fired by Sacco's gun? And he had stated he would answer "No" to such a question. Instead Katzman asked him a question so artfully designed that he could answer, "My opinion is that it is consistent with being fired by that pistol." This was used as a direct affirmation by both the prosecutor and the judge during the trial and afterward.

In November 1924, the sadistic and shameful Judge Thayer once again dismissed motions for a new trial on the Proctor motion, and then went to Dartmouth College to a football game, where he made his disgraceful remark to Professor James Richardson (which I quoted above) about the defendants. The professor was so shocked and horrified that he made an affidavit about it. By this time, practically every big trade union in the United States, state federations, central labor bodies and local unions had gone on record for a new trial. But a stubborn, poisonous, withered old man, full of hate and fear, stood between Sacco and Vanzetti and the simple justice of a new trial. A New Trial League was organized that year in Boston, called together by Mrs. Elizabeth Glendower Evans, Mrs. Anna D. Davis, Alice Stone Blackwell, John Codman and other notable New England liberals, and John Van Vaerenewyck of the Cigarmakers Union, who sent out a new appeal to all American trade unions.

The denial by Judge Thayer of the Proctor motion was a crowning disappointment to patient and controlled Vanzetti. At Christmas 1924 he declared a hunger strike in protest. On January 3, 1925, he was committed by Judge Raymond of the Superior Court to the Bridgewater State Hospital, following reports by state alienists. The defense attorneys secured the services of a well-known psychiatrist, Dr. Abraham Meyerson, who examined Vanzetti. In his report he stated:

I believe he is suffering from a prison psychosis of temporary nature brought on by the extraordinary conditions in which a man of intense mental life finds himself. The long legal battle, the bombardment of attention on the part of the press of the world, and of international organizations, the impending sentence of death, prison discipline, confinement with lack of outdoors, have brought on a transient paranoid state. In my opinion, he would be better off in a hospital than in his present environment.

After five years of calm endurance of intolerable pressures, Vanzetti had broken under the strain and suspense. But what he suffered from was a grim horrible reality and not delusions! It was with this grave new development that we entered the fifth year of their living hell.

All the motions for a new trial were exhausted and rejected by Judge Thayer. He had closed every door there. The case was due to be heard by the Massachusetts Supreme Court in the spring. I was in Massachusetts during December 1924, at the request of the Sacco-Vanzetti Committee and the American Civil Liberties Union. New life began to flow into the defense movement again as it moved forward, out of the long dreary hiatus of delays and stalling in Thayer's court. The Sacco-Vanzetti Committee agreed to enlarge the committee to include representatives from the Boston labor movement to direct the renewed agitation and raise the funds necessary for the costly appeal to the higher court. John Barry, a steel worker, was elected chairman of the enlarged committee; Michael Flaherty, vice-chairman, was a painter and a member of the Boston Central Labor Union. The treasurer remained the faithful and hard-working linotype operator, A. Felicani, who worked every day in a shop and gave all his leisure time for seven years to the defense of his comrades. A coal miner, Emilio Coda, became the secretary. He sent out an appeal to all the locals of the United Mine Workers, which brought in $5,000 immediately. He also addressed a letter to all the locals of the International Ladies Garment Workers Union, reminding them of their generosity at two conventions and that their president, Morris Sigmen, had visited Sacco and Vanzetti in prison to extend the union's greetings.

NOW THE HIGHER COURTS

It was decided in the Fall of 1924 by the Sacco-Vanzetti Committee to explore the necessity of reorganizing the legal team to present the appeal to the Massachusetts Supreme Court. It was argued strongly that a leading New England lawyer was now required, that Fred Moore, as an outsider, had two strikes against him. He had created animosities by his fighting attitude; the long delays, the complicated legal procedures and especially his insistence on "finding out who did it," had antagonized the defendants and their anarchist comrades beyond repair. The Sacco-Vanzetti Committee took up the question with the American Civil Liberties Union and the Workers Defense Union in order to secure their further financial support if such a move was made. It was agreed that as a person familiar with the whole situation and all the people involved, I should go to Boston and privately survey the matter among all interested parties, and then make a recommendation.

I first saw Fred Moore and told him of my assignment. It was not a pleasant one, in view of our 15 years of cooperation and friendship. He assured me there were no hard feelings; I should go ahead and if I returned finally to tell him that the consensus of opinion was that he should withdraw, he would do so. I then had prolonged conferences in which I interviewed every element—from conservative trade unionists, Socialists, anarchists, Communists, and Liberals, including Professor Frankfurter at Harvard University. The universal opinion was that new, distinguished local counsel was imperative. The reasons were not identical, nor did all I talked to share in the criticism of Fred Moore. But the insistence, especially of Sacco, that he must go and his threat to write a letter to the court discharging Moore as his lawyer if we did not act was decisive. So I returned to Fred's office with some members of the Sacco-Vanzetti Committee to tell him I saw no alternative but to release him from the case. It was a devastating blow to him, needless to say, but he was sufficiently objective and devoted to the cause to cooperate at all times whenever the lawyers called upon him to do so. He died of cancer in Los Angeles in the early 30s. He was a great labor lawyer.

On the recommendation of Professor Frankfurter, we interviewed William G. Thompson, a former Boston district attorney, who was not too anxious to take the case and insisted upon $25,000 payable in advance. I went hurriedly to New York City and was able to make arrangements with the Garland Fund to lend the Sacco-Vanzetti Committee $20,000 to supplement what the Boston committee could raise. The Amalgamated Clothing Workers and the International Ladies Garment Workers underwrote the loan for me and I returned with the money to Boston to see Mr. Thompson. He was a big, handsome, gray-headed man. He smiled ruefully when we gave him the check and said: "I thought sure you couldn't raise it, Miss Flynn. I can't say that I'm glad!" But before he was through, he too, like Fred Moore, became personally devoted to the defendants, especially Vanzetti, was deeply convinced of their innocence and battled heroically for them on the legal front. He objected however to "propaganda" and public meetings, and the defense committee found itself at odds with him over this crucial issue. Fred Moore, the fighting labor champion, had encouraged them in this field. He had understood that the only chance to save Sacco and Vanzetti was in the mobilization of millions outside the courtroom and that only by such agitation could the necessary funds be raised.

The whole frustrating pattern started all over again with the Massachusetts Supreme Court. The distinguished New England counsel made no more impression on the State Justices than he would have on Judge Thayer, whom it was plain they were determined to uphold. On May 12, 1926, in a document of 22,000 words on 66 separate motions, they declared Judge Thayer was correct in every ruling, that he had not exceeded his discretionary powers. They denied all motions for a new trial and declared that Sacco and Vanzetti were legally convicted. This long drawn-out process had dragged on throughout the years 1925 and 1926. The fateful decision shattered the legal illusions of all concerned that justice could be secured—at least in the courts of Massachusetts. Apparently the State Justices had considered Mr. Thompson a traitor to his class and gave all his arguments short shrift.

But hope was born anew from a strange new development, bearing out the rejected investigations of Fred Moore. A young Portuguese prisoner in Dedham Jail, Celestina F. Madieros, was awaiting an appeal from a conviction for bank robbery in Wrentham, in which a cashier was killed. He saw Rose Sacco visiting Nick with her baby and became greatly troubled. Finally in November 1925 he wrote a note which said, "I hereby confess to being in the South Braintree shoe company crime, and Sacco and Vanzetti was not in said crime." He passed this to Sacco via a trusty. While Madieros refused to name his associates, it was easily established, after investigation, to be the well-known Morrelli gang from Providence, Rhode Island. Mr. Thompson, overriding the same anarchist objections which had caused Fred Moore so much heartache, went ahead in May of 1926, before Judge Thayer, with a motion for a new trial based on this new evidence.

One of the most dramatic episodes of 1925 in the Sacco-Vanzetti defense was the return of Joseph J. Ettor and Arthuro Giovannitti to speak on their behalf. The leaders of the famous Lawrence strike in

1912 who had sat in a cage in Salem, Massachusetts, in the shadow of death on similar charges for many months, spoke eloquently for their two imprisoned comrades. Since Captain Proctor had been a star witness against them in their trial 13 years before, they laid great stress that his affidavit in this case showed that he was certainly not prejudiced in favor of the defendants when he exonerated them. The Ettor-Giovannitti meetings were a great success everywhere. I made trips with them, with Professor Guadagni and with the editor of an Italian anarchist paper named Calvani, who made a fiery and eloquent speech, but the identical one every time, so eventually I knew it by heart. Once, on a visit to Vanzetti, I quoted some to him. He laughed heartily and said: "Elizabetta, you must get tired of talking about us!" I assured him I did not. I had a system to vary it. Sometimes I started with their youth and worked forward, sometimes with the present and worked backward and sometimes in the middle and went both ways. He was greatly amused. Rarely did his sense of humor desert this noble man.

NOT MUCH PERSONAL LIFE

My ex-husband had completely dropped out of my life. I knew he was in Chicago and had left the IWW with Foster in 1911, had joined the Syndicalist League, went into the Painters Union of the AFL, was a delegate to the Chicago Federation of Labor, and was very active in the local labor movement then. Finally, in 1920 he served me a notice of divorce based on desertion. He agreed that I should keep custody of Fred, and soon after he remarried. But, erratic as usual, he had built a boat in his backyard and put it afloat on Lake Michigan. He and his bride set out on their honeymoon. A terrible storm came up and wrecked the boat; he held her up, clinging to the wreckage until he became unconscious. She was drowned and he was washed ashore, battered and bruised and nearly dead. A Socialist sheriff took him in custody in Wisconsin.

Detectives came to interview me in New York as to whether I thought he was capable of killing his wife. I replied indignantly, sensing a frame-up in the offing, "Indeed not, he is a kind and good man. He never killed me and he had plenty of provocation!" The Irish "dick" said: "I bet he did at that!" and left. Jones was released. Later I saw him at the IWW headquarters in Chicago, looking thinner and

older, with whitening hair. He was the proprietor of The Dill Pickle
—a radical night club on the North Side for many years. St. John visited him whenever he passed through Chicago. After one occasion he
said, "Well, Fred may inherit a fortune yet!" and told us a tall tale of
"Jonesey and his duck." It was a self-propelling duck on which he was
then working. Rumor had it that Donald Duck was an offspring of
Jones' duck. Jones died in Chicago in 1940.

My life with Carlo was tempestuous, undoubtedly because we were
both strong personalities with separate and often divided interests. After the strike on the Mesabi Range he severed his connections with the
IWW and became quite scornful of it. He identified himself with the
Amalgamated Textile Workers and several insurgent movements within the United Mine Workers, where Italian workers were involved. He
wrote and spoke only in Italian and made little or no effort to learn
English or to participate in American affairs. His preoccupation was
with Italian affairs, his friends were predominantly Italian anarchists
—a strange yet simple and earnest people who could be both exasper-
ating and amusing. I recall a "comrade" of Carlo's—a barber with a
large family—who was an enthusiastic anarchist, so much so that he
gave his children what he considered appropriate names—like "Liber-
ta" (Liberty); "Athee" (Atheist); "Bruno" (for Giordano Bruno),
etc. He was an extremely excitable man, though really a good father.
We sat down to an enormous dinner and the children hollered loudly
for whatever they wanted. Finally in exasperation he shouted, "Liber-
ta, shut up!" and "Athee, per Jesus Christo, I beat you up!" and
"Bruno, you are a fool!"

There were practically no women in the Italian movement—anarchist or socialist. Whatever homes I went into with Carlo the women
were always in the background, cooking in the kitchen, and seldom
even sitting down to eat with the men. Some were strong Catholics and
resented me very much; they were very disapproving of my way of
life. I became more and more immersed in my own field of labor defense work. Carlo's Italian comrades realized we had drifted apart and
had many differences which were fundamental because I was not an
anarchist—I was a Socialist, and an industrial unionist, a strong believer in organization. True, I had wandered afield into the path of
syndicalism, but still I was a Socialist. They tried to tell me that if I
would only stay home and "keep house" for Carlo, all would be well.
But I rejected that solution. I said: "He had a good Italian wife who

cooked spaghetti and was a model housekeeper. Why didn't he stay with her?" They knew the answer, and so did I then. Carlo had a roving eye that had roved in my direction in Lawrence but then, some ten years later, was roving elsewhere.

We separated in 1925, and would probably have separated sooner except that two cases in which we were mutually interested held us together. One was the Sacco-Vanzetti case; the other was his own arrest in the summer of 1923 under a Federal Obscenity Law. It sounds worse than it really was. It involved Italian pamphlets on birth control, then a very popular subject, and was merely a pretext for Carlo's political enemies to get him. With the rise of Mussolini, whom Carlo and others here had known as a Socialist in Italy, then the leader of fascism—a violent, brutal and anti-democratic ultra-nationalist movement, directed against Socialists, trade unionists and aliens—a united Italian anti-fascist movement emerged in this country in 1921. It was of wide proportions and embraced all political faiths. Arturo Giovannitti, Pietro Allegra, and Carlos Contreras, then known as Erneo Sormenti (who was later deported and then became leader of the Communist Party in Trieste), were all extremely active in it. *Il Progresso*—owned by Generoso Pope—was pro-Mussolini. The Sons of Italy was almost split asunder by the issue of fascism.

The fake march on Rome in October 1922 and the craven capitulation of King Victor Emanuel, who made Mussolini Prime Minister, preceded a reign of terror by the Black Shirts—jailings, burnings of union and newspaper offices, gagging of the press, beatings and the horrible castor oil treatment of hundreds of Italian men and women. The climax was the brutal murder of Socialist deputy Matteotti in 1924, committed by order of Mussolini to silence the bravest voice in Italy which had courageously exposed these monstrous deeds. The murder of Matteotti was shockingly similar to the murder of Karl Leibknecht and Rosa Luxemburg in Germany in 1919, and aroused world-wide protest, not confined to Italian people although they were particularly disturbed.

Carlo's arrest and trial, which resulted in conviction, hampered him considerably in his anti-fascist agitation. He was defended by our one-time prosecutor, Harold Content, now in private practice. When his conviction was confirmed after appeal, he was sentenced by Judge Goddard to a year and a day in Atlanta Penitentiary. But through the efforts of Roger Baldwin and myself, supported by the American Civil

Liberties Union and several large Italian trade union locals in New York, especially Locals 48 and 89 of the ILGWU, a reduction of sentence to three months was secured from President Coolidge. Another person who came to the aid of Carlo was Fiorello LaGuardia. He was then in Congress. I recall going to Washington to see him on Carlo's behalf. He took me to dinner at the Mayflower Hotel and got an enormous kick out of introducing me in the most innocent manner to stodgy Southern congressmen and then saying, after they politely greeted me, "She's an IWW, you know!"

He came to Judge Goddard's chambers to plead for a lighter sentence and to explain the Italian political overtones behind the charges. We walked out on the street together and stood on Broadway in front of the Woolworth Building. I felt badly because Carlo had just been taken to the Tombs and I knew we were also parting our ways when this ordeal was finished. A man had come to my office with a package of love letters Carlo had written to the man's wife, of such a nature that I had no choice. LaGuardia, of course, knew nothing of this at the time. But he sensed my great unhappiness and suddenly made a most penetrating and unexpected remark: "Elizabeth, why don't you stop mixing up with all these Italian anarchists and go back into the American labor movement where you belong?"

Years later, in 1940, after my son's death, I saw LaGuardia then Mayor of New York City out at Flushing Meadows. He said, "Elizabeth, I hear you joined the Communist Party!" I said, "Yes, Fiorello, don't you remember you told me to leave the Italian anarchists and get back where I belong?" He laughed his hearty, roaring laughter and said, "Well, I'd rather see you with the Communists than with those freaks!" But I had not been able or willing to take his advice in 1924 because I was then too deeply involved in a battle for justice for two anarchists who were not freaks but honest workers. I was fighting against a damnable frame-up in Boston, Massachusetts—fighting for the lives of "the good shoemaker and the poor fish peddler"—Sacco and Vanzetti.

Index